CEYLON AT WAR 1939-45

War and Military Culture in South Asia, 1757–1947

www.helion.co.uk/warandmilitarycultureinsouthasia

Submissions

The publishers would be pleased to receive submissions for this series. Please contact us via email (info@helion.co.uk), or in writing to Helion & Company Limited, Unit 8 Amherst Business Centre, Budbrooke Road, Warwick, CV34 5WE

Titles

No 1 *'Swords Trembling In Their Scabbards'. The Changing Status of Indian Officers in the Indian Army 1757–1947* Michael Creese (ISBN 978-1-909982-81-9)

No 2 *'Discipline, System and Style'. The Sixteenth Lancers and British Soldiering in India 1822-1846* John H. Rumsby (ISBN 978-1-909982-91-8)

No 3 *Die in Battle, Do not Despair. The Indians on Gallipoli, 1915* Peter Stanley (ISBN 978-1-910294-67-3)

No 4 *Brave as a Lion. The Life and Times of Field Marshal Hugh Gough, 1st Viscount Gough* Christopher Brice (ISBN 978-1-910294-61-1)

No 5 *Approach to Battle. Training the Indian Army during the Second World War* Alan Jeffreys (ISBN 978-1-911096-51-1)

No 6 *The Indian Army in The First World War: New Perspectives* Edited by Alan Jeffreys (ISBN 978-1-911512-78-3)

No 7 *War without Pity in the South Indian Peninsula 1798–1813: The Letter Book of Lieutenant-Colonel Valentine Blacker* Edited and with introductory notes by David Howell (ISBN 978-1-912390-86-1)

No 8 *Of Islands, Ports and Sea Lanes: Africa and the Indian Ocean in the Second World War* Ashley Jackson (ISBN 978-1-912390-74-8)

This book is dedicated to my extraordinary mother, Lesley Vivienne Jackson née Townshend, whose lifelong appetite for knowledge, and relish in people and places and 'things', has always been an inspiration.

The original poster on which the jacket design is based. It was issued by the Department of Information, Colombo, in January 1943.

Ceylon at War 1939-45

War and Military Culture in South Asia, 1757–1947 No. 9

Ashley Jackson

Helion & Company

Helion & Company Limited
Unit 8 Amherst Business Centre
Budbrooke Road
Warwick
CV34 5WE
England
Tel. 01926 499 619
Fax 0121 711 4075
Email: info@helion.co.uk
Website: www.helion.co.uk
Twitter: @helionbooks
Visit our blog http://blog.helion.co.uk/

Published by Helion & Company 2018
Designed and typeset by Mach 3 Solutions Ltd (www.mach3solutions.co.uk)
Cover designed by Paul Hewitt, Battlefield Design (www.battlefield-design.co.uk)
Printed by Lightning Source Limited, Milton Keynes, Buckinghamshire

ISBN 978-1-912390-65-6

British Library Cataloguing-in-Publication Data.
A catalogue record for this book is available from the British Library.

Contents

War and Military Culture in South Asia, 1757–1947
Series Editor's Preface

The aim of this academic historical series is to produce well-researched monographs on the wars and armed forces of South Asia, concentrating mainly on the East India Company and the Indian armed forces from 1757 until 1947. Books in the series will examine the military history of the period as well as social, cultural, political and economic factors, although inevitably the armies of the East India Company and the Indian Army will dominate the series. In addition, edited volumes of conference papers, memoirs and campaign histories will also be published. It is hoped this series will be of interest to both serious historians and the general military history reader.

The resurgence of interest in the history of warfare in South Asia has been very apparent in the growing historiography of the colonial period, particularly in the era of the World Wars. For example in the field of Second World War studies and the period until Partition, Daniel Marston and Tim Moreman have spearheaded this historical research with their volumes: the prize-winning *Phoenix from the Ashes: The Indian Army in the Burma Campaign* (2003), *The Indian Army and the End of the Raj* (2014) and *The Jungle, the Japanese and the Commonwealth Armies at War* (2005) respectively. These are complemented by Raymond Callahan's *Churchill and His Generals* (2007), a seminal work published in the United States that deserves better attention in the United Kingdom, and Steven Wilkinson's *Army and Nation: The Military and Indian Democracy since Independence* (2015). In addition, are the important wider studies of Christopher Bayly and Tim Harper, *Forgotten Armies: The Fall of British Asia, 1941-1945* (2004) and Ashley Jackson on *The British Empire and the Second World War* (2006). The most recent publications include *Approach to Battle: Training the Indian Army during the Second World War* (2017) published in this series, as well as Tarak Barkawi's *Soldiers of Empire: Indian and British Armies in World War II* (2017) and Raymond Callahan's *Triumph at Imphal-Kohima: How the Indian Army Finally Stopped the Japanese Juggernaut* (2017). Furthermore the Indian home front has been covered in Yasmin Khan's social history of the period entitled *The Raj at War: A People's History of India's Second World War* (2015).

The aforementioned rise in interest has been mirrored in India as eight volumes of the official histories of the Indian Armed Forces during the Second World War were reprinted in India in 2012 and another four in 2014 (they were originally published between 1954 and 1960). As Squadron Leader Rana Chhina stated at the launch of the reprints: 'As a resurgent India seeks to be a major player on the world stage, it behoves it to discard its narrow post-colonial world view to step up to reclaim the role that its armed forces played out on a global scale' during the Second World War. This resurgence is amply demonstrated by the publication of Srinath Raghavan's excellent overview *India's Wars : The Making of Modern South Asia* (2016), alongside the Kaushik Roy's *India and World II: War, Armed Forces, and Society, 1939-45* (2016) snd Anirudh Deshpande's *Hope and Despair: Mutiny, Rebellion and Death in India, 1946* (2016). However, even in this crowded arena, there is still much research and work to be published on both war and military culture in South Asia during the Second World War.

The series editors, members of the editorial advisory board and our publisher, Duncan Rogers of Helion, are all delighted to be involved in this series, most of the volumes of which are also being published in India under the Primus imprint. We hope it will be of interest in the UK, India but also globally.

Alan Jeffreys

Introduction and acknowledgements

This book is the culmination of sporadic work on Ceylon and the Indian Ocean during the Second World War that began in the 1990s. After completing a doctoral thesis on wartime Bechuanaland, I decided to attempt a similar study of another British colony, choosing Mauritius on the strictly scientific grounds that it would probably be a nice place to visit.[1] This provided an introduction to the fascinating story of the Indian Ocean during the war, a neglected but vital theatre of operations because of its status as a global transport and communications hub essential for supporting Allied battlefronts in the Western Desert, the Caucasus, China, and South Asia. It was also a region highly prized because of the raw materials and foodstuffs its territories yielded to the Allied war effort, not least oil and rubber, and was central to the trading life of the British Empire and indeed the whole world. As the Mauritian project developed, I was drawn to Ceylon as a further potential case study, partly through contact with a friend's family, the older generation of which, in another life far away from their Sussex demesne, had been tea planters there. Cursory research revealed two things: that Ceylon was a really rather significant colony (in the same way that Bechuanaland and Mauritius were rather minor ones), and, secondly, that it had played a very prominent role in the war.

While Singapore is famed as an imperial base that failed, and Egypt and Malta heralded as bases that held, Ceylon remains uncelebrated in general histories of the war. But it too was an important base camp for Allied operations and global logistics, and a headquarters establishment for the higher direction of war in the surrounding region. For various reasons the island assumed unexpected strategic importance, and at a critical juncture in 1942 attracted the concentrated attention of the prime minister, the War Cabinet, the Chiefs of Staff, and the lords of the Admiralty, its significance acknowledged in Washington, too, even in the White House. At a meeting of the British Cabinet on 12 August 1942, Australia's accredited representative, S. M. Bruce, said that Ceylon's defence was 'a matter of importance second only to that of the British Isles'.[2] I soon began to discover why it was so important: it was because of the scale of Allied defeats in the early stages of the war against Japan, and, in particular, the loss of Britain's great naval bulwark in the east, Singapore, and the global crisis engendered as Japanese forces advanced with precipitate speed. Singapore's surrender on 15 February 1942, and the series of Allied defeats that occurred all around it, transformed Ceylon into a major strategic redoubt

1 Ashley Jackson, *Botswana 1939-1945: An African Country at War* (Oxford: Clarendon Press, 1999) and Jackson, *War and Empire in Mauritius and the Indian Ocean* (Basingstoke: Palgrave Macmillan, 2001).

2 Stephen Roskill, *The War at Sea*, volume 2, The Period of Balance (London: HMSO, 1956), p. 87.

because of its geographical position relative to key sea lanes and its possession of valuable port and naval facilities.

Following the string of astonishing Japanese victories in the three months after Pearl Harbor, Ceylon became central to British and Allied defensive strategy. The Indian Ocean sea lanes that it helped operate and protect had become even more pivotal with the closure of the Mediterranean to Allied shipping. For most of the period 1940-1943, supplies and reinforcements for the armies and air forces fighting in the North African theatre had to round the Cape and progress north through the Mozambique Channel and the Red Sea. The Indian Ocean was also the conveyor belt used to build up and supply, from America, Britain, the Middle East, and India, the large British Empire force massed in Iran and Iraq in 1941-42 in order to forestall a possible German bid for the region's oil. Related to this, with the virtual closure of the Arctic convoy route, all Anglo-American military aid to the Soviet Union had to cross the Indian Ocean and make for ports at the head of the Persian Gulf, for onward movement overland via the commandeered transport infrastructure of Iran.

Ceylon's value was further augmented because of the Allies' need to utilize its resources, which included their largest remaining source of natural rubber, and the need to deny its harbours, bases, and resources to the enemy. Its conquest and occupation by the Japanese, a scenario anticipated by Churchill and the Chiefs of Staff, would have gifted the enemy a stepping stone from which to assault India and plunder the sea lanes on which the Allied war effort had come to depend. Furthermore, when the day came for the Allies to stop retreating and advance to the attack, the island would provide *them* with a stepping stone as they moved eastwards to drive the Japanese from Asia and the East Indies.

Ceylon had always been an important port of call for shipping, and for a century and a half had been a junction and gathering point for the merchantmen that kept the eastern and western territories of the British Empire connected, illustrated by the fact that in the 1930s Colombo received a greater annual tonnage of shipping than all the harbours of British India combined. The island had always had significance as a naval base, too, having originally been seized lest Colombo and Trincomalee fall into the hands of the French during the Revolutionary and Napoleonic Wars, important as they were for the security of the sea lanes.

But nothing could have prepared Ceylon for the role it was called upon to perform following the sinking of *Prince of Wales* and *Repulse*, the surrender of Singapore, and Allied defeats across South-east Asia and the East Indies, extending even into the Bay of Bengal with the conquest of Burma and the Andaman and Nicobar Islands. Now, Ceylon became an essential strongpoint because of its proximity to the sea lanes funnelling resources to the Western Desert and the Soviet Union, Britain's only major naval base between the Cape of Good Hope and Australia. It became, in John Darwin's memorable analogy, a second Egypt.[3] Singapore had been intended as the eastern equivalent of that great military encampment, a haven and *place d'armes* for British and Allied forces and a hub from which to project military power in the surrounding region. Yet by default it was to be Ceylon that was called upon to perform this role in support of its giant neighbour India, though it has not attracted the attention of Malta besieged, Cairo within an ace of conquest by the Afrika Korps, or Singapore's last desperate days.

3 A term used by John Darwin in conversation with the author at Reading Station, 28/4/98. In the crisis months of 1941-42, the British government and Chiefs of Staff put Ceylon, Indian Ocean sea lanes, and the Persian Gulf ahead of Egypt and the Suez Canal in the order of strategic priorities.

Nevertheless, it was as important and as alive as these other imperial battle bases, packed with men and women of all races, Kenyan askaris rubbing shoulders with Indian gunners, Rhodesian lorry drivers, Australian infantrymen, British sailors, Burgher cipher clerks, Canadian pilots, Tamil dockers, and third generation tea planters. Along with civilian refugees fleeing colonies overrun by the Japanese and even a number of Axis prisoners of war, thousands of military migrants came to an island inhabited at the time by 6,010,000 people. This figure was broken down in a 1941 estimate into 2,596,000 'Low Country' and 1,467,000 'Kandyan' Sinhalese; 697,000 Ceylonese Tamils, 650,000 Indian Tamils, and 167,000 'other' Tamils; 380,000 'Moors', 18,000 Malays, 30,000 Burghers and 10,000 Europeans.[4]

Initially, these wartime migrants arrived as refugees and as reinforcements at a moment of great peril, when Allied colonies were falling to the Japanese and their mighty navy sought to destroy British sea power in the Indian Ocean. This featured an assault on Ceylon intended to 'Pearl Harbor' the Royal Navy and finish what had been started with the sinking of *Prince of Wales* and *Repulse* on 10 December 1941. Later, as the tide of war turned in the Allies' favour, Ceylon became an offensive base where imperial forces gathered ahead of anticipated attempts to reoccupy the lost colonies stretching all the way from the Burma-India border to Java and Indo-China. From Ceylon, aircraft and warships helped sweep the eastern Indian Ocean clear of Japanese forces, while imperial divisions involved in the Burma campaign trained and recuperated there. The island became a giant naval base, aircraft carrier, and military nerve-centre for forces massing under Admiral Lord Louis Mountbatten, Supreme Allied Commander South East Asia, headquartered in Ceylon's Central Highlands with a staff of over 5,000 men and women.

* * *

Using archival material from Britain and Sri Lanka and a range of secondary sources never before brought together in such a fashion, the book provides the first comprehensive single-volume study of Ceylon's war, collating, extending, and augmenting previous work that I have undertaken.[5] It also significantly broadens and deepens the subject's scant historiography,

4 These figures are from The National Archives (TNA), London, 940.531 SHU, John Shuckburgh, 'Colonial Civil History of the War',(4 volumes), volume 3, part 4, 'Major Political Developments Arising Out of the War', 4, 'Ceylon', p. 41. Ceylon administrative reports for 1945 gives a population of 6.6 million. See Sri Lanka National Archives (SNLA), Colombo, Lot 5/439, 12/170. Colonial Office figures for May 1941 showed a population of 5.5 million including 3.5 million Sinhalese, 380,000 'Moslems', 30,000 Burghers, 10,000 Europeans, and 1.5 million Tamils. 'Of the latter a substantial number have for generations past been settled in the Island and others come to and fro between the Island and India – in 1938, 180,000 Indians including 50,000 labourers were recorded in such migration'. See K. M. De Silva (ed.), *Sri Lanka*, part 1, *The Second World War and the Soulbury Commission 1939-1945*, British Documents on the End of Empire (London: The Stationery Office, 1997), pp. 175-76, CO 54/981/14, no. 10, Indians in Ceylon, May 1941.

5 See Ashley Jackson, chapter 10, 'The Indian Ocean' and chapter 11, 'Islands of the Indian Ocean', in Jackson, *The British Empire and the Second World War* (London: Continuum, 2006); Jackson, 'Refitting the Fleet in Ceylon: The War Record of Walker Sons and Company', *Journal of Indian Ocean Studies*, 10, 3 (2002); Jackson, 'The Colonial Empire and Imperial Defence', in Greg Kennedy (ed.), *Old World Order: Imperial Defence, 1856-1956* (London: Routledge, 2007); Jackson, '"Defend Lanka Your Home": War on the Home Front in Ceylon, 1939-1945', *War in History*, 16, 2 (2009); Jackson,

which offers very few publications relating directly to the island's war experience. The limited focus on the wartime Indian Ocean relevant to Ceylon has been dominated by accounts of the brief Japanese raid of April 1942, the naval manoeuvres that took place, and the aerial combat between British and Japanese forces over Colombo and Trincomalee.

The book's chapters explain why Ceylon was so important, how it became a refugee base for people escaping calamities in neighbouring colonies, and charts the organizational and military preparations undertaken in order to prepare the island for invasion. It offers a detailed account of the Japanese raids of April 1942 before explaining how Ceylon became the base for South East Asia Command, chronicling the range of activities Mountbatten undertook from his Kandy headquarters following its arrival in spring 1944. The book also offers a detailed description of what life was like in Ceylon for the imperial service personnel stationed there, their professional and recreational activities, and presents a multi-faceted account of the war's impact on the island's home front. It is best read in conjunction with its partner volume, *Of Islands, Ports, and Sea Lanes: Africa and the Indian Ocean in the Second World War*, which chronicles the war in the wider region.[6] In turn, these two books compliment another recent study, *Persian Gulf Command: A History of the Second World War in Iran and Iraq*, because this region abutted the Indian Ocean and depended on its sea lanes in order to play its own important role in Allied strategy.[7]

Having said all of that, it is necessary to convey to the reader the author's awareness that this is by no means an exhaustive study; even when dealing with a relatively tightly-bounded and defined topic – such as a single colonial territory during the war – there is always *plenty* more work to be done. This is particularly the case if one has attempted to write a book that covers a lot of ground – looking at strategic and military perspectives along with political, social, and economic ones, while also trying to blend in the experiences and impressions of 'those who were there'. Making a contribution that others might supplement and build upon is part of the pleasure of working in a field where one knows there is so much more material to be uncovered, assessed, and presented in published form. It is also a reason why reviews of books that take a 'they didn't look at such-and-such' or 'they don't adequately address the indigenous experience' etcetera line are greeted with chagrin; unless such omissions invalidate what *is* actually proffered, such reviews can tell us more about the reviewer's own preoccupations, and the sometimes irresistible desire to get one over on the author under the microscope. In such cases, the author's natural response is: 'Well, go and write it then. This is what I've done, and I hope it's a contribution to the field'.

chapter 3, 'The Evolution of Ceylon as a Martial Colony, 1760-1960' and chapter 10, 'Ceylon, Mauritius, and the Indian Ocean in the Second World War', in Jackson, *Distant Drums: The Role of Colonies in British Imperial Warfare* (Brighton: Sussex Academic Press, 2010); Jackson, 'Military Migrants: British Service Personnel in Ceylon during the Second World War', *Britain and the World*, 6, 1 (2013); and Jackson, 'Ceylon's Home Front during the Second World War', in Mark Crowley and Sandra Trudgen Dawson (eds), *Home Fronts: Britain and the Empire at War, 1939-1945* (Martlesham, Suffolk: Boydell and Brewer, 2017).

6 Ashley Jackson, *Of Islands, Ports, and Sea Lanes: Africa and the Indian Ocean in the Second World War* (Solihull: Helion, 2018).

7 Ashley Jackson, *Persian Gulf Command: A History of the Second World War in Iran and Iraq* (London: Yale University Press, 2018).

One makes this point not to goad potential readers and reviewers, or to 'get one's apologies in early', but to display an awareness of the work's limitations and a sense of what else might be done to further the study of Ceylon during the war. From the vantage point of this author's research, several things come to mind. Firstly, the British national archives at Kew alone contain shelves full of untapped material. Just a cursory search of 'Ceylon 1939-1945' yields 3,386 files. Secondly, a great deal of memoir-type material exists in the Imperial War Museum and the National Army Museum that would allow a much more comprehensive military history to be approached. Thirdly, the Sri Lanka national archives, in which I conducted some research, needs to be properly mined, along with the archives that will undoubtedly exist in other Sri Lankan institutions, as well as those in related national collections, such as those of Singapore.[8] Fourthly, it would be a boon if one day someone with the requisite language skills were to examine Japanese military thinking and deployments in the Indian Ocean, including the attacks on Ceylon, starting, perhaps, with translations of the relevant sections of the Japanese official history. Finally, and a subject not directly addressed in this book, there is clearly plenty of potential for a scholar with the necessary academic and linguistic skills to produce a history of the war centred on the experience of the island's people, especially its Sinhalese and Tamil communities. Though time is fast running out, a comprehensive oral history of the war in Ceylon would be of inestimable benefit.[9]

In preparing this book I have incurred numerous debts of gratitude. In Sri Lanka in 2007, during a visit generously supported by the British Academy, my research was greatly aided by W. A. Upali Senaratne who as a driver and guide was able to answer all my questions about the country, its people, flora and fauna, as well as the then British High Commissioner, Dominick Chilcott. Thanks are also due to Lieutenant Colonel Anton Gash, Defence Attaché at the British High Commission, who provided both hospitality and generous assistance. Thanks also to Major-General N. A. Ranasinghe, Commandant, Sri Lanka Defence Services Command and Staff College, for allowing me to lecture to the college. Also, to Dr Saroja Wettasinghe, Director of the National Archives of Sri Lanka and her staff, and Wester Felthman, General Manager of the St Andrew's Hotel Nuwara Eliya. My colleague Professor Andrew Stewart has provided much help in my recent Indian Ocean researches; Dr Sarah Butler very kindly allowed me to see the papers of the wartime Chief Censor Ceylon, Frederick Tippet; and Duncan Rogers graciously allowed me to publish two Indian Ocean books with his publishing house, Helion. George Anderson provided the maps for this and *Of Islands, Ports and Sea Lanes*, and

8 During a research trip to Singapore in 2012 I was able to visit the National Archives but did not have time to do anything other than search the online collection. The archive holds an impressive oral history collection, and many of the items refer to people who were evacuated or escaped from Singapore to Ceylon, detailing what they did while they were there.

9 De Silva makes the point that, under the constitution of 1931 'responsibility over large and important areas of government activity was transferred to the Board of Ministers and the executive committees [of the State Council].', De Silva (ed.), *Sri Lanka*, p. xxxii. This means that there is very little on social policy in the Colonial Office archives held in London, though radical changes in education and language policy were being adopted and an embryo welfare state was in the process of creation. What one doesn't get – or, rather, what I haven't seen – are the kind of district reports common in the African colonial empire.

Kim McSweeney has brought her excellent typesetting skills to both titles. My wife Andrea has assisted in the manuscript's preparation in several important ways.

I must also acknowledge authors whose works offer specialist help on aspects of Ceylon's wartime story. Rob Stuart's articles offers the best detail on the Japanese air raids on Colombo and Trincomalee , and I am indebted to John Barrass for his work on the RAF during the raids and his helpfulness in tracing sources; Ralph Ferdinands's *Proud and Prejudiced* history of the island's Burgher community provides some fine recollections from those who lived through the war; James Thompson's exquisite memoir-story of his time in Ceylon and other Indian Ocean islands during the war has added rich tones to both this book and *Of Islands, Ports, and Sea Lanes*; Andrew Boyd's *The Royal Navy in Eastern Waters* has taken the study of the strategic situation in the Indian Ocean up to 1942 to another level; and K. M. De Silva's *Sri Lanka: The Second World War and the Soulbury Commission*, part of the British Documents on the End of Empire project, is a must-read for anyone interested in the island's wartime history.

I am particularly indebted to the authors of the memoirs I have used here. These include the many people who contributed their stories to the excellent BBC World War Two People's War oral history initiative in the early 2000s. Special thanks are due to the men and women who in the late 1990s corresponded with me and sent me their reminiscences, handwritten, often on air mail letter paper, or hammered out on typewriters. This was in response to an advertisement placed in the *Ceylon Association Bulletin*, 232 (January 1999). These generous people sent their reminiscences and extracts from books, and put me in touch with other people, a network that came to encompass correspondents in America, Australia, Britain, Jersey, New Zealand, and Sri Lanka. I became a member of the Ceylon Association, and attended a Ceylon Comrades Reunion at the Victory Services Club, Seymour Street, London W2. I am only sorry that few of those people who offered me their assistance for this project will be alive, 20 years later, to see the result. But some of them will be, along with their children, and it is important to name them in order to thank them and to acknowledge their aid. So, thank you to Gerard Robinson, J. D. N. Banks, George Shepperson, Tom Barron, Monica Hulme, William Barry Cameron, Jack Thornhill, Peter Beauchamp, Alistair Jackson-Smale, John Rogers, Ronald Barber, Cynthia Samuel, Joan Gottelier, Bubbles Mullins, Ian Bennett, Jane Bennett, Trevor St. C Anghie, Daniel Parker, Mahinda and Deanna Abeykoon, Lerenz Pereira, Mavis Pereira, Ralph Banks, Ivor Ferdinands, and I. P. Domingopillai of the Ceylon Chamber of Commerce.

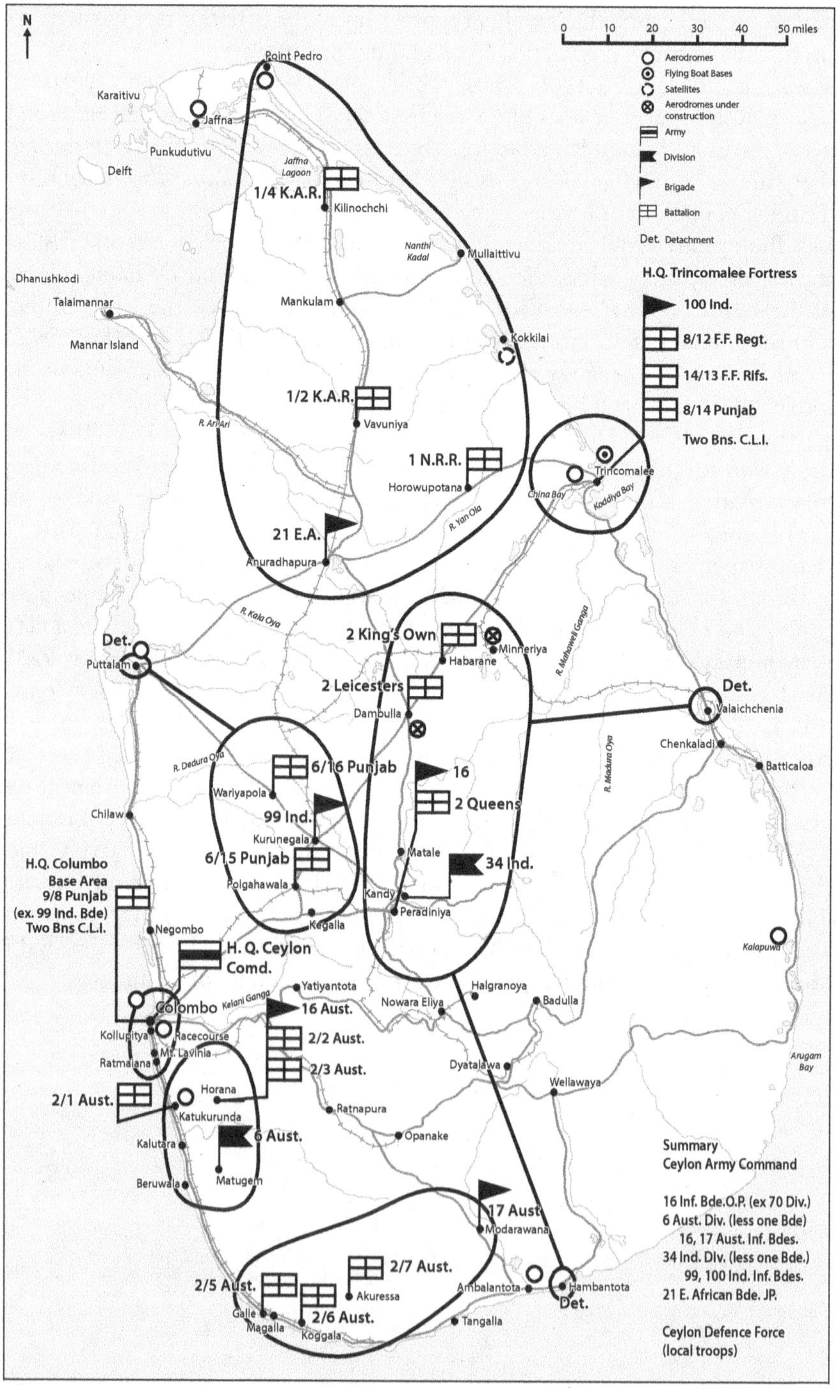

This map is based on a May 1942 War Office map entitled 'Dispositions – Ceylon Army Command', showing the positions and defensive responsibilities of the army units stationed on the island at the time of the Japanese raids.

1

The surrogate Singapore

Like most British colonies east of Suez, Ceylon experienced a war of two halves. In the first half the fighting was a distant, primarily European affair. On 28 December 1939 Governor Sir Andrew Caldecott told the Colonial Office that the State Council, the colony's unicameral legislature, had passed a resolution of loyalty.[1] While keen to drive forward their nationalist agenda and constantly drawing Whitehall's attention to the more fractious stance of the Indian National Congress, the politicians of the Ceylon National Congress 'do not question the certainty of our victory ... Outside the ranks of politicians considerable interest in the war is evidenced by an enormous increase in the circulation of vernacular newspapers. The great majority of these emanate from Lake House (the home of the Ceylon Daily News) and are sane, sound and loyal'.[2]

'The first general reaction to the declaration of war', the Governor continued, 'was a sense of relief from long suspense and of duty at last begun. This was manifested in the speed with which mobilization of local forces was effected and in the cooperation of the public with observing the coastal black-out'.[3] But the second reaction, Caldecott wrote:

> was a wave of unfortunate memories of the [heavily suppressed] riots of 1915, resulting in suspicion and criticism of Defence measures already taken and of those thought likely to be taken. In view of the fact that four of my seven Ministers, the Deputy Speaker and the Proprietor of the Daily News group of newspapers were all arrested, imprisoned and in fear of having to face a firing squad in 1915 this second reaction, however regrettable, need cause neither surprise nor undue concern.[4]

1 De Silva (ed.), *Sri Lanka*, CO 54/971/11, no. 7, Things Ceylonese (a regular informal review of Ceylon affairs sent by Caldecott to the Colonial Office), 28/12/39, p. 26. Ceylon was one of the most constitutionally advanced colonies in the British Empire. The State Council had replaced the old legislative council under the Donoughmore constitution of 1931. From it, Ceylonese ministers were drawn who formed part of the government in a Board of Ministers, a most unusual situation in a British colony (as opposed to the 'white' dominions and the politically mature India), where although legislative councils (consultative, not executive, bodies) usually existed, executive power was fully concentrated in the hands of the governor.

2 Ibid.

3 Ibid., CO 54/971/11, no. 1, Things Ceylonese, 7/9/39, p. 2.

4 Ibid., pp. 2-3. Occurring on the centenary of the Kingdom of Kandy's secession to British rule, the riots led to the mobilization of the Ceylon Defence Force and communal disturbances robustly suppressed by the garrison troops of the 28th Punjabi Regiment.

Even at this early stage of the war, the dramatic events of spring-summer 1940, as Germany invaded the Low Countries and conquered France, could not help but engage the interest of the people of Ceylon, especially its European and westernized communities. From the east, meanwhile, news of Japan's war in China had been followed for some years, including horrifying tales of atrocities committed in captured towns and cities.

Nevertheless, with the war apparently distant and Ceylon being considered 'out of the zone of hostilities', as the Governor phrased it, indigenous politicians adopted a 'business as usual' approach to their politics, which revolved around an intense and protracted dispute with the Government of India regarding the issue of Indian immigration and strident calls for constitutional advancement towards full self-governing status.[5] In May 1940 Caldecott reported that most ministers do not 'appear in the least worried about the Empire's ordeal. I have noticed no worthy response from them to appeals for War Charities'.

Their present political philosophy seems to be founded on three considerations:

> 1. The British Naval and Mercantile Marine are invincible, and Ceylon has therefore no need to envisage any change of her world-status arising out of the war;
> 2. This being so her politicians can go on with, nay intensify, their usual game of pinpricks [sniping at the colonial government] and with impunity blame Britain for everything that Ceylon has got and everything she hasn't.[6]

The third 'consideration' was the politicians' desire for a general election in order, Caldecott claimed, to secure re-election into a parliament where there was no opposition party, securing 'thereby a further provision of livelihood from State Funds'.[7]

In June Caldecott reported on the 'general situation in the island', dividing the population into the 'left-wing Samajists [members of the Communist/Trotskyist Lanka Sama Samaja Party] ... who in these dark days have come out definitely anti-British', and the 'non-English speaking classes', urban, agricultural, and labour, among whom there was no 'inherent antipathy' towards Britain but comprising people easily swayed by politicians. There were then the 'clerical classes', generally pro-British, and the 'upper native classes', divided between those who were pro-British and those who were 'pro-Ceylonese' and in favour of Ceylon's elevation to dominion status, which would put it on an autonomous constitutional par with Australia, Canada, New Zealand, and South Africa. Not anti-British, the recent fall of France and Italy's subsequent declaration of war had caused this group to rally to the Empire's cause, and 'the Ministers and nearly all of the State Councillors and politicians belong to this stratum'. There was then the 'European community', divided between 'the reactionaries' who opposed the involvement of indigenous Ceylonese people in the island's governance (a horse that had already well and truly bolted), and 'the moderates'.[8]

The war had moved a step closer when Italy joined the fray in June 1940, extending the fighting into the Indian Ocean courtesy of the East Africa campaign fought between British and Italian forces on land, sea, and in the air. But signs of war in Ceylon remained discreet,

5 Ibid., CO 54/971/11, no. 7, p. 26.
6 Ibid, CO 54/977/7, no. 6, Things Ceylonese, 20/5/40, p. 82.
7 Ibid.
8 Ibid., CO 54/977/7, no. 9, Things Ceylonese, 29/6/40, pp. 106-07.

if visible at all. Colombo and Trincomalee, and the warships of the East Indies Station they accommodated, became busier as German raiders were hunted across the Indian Ocean and the navy operated off East Africa and in the Red Sea in support of troops on land; the odd Australasian troop convoy began to appear in Colombo harbour en route to the Middle East; and 200 miles south of Colombo, parts of the Maldive Islands, a British protectorate administered as a dependency of Ceylon though internally self-governing under a sultanate, were gradually prepared for service as a naval base in the event of Singapore being incapacitated. But with the fighting fronts far away and little expectation that Japan would dare challenge Anglo-American hegemony, the conflict's effects were hardly alarming. 'We had absolute faith in our navy', said Joan Gottelier, a 21 year old planter's daughter working in the signals reference library at the shore base HMS *Lanka* in Colombo.[9] The European community was confident, Singapore and Trincomalee were considered mighty naval bases, British prestige stood high, and if it came to war, the Japanese would be no match when confronted with the discipline and traditions of British troops, whatever they had achieved in China.

Nevertheless, even at this early stage of the conflict Caldecott was keen to ensure that London understood the strength of nationalist feeling in Ceylon and the root causes of the 'loyalty' evinced by its leaders towards Britain vis-à-vis the war. In September 1940 he wrote:

> I can also state without doubt or hesitation that social and political opinion in this Island among all non-European communities is predominantly and progressively nationalistic and thereby in effect, if not in essence, anti-British. The great majority of Sinhalese and Tamils want to see as many Britishers out of the Island as possible, and as few of them into it as possible …
>
> Ceylon's loyalty to the Empire during the war, which I assess at over 99 per cent, should not be mistaken for something that it is not. It is due to two things, first, the realization that Nazi victory would set an end to Ceylonese nationalism; second, a high sentimental regard for the King's Person and Throne.[10]

Ceylon's strategic position was also being monitored in Whitehall in these early stages of the conflict. In November 1940 the Chiefs of Staff considered an 'appreciation of the situation at Ceylon', a 14 page document prepared following meetings of the combined military staffs of India and Ceylon. Their rationale was that with the recent creation of Far East Command in Singapore, and in case of war with Japan, joint staff talks were prudent. They were very clear on the value of Ceylon: 'the strategic position of Ceylon and the facilities it offers as a Naval base far outweigh those which could be provided by any port on the coast of India'.[11]

9 Joan Gottelier, letters to the author 4/3/99, and interview, Martock, Somerset, April 1999. In August 1940 Joan went with her father for an interview, and was called to start work less than two days later, missing her own 21st birthday party. She worked in ciphers and signals, and along with other locally-recruited employees, 'carried' the naval shore headquarters until the arrival of members of the Women's Royal Naval Service (Wrens) from Britain.

10 De Silva (ed.), *Sri Lanka*, CO 54/974/1, no. 2, Caldecott to Colonial Secretary Lord Lloyd, 17/9/40, p. 126 and p. 129.

11 TNA, AIR 20/4689, Ceylon: Defence appreciation, 28/11/40. The report's appendices detailed the island's defence forces, military facilities, railway rolling stock, topography, and the essential needs of the civilian population.

As the situation darkened in 1941, the British prepared to defend the island, the Chiefs of Staff considering the matter as early as February and decreeing that the garrison would need to be increased.[12] The ensuing plan for the reinforcement of the garrison was known as scheme Lancelot.[13] Reinforcement would come from the Indian Army, and the commanding officer of that force, when it arrived, would take over from the Officer Commanding Troops Ceylon as the island's most senior military figure. A War Office document, 'Administrative appreciation relative to the reinforcement of Ceylon', said that Colombo and Trincomalee would be the obvious targets if an enemy force landed on the island. Ceylon's defenders would also need to protect the ferry point giving access to India, as an enemy would likely try and prevent further reinforcement. It was assessed that the most that could be done by the garrison would be to stop a landed enemy getting to Colombo and Trincomalee and to hold such a force until it could be rounded up or cut off by sea. The minimum defensive requirement was an infantry brigade in each place. They would need to operate on interior lines and not be drawn too far away from their positions. 'River lines approximately 25 miles NORTH and SOUTH of COLOMBO and TRINCOMALEE appear to be suitable natural obstacles on which to hold the enemy and it is not expected that troops will be called upon to operate outside this 25 mile radius'.[14] Ceylon Command was advised to take in hand preparatory work essential to the operation of such a force if it were deployed. Cement pill boxes and anti-tank ditches would be needed and the water supply to Trincomalee improved, and each brigade would require 50 20-seater buses, this number being considered 'sufficient, working on a 25 mile radius, to move a whole Brigade within 12 hours'.[15] At this stage, it was envisaged that:

> The reinforcements will comprise two infantry brigades, two howitzer batteries (3.7 or 4.5), one anti-tank battery, one field coy. together with Force H. Q. of which the Commander will assume command of all troops in Ceylon on arrival. They will not be sent until the first sign of a definite threat – i. e. the first indications that the enemy is in a position to advance West of Singapore or East of Aden – but when the decision to reinforce is made, it may only be a matter of hours before the troops arrive in Ceylon. The decision to despatch will be taken by H. M. G. in London.[16]

Tangible echoes now protruded into Ceylonese life more frequently, including the arrival on 6 October 1941 of 2,500 Italian prisoners of war who had been interned in Malaya.[17] Later in the month, the Colombo-bound portion of convoy WS 11 arrived from Bombay, *Largs Bay* bringing 1,000 all ranks, *Nieuw Amsterdam* 250 all ranks, *Johan de Witt* 1,000 all ranks, and *Orion* 500 men of the 5th Field Regiment along with supplies and ration packs.[18] Unaware of the full gravity of the situation, Ceylonese politicians remained preoccupied with proposals for

12 TNA, WO 106/4151, Ceylon defence, 10/2/41 to 30/8/41.
13 TNA, WO 106/4485, Ceylon reinforcement.
14 Ibid.
15 Ibid.
16 Ibid., minute, October 1941.
17 Butler Papers, private collection, the papers of Frederick Tippet.
18 TNA, WO 106/4485, secret cipher telegram, Embarkation Officer Bombay to GOC Malay and Officer Commanding Troops Ceylon, 27/10/41.

constitutional reform, the ramifications of labour unrest, and the issue of Indian immigration and the 'Indophobia' that it bred among the local population. 'Nationalistic feeling', a Colonial Office minute explained,

> has increased in India and in Ceylon ... [and] of late there has grown up a feeling in Ceylon, particularly among the Sinhalese, that there are too many Indians in the island, and that they are taking away work from the Sinhalese. The Government of India, in turn, have felt constrained to press for fuller recognition of the rights of Indians who have settled down in the island and have the intention of making it their home.[19]

While the general public were not insensitive to the Japanese threat, its character was that of distant thunder, not expected to develop into a storm. The thought that war could possibly ravage Ceylon and its neighbourhood would have been considered frankly preposterous, as people here and in places such as India and Burma had for long been inured to the security provided by 'fortress' Singapore and the umbrella of British seapower. As a 1940 British Pathé news film put it, Ceylon was 'as safe and sound as the British Empire of which it is part'.[20] On 8 December 1941 – the day after the Japanese attacked Pearl Harbor – the *Times of Ceylon* reassured readers that 'frequently it has been stated that the defence of Ceylon is assured by the huge perimeter stretching from Egypt across the Himalayas to Singapore'.[21] 'Ceylon is still a place of safety', the paper claimed a fortnight later.[22] Schoolboy Gerard Robinson's father had driven him to see *Prince of Wales* and *Repulse* docked in Colombo harbour, and he had felt sorry for the Japanese who might have to face them.[23] Admiral Sir Tom Phillips, the Commander-in-Chief of the newly-formed Eastern Fleet of which these two great ships were the vanguard, had broken his journey for a few hours at Colombo. Here he lunched with Governor Caldecott at his official residence, Queen's House, right by the harbour, before flying on to Singapore ahead of his ships. Less than two weeks later

19 De Silva (ed.), *Sri Lanka*, CO 54/981/14, May 1941.

20 See 'Safe and Sound' film footage, at https://www.youtube.com/watch?v=VkSoZmhBXDI

21 Sri Lanka National Archives (SNLA), *Times of Ceylon*, 8/12/41. This was a common theme of imperial propaganda. The 1938 Ministry of Information film 'Alert in the East' explained: 'Stronghold, naval base, strategic centre, Singapore is above all one of the ramparts of that freedom for which the British Empire stands ... As Singapore commands the eastern entrance to the Indian Ocean, so the security of the great Indian empire has been enormously increased. That home of magnificent fighting men is able to mass her resources for the conflict in which her destiny is vitally at stake. Undistracted by the worries of self defence, she has been able to send large numbers of experienced fighting men overseas to serve under General Wavell [in the Middle East]'. See https://www.youtube.com/watch?v=AqoCNsFFq7k. The 8 December edition of the *Times of Ceylon* also announced a black out that evening, though said that the threat of air attack was remote. It reported that Japanese nationals had been rounded up and the Japanese consulate's communications severed; seven Hungarian nationals were also removed to the internment camp opened at the Diyatalawa military base. The headline ran: 'Whole world at war: Japanese challenge: Singapore, Thailand, Hong Kong, Malaya, Hawaii, Manila attacked'.

22 SNLA, *Times of Ceylon*, 23/12/41.

23 Gerard Robinson, *Fading Edge of Empire* (Sydney: The Author, 1998), p. 70.

both were at the bottom of the Gulf of Siam and 840 members of their crew dead, Admiral Phillips among them.[24]

Pearl Harbor and its immediate aftermath changed things dramatically. Royal Marines officer James Thompson arrived in Ceylon on that fateful day:

> On a famous night in December, 1941, the island first came into my heart; the night when the lights of Colombo were lowered and the years of darkness gathered around that lovely, tawdry city.
>
> On the night we arrived in Colombo harbour the lights faded and grew cold on the legendary sign which proudly blazed over the harbour and out to sea and 'Ceylon for Good Tea' remained a gaunt and rusting memory through all the years.
>
> Pearl Harbour [sic] Day; and the city lights were mechanically snuffed, as the rattle of the bombs fallen on distant Hawaii echoed across the Pacific. I stepped ashore into a blundering, bewildered and darkened city. I felt as though I was on the fringe of the plague, advance germ or microbe in a disease which stretched scabrous hands from East to West. We were the harbingers of darkness, the wingless angels of unnatural shadow, the lights died on our coming to continent and city; we were the khaki plague.
>
> In near darkness we sat in the near deserted hotels, the Grand Oriental, the Galle Face; disappointed, depressed, all pleasures soured, our high spirits deflated like punctured bladders. Four young men in a startled, uncertain city, groping in its first chaotic darkness, a city afraid of the high drone in the night sky, the natives restless, uneasy, the Europeans calm, heroically helpless.
>
> There were few troops in the island and we enjoyed a certain illustrious, privileged isolation; four uniformed young men in the empty hotel lounges, returned from island sickness and squalor to a lonely hour in a quiet room, drinking expensive beer under the revolving fans. The city to which we came so eagerly was dark and disturbed; there were few European women, the mirrored bars bare, the high stools unweighted by the svelte flanks of the anxious girls so vividly conceived in our foetid tents [the men had been based in very trying conditions in the Chagos Archipelago]; taxi drivers, rickshaw wallahs, waiters clustered anxiously together, the hotel telephone kiosks never empty. From the heights of our European experience we watched the routine antics.[25]

24 Joan Gottelier recounts a tragicomic story: 'When *Prince of Wales* and *Repulse* passed through, everything had to be absolutely ship shape in the office and our cypher officer stood at the window [as the warships left for Singapore] and said "I hope I never see those ships again". Did he eat his words!'. Gottelier interview, April 1999.

25 J. Alan Thompson, *Only the Sun Remembers* (London: Andrew Dakers, 1950), p. 185-86. Chapter 8, 'Island of the Heart', Thompson's love letter to wartime Ceylon, and to Jeanette. 'The evening was stillborn', the passage continued; 'we carried our darkness. But I found splendour and beauty in the perfect sweep of the Galle Face Green, the feel of rare, good grass to my soft feet, the first realisation of the great mass of the [Galle Face] Hotel now dark against the night-blue sky, the garden palms leaning over the surf ... Suddenly I knew; I knew there was grandeur in this city'. A couple of days later, Thompson was in the Central Highlands at the Diyatalawa military rest camp. Out for an evening's drinking with friends, he was dumbfounded to learn, on returning drunk to base, of the sinking of *Prince of Wales* and *Repulse*. The passage is reproduced in Jackson, *Of Islands, Ports, and Sea Lanes.*

The year 1942 was the hinge on which the fortunes of the British Empire rested, the year in which it seemed that all that could go wrong did, culminating in a breath-taking series of reverses for both the British and their allies. British imperial forces were thrown back in the Western Desert and Tobruk was captured along with its 33,000-strong garrison; the Battle of the Atlantic entered its bleakest phase and the U-boats enjoyed their 'happy time' off America's eastern seaboard; the disastrous Dieppe raid underlined the enormous difficulties the Allies faced in breaching Hitler's Fortress Europe; the Japanese conquest of the Malayan peninsula led to the fall of Singapore that shocked the world; Burma was invaded by Japanese troops advancing in the wake of hundreds of thousands of retreating soldiers and civilians, all scrambling to get to India; and the Germans launched their summer offensive in the Soviet Union, which, in the light of the Barbarossa offensive to date, appeared to have every chance of success.

In the Pacific, the Japanese conquered strategic American islands such Guam and Wake, as well as British and Australian territories in the Bismarck Archipelago, the Gilbert and Ellice Islands, New Guinea, and the Solomons. In February the Dutch East Indies were invaded and remaining Allied naval power in the East Indies and south-west Pacific fought a last-stand battle in the Java Sea. The annihilation of the participating American, Australian, British, and Dutch cruisers and destroyers on 27-28 February led rapidly to the collapse of General Sir Archibald Wavell's stillborn American-British-Dutch-Australian (ABDA) Command, a mere six weeks after Churchill and Roosevelt and the combined Allied chiefs of staff had created it.[26] In March Rangoon fell, the Dutch East Indies capitulated, and in May the conquest of Burma was completed and all resistance in the Philippines ceased, though General Douglas MacArthur vowed to return. The Bay of Bengal now belonged to the Japanese, and the Andaman and Nicobar Islands were taken, beginning years of brutal occupation that would wipe out 10 per cent of the population.

After the frenzied conquest of a vast new empire, the Japanese looked set to invade Australia, Ceylon, and India, seemingly capable of doing whatever they turned their hands to. Following Pearl Harbor and the raid on Darwin in Western Australia (19 February), Vice Admiral Chuichi Nagumo's fleet of carriers and battleships searched for its next challenge. This he found when he led his fleet through the Sunda Strait separating Java from Sumatra and entered the Indian Ocean, on course for Ceylon where he intended to destroy the Royal Navy's Eastern Fleet, simultaneously paralyzing shipping by air raids and shore bombardments along India's coast. Now, the veils were removed from everyone's eyes, and people in Ceylon had cause to worry. 'We felt there was a real chance of invasion', said Joan Gottelier, and 'many planters sent their wives and kids down to South Africa'.[27] Schoolboy William Cameron, a member of a tea planting family, recalled the 'serious faces of parents and grandparents listening to Radio Ceylon evening news', and felt prompted to ask his father if the Japanese were going to come and kill them.[28]

Yet the island was not entirely unprepared; in line with every territory of the British Empire – even those almost inconceivably remote from any likely battlefield or threat of invasion – there was a defence scheme in place and locally-recruited defence forces waiting. In 1940, for example, the 2nd Battalion The Ceylon Light Infantry was route marching around the island to places

26 See Jackson, *Of Islands, Ports, and Sea Lanes.*
27 Gottelier interview, April, 1999.
28 William Barry Cameron, letter to author, 26/5/99, and enclosed typescript, 'Bits and Pieces'.

such as Colombo, Diyatalawa, and Ratmalana airport, mounting guards for Ceylon Garrison Artillery anti-aircraft units and around key installations such as the Pettah Power House, the Pettah Pump House, and the broadcasting station.[29] In October 1941 Major-General H. V. Lewis, commander of the 17th Indian Division, was detailed to prepare a report on the defence of Ceylon for Wavell. He assumed a Japanese scale of attack amounting to two infantry divisions, and that their intent would be to destroy the port facilities of Colombo and Trincomalee and cut rail and sea communications with India. 'The forces available to defend these objectives are inadequate and a third Brigade is urgently required to ensure the efficient defence of the Island'.[30]

Though there were no air force assets to speak of, as a naval base Ceylon's ports had been afforded a degree of protection. The island also possessed a small imperial garrison and a Ceylon Defence Force that was approaching a strength of 5,000 as the year 1941 matured, bolstered in January 1942 by the arrival of two brigades of the 34th Indian Division, its 99th Indian Infantry Brigade deployed for the defence of Colombo, the 100th Indian Infantry Brigade for Trincomalee.[31] Writing in the *Spectator* on 20 March 1942, J. Tudor Jones said that

> Ceylon has for years been fully alive to the responsibilities of her position. She has endeavoured, even though the means at hand were small, to train and expand a defence force composed of her nationalities, and to create in all minds an awareness of things which might happen, and of what all men and women might some day be called upon to do. As a member of the Volunteer Defence Force, I was fighting imaginary Japanese landings four years ago. We might call the enemy Sabronians or Illubullians, but we knew who they were. Our exercises were amongst tea and rubber plantations, and in jungle ways, as in Malaya and Java; making full use both of the excellent roads and railways and of the bullock-cart tracks. Sometimes we made these battles more real by joining with the Navy and the Fleet Air Arm.[32]

29 TNA, WO 172/1558, 2nd Battalion The Ceylon Light Infantry, war diaries, October 1940 to November 1941.

30 TNA, WO 106/4516, Ceylon defence, 1/9/41 to 10/2/42, Major-General Lewis, Precis of the report on the defence of Ceylon, 6/10/41. Lewis's plan envisaged the defence of Colombo and Trincomalee by a brigade apiece with army headquarters and a reserve at Kandy, a Ceylon Light Infantry force defending the ferry point to India as well as Mannar Island, and armed patrols in armoured fighting vehicles deployed to guard the railway lines. 'Mobile Forces from KANDY, COLOMBO, or TRINCOMALEE will be utilised to deal with raiding parties'. At Trincomalee, two battalions would 'retain their mobility to counter landings between MULLAITTIVU and BATTICALOA. The equivalent of Two Bns [battalions]. and One Indian Bn. of the C. L. I. [Ceylon Light Infantry] will man the beach defence pillboxes and will be utilised for Aerodrome defence'. In the Colombo sector, Lewis recommended, 'Two Indian Infantry Bns. will be utilised to counter enemy landings between the rivers MAMA OYA in the North, and the KALUGANGA in the South. The 2nd and 3rd Bns. C. L. I., One Indian Bn. and First Reinforcements from the Indian Bde [brigade]. to form the defence of Colombo in pillboxes etc'.

31 Ibid., order of battle. An Indian infantry company was also deployed to defend Galle. The Ceylon Defence Force's headquarters was at Diyatalawa.

32 J. Tudor Jones, 'Ceylon on Guard', *The Spectator*, 20/3/42.

But it was abundantly clear that Britain did not at that moment have sufficient naval resources in the Indian Ocean to prevent a determined Japanese bid to take the island, and that along with an Eastern Fleet being assembled following the loss of *Prince of Wales* and *Repulse*, air and land reinforcements would be needed if an invasion force were to appear on the horizon under the wings of the Imperial Japanese Navy's awesome carrier-borne air force.

Why Ceylon?

For some time before war with Japan erupted, British strategy had ascribed to Ceylon and the Maldives an important role in sustaining the naval power required in the Indian Ocean in order to confront Japan, should that become necessary. They were already regarded as important way-stations on the route east, and as possible fall-back positions should Singapore be threatened, or worse. Furthermore, before the decision was taken, late in the day, to send Force Z – the capital ships *Prince of Wales* and *Repulse* and their attendant destroyers, along with the carrier *Illustrious* – to Singapore, any required build up of naval forces in the Indian Ocean was conceived of as being based on Ceylon.[33] As Churchill wrote to the prime ministers of Australia and New Zealand on 2 August 1940, though Britain was trying its best to avoid war with Japan, if it came Singapore should be able to withstand a long siege. Furthermore, 'We should also be able to base on Ceylon a battle-cruiser and fast aircraft-carrier, which, with all the Australian and New Zealand cruisers and destroyers, which would return to you, would act as a very powerful deterrent upon the hostile raiding cruisers'. In addition, the Mediterranean Fleet could at any time be sent through the Suez Canal to operate in the Indian Ocean.[34]

But the rapidity of Japan's advance between December 1941 and February 1942, and the imperious destruction of all Allied forces in its way, upset such leisurely and hypothetical calculations. Completely unforeseen, the turn of events from Pearl Harbor onwards shocked everyone and elicited the urgent need to reinforce the Indian Ocean, a challenge for the British because their land, sea, and air forces were already stretched across several active theatres of operations. The naval disaster in the Gulf of Siam on 10 December 1941 and the loss of control of the sea that the destruction of Force Z caused, combined with the eradication of British air power in the Malayan peninsula, meant that there was little hope for forces on land as they retired in the face of the Japanese, retreating across the Straits of Johore for a hopeless last stand in Singapore, and, in the north, retreating towards India from Burma in disorder if not entirely in disarray. Vice Admiral Sir Geoffrey Layton, former Commander-in-Chief China Station, now replaced Phillips as interim Commander-in-Chief Eastern Fleet and Britain's most senior naval officer east of Suez. With Singapore doomed, Layton removed his flag and his headquarters temporarily to Java on 5 January and then to Colombo, in order to better organize sea lane protection and convoy escort work across the Indian Ocean region, and because the Allied naval forces assigned to ABDA Command were led by an American admiral. Ultimately, Layton moved

33 For the latest scholarship on the deployment of Force Z and the defence of the Indian Ocean, see Andrew Boyd, *The Royal Navy in Eastern Waters: Linchpin of Victory, 1935-1942* (Barnsley: Seaforth, 2017).

34 Winston Churchill, *The Second World War*, volume 2, *Their Finest Hour* (London: Cassell, 1949), p. 385.

to Ceylon because the strategic bottom line for the British lay in protecting the sea lanes that connected them to the fighting fronts of the Middle East, the oil of the Persian Gulf, and the Indian and Australasian dominions. In order to achieve this, possession of Ceylon, and the integrity of the remaining ships of the Eastern Fleet, was judged to be essential.[35]

Though the British had pledged to support ABDA Command, stood up on 10 January to regroup Allied forces in order to make a fight of it in the East Indies-south-west Pacific region, this could not be the main fight for the British. Effectively, they had to fall back in order to defend the Empire's core interests, which were located further west. Layton left a staff in the Dutch East Indies to supervise Britain's naval contribution to their defence, but along with his masters in London knew that the game was up there. While they could not scuttle and run, equally they could not continue to pump resources into a position that almost certainly could not be held.[36] Layton's clear priority lay in the western Indian Ocean, protecting sea lanes on which the Empire and the Allied war effort depended – which in turn depended on protecting, retaining, and utilizing Ceylon and its ports and denying them to the enemy. Singapore's failure had thrust Ceylon into the strategic limelight.

After its sweeping victories and the decimation of American, British, and Dutch military power in the region, Japan was in a position to challenge Britain's control of the Indian Ocean, a bonus opportunity earned by the ease of conquest thus far.[37] Basically, the Japanese had encountered such slight resistance that they had just kept on going, through South-east Asia and into Burma, and now wolfishly eyed India and stared across a weakly-defended Indian Ocean towards glittering prizes further west. If this was continued and the Japanese neutered the Royal Navy in the Indian Ocean and took Ceylon, they would be in a position to prevent the movement of military material and trade goods between Europe and Asia, prevent supplies and reinforcements from reaching otherwise isolated battlefronts in the Middle East, including Iran and Iraq, deny the British the Gulf oil on which they depended, and be in a position to link hands with German forces pushing for Cairo and the Suez Canal. It would have shown strategic acumen if the Japanese had attempted to do so, while the window of opportunity was wide open and they had their chance. Indian Ocean sea lanes were indispensable for the Allies for other reasons too. America relied on them in order to send aid to British and Chinese forces via the Red Sea and the Bay of Bengal, and since June 1941 a crucial supply line channelling Anglo-American aid to the Soviet Union via the Indian Ocean and the Persian Gulf had been developing, expedited by the Anglo-Soviet invasion of Iran in August 1941 and the control of Iran's transport infrastructure that it yielded.

Singapore's spectacular failure meant that a rapid recalibration of British strategy was required. The 'fortress' on the Malacca Strait no longer barred an enemy approach from the east as two decades of propaganda had led everyone to believe it would. The Indian Ocean's

35 With the closure of the Mediterranean to shipping, reinforcements for imperial forces fighting in North Africa and the eastern Mediterranean had to travel around the Cape and along East Africa's coast, through the Mozambique Channel and into the Red Sea.

36 One of Layton's most important decisions at this point was diverting a carrier-load of Hurricanes, destined for the Dutch East Indies, to Ceylon in early March.

37 The Japanese had what in modern parlance we might call a 'free hit'; Churchill described it as 'a move either way'. Charles Eade (ed.), *Secret Session Speeches by the Right Honourable Winston S. Churchill* (London: Cassell, 1946), p. 47.

sea lanes, supposedly safe behind Singapore's ramparts, now lay exposed; India itself, for long expected to act as a reservoir of troops to meet the Axis threat in the west, suddenly found itself naked on its eastern borders, watching with alarm as Japanese soldiers moved ever closer.

The key thing now was for the British to protect their core interests and draw a line in the sand. As the Japanese scurried westwards in the first quarter of 1942, the British government realized that it was in the Indian Ocean that maritime power would have to be reconstituted, with Ceylon acting as the main base of a fleet kept 'in being', preparing to meet a Japanese foray or further invasions, protecting the sea lanes through convoy escort and tireless patrol, and building for future offensive operations. Meanwhile, it had to be accepted that in the waters east of Ceylon the Royal Navy was a spent force and must await a return to the Far East as and when the general war situation permitted. In the here and now, there were convoys of troops and supplies that needed protection if the Empire was to survive. Hopefully, the Japanese tide would abate sooner rather than later, as they reached the end of their logistical tether and their front line strength, in key assets such as maritime aircraft and pilots, became exhausted, and American power regenerated in the Pacific.

Ceylon thus became the surrogate Singapore, an imperial base camp, a platform for military forces and a conduit giving access to nearby theatres of operations. In conversation with Dr Herbert Evatt, Australia's Minister for External Affairs, Admiral Sir James Somerville – sent to replace Tom Phillip's after his death – explained why Ceylon was the best location for the Empire's main naval base in the war against Japan, as opposed to Australia. Ceylon, he said, 'flanks or covers all vital lines of communication to the Middle East, India, and Australia'.[38] Australia, on the other hand, was at 'the terminal end of a line of communication' and therefore 'unsound and ineffective' as the base for a fleet dedicated to protecting the sea lanes of the Indian Ocean. From Ceylon and the new naval base being developed in the Maldives the Eastern Fleet, it was hoped, could defend the Indian Ocean, supplemented by important African ports such as Durban and Mombasa. Ceylon's strategic value rocketed for other reasons too, for with the loss of Malaya, it became the Allies most important source of that most strategic of raw materials, rubber. But whatever the strategists hopes and plans for Ceylon might now be, as the Allied position disintegrated in South-east Asia and the Dutch East Indies in February-March 1942, for many thousands of ordinary men and women, Ceylon appeared as a beacon of hope as they attempted to escape the clutches of an advancing enemy.

38 Michael Simpson (ed.), *The Somerville Papers: Selections from the Private and Official Correspondence of Admiral of the Fleet Sir James Somerville, GCB, GBE, DSO* (Aldershot: Scholar Press for the Navy Records Society, 1995), letter to Admiral Sir Guy Royle, 17/7/43, p. 463. The occasion was an interview with Evatt in Washington, during which he asked why the Eastern Fleet wasn't stationed in Western Australia.

2

Refugee island: The flight to Colombo

And so began a new chapter in the story of Ceylon, a nascent military redoubt but first, as the Allied position in the surrounding region crumbled, a place of sanctuary. Swept away in the maelstrom of Japanese invasion, remnants of defeated imperial and Allied formations that had cheated death or captivity reached the shores of Australia and Ceylon, as did thousands of evacuated civilians. For many people Ceylon was a last chance saloon, a refuge for those whom the Japanese tide threatened to engulf. Indicating the way the wind was blowing, in the last days of January Singapore naval base was quietly abandoned. Ernest 'Jackie' Spooner, Admiral Superintendent Singapore Dock Yard and Rear Admiral Malaya, ordered 'the entire European naval and civilian dockyard staff to quit the base and fall back on Singapore City, from where they were shipped off to Ceylon'.[1]

The following week, more refugees arrived in Colombo. On 6 February 3,000 women and children were greeted on the dockside by the Colombo Evacuees Committee led by Mrs G. S. Arbuthnot, wife of the Commander-in-Chief East Indies.[2] Some who made it to Ceylon brought specialist skills that were immediately put to good use, such as the chairmen of the Singapore and Rangoon docks, men who were to be integral to the process of readying Colombo and Trincomalee for attack. The men of the Malaya Meteorological Service were sent to Ceylon three days before Singapore's capitulation in order to form a new Air Ministry meteorological service for the RAF, as the island stepped into the shoes of the captured peninsula.[3] Another specialist who arrived in Colombo was W. F. Wegener, Chief Mechanical Engineer of the Federated States of Malaya Railways. Now installed at the Mechanical Engineer's Office of the Ceylon General Railways, he produced an inventory of the rolling stock that his organization had destroyed prior to the Japanese conquest as part of the 'scorched earth' retreat: very little had been left of the Malayan railway's 185 locomotives, 515 coaches, and 55,159 four-wheelers.[4] Valuable non-human cargo also arrived in Ceylon, including fighter aircraft originally destined for Sumatra and 'vast quantities of naval stores' that had been on their way to Malaya and

1 Peter Thompson, *The Battle for Singapore: The True Story of the Greatest Catastrophe of World War Two* (London: Portrait, 2006), p. 9.
2 SNLA, *Times of Ceylon*, 7/2/42.
3 SNLA, Dispatches 441.
4 SNLA, Dispatches 440, 26/1/43.

Singapore.[5] A Ceylonese employee of Cable and Wireless sent what was thought to be the last telegram out of Singapore before the Japanese took over. 'This is my last to you till we meet again kiss children for me', wrote Harry Rappa to his family in the Borella district of Colombo.[6]

The heavy cruiser *Dorsetshire* was one of the many ships caught up in the churning current of retreat caused by Japan's thrust westwards. February saw her tearing around between the ports of the eastern Indian Ocean trying to salvage something from the wreckage. 'Then to Singapore', wrote her skipper, Captain Augustus Agar, 'to evacuate civilians and any of the garrison who could get away. For us it was a complete reversal of procedure. Instead of taking reinforcements in, we were now bringing them out'.[7]

> This was the last refugee convoy to leave Singapore. Led by the *Manchester City*, it consisted of every conceivable kind of craft, but we got them safely at last to Colombo, which was rapidly becoming a refugee centre.[8]

Here many who had spent their entire lives in the Far East had now to sort themselves out and start a new life without goods, money, and friends. Many women had to leave behind their husbands, fathers, and brothers.

In the midst of all this, Ceylon still needed to operate as a naval headquarters and convoy assembly port. On 22 March *Dorsetshire* entered a very crowded Colombo harbour, managing to find a birth next to her sister ship, *Cornwall.* By this time, Agar wrote, 'Colombo might well have been called "Refuge Harbour", which indeed it was. The conglomeration of ships of all shapes and sizes was beyond belief, from large liners used as troop transports to small Dutch coasting vessels which had escaped from the Java Seas. The target thus presented can well be imagined, while the anti-aircraft defences were negligible'.[9] Vice Admiral Arbuthnot, Commander-in-Chief East Indies, reported to the Admiralty that:

> When Singapore fell and Java was attacked, Colombo became the terminal port for Eastern trade and the focal point for all convoys in the Eastern Theatre. The port facilities were naturally quite inadequate for this unexpected aggregation of shipping and I was caused much anxiety by the slow turn around of the ships and the vulnerable target presented by the crowded port and examination anchorage. There were regularly between 100 and 110 ships in a harbour whose official berthing capacity was 45.[10]

5 'Admiralty War Diaries of World War II', transcribed by Don Kindell, available at http://www.naval-history.net/xDKWarDiaries-Contents.htm. Vice Admiral Arbuthnot, secret despatch, Colombo, 18/6/42. Much of this material was transferred to Kilindini when the Fleet's headquarters relocated there in April.

6 Butler Papers, F. S. Tippet, 'Report and History of the Ceylon Censorship, September 1939-November 1945'. At the time Tippet was an Assistant Censor in Ceylon. He wrote on the Ceylon Telegraph Censorship information slip: 'Probably the last cable out of Singapore. Sender is an operative of Cable and Wireless there'. Tippet, 13/2/42. The message was from PCO Singapore, from Harry Rappa to Rappa, Turourrd, Borella, Colombo.

7 Augustus Agar, *Footprints in the Sea* (London: Evans, 1961), p. 171.

8 Ibid.

9 Agar, *Footprints in the Sea*, p. 172.

10 'Admiralty War Diaries of World War II', Vice Admiral Arbuthnot, secret Colombo, 18/6/42.

This was a major concern because Colombo, 'full to overflowing with shipping, offered a tempting target to Nagumo's powerful striking force of battleships, carriers, and cruisers'.[11] When the Japanese admiral had struck Darwin on 19 February, 'like Colombo, the harbour was full of shipping which had gravitated there from the invaded areas … and the same fate might soon overtake Colombo'.[12] History, unpleasant and very recent history, appeared to be repeating itself, and Nagumo and his superiors were indeed now looking towards the Indian Ocean island as they contemplated their next move: Operation C, an attack on Ceylon and the Eastern Fleet.[13]

Meanwhile, an exodus of imperial and Allied servicemen and civilians was taking place as the Japanese surged. They fled Singapore and the East Indies aboard overcrowded destroyers and a gallimaufry of merchantmen, warships, submarines, yachts, river steamers, and liners, a few proceeding by air, some by remarkable open boat endeavours. They headed for Australia and Ceylon, some moved on within sight of Colombo because of its overcrowded state and the fear of attack, and ushered on instead towards Bombay. Many were lost on the way, and between 16 January and 8 March, the day the Dutch finally capitulated in Java, nearly 60 evacuation and rescue ships were sunk in and around Singapore and the East Indies.[14]

Between 18 February and 8 March 1942 the destroyers *Scout* and *Tenedos* took part in an operation involving ten ships which evacuated 2,600 people from Padang. Between them the two destroyers ferried 1,800 people to waiting cruisers, to be conveyed to safety. On 27 February *Scout* escorted the cruisers *Danae*, *Dragon*, and *Hobart* to Colombo. All of these ships had been part of the Allied naval force deployed to defend the Dutch East Indies. Other ships making the dash for safety were not so lucky. The 1,000-ton Dutch steamer *Rooseboom* was employed in peacetime on the coastal run between the ports of Java and Sumatra. At the end of February she tried to escape from Batavia to Ceylon, and was ordered to put into Padang en route to pick up more civilian and military evacuees, mainly British and numbering around 500. The *Rooseboom* was taking them, wrote Corporal Walter Gibson of the Argyll and Sutherland Highlanders, 'crowded in her cabins and on her decks, to Ceylon and safety – there, it was hoped, for the regiments broken in the Malaya debacle to be formed again'.[15] But it was not to be, and things were to turn out very differently to how Gibson hoped. At midnight on 1 March, halfway to Ceylon, *Rooseboom* was located and torpedoed by Lieutenant Commander Yoshimatsu's submarine *I-59*. Only one lifeboat survived the attack, the others damaged or breaking up in the sea. Twenty-eight feet long and eight feet at its widest point, built to carry 28 people, this lifeboat was packed with 80 souls, another 50 clinging to the sides.

Thus began a horrendous period of weeks at sea, during which time most of the people died, some through exhaustion, others by suicide, some murdered and pushed overboard in order to reduce the boat's burden, some killed with cannibalistic intent. At one point, Gibson and 14

11 Agar, *Footprints in the Sea*, p. 171.
12 Ibid.
13 See Jackson, *Of Islands, Ports, and Sea Lanes* for an explanation of Japanese strategy.
14 'Evacuation and Rescue Ships 1942', at https://www.cofepow.org.uk/armed-forces-stories-list/evacuation-rescue-ships-1942.
15 Walter Gibson, *The Boat* (London: W. H. Allen, 1952), p. 8. Gibson was (as he put it) 'the only white survivor'.

other men rushed the 'murder gang', led by a Liverpudlian soldier, and after a brief struggle involving bottles and the jagged remnants of tinned cans, pushed them overboard.

> Three, as they came to the surface, got their hands to the gunwale and tried to drag themselves back. It was a confusion of pleadings and curses and choking half-smothered obscenities. Relentlessly we battered at their fingers with the rowlocks. We were down to the elemental now. It was, we told ourselves, a dozen times that night, either them or us.[16]

Later, Gibson witnessed the only other remaining European battered to death with rowlocks by four Javanese men, who then proceeded to gorge from a wound made in his body by a blade formed from a tin.[17] Now the only people left alive, Gibson and the Chinese woman Doris Lim watched the Javanese, one of whom died that night, with fear and suspicion. And then, land. The boat had drifted back to Sipora Island off Sumatra, 1,000 miles away and not far from *Rooseboom*'s original point of departure. Five people remained alive; Gibson, Lim, and the three Javanese sailors.[18]

Thomas Kenneth escaped Singapore during the final chaotic days of British rule. His RAF unit, 258 Squadron, had become operational in Singapore on 1 February. Just three days later, with the writing on the wall for the island fortress, the squadron moved to P (Palembang) 1 airbase at Palembang in Sumatra for the defence of the city.[19] While the aircraft were away from the base on an operational sortie on 14 February, however, Japanese paratroops encircled the airfield, so the Hurricanes were diverted to P2, another airbase. Here the squadron was disbanded, leaving only 232 and 605 Hurricane squadrons still operational as a British air contribution to the forlorn defence of the Dutch East Indies. Some of 258 Squadron's pilots and ground crew were killed or captured in Sumatra, others escaped to Java. The depressing process of deployment, redeployment, hasty defence, and then evacuation was repeated when Java fell, and the remaining men boarded ships ordered to make for Australia. For 258 Squadron, the process was soon to be repeated again in Ceylon, though this time there was to be no retreat.

The skipper of the tramp steamer that Kennedy boarded, the *Kota Gede*, decided to try and make it to Ceylon, an inspired decision as the four ships that set out for Australia as instructed were all sunk en route. On the day *Kota Gede* left Tjilitjap, 27 February, 24 other ships also departed the port loaded with evacuees. A dozen of them were sunk en route. With over 2,500 men aboard, *Kota Gede* was grossly overcrowded. Another airman aboard the ship was Harry

16 Ibid., p. 41.

17 Ibid., p. 48.

18 A press cutting in my first edition copy of *The Boat*, entitled 'The Fate of Doris Lim' and almost certainly from 1953, reports that she had become a double agent, working for the Allies in Japanese employment. 'Then a Chinese fell in love with her. He couldn't understand her friendship with the Japanese. After a bitter quarrel he stabbed her to death'. According to Gibson's account, she had previously worked for British intelligence in northern China, escaping from Tientsin before the Japanese occupation, escaping ahead of them from Shanghai and Hong Kong, and taking a post as assistant to a Chinese news cameraman in Singapore.

19 BBC World War Two People's War oral history archive, Thomas Kenneth, 'The Squadron that Vanished', A4204702. See Terence Kelly, *Battle for Palembang* (London: Robert Hale, 1985); Kelly, *Hurricane in Sumatra* (London: Arrow Books, 1991); and Kelly, *Hurricanes Over the Jungle* (Barnsley: Pen and Sword, 2004).

Tweedale of 232 Squadron. Amidst the cramped conditions on board, using steel helmets as pillows and queuing for hours for meagre rations, he was able nonetheless to reflect on his good fortune, and to take stock. 'It seemed incredible that I had survived Malaya, Singapore, Sumatra, and Java and was still alive to tell the tale'.[20]

Another refugee bound for Ceylon aboard the *Kota Gede* was Leslie Baker. In a letter to his mother he described how he had been in Batavia when the Japanese landed, the airmen and soldiers subsequently ordered to make their own way to a port in south Java for evacuation. 'A few thousands of us boarded a train for a ten hour journey to the port of Tjilatjap', a harbour designated as a rendezvous point for Allied troopships awaiting escort away from the East Indies. Upon arrival they had a three mile walk to the docks, where they all piled onto the *Kota Gede*, 'a 5,000 ton vessel soon to be sunk. [We] had a lot of Aussies with us and the ship was packed full on the decks. All the ships in harbour left, the Japanese only three hours from arriving at the port'.[21] The ship zig-zagged all the way across the sea to Ceylon, at one point sailing through a minefield with mines visible on either side. It took three and a half hours in a queue to get fed, and there was no bedding, cigarettes, or life jackets. Upon arrival in Ceylon, Baker was allowed to eat as much as he wanted, and like many other escapees, soon contracted dysentery.

Basil Lawrence was another 232 Squadron airman driven out of P1 and P2. A train took him and other men of his unit from Palembang to Oosthaven, where they took passage by sea to Batavia, there to embark on another train journey to Tjilatjap and the waiting *Kota Gede*.

> This ship was a really old cargo boat and everything on it was the worst I have ever seen. For sleeping we were in the holds on the bare boards and only a blanket for bedding. The conditions in the hold were terrible and during the night rats ran across the beams overhead and water dripped down from the roof; the stench there was overpowering.
>
> Food was a great problem. Usually we began the day with some dried bacon, biscuits and tea. At mid-day we had three 'dog' biscuits, a bit of jam and tea if we were lucky. In the evening more biscuits, a bit of bully beef or a couple of spoonfuls of mixed stew (tinned) and a mug of tea. There was no variety at all and very soon all we had was nothing but biscuits and bully beef. It hardly seems possible that literally hundreds of service men would queue for hours for such rations. I remember that one day I queued up with several others to scrape out some cheese tins in case a morsel had been left in the tins when the cooks opened them. We were very hungry.
>
> The drinking water was usually red with rust from the tanks that had not been used for water for years and for washing there was only salt water and as we did not have salt water soap, the situation was hopeless. Sanitary arrangements were also very bad and often it was impossible to use the lavatories. No-one could keep clean under these conditions and space was so limited.
>
> As can be expected the chaps could not last long in these conditions and an outbreak of dysentery occurred on board on 5th March. Two men died from this as there was not

20 BBC World War Two People's War oral history archive, Harry Tweedale, 'Tweedale's War', part 10, A6665114.

21 BBC World War Two People's War oral history archive, Leslie Baker, 'Les Baker's Letters Home', part 4, 'Journey to Ceylon', A2564967.

> sufficient medical kit on the boat. I had trouble with stomach pains and the 'runs'. It got worse until on Monday 9th March I reported sick with a temperature of 103 degrees. I was told to get my kit together in order to go into hospital when we reached port. I was on the 'Kota Gede' from 27th February to 9th March.
>
> COMBINED MILITARY HOSPITAL, COLOMBO, CEYLON.
> I was admitted into hospital on Monday 9th March, the hospital being a converted part of the Royal College [the 'Eton of Ceylon'] and similar to the school billets in Java. After being treated for Dengue fever and a leg wound I eventually left the hospital.[22]

Lieutenant Colonel Frank Rose of the Jat Regiment also made the harrowing journey from Singapore to Java, in his case aboard the commandeered yacht of the Sultan of Johore, before sailing on to Ceylon in the teeth of the advancing enemy.[23] On 28 February he was at Tjilatjap, where 32 Allied ships were bottled up by waiting Japanese submarines with enemy land forces only 30 miles away following the capture of Batavia two days before. The ships included cargo and passenger liners such as *City of Manchester*, the latter sunk south-east of Tjilatjap by *I-153* later that day.

Rose now boarded the decrepit steamer *Wuchang*, joining over 400 officers and men, all ex-Singapore. *Wuchang* had already had quite a war; a China Navigation Company Yangtze river steamer, she had been requisitioned by the Ministry of War Transport at Shanghai and sent to Singapore to become an ammunition ship for the flying-boats of the RAF's 205 Squadron, painted 'a virulent orange' to warn other ships to keep clear.[24] Earning a last minute reprieve when an order to blow her up as Singapore was about to fall was countermanded, on 11 February *Wuchang*'s skipper was ordered to try and escape as British and Japanese forces exchanged fire around Keppel harbour. En route to Batavia she was subjected to Japanese air attack and inspected by a Japanese destroyer, but arrived intact. Here she was rebunkered, a new Royal Navy Volunteer Reserve crew put aboard, and sent on to Tjilatjap.

Packed with 400 RAF and army men, getting out of the crowded port was *Wuchang*'s next challenge. In discussions with the British captain and Dutch engineer, it was decided that the only chance of escape was if a storm of such violence blew up that it scattered the waiting enemy submarines, allowing the Allied vessels to make a dash for it. It was an incredibly risky plan, particularly as *Wuchang* was barely seaworthy. Although 205 Squadron's aircraft and personnel had been destroyed or scattered, the Dutch authorities would not permit *Wuchang*'s captain to jettison the ammunition in the holds, adding to the danger of being aboard the ship at sea, especially during a storm. 'The decision, however, that the attempt should be made was instant and unanimous'.[25] Communal discussions decided that the ship would try and make it to Ceylon; it was known that most of the other ships would head for Australia, in convoys too

22 BBC World War Two People's War oral history archive, Basil Lawrence, 'The Evacuation of Palambang [sic] and Java', A2815562. The college had been taken over by the British Army and turned into a hospital, the school moving into four private villas on Turret Street.

23 National Army Museum (NAM), 9509-93, Frank Rose, 'The Last Voyage of the *Wuchang*', unpublished typescript.

24 '*Wuchang II*' at, http://wikiswire.com/wiki/Wuchang_II

25 NAM, 9509-93, Rose, 'The Last Voyage of the *Woo Chang*'.

fast for *Wuchang* to keep pace with, and that they would likely be spotted by Japanese aerial reconnaissance. This proved to be the case, and when the opportunity to escape arose with the development of a 'Sumatran', *Wuchang* heard the radio signals as other ships were located by Japanese aircraft and attacked.

Wuchang made it off Java and survived the storm, but there was still the small matter of a treacherous sea passage to Ceylon across waters now combed by Japanese ships and aircraft. Conditions were cramped, and most men lay where they were, apart from when drawing their thin rations. Most, according to Rose, were glad of the rest, exhausted after their exploits in Singapore and the exertion of reaching Java via the planned escape route. Known as the 'tourist route', this 'was a lifeline that stretched from Tembilahan, near the mouth of the Indragiri river, across the island of Sumatra to Padang' from where boats would take the Singapore escapees to safety.[26] It had been 'set up secretly before Malaya fell by a small group of men, some of them civilians, who had mapped out an escape road which had its clearing house at Rengat. From there the escapers were taken 250 miles by truck and train across the island to Padang'.[27] On board *Wuchang* 'every major unit of what had been the 3rd Indian Corps and the Garrisons of Penang and Singapore was represented'. There were also elements of the unfortunate 18th British Division that had had the experience of sailing into Singapore at the eleventh hour and almost straight into Japanese captivity.

A mood of 'hopeful expectation and cheerfulness' pervaded the atmosphere aboard the ship, in spite – or perhaps because of – their experiences.[28] But nervousness soon crept in as the prospect of Ceylon and safety diminished with the imminence of danger; on the second day out, there was a general alarm when a whale was mistaken for an enemy submarine, and on the morning of the third day the report 'submarine on starboard bow' was heard. This time it was the real thing, and a Japanese submarine surfaced close by. Men were visible on the conning tower, as were the tracks of the three torpedoes that were subsequently fired at *Wuchang*. Miraculously, all three missed, and there was brief elation. But soon after, the submarine surfaced again, only 300 yards away, and Rose and 400 other watching men expected the same sequence of events, this time without such a deliverance. But then, to everyone's great surprise, the sailors left the conning tower and the submarine crash dived. What had caused this extraordinary about turn was a 'ten foot length of spar and four indomitable men'; the previous day, these men had tied a lengthy piece of metal to the stern railing of the saloon shelter deck, and had pretended to harpoon whales. Now, with the enemy nearby, they had 'aligned it on the conning tower of the submarine, and obviously given the bulging eyed Jap Commander the fright of his yellow life', as Rose phrased it.[29] Admiral Layton reported to the Admiralty that 'S.S. WUCHANG, with 400 evacuated troops on board, on passage from Tjilatjap to Colombo was attacked by enemy submarine in 3-25S, 91-35E at 1045LT. Three torpedoes were fired, one missed ahead, the other two passed underneath the ship (a shallow draught river steamer). Enemy submarine abandoned

26 Ian Skidmore, *Escape from the Rising Sun: The Incredible Journey of the* Sederhana Djohanis (London: Futura, 1974), p. 82.
27 Ibid.
28 NAM, 9509-93, Rose, 'The Last Voyage of the *Woo Chang*'.
29 Frank Rose, 'Last Voyage of the *Wuchang*', posted by his daughter Aline Dobbie, at http://www.thepeacockscall.co.uk/sites/thepeacockscall.co.uk/files/images/Voyage-Woo-Chang.pdf

attack after observing ship at short range'.[30] Understandably, the Japanese commander had not been expecting to encounter a river steamer in mid-ocean, and had overestimated *Wuchang*'s draft because of her above-water height and the large number of men visible on deck. Or perhaps he had just been a bad shot.

After her providential escape, *Wuchang* sailed on for another ten days until the report 'land in sight' was heard. 'Late in the morning more palm trees and land did come into sight – the coast of Ceylon'.[31] It was not until about 5pm that Colombo was sighted 'and how welcome that sight!, magnificently lit up by the lowering rays of the Westering sun'.[32] As she approached the harbour, *Wuchang* was inspected by a 'fussy little Walrus' seaplane, and then an armed patrol vessel. Given the situation, the authorities in Ceylon were clearly taking no chances. A shot was even fired across her bows, and she was told to anchor in the Roads and not to attempt to enter the harbour until the following morning, as the boom defences were already in place for the night. Despite these wise defensive precautions, Rose was struck by the fact that the city was not blacked out. It reminded him of Singapore, where the sense that the war was distant had prevailed until its final days. Here in Colombo were visible neon cinemas signs, including one advertising the film *The Major and the Minor* (a new American comedy starring Ginger Rogers), which vied 'with equally large and brilliantly lit advertisements for well-known brands of tea and aerated water, beer and spirits'.[33]

Eventually a crisply-dressed naval officer was put aboard, who reported that Naval Headquarters were thinking of sending *Wuchang* on to Bombay. He was immediately presented with the prospect of being thrown overboard.

> A couple of hours later a signal was received to enter the harbour and tie up; this was eventually completed just before noon, between a tanker with most of her bows blown off and the battleship 'HMS Ramillies'. Finally at about 4.00pm orders were received to disembark and assemble on the pier. Here the officers were separated from the men, the former to be taken to one of the leading hotels and the latter to a transit camp which had just been prepared for a British Brigade which was due to arrive. It was well organized, clean and comfortable. NOT so the arrangements at the hotel. ALL available accommodation had already been taken over for the Staff of Ceylon Command, then in the process of being formed, and the only space available was the hotel swimming bath alongside the beach. The eighty odd Officers from the 'Woo Chang' were given string beds, without any sort of mattress, pillow or other covering, in the covered area round the emptied bath and allowed the privilege of using the lavatories and the changing rooms. Also, as they were not in a position to turn themselves out as well dressed Officers should, they could not of course be permitted to use the public dining rooms and had to content themselves with 'bully and potatoes' on tables set out in an out of the way veranda.[34]

30 'Admiralty War Diaries of World War II', Layton's diary, November 1941-March 1942.
31 NAM, Rose, 'The Last Voyage of the *Woo Chang*'.
32 Ibid.
33 Ibid.
34 Rose, 'The Last Voyage of the *Wuchang*', at http://www.thepeacockscall.co.uk/sites/thepeacockscall.co.uk/files/images/Voyage-Woo-Chang.pdf

Though reluctant to accommodate *Wuchang*'s human cargo, the authorities in Ceylon welcomed its valuable consignment of ammunition. 'It was an ironic anomaly indeed', wrote Rose, 'that, whereas the men from the 'Woo Chang' were scarcely welcome, her cargo of bombs and in particular aircraft ammunition, which were in considerably short supply in Colombo, were looked upon almost as manna from heaven and were immediately unloaded for use by the incoming reinforcements of the RAF'.[35] On 11 May, *Wuchang* was taken over by the navy and turned into a submarine accommodation ship, soon commissioned as HMS *Wuchang*.[36]

Thomas Carter was another escapee from both Singapore and Java. He had been part of a Radio Installation and Maintenance Unit in Singapore when orders were given to destroy the equipment apart from 243 Air Ministry Experimental Station, a radar outfit, which moved location for a third time on 13 February.[37] Word came from Air Vice-Marshal Conway Pulford that evacuation space for RAF personnel was available on a flotilla of 44 small vessels making a break for Java many of which were sunk en route. Carter made it safely to a small port in eastern Sumatra, and then trekked to Padang along the escape route reconnoitred by, among others, men of the Special Operations Executive. He and the other survivors were then taken to Ceylon by *Dragon*, *Hobart*, and *Tenedos*, only 34 of the 250 RAF personnel who had left Singapore being counted upon arrival.

> The dockside at Colombo was jammed with stores and equipment that had been shipped from the UK intended for the Middle East, diverted towards Singapore after rounding the Cape, and rediverted to Colombo when it became apparent that Singapore would fall. It included equipment for at least one Mobile Radio Unit. The RAF in Ceylon had by now been transferred to India Command, which had no radar whatsoever. It had been decided to form a Radio Branch at Air Headquarters India, and Group Captain C. C. Morton had just arrived in Delhi, from Iceland, to become the first Command Radio Officer. He had no staff and there were no transport or communications aircraft in India, so when he heard that we had arrived in Ceylon he borrowed a Hawker Hart trainer of the RIAFVR [Royal Indian Air Force Volunteer Reserve], flew to Colombo and gave me orders. Equipment for an MRU [mobile radio unit] was to be collected together in Colombo and taken by ex-Far East radar personnel to Trincomalee, where it should be brought into operation as soon as possible, telling to the RAF station at China Bay, where some Hurricane fighters were expected shortly. I was also to choose a site for a COL [Chain Overseas Low-flying] at Mount Lavinia, near Colombo.[38]

Also caught up in the chaos on the quaysides in Java and Singapore and fighting to get to Ceylon was 'Phil' of the Royal Signals. He boarded *Kedah* on 26 February, the overcrowded ship leaving

35 Ibid.

36 'Admiralty War Diaries of World War II', Eastern Fleet war diary, May 1942. *Wuchang* was part of the 'Allied China Fleet' or 'Allied Chinese Ships', 32 vessels of the China Navigation Company requisitioned by the Royal Navy and Royal Australian Navy. See 'Allied Chinese Ships', https://en.wikipedia.org/wiki/Allied_Chinese_Ships

37 BBC World War Two People's War oral history archive, Thomas Carter, 'Eight Years in the RAFVR [RAF Volunteer Reserve]', part 6, 'Escape from Singapore', A3146771.

38 Ibid.

port 'with some strafing to see us off'.[39] Arriving at Colombo on 7 March, he proceeded to establish communications at Army Headquarters Ceylon in the recently requisitioned premises of the Colombo museum. *Kedah*'s was an important voyage given the passengers she carried. Requisitioned by the Royal Navy in December 1939, she had been converted into an armed auxiliary vessel. The navy made various changes, which included removing the top section of the funnel, the erection of new, taller, masts, and the mounting of two four-inch guns and one three-inch anti-aircraft gun, with depth charge launchers on the after deck. She had served around North Borneo and then been used as an evacuation ship prior the fall of Singapore. On her last trip out of Singapore she had been under constant attack from the air, remaining undamaged thanks to the brilliant seamanship of Captain J. L. Sinclair. But the massive vibrations caused by bombs falling close to her hull had damaged the engines, and she could now only manage a speed of seven knots. In Batavia, although in urgent need of an overhaul, she was ordered to sail to Tjilatjap and take on board the headquarters staff of General Wavell's ABDA Command, along with some 400 refugees, and to evacuate them to Colombo. En route she was once again attacked from the air, after which her machinery failed completely, leaving her becalmed. Fortunately, she was soon taken in tow by the light cruiser *Dragon*.

Lieutenant-General Sir Henry Pownall, erstwhile ABDA Chief of Staff and former Commander-in-Chief Far East, was one of the senior officers escaping aboard *Kedah*.[40] As he wrote at sea on 27 February, 'yesterday at crack of dawn – indeed two hours before it – we left Lembang for Tjilatjap and embarked on HMS *Kedah*'.[41] On 2 March he wrote:

> The voyage creeps on miserably slowly. This ship is supposed to be capable of seventeen knots and did that for a few hours. Since then one thing after another has gone wrong in the engine room and we stop, or nearly stop, for several hours every day. It is a very poor show indeed. We should have been at Colombo two days from now. I doubt if we shall get in in four. Luckily food is plentiful if plain (since it all comes from tins) but our water supply is running very short ... On 27 February there was fought the battle of the Java Sea, during and after which our combined naval forces were practically annihilated. The Japanese landed at several points on the north coast of Java on 28 February. On 2 March, Admiral Helfrich [Dutch naval commander-in-chief] and the Naval HQ disbanded, going

39 BBC World War Two People's War oral history archive, 'Phil', 'Two Evacuations: France 1940 and Java 1942', A2755235.

40 *Kedah* had been built for the Blue Funnel Line's Straits Steamship Company and worked on the Singapore-Penang route. In December 1939 she was requisitioned by the Royal Navy and kitted out as an 'armed auxiliary patrol vessel'. She patrolled around North Borneo and was one of the last ships out of Singapore, damaged by near-miss bombs as she departed. She was one of the escorts for the 16 vessels of the so-called 'Empire Star Convoy' departing Singapore on 'Black Friday', 12 February. See http://pwencycl.kgbudge.com/K/e/Kedah_class.htm and http://singaporeevacuation1942.blogspot.co.uk/2007/02/hms-kedah.html. Pownall wrote on 25 February: 'we are leaving some 5,000 British troops here, mostly in the form of A. A. units and their ancillaries. There are about 2-3,000 RAF personnel here with their aircraft (and about 6,000 to be evacuated as superfluous). About 3,000 Australians'. Brian Bond (ed.), *Chief of Staff: The Diaries of Lieutenant-General Sir Henry Pownall*, volume 2, *1940-1944* (London: Leo Cooper, 1974), 25/2/42, p. 90.

41 Ibid., p. 92.

> by air to Ceylon, some to Australia. ABDA Command HQ did not have much time to spare in making their getaway.[42]

On 7 March *Kedah* arrived at Colombo, and 'mighty glad to get there', wrote Pownall.

> We were in tow for some 300 miles by HMS *Dragon* who had come to our assistance as the result of our W/T [wireless telegraphy] messages. We had no incidents at all as we might well have done, not only while we lay motionless but also when we were being towed along at six knots. Another ship with refugees had three torpedoes fired at her not far from where we were by a Jap submarine [this was the *Wuchang*]. She was of shallow draught and all passed under her. We might not have been so fortunate.
>
> So it was a nine days' voyage instead of the five and a half to six originally calculated. The food just held, but the water didn't. There was enough to drink but none available for washing. Another day and I don't think there would have been enough even to drink.
>
> And so we got ashore, sent off telegrams to say we have arrived, and asked for disposal orders.[43]

As well as escaping from Malaya, Singapore, Java, and Sumatra, some people also managed to get away from the Andaman and Nicobar Islands before the Japanese arrived. Denis McCarthy had served in the Andamans for five years as Commandant of the Military Police Battalion and District Superintendent of Police. Along with a dozen others he escaped on a motor launch when the islands were invaded, navigating to Ceylon 'using a hydrographic quintant in lieu of a magnetic compass'.[44]

Comparatively late arrivals in Ceylon included Lieutenant Commander Geoffrey Brooke and a group of ex-Singapore escapees, following an epic journey.[45] Brooke had been aboard *Prince of Wales* when she sank and two months later, on 13 February, had managed to get away from Singapore before the Japanese landed. Along with 140 others he made it off aboard a Yangtze river steamer already damaged by bombs and machine-gun fire. The vessel caught fire 80 miles off Singapore and the passengers were forced to abandon ship and paddle to a deserted island. Over the course of the next week Brooke used a motor boat to bring in the wounded from two other stricken ships, laying them down on the beach where their clothes were ripped up to make bandages. Brooke and Lieutenant Commander A. H. Terry then loaded the most seriously wounded on to rafts to be towed to Sumatra while he and 60 other men, mainly survivors from *Prince of Wales* and *Repulse*, volunteered to remain. After a further seven days passing Chinese traders were persuaded to take them to Sinkep Island. There the Dutch administrator gave them opium, which was rationed to pay Chinese people who took them to the mouth of the Indragiri river.

Towing and polling small boats and now numbering 600, Brooke's party eventually reached a small town. There they were held up for five days and so missed the last ship to sail from Padang, which was torpedoed. On resuming his journey after a 24-hour road trip over the mountains

42 Ibid., pp. 92-3.
43 Ibid., p. 93.
44 Ian Trenowden, *Operations Most Secret: SOE, the Malayan Theatre* (N. P.: Crécy Books, 1978), p. 62.
45 'Lieutenant Commander Geoffrey Brooke', obituary, *Daily Telegraph*, 30/1/09.

to the railhead leading to Padang, Brooke was ordered by the Royal Marines heading the SOE resistance to board a Malay prahu and attempt passage to Ceylon, he and 17 officers being selected because it was thought that they would be most useful to the war effort if they survived. Others who boarded the 30-ton *Sederhana Djohanis* included John Davis, a police officer, and Richard Broome, a former District Officer in Ipoh, Perak.[46]

The vessel, helmed by Captain Ivan Lyon of the Gordon Highlanders, seconded to SOE, endured a hazardous 35-day voyage with precious little food and with water gathered during rain squalls. At one point they survived a machine-gun attack from the air and, as they neared Ceylon, inadvertently sailed through the middle of Vice Admiral Nagumo's fleet as it prowled off the island. Though unmolested, they feared that Ceylon had fallen, possibly India too. The navigator, Gorham, said: 'That cloud on the horizon. I'm pretty sure it isn't a cloud at all. It's Adam's Peak'.[47] They had sighted Ceylon after sailing a total of 1,660 miles and subsisting on a diet consisting mainly of bully beef and tinned salmon. Off the island's south-east coast they were rescued on 14 April by the merchantman *Anglo-Canadian*, which proceeded to sink *Sederhana Djohanis* with gunfire so that she did not present a floating obstacle in a busy shipping lane. The men were taken to Bombay, by this time already packed with ships along with the main striking force of the Eastern Fleet, which had fled there following the Japanese raid on Ceylon and the sinking of the heavy cruisers *Cornwall* and *Dorsetshire* on 5 April.[48]

Another safe arrival in Ceylon was Tom Simkins, who had been chief radio operator of *Pinna*, wrecked by Japanese bombs as it attempted to take 19,000 tins of petrol from Pladjoe, where the Royal Dutch Shell refineries were located, to Singapore. Having subsequently escaped Singapore back to the Dutch East Indies, it was time to escape again, Simkins this time departing Tanjong Priok in Java aboard *Perak* on 27 February, having made it away from Singapore and Benkulen in the face of the enemy. Creeping along at five or six knots, the vessel had a narrow escape from a Japanese submarine, but managed to make it to Ceylon.

> As we paralleled the coast of Ceylon … I had a lovely feeling of well-being that I had not experienced since that early morning on the 'Pinna' when the Captain had awoken me. And I was clean too, I had just had a shower – the first one since leaving Batavia, because of the water shortage – and then a second one with my shorts and shirt on because it was more convenient to wash them that way … As I dried out on deck in the hot sun, the Japanese war was 2,000 miles away, and ahead, shimmering in the heat, Colombo looked beautiful, and this time, it just had to be the right island – a safe one.[49]

Ceylon was also a destination for escaping aircraft, warships, and naval support vessels. In late March, Agar wrote, 'Colombo was so overcrowded we now worked from Trincomalee … The

46 Skidmore, *Escape from the Rising Sun*.
47 Ibid., p. 173.
48 In Delhi in May 1942, he talked to Brigadier Bernard Fergusson, Wavell's ADC, and they hatched the plan that led to Operation Jaywick. See Ian Skidmore, *Escape from the Rising Sun*. Also John Clancy, *'The Most Dangerous Moment of the War': Japan's Attack on the Indian Ocean, 1942* (Oxford: Casemate, 2015), p. 140.
49 BBC World War Two People's War oral history archive, Tom Simkins, 'Another Door', part 7, 'Another Wrong Island', A1118486.

small aircraft carrier *Hermes* turned up from Cape Town while we were there ... There were also in harbour a number of storeships, fleet auxiliaries, ammunition ships, oilers, all ex-Singapore'.[50] The American light cruiser *Marblehead* made it to Trincomalee on 21 February after sustaining serious damage during the Battle of the Makassar Strait, before proceeding to South Africa for repairs on 2 March. British and Dutch ships hastened to Colombo and Trincomalee after the Battle of the Java Sea, and the Dutch commander-in-chief transferred his headquarters to the island and placed his remaining warships under British command. Of the seven Dutch submarines sent to operate in defence of Malaya on the outbreak of war with Japan, four had been lost by Christmas 1941.[51] With Singapore about to fall, these vessels were moved to Surabaya in Java. This base in turn was evacuated and the remaining Dutch submarines were dispersed to Ceylon and Fremantle.

Captain H. C. J. Coumou's submarine *KXII* had remained in Surabaya to embark Rear Admiral Pieter Koenraad together with key officers and men of the base staff, and sailed for Colombo on 5 March, leaving the burning and wrecked naval base at virtually the same time as Japanese troops entered the town.[52] For the next few days *KXII* successfully evaded Japanese ships and aircraft. Emergency dives became more frequent as Coumou vainly sought a way through the heavily patrolled straits of Bali, then Lombok and finally Alas, a strait leading south through the island chain. On one occasion, while passing through the safe channel of a Dutch defensive minefield, the submarine had to dive quickly because of the close proximity of the enemy. On the 8 March, while attempting to evade an enemy destroyer, *KXII* was illuminated by a searchlight as it dived and shortly afterwards two patterns of six depth charges exploded some 200 yards away. Two more enemy destroyers were encountered and successfully evaded before the submarine escaped through the Sape Strait. By this time Coumou realized that he would have insufficient fuel to reach Colombo and adjusted course for Fremantle.

Lieutenant Commander A. H. Deketh's submarine *KXI* left Surabaya for Colombo with the captain and staff of the submarine base and some spare crew. When south of Java she came upon the survivors of the Australian sloop *Yarra* which had been sunk by aircraft while escorting a convoy of refugees to Australia. Though desperately overcrowded *KXI* took 28 men on board, many badly wounded, and conveyed them to safety in Ceylon.[53] At Colombo the Dutch submarines came under British command and joined the only two Royal Navy submarines in the area, *Truant* and *Trusty*, which had been detached from British forces supporting operations in the East Indies in order to patrol the Malacca Strait. The Dutch submarines were supported by the Dutch submarine depot *Colombia*, the latter by the British submarine depot ship *Lucia*. Their initial task was to detect any Japanese threat to the island. Victory had given the Japanese new bases from which to operate their own submarines in the Indian Ocean, and as early as January the 5th Submarine Squadron had been ordered from French Indo-China to Penang and soon began to reconnoitre the area around Ceylon and up the west coast of India in anticipation of a Japanese sortie. The Japanese did not have it all their own way, and on 17 January *I-60* was detected en route to Penang, blown to the surface, and sunk in the southern entrance to the

50 Agar, *Footprints in the Sea*, p. 172.
51 Brian Wilson, *A Submariners' War in the Indian Ocean, 1939-45* (Stroud: Tempus, 2000), p. 63.
52 Ibid., p. 64.
53 Ibid., p. 64. For *Yarra* see J. E. Macdonnell, *Valiant Occasions* (London: Constable, 1952), Chapter 9, 'Sloop *versus* Jap Squadron'.

Sunda Strait by the destroyer *Jupiter*, the Royal Navy's first Japanese victim of the war.[54] Later, Hudsons attacked and destroyed a number of Japanese flying-boats moored at Port Blair in the Andamans.

In addition to those people arriving in Colombo as they escaped the Japanese, some needed to leave the harbour, including thousands of Australian troops returning from the Middle East to defend their homeland. This was hazardous business because of intensifying Japanese activity and the commensurate diminution of British seapower in the waters of the eastern Indian Ocean. Involved in escorting Australian troops and other military convoys through these dangerous waters was the cruiser *Cornwall.* Throughout February she was kept very busy ferrying convoys, collecting eight ships at Aden and bringing them to Colombo, then escorting ships from Colombo bound for Singapore and the East Indies, returning to Colombo on 13 February and picking up a convoy destined for Rangoon. Back in Colombo on 24 February, she moored directly ahead of a liner packed with Australian troops. 'The Aussies on deck greeted us with remarks such as "Where was the Navy at Singapore?" … "What are you doing in port?" … "Why aren't you at sea?"'.[55] The sailors bantered back. It was then *Cornwall*'s pleasant duty, wrote crewman Ken Dimbleby,

> to escort the convoy of Australian troops to Fremantle. We were due to sail on the evening of 28 February [the day of the Battle of the Java Sea]. The wires to the buoys had been slipped and *Cornwall*'s screws were already churning up the dirty water in the harbour as a tug eased her bows round. The Aussies in the liner nearby crowded the rails on deck to watch the warship leave harbour, when suddenly there was a change of orders. *Cornwall*'s engines stopped and we started to make fast to the buoys again.
>
> 'Wot's up, scared?' shouted some of the Aussies on the deck of the liner.[56]

Australian Freddie Mathieson remembers the occasion as the convoy made its abortive attempt to get underway. His troopship made it out, but then 'all hell broke loose. The destroyers were tearing all over the place relaying signals, flashing lights, sirens going. Everyone upon deck to see what was going on. We soon found out as the whole convoy did a complete turn and headed back to Colombo'.

The following morning, 1 March, the process was repeated, this time the entire convoy leaving port and getting underway for Australia.

> At dawn we were in the outer harbour. Our destination was Java, but it has fallen, we are very lucky indeed. We hear that some of the ships that sailed from Colombo while we were there got to Java, landed troops without their equipment, as it was on other ships. They were just in time to be P. O. W.'s. What a way to go into the bag, if we had sailed a day sooner that would have been our fate.[57]

54 Wilson, *A Submariners' War*, p. 80.
55 Ken Dimbleby, *Turns of Fate: The Drama of HMS* Cornwall (London: William Kimber, 1984), p. 138.
56 Ibid.
57 Freddie Mathieson quoted in Richard Aldrich, *The Faraway War: Personal Diaries of the Second World War in Asia and the Pacific* (London: Corgi, 2010), pp. 215-16.

> Just after breakfast, we up anchor once more, out to the assembly area. Fourteen ships now, all troopers and freighters, the cruiser HMS *Cornwall* and two destroyers, looks like Aussie now. Our course is a general S. S. E. The convoy looks a picture, the *Cornwall* to our stern and the destroyers like sheep dogs, very busy. Also a tanker with us. As we departed Colombo we noticed something that was not there before, two Australian Soldiers wearing all new gear have 'appeared' one plays guitar, the other clarinet. They just sit around playing great music and it goes down well with all the troops – a real touch of home. No one knows where this pair came from and who cares, their playing in the early evening settles the whole ship down, this could be one of those strokes of genius the Army has at times, to smuggle a couple of good musicians on to all the troop ships, as good music could help soothe the lousy news we have had on this trip.[58]

This was convoy SU1, comprising 12 troopships carrying 11,000 Australian and New Zealand troops hastening home from the Middle East. It was escorted out of Colombo by *Cornwall*, the battleship *Royal Sovereign*, the destroyers *Express*, *Nizam*, and *Vampire*, the corvette *Hollyhock*, and the armed merchant cruiser *Manoora*. There were also civilians leaving Ceylon because on 14 March Admiral Layton, now appointed Commander-in-Chief Ceylon, issued an order 'directing the evacuation from Ceylon of all non residents (this included all Service wives) and advising the evacuation of other European women and children. The order excepted those on essential war work'.[59]

As some of his ships worked hard to support the evacuations from Malaya and the East Indies while others conducted escort duties the length and breadth of the Indian Ocean, sometimes escorting convoys bringing reinforcements to Ceylon, Layton kept Whitehall abreast of proceedings. On 4 March, for instance, he wrote: 'YARRA [sloop], ANKING [base depot ship], FRANCOL [oil tanker], and MMS [motor minesweeper] 51 were intercepted by an enemy force of 3 cruisers (two of the NACHI class) and 2 destroyers in 11-30S, 109-03E at 0615GH/4 and sunk by gunfire. A few survivors were picked up by Dutch Merchant Vessels and brought to Colombo or taken to Western Australia'.[60] On the same day he also reported that 'DECOY, FORTUNE, SWEERS, GUARDIAN, RAMILLIES, NORMAN, COLUMBIA, and RANCHI arrived Colombo. DURBAN arrived Mauritius. Convoy DM 3 (STAFFORDSHIRE, AUTOLYCUS, and PARDO) arrived Colombo with A.A. Units and R.A.F. personnel (65th Heavy A.A. Regiment and 43rd Light A.A. Regiment)'.[61] It was all go as in defeat the British and their allies attempted to rescue what they could and prepare for the next battle.

In addition to all of the people escaping from Singapore via the East Indies, survivors of *Prince of Wales* and *Repulse* and personnel evacuated from Malaya arrived direct, and there were new drafts of men originally destined for the Dutch East Indies as well as those being sent for scheduled duties in Ceylon. Arriving all together in the space of a few short weeks, their accommodation and organization presented the island's military and civilian authorities with a considerable problem: 'When the numbers had been reduced to more manageable proportions', wrote the Commander-in-Chief East Indies, 'I approved the requisitioning of two schools for conversion to barracks, St Joseph's College for men and St Thomas's for officers'. Though the

58 Ibid.
59 'Admiralty War Diaries of World War II', Arbuthnot secret despatch, Colombo, 18/6/42.
60 'Admiralty War Diaries of World War II', Layton's diary, November 1941-March 1942.
61 Ibid.

men were to prove useful later on when manpower was needed to work the ports of Ceylon in the aftermath of a Japanese attack, there were problems.

> A less satisfactory aspect was the low state of discipline of many of the men. For various reasons the vast majority were young, half trained ratings; under proper leadership they would have done well enough, but practically the only officers were R.N.R. [Royal Naval Reserve] or Straits Settlements R.N.V.R. [Royal Navy Volunteer Reserve] and Petty Officers were lacking. Every effort was made to get these young men to sea, as reliefs, to complete complements, or, in some cases in exchange for men who would benefit by a spell on shore, and the numbers were gradually reduced. However, from the first to last they caused me much concern.[62]

Things were moving swiftly amid chaotic conditions. *Time* magazine, with its customary grasp of the strategic situation, captured the importance of Ceylon and the unhealthy state of the Allied position in the Indian Ocean at this moment:

> At the southern nub of India, where the Indian Ocean meets the Bay of Bengal and the Arabian Sea, lies a focal centre of General Wavell's task: Britain's island of Ceylon. Holding Ceylon, Wavell holds the sea entrances to India's eastern ports (Madras and Calcutta) which are also inlets for China's supplies. On Ceylon is Trincomalee, Britain's secondary naval base, immensely important now that Singapore is gone. Trincomalee is now the Allies only useful naval base north of Cape Town and east of Suez.
>
> Whoever holds Trincomalee and Ceylon's aerodromes holds the key to the Indian Ocean and all its vital sea routes between Africa, Australia, India, and the Middle East. Without Japan and Ceylon, the Japs can make Allied transport in the Indian Ocean dangerous and expensive. With Ceylon, they could make it almost impossible.
>
> Last week, when the Japs bombed the Andaman Islands in the Bay of Bengal, they were softening up the way station on the invasion route to Ceylon. And Ceylon, just sixty miles off southern India, is a way to invasion of India itself. It could even be a substitute for invasion. With eastern India bottled up and with ships and planes in position in Ceylon to raid even the Indian routes to the vital ports of Bombay and Karachi on the Arabian Sea, Japan could well let India to soften and crumble under blockade.[63]

The British government was pulling out all the stops in order to reinforce the Indian Ocean and get troops and aircraft to Ceylon, but things took time to move across vast distances. It was a race against time, and as Allied war leaders attempted to divine Tokyo's intent, it was imperative that Ceylon do all it could to prepare itself for attack. 'A descent upon Ceylon', wrote Sir John Shuckburgh in his exhaustive yet unpublished history of the colonial empire at war, 'seemed for months on end to be among the immediate possibilities of the hour'.[64] As the dust settled in the Dutch East Indies and the Governor-General formally surrendered to the Japanese, it looked as if the hour had come.

62 Ibid., Arbuthnot secret despatch, Colombo, 18/6/42.
63 *Time* magazine online archive, 'World Battlefronts: New Pacific', *Time*, 16/3/42.
64 TNA, 940.531 SHU, Shuckburgh, 'Colonial Civil History of the War', volume 1, 'Introductory', part 2, 'Military Services', 'Eastern Area', 'Ceylon', p. 55.

3

Admirals Layton and Somerville and the defence of Ceylon

The second half of Ceylon's war had commenced with the coordinated attacks on British and American territories in December 1941. Japan's entry into the war, wrote Sir Andrew Caldecott, 'thrust every other consideration out of minds'; Ceylon's officials and politicians now had 'plenty to do in organizing services and preventing panic'.[1] The surrender of Hong Kong on Christmas Day was a sobering moment, felt keenly by members of Ceylon's civil service. Caldecott had been governor of the conquered colony before moving to his present appointment in Colombo, and the now deposed and interned incumbent, Sir Mark Young, along with his deputy, Franklin Gimson, were both former members of the Ceylon service. After the subsequent collapse of Singapore and with Burma and the Dutch East Indies teetering on the brink of surrender, Ceylon became an 'indispensable island' at the top of Whitehall's strategic agenda as the war in the east expanded.[2]

The strategic logic of a move against Ceylon was fully appreciated by the British government, Tokyo's intent confirmed by intelligence reports, such as the one received by MI6 from a 'reliable source' in France: 'The Japanese embassy has recently bought a great quantity of charts and maps for the Ceylon and East Indies areas from the Hydrographic Section of the French Admiralty in Paris'.[3] The course of the contest between the Allies and the Japanese in its early weeks decreed that Ceylon was not to be a colonial backwater diligently but peripherally 'doing its bit' for the war, but would instead become a major strategic base, integral both to the defence of the Indian Ocean's sea lanes and to plans to one day strike back at the enemy. It was, Churchill told Roosevelt, 'the vital point now that Singapore is gone'.[4] He had already told Wavell, the man charged with the thankless task of defending the region, that the president 'realises [the] vital importance of Ceylon, which is our key of naval re-entry'.[5]

But a re-entry into the lost eastern empire would have to wait; for the foreseeable future, it was all about just holding on. The Lords of the Admiralty were well aware of the global significance

1 De Silva (ed.), *Sri Lanka*, p. lv.
2 Roskill, *The War at Sea*, p. 31.
3 TNA, WO 208/924, Ceylon: Possible Japanese invasion, February 1942-January 1943, MI6 document, 10/2/42.
4 Churchill, *The Second World War*, volume 4, *The Hinge of Fate* (London: Cassell, 1951), p. 169, Churchill to Roosevelt, 5/3/42. See chapter 10,'Ceylon and the Bay of Bengal'.
5 Ibid., p. 172, Churchill to Wavell, 20/2/42.

of events unfolding in the Indian Ocean, and told Admiral Sir James Somerville, on his way by sea to take over the Eastern Fleet following Tom Phillips's death, that the 'worse thing the Japanese could do would be to take Ceylon from us, as this would undermine our whole naval position in the East ... We rate the chance of the Japanese "Pearl Harbouring" very high and hope you will take all possible precautions'.[6] Loss of Ceylon and the Eastern Fleet would put the Indian Ocean's sea lanes at the mercy of the enemy; as Captain Agar phrased it, 'defeat would uncover these routes and lay open the way, not only for an invasion of India (where there were no defences worth considering), but also cut us off from the Middle East until the position could be restored'.[7] Churchill was fully cognizant of the threat, writing that after the enormous Japanese advances to date, India itself was now menaced. 'The coasts of India and Ceylon, and, farther west, the vital sea route by which alone we sustained the armies in the Middle East, lay open to raids on the largest scale'.[8] As he told the Australian prime minister, the 'Winston Special' (WS) convoys to India and the Middle East were conveying nearly 50,000 men a month, not to mention other troops movements in the Indian Ocean and the transit of military hardware and supplies across its waters to a range of battlefronts and defensive positions.[9]

At the highest level of war direction, Churchill and the Chiefs of Staff determined that Ceylon could not be allowed to fall and pumped in troops and aircraft while strengthening the island's shore defences and base infrastructure as quickly as they could. They were wise to do so, because following their conquest of the Dutch East Indies, the Japanese were free to turn Vice Admiral Nagumo's marauding carriers and battleships westwards in order to destroy British naval forces in the Indian Ocean, finishing the job begun with the destruction of *Prince of Wales* and *Repulse*. In the process, they would shore up their gains to date, securing the western perimeter of the nascent Greater East Asian Co-Prosperity Sphere. To achieve this meant attacking Ceylon, where they expected to find the Eastern Fleet, believed to be even stronger than the American Pacific Fleet. Though for logistical reasons Japanese generals opposed the navy's plan to invade and occupy Ceylon, the navy, at the height of its swagger, confidently believed that, offered the example of a crushing naval victory, the army would be forced to change its mind.

The Germans had their eyes on the situation too, alive to its rich strategic potential. On 13 February Grand Admiral Erich Raeder told Hitler that Rangoon, Singapore and probably Darwin would be in Japanese hands at any moment with Java and Sumatra soon to follow. Japan planned to protect this Indian Ocean front, Raeder continued, by capturing the key position of Ceylon, 'and she plans to gain control of the sea lanes in that area by means of superior naval forces'. Once Japanese forces were installed in Ceylon, 'Britain will be forced to resort to heavily escorted convoys if she desires to maintain communications with India and the Near East' (meaning the Western Desert and eastern Mediterranean theatre), further draining its already overstretched naval and merchant marine resources.[10]

The day after the surrender of Singapore, 16 February, the Chiefs of Staff articulated Britain's new strategic position:

6 Churchill Archives Centre (CAC), Cambridge, Papers of Sir Ralph Bevan Edwards, REDW 2/8.
7 Agar, *Footprints in the Sea*, pp. 176-77.
8 Churchill, *The Second World War*, volume 4, p. 152.
9 Ibid., p. 156, Churchill to Australian prime minister, 20/3/42.
10 Ibid., p. 122.

> The basis of our general strategy lies in the safety of our sea communications for which secure naval and air bases are essential. We must therefore make certain of our main bases i.e. Burma, India, Ceylon, Australia, and New Zealand ... For the defence of our Indian Ocean sea communications, we are building up our Eastern Fleet. At present there is no secure base in the Indian Ocean. Thus we must:
>
> a) Secure Ceylon;
> b) Develop Addu Atoll;
> c) Develop additional bases for reconnaissance and striking forces ...
>
> Our sound policy strategically is to withhold major reinforcements from Java and to concentrate on holding Burma, Ceylon, India, Australia, and New Zealand ... The loss of Ceylon will imperil our whole British war effort in the Middle East and Far East, owing to its position in relation to our sea communications.[11]

Churchill kept a daily watch on the situation, telling the Chiefs of Staff the following day that the 70th British Division needed to get to Bombay immediately, dropping off a brigade at Ceylon on the way, and that they must 'make absolutely sure of Trincomalee by A. A. [anti-aircraft] reinforcements from Convoy W. S. 17'.[12] Ten days later, he was again badgering the Chiefs of Staff, telling them to give him figures for the 'exact state of the garrison of Ceylon, naval, air, and military and the dates of air and military reinforcements'.[13] On 3 March the prime minister was back on the case, telling the Chiefs that 'the leading brigade of the 70th Division must reach Ceylon at the earliest moment (when?). Also the big convoy of anti-aircraft and anti-tank'.[14]

Churchill was crystal clear on the importance of Ceylon throughout this period: it was the 'only really good base for the Eastern Fleet which we were forming', he said, and as a result '[e]nergetic and almost frantic efforts were being made by us to procure a sufficient force of fighter aircraft for the island before the expected Japanese attack'.[15] Another reason for Churchill's keen interest in the affairs of the Indian Ocean at this stage, aside from the very obvious strategic ones, was distinctly political. With the loss of *Prince of Wales* and *Repulse*, the surrender of Singapore, and the raid on Darwin all fresh in the memory, Churchill's premiership was on rocky ground. A no confidence vote in the House of Commons had been seen off only weeks before, and a resounding defeat in and around Ceylon could prove to be one defeat too many for the embattled prime minister.

With the eyes of Churchill, the Chiefs of Staff, and the Lords of the Admiralty firmly fixed on the island, the Secretary of State for the Colonies, Lord Moyne, now took his cue from the highest authorities. Reflecting this, he left his governor in Colombo in no doubt as to the

11 TNA, CAB 66/22/24, War Cabinet, 'Far East Appreciation', Report by the Chiefs of Staff (Brooke, Portal, and Pound), 21/2/42.
12 Churchill, *The Second World War*, volume 4, p. 125, Churchill to Ismay for Chiefs of Staff, 17/2/42.
13 Ibid., p.146, Churchill to Ismay for Chiefs of Staff, 27/2/42.
14 Ibid., p. 154, Churchill to Ismay for Chiefs of Staff, 4/3/42.
15 Ibid., p. 152.

situation now pertaining and what was expected of him. A matter of days after the Chiefs of Staff had underlined Ceylon's strategic value, Moyne told Caldecott that:

> With the fall of Singapore and the enemy's penetration of Burma and the Netherlands East Indies, Ceylon has become a vital point in our Indian Ocean defence area, and particularly the security of the island as a naval and air base for our future operations against Japan is a matter of the very highest importance. Much planning is now concentrated on strengthening the defences of Ceylon.
>
> I have addressed you in separate telegrams on various aspects of civil defence in the island in which immediate and thorough-going action is required by the Government of Ceylon to meet the difficulties with labour which have already appeared in essential services, and to instil a sense of security and resolution in the general population.
>
> You have, under the Constitution, powers in an emergency such as we are now faced with, to assume the direct administration of any Department of Government, and it will be essential that this power should be used without hesitation if in any matter such action will conduce to the strengthening of the island's capacity for defence and of its usefulness to the Allied war effort. I appreciate, of course, that if such action needs to be taken, it is likely to be at the expense of good relations with the Board of Ministers and the State Council, but unfortunate as that may be, it must have no more weight than it is worth in the scales of Empire Defence ... It is for that reason that I feel it necessary to impress upon you that the Government of Ceylon must not fail in the present crisis at any point, and that you must be prepared at any time to take up your emergency powers.[16]

From not being in the 'war zone', as the Governor had phrased it, Ceylon was now at the eye of the storm. The message from the Colonial Secretary was very clear; Caldecott was to take any steps necessary to ready Ceylon for war and brook no opposition in doing so, whatever the longer-term consequences; the future of the British Empire, no less, was at stake. Not only did the civil authorities along with their military counterparts need to deal with the refugees now arriving in Ceylon's ports, they had to get their house in order and prepare for an imminent attack, while readying the island for the new wave of reinforcements it was about to receive. During this crucial period, the Colonial Secretary in London kept a very close eye on Caldecott and his administration; Admiral Somerville, lunching with the Governor at Queen's House shortly after his arrival, wrote that he had found him 'most indignant at telegrams from Colonial Office saying Ceylon not doing its stuff'.[17]

Initially, things did not looking promising, and there risked developing a situation in which there were too many uncoordinated leaders. Alongside the civilian authorities, there was a host of military commands too. Headquartered on Ceylon was the Commander-in-Chief East Indies, Arbuthnot, subordinate in some regards to the recently-created Commander-in-Chief Eastern Fleet though with his own distinct local defensive responsibilities and resources. The interim Commander-in-Chief Eastern Fleet, Vice Admiral Sir Geoffrey Layton, was also now present on the island. Both men were directly responsible to the Admiralty. There was also

16 De Silva (ed.), *Sri Lanka*, CO 54/985/5, no. 1, Moyne to Caldecott, 19/2/42, pp. 192-3.
17 Simpson (ed.), *The Somerville Papers*, p. 397, diary, 29/3/42.

a General Officer Commanding Troops, Major General Roland Inskip, who had arrived the previous November, and the major-general commanding the 34th Indian Division which had been deployed to defend the island.[18] There was then an air vice marshal in charge of 222 Group RAF, which had stood up in September, though in February his command possessed little more than two squadrons of Fulmars, some Vildebeest torpedo-bombers, and a tiny detachment of 205 Squadron flying-boats. Both the land and air commanders were subordinate to Wavell as Commander-in-Chief India.

Not only was there the possibility of civil-military disjointedness, but also inter-service friction and a confused command picture. Commodore Ralph Edwards had been on his way to join *Price of Wales* when, breaking his flying-boat journey at Cairo, he had learned of her destruction. Continuing eastwards, at Basrah a few days later he was instructed instead to proceed to Colombo to assist Arbuthnot. Arriving on 15 December, he was unimpressed by the situation he encountered as Ceylon adjusted to the startling events of the first week of the Japanese war. 'The muddle here is appalling and old Arbuthnot and his people just don't understand', he wrote.[19] Following his arrival in Ceylon in late January, Layton endorsed this poor opinion of Arbuthnot, writing that although he had been a very brave officer, 'he seemed to have aged prematurely and was incapable of decisive action'.[20] Later, on his arrival in Ceylon, Somerville confirmed this view: 'Lunched with the Arbuthnots', he wrote on 28 March, 'he full of moans and grievances'.[21] Somerville found 'a confused situation and uncertainty over the enemy's next move, compounded by a lack of intelligence and reconnaissance, panic and gloom in much of the high command, and inter-service ignorance about each other's functions and forces'.[22] Clearly, the command situation in Ceylon needed to be very firmly gripped if the British were to avoid another debacle.

Layton, the ranking military officer on the island, became increasingly prominent in Ceylon's war councils. He was one of Britain's wiliest sea dogs, and one of its most important wartime naval commanders because of the leadership he showed in the desperate weeks following the opening of the war with Japan. He had been Commander-in-Chief China until the position lapsed when Admiral Phillips took up the newly-created position of Commander-in-Chief Eastern Fleet on 2 December 1941 after *Prince of Wales* and *Repulse* had docked at Singapore's Sembawang naval base. Layton had then replaced Phillips immediately news came through of his death a week later, disembarking from a troopship about to take him from Singapore to Britain, where he had been scheduled to assume the role of Commander-in-Chief Portsmouth. Now, in a very dark hour, his country needed him. Having briefly based himself in Batavia after removing his flag from Singapore, he considered Ceylon the best place from which to work

18 The *Times of Ceylon* reported Inskip's arrival on 21 November, and that he was staying at the Galle Face Hotel. SNLA, *Times of Ceylon*, 21/11/41.

19 CAC, Edwards Papers, REDW 2/7, Diary extracts November 1941-May 1942. Agar and Loveridge dissented from this portrayal of 'Buffy'. See Jackson, *Of Islands, Ports, and Sea Lanes.*

20 Quoted in Peter Smith, *Fist from the Sky: Japan's Dive-Bomber Ace of World War Two* (Mechanicsburg, PA: Stackpole Books, 2006), footnote 158. Here Smith makes reference to the Layton papers stored in TNA, ADM 1472A and B, along with the Layton Papers held at the British Library, 74796 to 74806 Correspondence and papers of Sir Geoffrey Layton relating to the naval war in the Pacific, 1940-45.

21 Simpson (ed.), *The Somerville Papers*, 28/3/42, p. 396.

22 Ibid., p. 357.

given the situation that was unfolding and the fact that ABDA's naval forces were under the command of the American admiral Thomas Hart.[23] He had arrived in Colombo on 21 January aboard the light cruiser *Emerald*, wearing the flag of the Commander-in Chief Eastern Fleet, a position which he was to fill until the arrival of Somerville, whom he was told on 27 January was being sent out to take over the fleet.[24]

But that would take nearly two months to transpire, Somerville not leaving Britain until mid-February and not arriving in Colombo until 24 March. In the crucial interim, Layton was responsible for supervising Britain's naval war in the region, which entailed defending the sea lanes to the Middle East and Persian Gulf as well as contributing to the defence of Burma, Malaya, and the Dutch East Indies – which increasingly meant assisting the retreat and evacuation from them. In addition to supervising – as far as was possible amid the prevailing chaos – the collapse of the Allied position in the great arc of territory that had supposedly formed a barrier against the Japanese, he was intimately involved in drawing the new defensive line that the British knew they would have to hold – and this meant preparing to defend the sea lanes of the western Indian Ocean while holding on to Ceylon.

Inevitably, therefore, Layton became embroiled in the defence of the island itself. Here he was determined to sort things out, aware that Ceylon's retention was vital to the British cause and that the Japanese were already sniffing around, probing Ceylon's defences.[25] On 28 January, for example, he reported that a Japanese submarine had appeared off the north-east coast and attacked the paddle steamer *Idar*, which was set ablaze by gunfire. Soon after, there were false reports of enemy aircraft landing 30 miles north of Mannar on the west coast, leading to precautionary measures.[26] The Japanese were probing the waters around the island in anticipation of an attack, British anti-submarine vessels vying with Japanese submarines off Ceylon's coast, though with little effect on either side so far. On 1 February Arbuthnot suggested that a strategic minefield be laid off Colombo, but the Admiralty, at this stage, demurred.[27]

Commander-in-Chief Ceylon

In Ceylon Layton had found 'something of an Augean stable'. He told Pound that he was 'profoundly shocked by [the] state of unreadiness and unjustified complacency in nearly all circles'.[28] He told London that Ceylon 'was virtually defenceless':

23 Replaced by the Dutch admiral Conrad Helfrich on 12 February.

24 One of those accompanying Layton on board *Emerald*, which left Java on 16 February, was Paymaster Sub-Lieutenant R. V. Ward. He had been aboard *Prince of Wales* when she was sunk, spending an hour and a half in the water, with the sharks. He then spent two weeks in Singapore attached to Layton's staff, moving to Java aboard *Durban*. 'There we worked in Lever Building, then in the French Consulate from 6 January to 16 January'. BBC World War Two People's War oral history archive, R. V. Ward, 'The Sinking of HMS *Prince of Wales* and HMS *Repulse*, A4217979.

25 All from 'Admiralty War Diaries of World War II', Layton's diary, November 1941-March 1942.

26 Ibid., 1/3/42.

27 Ibid., 1/2/42.

28 Layton to Pound, 27/2/42, quoted in Stephen Roskill, *Churchill and the Admirals* (Barnsley: Pen and Sword, 2004), p. 202.

> By 7th February, it was obvious that the Malaya – N.E.I. [Netherlands East Indies] barrier, on which it had really depended for its defence against the enemy, was about to collapse, and I represented to the Admiralty its deficiencies. The first essential was clearly a strong fighter force at Colombo and Trincomalee, and adequate R.D.F. [radio direction finding – radar] at these places to give warning of attack.[29]

In order to orchestrate Ceylon's defence and maximize its potential, the creation of an efficient command structure was imperative. There could be no repeat of the farrago of civil-military, and army, navy, air force, confusion and dissension that had so blighted the defence of Malaya and Singapore. It was clear that what was required to supercharge and streamline Ceylon's war effort and coordinate its defences was a dynamic individual empowered with supreme authority. On 26 February Churchill asked Wavell, en route to Ceylon, to 'pray consider whether key situation Ceylon does not require a first-rate soldier in supreme command of all local services, including civil government, and whether Pownall is not the man. We do not want another Singapore'.[30] Wavell agreed that Pownall was ideal for the role, but the fact was that at this particular moment he was still in Java awaiting evacuation. In their wisdom, therefore, the government decided that there was no better person for the role than Layton, already on the spot, already wise to the theatre and its challenges, and, what is more, already in Ceylon grappling with them.

Layton was convinced that the change proposed by Churchill with regard to the command structure 'was not only desirable and necessary but imperative and urgent'.[31] 'On reading this message', Roskill writes, 'Churchill discussed matters with Pound, and proposed that Layton should be appointed in supreme command of all forces and authorities in Ceylon'. Alanbrooke's diary records discussion of a 'Military Governor for Ceylon' at the Chiefs of Staff meeting of 3 March.[32] The following day, he wrote:

> A long and protracted COS taken up mainly with a heated argument as regards the relative advantages between a single commander (or generalissimo), as opposed to the usual trinity of three services. I was supporting the former and was being strongly opposed by CNS [Chief of the Naval Staff] and CAS [Chief of the Air Staff]! The case in point being Ceylon, and our attempt at producing a military commander instead of the usual civil Governor. The argument itself and impossibility of arriving at any agreement convinced me more than anything else that I was right! But argument went on for close on 2 hours.[33]

29 'Admiralty War Diaries of World War II', Layton's diary, November 1941 to March 1942, 15/2/42.

30 Churchill, *The Second World War*, volume 4, p. 129. Pownall, Churchill continued, 'assumed command of the garrison on March 6'. (Ibid.) In this brief passage in his history of the war, Churchill is in error, conflating Layton and Pownall, and the respective roles that they now assumed – the former, Commander-in-Chief Ceylon, the latter, General Officer Commanding Troops Ceylon. Pownall did not land in Ceylon until the following day, 7 March, and Churchill is clearly thinking of Layton, who was indeed officially appointed Commander-in-Chief Ceylon – obviously the role Churchill is describing – on 5 March.

31 Roskill, *Churchill and the Admirals*, Layton to Pound, 27/2/42, p. 202.

32 Alex Danchev and Dan Todman (eds), *War Diaries, 1939-1945: Field Marshal Lord Alanbrooke* (London: Phoenix, 2002), 4/3/42, p. 234.

33 Ibid., pp. 235-6.

As a consequence of these protracted Whitehall discussions, Layton was promoted acting admiral and formally appointed on 5 March to a brand new post, that of Commander-in-Chief Ceylon.[34] The appointment became effective on 5 March, 'and was without doubt one of the best Churchill ever made'.[35] Alanbrooke wrote on 6 March: 'COS mainly concerned with organization of defence of Ceylon and of organization of its supreme command'.[36]

To give him a fighting chance of succeeding in this new role, London took the drastic step of subordinating the island's civil authorities to military command; it was no time for half measures, and so the Governor and the Ceylonese Board of Ministers and State Council were placed under Layton's authority. Breaking the news of his demotion, the Secretary of State for the Colonies – now Lord Cranborne – told Caldecott that the War Cabinet had decreed that Ceylon and its dependencies were henceforth designated a 'military area' under a Commander-in-Chief Ceylon.

> Ceylon is now a key point for the concentration of forces and for defence of our communications in the Indian Ocean ... All civil and military authorities in the area will be subject to his directions ... I should have wished to give you time to explain the projected change to your Ministers but I fear that the military situation does not permit of the delay which that would occasion.[37]

As well as placing Layton in authority over the civil administration, he was also put in charge of the three armed services on the island, Britain's first experiment with a unified command structure in an operational theatre, the lessons of Malaya and Singapore being intelligently applied. The Chiefs of Staff's directive to Layton, issued on 5 March, ran:

> You are appointed Commander-in-Chief Ceylon. All naval, military, air, and civil authorities in the area, including the Governor and Civil Administration, will be subject to your direction.
>
> 2. Your immediate task is to ensure that all measures necessary for the defence of Ceylon are taken forthwith and that the military and civil measures are properly coordinated. The Governor has emergency powers under the Constitution, and the power of issuing Defence Regulations, which he can use to the extent that you may require any such measures.
>
> 3. You will convene and preside over any council or conference from time to time which you consider necessary for the effective cooperation of all services in Ceylon
>
> 4. You will report as soon as possible whether, in order to carry out the tasks specified in paragraphs 2 and 3 above, it is necessary for you to assume supreme command of all the fighting services allotted to the defence of Ceylon, and what staff and other arrangements this would entail.

34 He was promoted full admiral on 15 September 1942, TNA, ADM 199/663, War diary no. 4, 1/9/42-31/12/42.

35 Roskill, *Churchill and the Admirals*, pp. 202-03.

36 Danchev and Todman (eds), *War Diaries*, 6/3/42. The following day, he arrived for the Chiefs of Staff meeting to find a note from Churchill appointing him chairman of the committee.

37 De Silva (ed.), *Sri Lanka*, CO 54/985/6, Cranborne to Caldecott, 3/3/42, p. 195. On Layton's appointment see also documents 119, 120, and 124.

> 5. On all military matters your immediate superior will be the Commander-in-Chief India. As to civil matters, the Governor of Ceylon will remain at his post and will exercise the civil functions of Governor subject to your overriding authority and direction.[38]

As Axis broadcasts announced, 'feverish' preparations were taking place in Ceylon, and Layton immediately established a War Council, a crucial vehicle for preparing the island comprised of senior military and civilian leaders including the Governor and the British and Ceylonese members of the Board of Ministers.[39] Layton had been given almost dictatorial powers; 'Do not ask permission to do things. Do them and report afterwards what you have done', Pound told him. Initially it was feared that the transfer of power over civilian matters to Layton would lead to constitutional clashes and, potentially, a breakdown in the system of government. In fact, this did not occur. Through regular meetings of the War Council, Layton showed a greater appreciation of the island's political problems than if he had relied solely on the views of the Governor, and a remarkably effective system of wartime civil-military governance came into being.[40] Initially, there was some resistance from Don Senananyake, leader of the State Council, regarding the extent of Layton's powers, and extensive discussion. Layton wrote that when it 'became clear that the only alternative to loyal co-operation from the Board of Ministers ... would be a purely military regime, Mr Senananyake finally accepted the situation'.[41] Less than a week after taking over, Layton told Pound that he had 'weathered the storm' which he had expected to arise, and that 'after a slight outburst [presumably on the part of the Civil authorities] they had accepted the situation in what I can only describe as a very good spirit'.[42] Efforts were made in the press to fully explain the situation to the public. As one newspaper's headline and sub-headings read: 'War Council set up in Ceylon; Coordination of all defence measures; ministers included; function of Commander-in-Chief explained'. The article was at pains to explain the strategic situation that had made this change necessary, and that it would not entail the imposition of martial law.[43]

The position of the Eastern Fleet

So, plans were in hand to ready Ceylon for attack. But it was naturally to the navy that people looked for the first line of defence. In defending Ceylon and the sea lanes, the problem facing

38 SNLA, Sessional Papers, SP 3 1942, 'Directive issued by HMG to His Excellency Admiral Sir Geoffrey Layton KCB DSO' (Colombo: Ceylon Government Press, 1942). Reproduced in De Silva (ed.), *Sri Lanka*, CO 54/985/6, no. 9, p. 196.

39 Ibid. CO 54/985/6, Colonial Office minute.

40 De Silva (ed.), *Sri Lanka*, p. lv. He was also to take a lead in getting Whitehall to reopen, during the war, the issue of Ceylon's constitutional advancement.

41 TNA, ADM 199/663, Ceylon Command: War diaries. These are the war diaries of the Commander-in-Chief Ceylon, and contain the minutes of all War Council meetings and the regular Commanders' Meetings, as frequent as the War Council gatherings and bringing together all the island's main service commanders and on occasions representatives of India Command, sometimes including the Commander-in-Chief India himself.

42 Roskill, *Churchill and the Admirals*, Layton to Pound, 11/3/42, p. 203.

43 Butler Papers, F. S. Tippet, 'Report and History of the Ceylon Censorship, September 1939-November 1945', undated newspaper cutting.

the British was that at this juncture they did not have the naval wherewithal to meet the full force of the Japanese fleet likely to be deployed against the Eastern Fleet and Ceylon. This comprised, under Nagumo, the five carriers and four battleships of the First Air Fleet and the 3rd Battle Squadron, supported by Rear Admiral Jisaburo Ozawa's Second Expeditionary Fleet, built around a sixth carrier. Things had happened too quickly for the British to be adequately prepared; Force Z had been destroyed, practically ceding control of the eastern Indian Ocean to the enemy; a large army had surrendered at Singapore; the air power of Far East Command had been destroyed or scattered; a weak Burma Army was in retreat; and British air, land, and naval forces were even now supporting their allies in a forlorn defence of Java and Sumatra. It would take time to repair the damage and amass in Ceylon and India sufficient resources to provide an appropriate level of defence, and it would take time to reinforce the Eastern Fleet and better protect its bases in Ceylon and the Maldives in order to conduct the defence of the sea lanes.

Nevertheless, reinforcements were on their way, though distances were great and ships in dry dock or squadrons in the process of updating their aircraft could not be magically fixed and transported to where they were needed overnight. Troops, of which there were never enough to meet all actual and likely threats, needed to be shipped by sea, and the passage around Africa and across the Indian Ocean from Europe or the Mediterranean took many weeks. It was all a question of time; given Japan's astonishing success to date, the British government and commanders on the ground, aided by decent intelligence and a clear sense of what the enemy's next moves might be, thought an attack on Ceylon and India likely, centred on an attempt to cripple the Royal Navy in the Indian Ocean. The question was whether the British would have enough on the ground when this happened, along with the skill and luck required to meet the challenge.

In the first weeks of March a fascinating discussion regarding Ceylon's defence and the role of the Eastern Fleet developed between, on the one hand, admirals Layton, Somerville, and Vice Admiral Sir Algernon Willis (Commander-in-Chief South Atlantic, now appointed Somerville's deputy), and, on the other hand, the Admiralty. The Admiralty suggested that two of the Eastern Fleet's 'R' for 'Revenge' class battleships should be retained in Colombo harbour, where their powerful armaments would deter the Japanese from attacking and, if they did, offer a powerful supplement to the port's firepower. As the Admiralty told Somerville on 1 March, 'Attacks on Ceylon relative to Pearl Harbor type or full scale invasion considered possible … [Layton] has been instructed to keep 2 'R' class in Ceylon to operate against possible invasion'.[44]

Layton, Somerville, and Willis – and also Jan Smuts, with whom Somerville consulted as he broke his journey at Cape Town on 11-12 March – completely disagreed. They believed that keeping the Eastern Fleet intact was the single-most important strategic requirement. Disastrous though it might well prove to be, Ceylon could be lost, but the fleet simply could not, because then there would be nothing whatsoever between the Japanese and the sea lanes further west. Therefore, basing two of the fleet's most powerful units in Ceylon, old, of limited endurance, and ill-equipped to meet the Japanese at sea though they might be, would be sufficient to actually precipitate an enemy attack intended to destroy them, thereby greatly weakening the fleet, rather than deter it. As Somerville signalled to Pound, 'to prevent "Pearl Harbor" at Trincomalee and Colombo we must have an adequate scale of defence'; stationing two battleships

44 Simpson (ed.), *The Somerville Papers*, p 388.

there 'appears to afford a vulnerable target rather than an effective deterrent in view of what must be the very limited fighter protection available'.[45] The Admiralty, however, persisted. A week later Somerville received a 'signal from DP [Admiral Sir Dudley Pound, the First Sea Lord] to say they were prepared to expend 2 'R's' in defence of Ceylon providing expenditure effective'. Unimpressed, Somerville wrote that the plan '[s]eems a bit wet'.[46]

Somerville was having a strenuous journey out to Ceylon aboard the carrier *Formidable*, worrying about the lack of training and experience among his ships' captains and crews and the pilots of the Fleet Air Arm. While retaining a confident and humorous demeanour for the benefit of his men, he was also worrying about what on earth to do in terms of strategy against the Japanese. While at sea on the six week voyage out, he kept up a constant correspondence with the Admiralty on this matter. It must have come as a relief when he reached Cape Town and was able to talk strategy with his new deputy, Willis, as well as Smuts, whom he found to be wise and extremely personable.

Following their meeting at Cape Town, Somerville was able to articulate his thinking on matters in correspondence with the Admiralty. Before attempting to capture Ceylon, he believed, the Japanese would seek to reduce the Eastern Fleet, and would support an attack on the island with the greater part of their fleet. Stationing two battleships at Ceylon would provide a good opportunity for them to do this. Until reinforcements for the Eastern Fleet arrived, Somerville said that he would not be able to offer effective opposition to the greater part of the Japanese fleet if it were deployed to the Indian Ocean. He agreed that the loss of Ceylon would be a most serious matter, but that if the Japanese determined to do this with the support of the greater part of their fleet, the British could do very little about it.[47] But Somerville (erroneously, as it happened) believed that this was unlikely to occur, as the Japanese would be reluctant to denude their Pacific lines of communication of protection. If they were to attempt a sortie into the Indian Ocean or an assault on Ceylon with a lesser scale of naval power, the most effective defence and deterrence would be to keep the Eastern Fleet intact, best achieved by keeping it at sea and mounting feints east of Ceylon from time to time. What would be folly would be to allow the Eastern Fleet to be destroyed in penny packets. If Ceylon were lost it would be extremely difficult, but not impossible, to maintain the use of the all-important sea lanes leading to the Middle East and Persian Gulf, but if the enemy took Ceylon *and* destroyed most of the Eastern Fleet, things would become really desperate. 'The whole of our cause in the Indian Ocean must depend on the Eastern Fleet being kept in being. The crippling of this fleet would of course make the loss of Ceylon almost a certainty, but far more important it would open our vital supply lines both oil and to the Middle East to any enemy raiding force'.[48]

Fortunately, the will of the men on the spot was allowed to prevail. The Admiralty replied to Somerville's appreciation of the strategic situation and generally agreed with it, especially with the contention that the Eastern Fleet must not be sacrificed, and also offered an 'apologia' for the idea of stationing battleships in Ceylon's ports, which Somerville considered 'rather weak'.[49] What is interesting about these exchanges is that the Admiralty was prepared to risk so much to

45 Ibid., to Pound 2/3/42, p. 390.
46 Ibid., pocket diary 9/3/42, p. 392.
47 Ibid., pp. 392-3.
48 Ibid., pp. 395
49 Ibid.

defend Ceylon; the British had entered the war in 1939 with 14 battleships and 3 battlecruisers, but by early 1942 had lost three battleships and two battlecruisers sunk and two battleships were out of action having been badly damaged during the Italian frogmen attack on Alexandria harbour in December 1941. The battleship *Duke of York* had entered commission in November 1941, though the battleships *Anson* and *Howe* would not commission until April and August 1942 respectively. Down to 10 battleships and a single battlecruiser at this moment, the fact that the government regarded two of their number as expendable indicates the strategic importance ascribed to Ceylon.

Establishing Ceylon Command

Meanwhile, every effort was being made to ready Ceylon. Determined to avoid a repeat of Singapore's lethargy and disorder in the face of invasion, London conveyed explicit instructions to Layton to get rid 'without hesitation' of anyone who was 'inefficient or incapable of dealing with the emergency', and the British government was 'prepared to abrogate the Ceylon Constitution if ministers played up'. Granted such latitude, Layton immediately replaced the Chief Secretary and Deputy Governor Guy Wodeman.[50] Born in 1886 and having entered the Ceylon civil service in 1909, he was to be employed by the Colonial Office until the end of the war but not considered up to the challenges associated with Ceylon's administration at this crucial moment. Also in Layton's sights was Arbuthnot, whom he blamed for the unsatisfactory state of affairs in Ceylon, and Somerville agreed with him when he arrived and suggested abolishing the post of Commander-in-Chief East Indies (for these and other reasons this eventually transpired in June, the post being downgraded to the role of Flag Officer Ceylon).[51] Fortunately, Layton quickly concluded that in contrast to his deputy, Caldecott was a brilliant governor.[52] He was also impressed with the members of the Ceylonese elite occupying prominent political roles in Ceylon's unusual governance structure, such as Oliver Goonetilleke, who served throughout the war as head of the Civil Defence Department, particularly crucial at this moment of impending attack.

The War Council created by Layton was a central administrative machine in the new system, and was to meet between three and five times a month, the inaugural meeting occurring on 9 March. The minutes of that first meeting reveal the urgent business that Layton wanted taken in hand forthwith. The members discussed the penal code and penalties given the need to maintain public discipline in an emergency, underground subversive societies, the internment of enemy aliens, an order for 15,000 gas masks (raised to 30,000 at the 16 March meeting) and 1,000 decontamination suits, food control, fuel stocks (including coal, essential for the operation of the railways), censorship, and the need to declare all the island's provinces as defence areas.[53] Complete blackouts of the docks were trialled, and car headlights were dimmed. Orders were issued putting arrack shops in Colombo out of bounds to service personnel, there being

50 Wodeman tendered his resignation, expressing the sentiment that after 30 years service a younger man was needed in the role. TNA, ADM 199/663. War Council minutes, 4/4/42.

51 This was done in June. See Jackson, *Of Islands, Ports, and Sea Lanes.*

52 British Library (BL), Layton Papers, 74800, Part II 'Ceylon 1942-45'.

53 TNA, ADM, 199/663, War Council minutes, 9/3/42.

no wish to repeat a Singapore situation in which troops got drunk or – worse – the troops of an invading enemy got drunk, fuelling their predilection for committing atrocities.[54] The Port area of Colombo was searched for unguarded stores of liquor, to be removed if found.[55] New water wells were constructed in Colombo,[56] the fire brigade was brought under military law,[57] and road signs were removed to confuse an invading enemy (though commenced, the scheme was reversed because the signs were needed by imperial troops 'in a strange country'; confusing them was deemed to be more detrimental than confusing the enemy).[58] Lighthouses were camouflaged,[59] trenches dug and obstacles erected on possible landing sites,[60] and rewards for the apprehension of enemy agents publicly announced in the wake of a report from an army officer who had observed parachutists descending from a bomber-like aircraft.[61]

Information on the island's transport and communications networks and facilities was gathered and studied as defensive plans were enacted, a new military system developed, and maps and information produced for distribution to the tactical level commanders who would be responsible for leading troops into action if the enemy landed. The 'British Empire Report: Ceylon', for example, contained photographs of Colombo harbour, Colombo harbour breakwater, and the Ratmalana railway workshops, and map diagrams of Galle harbour, the city of Colombo, Trincomalee town, the railway telegraph system, the railway telephone system, the Ceylon Government Railway network, the electricity network, the telephone system, the telegraphy system, and malarial areas.[62] States of readiness and code words were put in place, standard military procedure to indicate the threat level and initiate defensive operations if this became necessary. At one stage, the code words were 'Wellington', 'Clive', 'Waterloo', and 'Plassey', the latter being the highest state of alert denoting that a raid or invasion was imminent.[63]

In getting to grips with his new role, the most immediate matters to be addressed, Layton wrote, related to civil defence as well as military preparation. There was no radar, the fire-fighting arrangements were rudimentary, and there were no gas masks. Efforts were now made to transform this situation by organizing civil defence on a professional basis, addressing the food supply situation, instituting a comprehensive air raid precautions (ARP) programme, and taking measures to get the ports running properly. In pursuing this, Layton appointed Mr Wilson, late chair of the Harbour Board in Penang, as Port Controller Colombo, and appointed Mr Strong, late of the Rangoon Port Authority, as chair of the Colombo Port Commission.[64] Getting the harbours sorted out was vital in preparing for a Japanese attack that would inevitably target merchant shipping as well as military installations and assets. It was also vital because

54 Ibid., War Council minutes, 31/3/42 and 3/4/42.
55 Ibid., Commanders' Meeting minutes, 14/4/42.
56 Ibid., Commander-in-Chief Ceylon war diary, 1/6/42-31/8/42.
57 Ibid., War Council minutes, 13/4/42.
58 Ibid., War Council minutes, 20/4/42.
59 Ibid., Commanders' Meeting minutes, 12/5/42.
60 Ibid., Commanders' Meeting minutes, 21/4/42.
61 Ibid., War Council minutes, 1/4/42.
62 TNA, WO 252/893, British Empire report: Ceylon, October 1942.
63 TNA, ADM 202/190, MNBDO, 3 Marines Naval Brigade, July 1943-May 1944.
64 In December 1942 people involved in the raids were honoured, including MBEs for men in the Harbour Engineers Department, Colombo Port Commission. SNLA, *Times of Ceylon*, 15/12/42. Conrad Helfrich was also awarded a KCB.

trade needed to be kept moving – already a stockpile of copra awaiting export was building up because of the lack of shipping – and food needed to be imported.[65] In sorting out the harbours alone Layton had his work cut out for him. There were go-slow strikes in Colombo on a regular basis, to the extent that sometimes as many as 50 valuable ships were lying exposed in the outer anchorage waiting to discharge their cargoes. Rice was already a major headache; in peacetime Ceylon imported 540,000 tons a year, though its chief supplier, Burma, was about to succumb to the enemy. Getting Ceylon onto a proper war footing also meant increasing rubber production, tightening censorship, and building new military bases and facilities across the island, sucking more and more civilians into the war economy in the process.

From a strictly military point of view, requisitioning was the order of the day, and buildings and tracts of land across the island were summarily taken over by the military. Schools and public buildings, hotels and houses, were requisitioned in order to accommodate the new forces pouring into the island along with all that was needed to support them, including military hospitals. Land was commandeered for new bases and for training grounds. Ratmalana, the island's civil airport, was commandeered by the RAF and its runway doubled in length; a new RAF airbase was rapidly developed at the Colombo racecourse; the Colombo museum was taken over as Army Headquarters; Koggala lagoon and its environs was declared a 'special area' and developed as a major flying-boat base; and the Welcome Hotel Trincomalee was commandeered as a combined headquarters.[66] New fighter airbases were developed at Dambulla, Minneriya, and Vavuniya.[67] At Katukurunda work on another large airbase was taken in hand, the facility eventually allocated to the navy for disembarked Fleet Air Arm squadrons from Royal Navy carriers. Compulsory evacuation legislation was put in place in case settlements in the vicinity of these bases needed to be emptied of civilians at short notice. Heavy and light anti-aircraft guns (62 of the former and 100 of the latter by the end of April), barrage balloons, searchlights, and radar units were rushed in, as well as smoke generators to conceal potential coastal landing points in the event of an invasion. Anti-submarine and anti-torpedo booms were installed and controlled minefields established off the ports and at potential enemy landing grounds.[68] The defences of Colombo and Trincomalee 'were being augmented by the day' and Captain Palliser of the Royal Navy was appointed Trincomalee Fortress Commander, and in his new position decided 'to annexe everything in Trincomalee required to build and run a port on a warlike

65 BL, Layton Papers, 74800, Part II 'Ceylon 1942-45'.

66 Ratmalana was the colony's first aerodrome. A De Havilland Puss Moth, flown by Harold Tyndale-Biscoe of the Madras Flying Club, was the first aircraft to land there on 27 November 1935. Welcome Hotel detail from TNA, ADM 199/663, Commanders' Meeting minutes, 27/3/42.

67 It was noted on 20 April that 600 more labourers were required for the development of the Colombo airbases and 2,000 for China Bay and its satellite at Kokkilai, TNA, ADM 199/663, War Council minutes, 20/4/42. The demand was constant throughout the war. A regular item on Commanders' Meeting minutes throughout 1943 had airbase construction progress as a standing item. In January 1943, for instance, there were over 6,500 labourers employed in the construction of the new airbases at Sigiriya and Vavuniya. TNA, CO 968/12/7, Commander-in-Chief Ceylon, war diaries, January to March 1943, War Council minutes, 18/1/43.

68 An observation minefield was established at Colombo. On one occasion it blew a junk, heavily loaded with iron ore, to pieces; faced with positive asdic echoes from a large mass of metal, the operator diagnosed a submarine. As the junk did not reply to hydrographic challenge, it was destroyed. Trenowden, *Operations Most Secret.*

footing'.[69] The civil government was told that Trincomalee and environs was a 'Special Area' for the military, taken over under the defence regulations.[70]

Layton set about his work with gusto. John O'Regan, a young colonial civil servant, was able to observe him at close quarters courtesy of his duties as one of the Governor's two private secretaries. The Admiral was as a brave, no-nonsense man, well known for his 'rough quarter-deck style'. O'Regan recounts a War Council meetings at which 'it was Layton's habit to review the past week's events. He would ask, for example, about the very slow progress with a road to the airport'.

> 'Kotalawala', he would demand.
>
> 'What the hell have you been doing in the last week?'
>
> To which [Sir John] Kotalawala, then Minister of Communications and Works, replied: 'The head overseer is having a lot of trouble with supplies'.
>
> 'Then give him six on the backside', Layton would bark.[71]

Admiral Lord Louis Mountbatten also had occasion to see Layton in action. '[T]he set up here is curious', he wrote: 'the Governor is definitely under the Commander-in-Chief's orders in all matters pertaining to the defence of the Island and operations generally'. Mountbatten stayed with Layton during his visit, recording in his diary that 'our host was my Captain in *K.6*, in the 12th Submarine Flotilla, when I was doing my midshipman's submarine time during the winter of 1917-1918. He seems quite unchanged, the typical, bluff, decided sailor. I hear that he keeps all the Ministers in proper order, with very strong language'.[72] On 26 March, two days after landing at Ratmalana to assume command of the Eastern Fleet, Somerville wrote that he

> [drove to] the Secretariat where Geoffrey [Layton] was presiding at a meeting as C-in-C Ceylon. There was little doubt as to who was master in *that* house and I was much impressed. He's very drastic but that is what is needed here ... He takes complete charge of Ceylon and stands no nonsense from anyone. He pulls all the Ministers legs and they work for him all the harder.[73]

Somerville's arrival added impetus to the process of centralizing command in Ceylon. He brushed aside Arbuthnot's complaints about Layton's ruthless approach. 'I told him that in my opinion Geoffrey Layton was saving Ceylon from itself. He's roaring up the Ministers, Editors of Papers and Harbour Authorities and is doing wonders ... He and I work absolutely hand in

69 CAC, REDW 2/7. Palliser was replaced by Brigadier Lomax (with the rank of acting major-general) on 31 May 1942. TNA, ADM 199/663, war diary 5/4/42-31/5/42.

70 SNLA, H. 29.4.12, CFD 306/38 Defence Regulations (Miscellaneous).

71 John O'Regan, *From Empire to Commonwealth: Reflections on a Career in Britain's Overseas Service* (London: Radcliffe Press, 1994). The correct spelling of the surname is 'Kotelawala'. Roskill tells the story of the recently appointed Civil Defence Commissioner, Oliver Goonetilleke, complaining to Caldecott that Layton had called him a 'black bastard'. 'My dear fellow that is nothing to what he calls me!', was the reply. Roskill, *Churchill and the Admirals*, footnote, p. 203.

72 Philip Ziegler (ed.), *Personal Diary of Admiral the Lord Louis Mountbatten, Supreme Allied Commander South-East Asia, 1943-1946* (London: Collins, 1988), 15/4/44, pp. 98-99.

73 Simpson (ed.), *The Somerville Papers*, p. 397.

hand and call each other the most frightful names'.[74] Somerville told Pound he was 'glad that Geoffrey Layton has been put in charge of Ceylon. From what I saw of the soldiers and the Governor I'm convinced that they want a good driving hand on them all the time', referring to his previous experience of Ceylon, where he had been stationed as Commander-in-Chief East Indies until shortly before the outbreak of war.[75]

Somerville was relieved that the creation of the Commander-in-Chief Ceylon post enabled him to concentrate on fleet operations at sea without having to worry about the defence of Ceylon from 'on board' the island itself. As he wrote to his wife, 'Geoffrey Layton has been made C-in-C Ceylon … I think it's a good plan as I certainly cannot tackle the defence of Ceylon and the Fleet'.[76] This was important, because Somerville was adamant that he needed to spend as much time at sea with his fleet as possible, not only in order to pursue his strategy, which was to move about using the region's various ports and naval bases in order to keep the Japanese guessing as to the fleet's whereabouts, but because he required as much time as possible to put his ships through their paces, to train his pilots and to get his captains used to operating as part of a large fleet, an experience that very few of them had ever had. After he had had some time to see Layton in action and work alongside him, Somerville told Pound: Layton 'takes complete charge of Ceylon and stands no nonsense from anyone. Sometimes tries to take charge of the Eastern Fleet also but fails. We are the best of friends'.[77] In a subsequent signal to the 1st Sea Lord he wrote that Layton had 'got everyone under his thumb in Ceylon'.[78]

Stephen Roskill, in the official British history of the war at sea, writes:

> Admirals Layton and Somerville were both strong personalities, and although there were occasional differences of opinion, notably over whether the Commander-in-Chief, Ceylon, exercised any measure of control over the Eastern Fleet, these were easily resolved. Between them they formed a powerful team to work for the ultimate restoration of British maritime power in the East … With General Wavell the Navy's relations were excellent, and that great soldier quickly grasped the diversity and magnitude of the problems with which the sister service was faced. As Somerville expressed it when the three of them were in conference, the Eastern Fleet not only shared in the defence of India and Ceylon, but was responsible for the security of the sea routes 'from the Cape eastwards to Australia and northwards to Aden and the Persian Gulf'. It was moreover 'an important force to be used in the ultimate operations of ejecting the enemy from Malaya and the Dutch East Indies'. But in April 1942, such plans were almost visionary, for the first need was to defend what we still held.[79]

74 Quoted in Donald Macintyre, *Fighting Admiral: The Life of Admiral of the Fleet Sir James Somerville, GCB, GBE, DSO* (London: Evans Brothers, 1961), p. 182.
75 Simpson (ed.), *The Somerville Papers*, 11/3/42, pp. 393-94. After returning to Britain he retired, only to be recalled by the outbreak of war.
76 Ibid., 8/3/42, p. 391.
77 Ibid., 20/6/42, p. 430. A spat between Layton and Somerville over division of responsibilities between their respective commands, centred on the control of intelligence personnel in Colombo, was played out in communications with the Admiralty in summer 1942. See TNA, ADM 20/2410, Defence of Ceylon, 3/3/42-2/9/42, Somerville to Admiralty, 4/7/42 and Layton to Chiefs of Staff, undated.
78 Simpson (ed.), *The Somerville Papers*, 15/7/42, p. 434.
79 Roskill, *The War at Sea*, volume 2, p. 59.

Given that it was essential for the three services to cooperate and coordinate their defence plans, proximity of headquarters' staffs was important. Naval Headquarters in Ceylon had been moved from Trincomalee to the shore base HMS *Lanka* in Colombo so as to be closer to the Governor and the seat of government. The naval operations room was 'a vast subterranean complex, with huge wall maps and concealed lighting'.[80] Nearby, Layton established his headquarters in the imposing Secretariat Building on the Galle Face, the main building of British colonial authority forming a fitting abode for the man now exercising supreme authority over the island. The main intelligence-gathering facility was established near Colombo at HMS *Anderson*, and the Fighter Operations Room at Bishops College, Boyd Place, Colombo.[81] On his arrival Somerville took over the house of the King's Harbour Master, adjoining the Victoria Arcade Navy Offices, for when he was ashore, while Army Headquarters was established a short distance away at the Colombo museum, another imposing building.

Most importantly, in fostering inter-service awareness and cooperation and ensuring a smooth chain of command, alongside the War Council Layton formed a Commanders' Committee, which first met on the day he assumed the role of Commander-in-Chief Ceylon, and was to meet four or five times a month thereafter. The boards and sub-committees established by Layton reveal the extent of the war-related work that came within the purview of the Commander-in-Chief and his War Council and Commanders' Committee. There was a Services Defence Committee, Air Defence Committee, Inter-Services Radio Direction Finding (radar) Technical Sub-Committee, Combined Signals Board, Combined Security Board, Works Priority Committee, Advisory Committee on Food Supplies, Requisitioning of School Buildings Board, War Publicity Committee, Shipping Priority Committee, Cargo Dispersal Committee, Petrol Board, and Manpower Board.[82] There was also the 'X' Committee, dealing with demolition and denial schemes in the event of an enemy takeover. It made detailed plans for the destruction or denial of road, rail, and communications infrastructure, industrial plant, machine tools, oil and petrol facilities and stores, alcohol supplies, railway rolling stock, power stations, and other assets. The committee decided, however, against a vigorous programme of tea and rubber denial, adjudging these commodities to be non-essential for the Japanese, and fearing that the destruction of stocks in Colombo 'might set the whole city ablaze'.[83]

A very important position in the new command structure was that of army commander, and on 10 March, three days after disembarking from *Kedah*, Lieutenant General Sir Henry Pownall was appointed General Officer Commanding-in-Chief Ceylon, in charge of the island's land forces and defences. Although this was Pownall's seventh job in the war to date, he applied himself with gusto to the task of preparing the island to resist Japanese invasion. 'At this time this was anything but a sinecure since a Japanese invasion seemed imminent. The appointment showed that, despite his association with two military disasters (Dunkirk and Singapore), Churchill still retained faith in Pownall … [and he] threw himself eagerly into organizing Ceylon's defences'.[84] Wavell visited Ceylon to check on the defences in this part of his sprawling domain:

80 Trenowden, *Operations Most Secret*, p. 92.
81 TNA, ADM 199/663, Commanders' Meeting minutes, 29/5/42.
82 TNA, ADM, 199/663.
83 TNA, WO 106/3715, Denial scheme Ceylon, April 1942.
84 Bond (ed.), *Chief of Staff*, p. xiii.

> Ceylon was at that time considered next on the list for Japanese aggression, the military resources were as usual quite inadequate to repel any invasion, and Ceylon was the last bastion before India. Pownall had done his best, but was in some trepidation as to whether Wavell would think that good enough. When nervous Pownall was at his most precise and concise (in contrast to Wavell [who was renowned for his awkward silences]) and Wavell was treated to 35 minutes' highly concentrated dissertation ending with 'That's the lot sir – as the Japs would no doubt be happy to learn'.
>
> 'I see', said Wavell. There was a long, long pause.
>
> 'Is there anywhere where I can have a pee?'
>
> 'From then on', Pownall commented, 'I knew I was in the clear.[85]

Another factor in preparing Ceylon was the recruitment and organization of local people into military and civil defence formations. In the light of the loss of Malaya and Singapore and the ensuing criticism of its civil defence preparations, the Colonial Office was particularly anxious that Ceylonese people be given every opportunity to serve in the forces. As K. W. Blaxter of the Colonial Office wrote to the War Office two days before the Japanese raid on Colombo:

> I am directed by Viscount Cranborne [the Colonial Secretary] to transmit, for the consideration of the Army Council, copies of telegrams exchanged with the Commander-in-Chief, Ceylon, regarding a debate on 24 March in the State Council of Ceylon on a motion for the adoption of compulsory military service for Ceylonese, and to draw their attention to the statement that all necessary recruits for the defence of the Island can be obtained by voluntary means.
>
> In view of the experience of Malaya and of the criticism which has been continually expressed in Parliament and the Press that insufficient opportunities for military service were accorded in that territory to the local population and in view of the threat to Ceylon which has been created by the Japanese successes in the East, Lord Cranborne would like to be certain that the fullest possible use is made of Ceylonese man-power in the military defence services of the Island, apart from the engagement of large numbers of Ceylonese for civil defence services and essential labour organizations.[86]

Layton subsequently reported to Cranborne 'on the expansion of local defence forces'. Two battalions of military pioneers had been raised and a third was forming. Since the start of the war the Ceylon Garrison Artillery had risen from 364 to 485 and the Ceylon Light Infantry had expanded from one battalion to four. Two battalions of military pioneers had been raised for the British Army and a third was forming, and the Ceylon engineers was in the process of increasing its strength from 264 to 3,585 men. The militarization of pivotal railway personnel was in hand and a similar scheme under way for posts and telegraphs. In Colombo, Layton reported, the town guard and Ceylon Planters Rifle Corps had an operational role in an emergency and a scheme was in hand to use local personnel to guard dispersed aircraft. Four battalions of the Essential Services Labour Corps, created to provide guaranteed and immediate

85 Ibid., pp. 95-96.

86 De Silva (ed.), *Sri Lanka*, CO 54/985/4, no. 11, 3/4/42, pp. 202-03.

labour when and where it was needed so that military work would not be hindered by strikes and labour shortages, had also been enrolled.

The 'GOC reports that all the above stretch military resources to the utmost. Neither weapons nor organizing and training staffs are available for extending Home Guard into rural districts on British lines'.[87] Weapons were, however, reaching the colony, Wavell asking Somerville in April to transport 400 rifles and bayonets from Bombay aboard *Warspite* for distribution in Ceylon.[88] All of this testified to the extent to which local people were involved in the war effort through membership of uniformed military or civil defence services, their significance being that in joining up they helped support imperial forces, relieving them of local duties and thereby allowing them to concentrate on prosecuting the war against the enemy closer to the frontline. Given the dire circumstance of the moment, Layton even proposed the formation of a guerrilla force, to be known as the Ceylon Levies, to supplement the island's military resources should the Japanese land. This appears to have gone ahead, minutes revealing the existence of three 500-man outfits, their role 'similar to the irregulars in Assam'.[89] There was then the Colombo Town Guard which, among other things, was detailed to help implement the city's oil denial scheme in the event of imminent invasion.[90]

Reinforcements

As the new command arrangements bedded in, Ceylon received significant reinforcements, as too did the Eastern Fleet. Given the enormous global demands on the Royal Navy, the naval reinforcement programme that was in progress in the hope of meeting the Japanese in battle if they entered the Indian Ocean in strength was impressive. The four 'R' class battleships would be concentrated in the Indian Ocean by March, Somerville arrived from Britain with reinforcements including *Formidable* late in the month, and the modernized battleship *Warspite* entered Trincomalee harbour on 22 March and assumed the role of Somerville's flagship. After ferrying aircraft around between North Africa, the Dutch East Indies, and Ceylon, the carrier *Indomitable* also joined Somerville's fleet and a third fleet carrier, *Illustrious* – originally designated as part of Force Z – was finally on the way. The fleet was also augmented by a range of Dutch warships escaping from the East Indies. On 1 March Layton wrote that 'Vice Admiral Helfrich reported that he was resigning the command of the Allied Naval Forces in the ABDA area, that Commodore [John] Collins had been directed to withdraw all British Naval Forces, and that U.S. Naval Forces, except submarines were also going. Surviving Dutch vessels would proceed to Colombo'.[91] The Dutch admiral duly arrived in Ceylon by air on 3 March and proceeded to set up his headquarters, and Dutch naval forces now came under command of the Eastern Fleet. The question on everyone's mind was whether the large Eastern Fleet now gathering, untrained, composite,

87 Ibid., CO 54/985/4, no. 16, 9/6/42, pp. 205-06.
88 'Admiralty War Diaries of World War II', Reports and proceedings of the Eastern Fleet, 13 April-1 May 1942.
89 TNA, ADM 199/663, Commanders' Meeting minutes, 10/11/42.
90 Ibid., Commanders' Meeting minutes, 29/4/42.
91 'Admiralty War Diaries of World War II', Layton's diary, November 1941 to March 1942, 1/3/42.

and weak in organic airpower as it was, would be sufficient should it be required to meet the Japanese in battle.

While the navy was king in Ceylon, the island had for long been home to units of the British Army as well as locally-recruited defence formations, and the prevailing situation led to a great increase in the number of troops based there as reinforcements were rushed in and locally-raised forces increased tenfold. The 34th Indian Division had arrived in January, and on 1 March Wavell informed Layton that further reinforcements were on their way to Colombo. The 16th British Infantry Brigade, which Churchill was so keen to get to the island, would arrive by 14 March; the 21st East African Brigade by 17 March; and the 16th and 17th brigades of the 6th (Australian) Division by 20 March. On their way home from the Middle East to help defend Australia, the loan of these Australian soldiers was, in Churchill's words, 'a welcome stop-gap'.[92]

All these forces duly arrived, and by the end of March the garrison was equivalent to over two divisions of regular troops, and there were also the local formations of the Ceylon Defence Force, including a brigade's-worth of light infantrymen. The 16th British Infantry Brigade, crack troops who had fought in the Western Desert including the breakout from Tobruk, disembarked on 14 March as scheduled. The East Africans arrived on 21 March, the Australian brigades two days later.[93] The ethnic mix of the forces assembling in Ceylon was testament to British imperial arms, the King's African Rifles alone containing men from the different tribal communities of Kenya, Northern Rhodesia, Somaliland, Tanganyika, and Uganda. All over the island British colonial civil servants liaised with army units, which required access to land, water, and lines of communication, as well as areas designated 'no go' to civilians in which to conduct their exercises, and the demarcation of 'prohibited places' for exclusive military use.[94] The entry of Japan into the war meant an increasing workload for the men of the colonial service, as the build up of forces on the island necessitated civil-military liaison work and its strength dwindled as members left to join the armed services.[95] In addition to his duties as secretary to

92 Churchill, *The Second World War*, volume 4, p. 153. In withdrawing Australian forces from the Middle East for home defence after the shock of the fall of Singapore and the raid on Darwin, prime minister John Curtin had consented to Churchill's request that two of the five Australian brigades be retained in Ceylon as a garrison force at this crucial moment.

93 TNA, ADM 199/663.

94 TNA, CO 968/13/1, Ceylon prohibited places. This could lead to disputes requiring very detailed historical and legal research, for example in defining exactly what, on Galle Face Green, was 'colonial military land'. See TNA, CO 968/136/3, Ceylon: Galle Face (Colombo).

95 O'Regan, *From Empire to Commonwealth*. For administrative purposes the island was already divided into nine provinces under the system of British colonial administration, each headed by a Government Agent. The provinces were subdivided into districts, each under an Assistant Government Agent. O'Regan's appointment to the Ceylon civil service had been heralded by the receipt of a document entitled 'Eastern No. 126 Notes for the Information of Candidates Appointed to Ceylon'. Among other things, it advised cadets to 'purchase a horse on arrival in Ceylon; bowler hats never worn – buy an Ellwood helmet with puggaree or a pigsticker helmet, evening dress, a deck chair, a rifle, a motor cycle, and a camp bed'. Arriving after a sea voyage familiar to countless thousands of Britons in the 1930s and 1940s – including stops at Gibraltar, Malta, and Port Said before the trek across the Indian Ocean – O'Regan began his career as an Assistant Government Agent. Like all new recruits, O'Regan was a bachelor and therefore found lodgings in a chummery (sleeping quarters for unmarried men, a name derived from British India), soon making friends. Just before the outbreak of war, having obviously impressed the right senior administrators, O'Regan was appointed Private Secretary to the Governor, Sir Andrew Caldecott.* A couple of years later, before

the Governor and an Assistant Government Agent, John O'Regan was appointed Chief Liaison Officer to Army Divisional Headquarters in Kandy, responsible for relations between civil and military authorities in the Central Provinces. This entailed working with the large army contingents now billeted in the region – which included the Indian division – responding to their needs and smoothing over any difficulties that their presence caused.

The photo scrapbook of one King's African Rifles officer documents the sudden build up of forces in Ceylon.[96] On 11 March the men of his battalion massed at Mombasa, about to leave for an 'unknown destination'. The safe money was on Rangoon, as it was known that it was threatened and in dire need of defensive reinforcement. The troops boarded ships and left in a convoy escorted by the cruiser *Ajax*. But it was to Ceylon that they were sent, soon billeted in a jungle camp near Jaffna, local people tending rice in paddy fields nearby. Soon, the 2nd (Nyasaland) Battalion was under canvas at Mile '18' Camp Jungle Side, men from Central Africa sent to defend Ceylon in its moment of peril.[97] These troops, along with the men of the Ceylon Light Infantry, were soon devoted to securing the island's key strategic sites and potential landing grounds. The regular troops were undergoing jungle training and forming a mobile striking force, and each main airbase was defended by a battalion.[98]

As Commander-in-Chief India Wavell disagreed with Churchill and the Chiefs of Staff regarding the maintenance of front-line British troops in Ceylon, and also argued that the island was receiving too much of the limited airpower available to defend his vast command, which he felt was particularly vulnerable in north-east India as the position in Burma crumbled. But the Chiefs of Staff explained that, following the loss of Singapore, the Eastern Fleet would have to be built up to defend the region's vital sea lanes, and for this it was essential that Ceylon be protected as its main base, requiring the insertion of substantial air and land forces. As they informed Wavell on 19 March, the function of the Eastern Fleet was 'to maintain control of the sea communications in the Indian Ocean. Both the Middle East and India depend on these. Such control would be at best precarious if Japan obtained and we were denied bases in Ceylon'.[99] The Chiefs were adamant that Wavell could not remove forces from Ceylon for India's defence, particularly the 16th British Infantry Brigade. 'We fully realise that the defence of Ceylon is essentially an air and naval problem', they told him. 'Land forces now there are intended as a deterrent to attempts at occupation by the Japanese until air forces in Ceylon and naval forces in the Indian Ocean are built up'.[100]

With the loss of Rangoon and the evacuation of the Andaman Islands between 8 and 12 March and their subsequent occupation by the Japanese, Ceylon and the coast of India had been placed under even greater threat (admirals Arbuthnot and Layton had opposed India

the outbreak of the Japanese war, he married the Governor's daughter, Joan. O'Regan was given a range of tasks as a colonial civil servant, including attendance at the coronation of the Sultan of the Maldives, which were administered from Ceylon and which contained the important naval base at Addu Atoll.

96 NAM, 1997-08-57, Photograph album of East African battalions in East Africa, Ceylon, Burma, and India.

97 In June 1944 the battalion left aboard the *Vasova* for Chittagong on route to the frontline in Burma where, in the battles around the Chindwin, it fought and walked for four months.

98 TNA, ADM 199/663, Commanders' Meeting minutes, 17/3/42.

99 Chiefs of Staff to Wavell quoted in Simpson (ed.), *The Somerville Papers*, p. 395.

100 Ibid.

Command's decision to evacuate the Andamans).[101] The Chiefs of Staff's resolve on this matter reflected Churchill's belief that the invasion of Ceylon was a distinct possibility, and that it must be held. Risk would have to be accepted in north-east India, where Wavell was planning for a last ditch defensive 'bastion' around Calcutta. Churchill spelled out to Wavell, with whom he was used to sparring, exactly where the main effort must lay: 'If Ceylon, especially Colombo is lost, all naval build up will be futile. Therefore the defence of Colombo by flak and aircraft must be considered as an object more urgent and not less important than the defence of Calcutta'.[102] Ramming home the point, he told the Chiefs of Staff:

> Let us be clear about Ceylon. What we want there is the integrity of the defences of the naval base. This is because we want the Fleet to operate from there into the Bay of Bengal, and not have to go 600 miles away to Port T [Addu Atoll]. Nothing must be taken from Ceylon which endangers the naval base or deters the Fleet from using it. [103]

Yet it was acknowledged that while the troops massing in Ceylon could act as a deterrent and would be in the forefront should Japanese soldiers land, the front line of defence had to be provided from the air if the navy proved incapable of preventing a concerted attack on the island. Unfortunately, as Somerville was keenly aware, the aircraft of the Fleet Air Arm were too few, too antiquated, and too untrained to be relied upon to interdict attacking Japanese forces. Shore-based aircraft would possibly be able to launch an attack on an enemy fleet and shore-based fighters would obviously be needed to meet enemy air raids on Ceylon's ports and vital infrastructure. In preparing Ceylon to meet the threat of Japanese invasion, therefore, the army formations were joined by RAF units rushed in from Britain and the Middle East and from squadrons escaping the Dutch East Indies or originally intended for deployment there. Elements of several British, Canadian, and Dutch flying-boat units, amounting to eight machines, had arrived in Ceylon by the beginning of April. Flying-boats were indispensable because of their unique ability to fly exceptionally long distances without landing, and to land on water. No other platform possessed these attributes or offered a similar reconnaissance capability, essential now in order to try and provide early warning of a Japanese attack. The limited radar coverage afforded Ceylon by late March would only be able to warn of an attack once enemy aircraft were close in to the island, and intelligence derived from signals intercepts was no substitute for the human intelligence that might be furnished if a flying-boat crew hundreds of miles out to sea succeeded in getting 'eyes on' an approaching enemy formation, or if one of

101 'Admiralty War Diaries of World War II', Arbuthnot, secret despatch, Colombo: 'It had been my view, and that of Admiral Layton that the Andamans should not be evacuated: their strategic importance was too great, and we felt that the Japanese should at least be made to fight for them. The Commander in Chief, India, however, considered that the only garrison he could spare was too weak to offer ay real opposition and could be better employed elsewhere, and the Andamans were therefore evacuated and in due course occupied by the Japanese who lost on time in basing Naval Forces and aircraft there. Shipping was not available to evacuate the civil population'. The British had suffered a casualty there when the Royal Indian Navy ship *Sophie Marie* had struck a mine on 1 March laid in January by *Abdiel*, sent there to mine Port Blair and other anchorages.

102 Churchill, *The Second World War*, volume 4, Churchill to Wavell,18/4/42, pp. 163-4.

103 Ibid., Churchill to Ismay for Chiefs of Staff, 27/3/42, p. 156.

the small number of British and Dutch submarines patrolling off the coast of Malaya managed to detect the enemy and signal a warning.

There was a detachment of 205 Squadron flying-boats in Ceylon by mid-March and 321 Dutch Squadron had a couple of Catalinas at Malay Cove, abutting Trincomalee harbour.[104] 413 Squadron, a Royal Canadian Air Force Catalina unit, began to arrive in the last days of March. Previously based at Sullom Voe in the Shetland Islands flying patrol sorties off Norway, the roulette wheel of wartime deployment now sent the squadron to Ceylon, which it reached by a series of hops across the Empire, calling at Gibraltar, Cairo, and Abukir.[105] Flight Lieutenant Rae Thomas and his Catalina were 'first to reach Koggala [on 28 March] where the base had been established among coconut plantations. The lake was full of obstructions and was surrounded by marshes and tall palms. Only a short clear stretch existed for landings and take-offs'.[106] The commanding officer, Squadron Leader Leonard Birchall, arrived with his machine on 2 April, the squadron's 331-strong ground crew not arriving until May aboard the troopship *Nieuw Holland*.[107]

Fighters and bombers also arrived. In February it had been decided to send 30 Squadron RAF, fresh from the fall of Crete, to Ceylon. Declared non-operational, it moved via Heliopolis to Port Tewfik on the Red Sea. The squadron was reformed and re-equipped with Hurricanes, the main party embarking for Ceylon aboard *Princess Kathleen* on 22 February.[108] The air party, including a 196-strong servicing team, embarked on *Indomitable*, sailing on 26 February.

> All available hands began assembling the crated Hurricanes on the hangar deck on 5 March, and on the following morning twenty Hurricanes took off, bound for Ratmalana airfield, Colombo ... Stores and personnel arrived at Ratmalana on 11 March, and the Squadron was declared operational on 19 March ... On 29 March, 30 Squadron had all 24 of its Hurricanes serviceable and airborne in mass formation over Colombo; morale was high and crews were reported as expectant and ready for operations.[109]

Another important reinforcement came with the arrival of 258 Squadron, also flying Hurricanes. Its ground crew and pilots had escaped from Malaya, where the squadron had flown Brewster Buffaloes, and then from the Dutch East Indies. On 23 February the first consignment of eight new Hurricanes had arrived in Ceylon from the RAF depot at Karachi to await the arrival of the squadron's air and ground crew, and it was officially re-formed in Ceylon on 30 March. It

104 'Admiralty War Diaries of World War II', Layton's diary, November 1941 to April 1942.
105 For Birchall, see Rob Stuart, 'Leonard Birchall and the Japanese Raid on Colombo', *Canadian Military Journal* (Winter 2006-2007); Sanji Gunasekara, 'Target Ceylon, 1942', *Travel Sri Lanka* (September 2008); and Michael Tomlinson, *The Most Dangerous Moment: The Japanese Assault on Ceylon, 1942* (London: Mayflower, 1979).
106 Arthur Banks, *Wings of the Dawning: The Battle for the Indian Ocean, 1939-1945* (Malvern Wells, Worcestershire: Images Publishing, 1996), p. 49.
107 On 1 March the Admiralty told Somerville that the Americans had agreed to turn over to the British 18 flying-boats that would enable three squadrons to be formed in the Indian Ocean. Simpson (ed.), *The Somerville Papers*, p 388.
108 John Barrass, 'The Battle of Ceylon – 1942 – Part 2','30 Squadron and the Air Battle Over Colombo – 5 April 1942', https://www.raf.mod.uk/history/ceylon2.html
109 Ibid.

started out at Ratmalana but then moved to the new RAF base at the Colombo racecourse on Reid Avenue and was housed in well-appointed bungalows in the Cinnamon Gardens district, though men would sleep in the grandstand during emergencies. The squadron was a typical imperial mixture; the commanding officer, Squadron Leader Peter Fletcher, was Rhodesian and his pilots were from America, Argentina, Australia, Britain, Canada, New Zealand and South Africa. A third Hurricane squadron was based at China Bay, adjoining Trincomalee harbour. This was 261 Squadron, which had previously served in India with Gladiator biplanes, as well as in Malta and Iraq. Subsequently slated for service in Singapore, it was diverted to Ceylon. On 6-7 March the carrier *Indomitable* flew off two squadrons-worth of Hurricanes for 261 and 30 squadrons, brought from North Africa and initially earmarked for Java though redirected on Layton's orders. Other units arrived to bolster Ceylon's air defences in anticipation of a Japanese attack following the fall of Singapore. On 28 February 11 Squadron, flying Blenheim Mark IV bombers and veterans of the Iraq campaign, arrived from the Middle East to be based initially at Ratmalana though soon moved to the racecourse. By the beginning of April, the Air Officer Commanding 222 Group Ceylon, Air Vice Marshal John D'Albiac, had 50-60 serviceable Hurricanes, 14 Blenheims, six Catalinas, and a few squadrons of Fulmars, Swordfish, and Vildebeest.

Thus Ceylon donned its armour, an island bastion thrust to prominence by the spectacular defeats of imperial and Allied forces in the Japanese war to date. An officer serving in Ceylon with the 34th Indian Division summed up the situation:

> By the end of February things looked black. Malaya had fallen and the situation in Netherlands East Indies was serious. Ceylon was right in the front rank and our brigades were still very raw; they were holding large areas and certain essential equipment had not been received ... In March, however, the whole situation suddenly changed. Ceylon was literally flooded with British and East African troops, regiments of Artillery, light and heavy AA batteries, all the equipment we wanted, and a large number of senior Naval, Army, and Air Force officers. Sir Geoffrey Layton was appointed Commander-in-Chief, with autocratic powers and General Sir Henry Pownall became GOC, Ceylon ... Battalions took over from platoons and squadrons of Hurricanes replaced the few obsolete aircraft we had relied on. New aerodromes were cut out of the jungle and all was hustle and bustle.[110]

While obviously not aware of the scale of the Japanese threat, defensive preparations impressed the local people. Brian Randall Kriekenbeek wrote that 'I accepted the fact that the British were occupiers, and felt the Empire was guarding Ceylon from the Japanese'.[111] Tea planter's son William Cameron was reassured by the fact that Ceylon seemed to be teeming with troops, Colombo positively 'seething with the Military'.[112] Ivor Ferdinands, a schoolboy living near Trincomalee where his father worked on the railways, wrote:

110 'Fan Tan', 'Soldiering in Ceylon', *Journal of the United Services Institute of India*, LXXIII (1943).
111 Sergei De Silva Ranasinghe, 'Forgotten Campaigns, Forgotten Veterans', *Sunday Times* (Sri Lanka), 5/11/06, at http://www.worldgenweb.org/lkawgw/burmacamp.htm. Kriekenbeek joined the Ceylon Light Infantry as a second lieutenant and later saw service with the Gurkhas in Burma.
112 Cameron typescript, 'Bits and Pieces'.

> The area around our house seemed thick with military installations. The British seemed to have done as much as they could to provide a defence for the railway terminus. There were batteries of light 3.7-inch and heavy 4.5-inch anti-aircraft guns, barrage balloons floated above like fat, silver sausages with fins, and military personnel of every nationality and colour filled the streets. The Empire was there with the British, the Indians, the Ceylonese, the East and West Africans, and numerous others we could not identify.[113]

It was just as well they were, for the Japanese were coming.

113 Ivor Ferdinands quoted in Rodney Ferdinands, *Proud and Prejudiced: The Story of the Burghers of Ceylon* (Melbourne: Rodney Ferdinands, 1995), p. 177.

4

The Japanese raid on Colombo[1]

Over after-dinner port and cigars at the British Embassy in Washington, Winston Churchill was asked what he considered to have been 'the most dangerous moment of the war'. His answer was that

> the one which caused him the greatest alarm, was when the news was received that the Japanese fleet was heading for Ceylon and the naval base there. The capture of Ceylon, the consequent [enemy] control of the Indian Ocean, and the possibility at the same time of a German conquest of Egypt would have closed the ring, and the future would have been bleak.[2]

As Churchill knew, if these events had come to pass the enemy would have been in a position to fracture the Allied war effort by seizing control of the Indian Ocean's sea lanes, access to which allowed them to support operations in the Middle East, extract Persian Gulf oil, send aid to the Soviet Union, and maintain contact with China and India.

This was the moment when the high command of the Imperial Japanese Navy sought to reprise Pearl Harbor with a battleship and carrier raid on Ceylon and the Eastern Fleet. The desired result – the destruction of British seapower east of Suez – would secure the western perimeter of the new Japanese Empire, growing daily before the eyes of an astonished world. With the threat of the Royal Navy eliminated, the Japanese would then be free to concentrate their full force on the US Navy in the South Pacific. Destroying the Eastern Fleet would also secure the sea lanes connecting Japan's westernmost territories, enabling the unhindered resupply of the hundreds of thousands of troops based as far away as Burma and the Andamans, and guarantee access to the valuable raw materials that were one of the

1 This and the following chapter are best read alongside 'The Japanese Raids in the Indian Ocean', chapter 9 in Jackson, *Of Islands, Ports, and Sea Lanes,* which concentrates on the naval dimensions of the Japanese operation. Overviews and detailed commentaries on the Japanese raids occur in works such as Tomlinson, *The Most Dangerous Moment* and Boyd, *The Royal Navy in Eastern Waters* – a section entitled 'The IJN Attack on Ceylon' – and in numerous officials files, such as the Layton Papers, the Eastern Fleet war diaries, and TNA, AIR 20/4698, Ceylon: Japanese attacks.

2 This tale is recounted in Tomlinson, *The Most Dangerous Moment,* p. 12, recalled by Lester Pearson, Canadian ambassador to Washington at the time. The occasion, in March 1946, was a dinner at the British Embassy in Washington.

major fruits of victory and the reason for going to war in the first place. Such a triumph would also unveil the exciting prospect of linking hands across the ocean with the Germans and Italians. As an added bonus, it would teach the people of Ceylon and India a graphic lesson regarding the proximity of Japanese power and the commensurate weakness of their British masters.

Fortuitously for the British, with a Japanese attack expected any day around the beginning of April, key military units and personnel had arrived in Ceylon just in the nick of time, thousands of extra troops disembarking in mid-March, Somerville touching down on 24 March, and the major fleet units *Formidable* and *Warspite* arriving at the same time to join the 4 'R' class battleships and the carrier *Indomitable* as 'the framework of a new Eastern Fleet'.[3] In the air, the Hurricane squadrons were coming up to strength right at the end of the month with additional Catalinas arriving in the first days of April. But it was all desperately last minute.

An imminent Japanese attack on Ceylon was reported on 28 March when Far East Combined Bureau, the island's Bletchley Park outstation, intercepted a Japanese signal: '[The cryptanalysts] were working one sultry afternoon in Colombo on a message that described plans for a massive attack somewhere. Then they spelt out the name of the place that was to be clobbered – KO-RO-N-BO; an electric shock ran through the up-to-then relaxed office'.[4] It was also known that an enemy force of cruisers and destroyers was operating near the Andaman Islands, accompanying the invasion force for their occupation. As soon as he landed in Ceylon, Somerville immediately set to work. 'To office early', he wrote on 29 March, 'and had a series of conferences all forenoon over possible Jap carrier attack. Decided land-based [RAF and Fleet Air Arm] striking force practically useless as Blenheims no experience and Swordfish have not got the range. So all depends on the carriers'.[5]

With Nagumo's fleet at large, Somerville put to sea on 30 March, hoping to intercept it south of the island and deliver a night attack. The Eastern Fleet's 29 major warships, divided into a 'Fast Division', Force A, and a 'Slow Division', Force B, came together off Ceylon to form the largest concentration of British warships then afloat. But while it was a large fleet – and a powerful one, by some measures – it was ill equipped to meet its current foe, for reasons of composition (too many unmodernised and slow battleships, not enough carriers, old-fashioned aircraft), and reasons of training (it was composite and lacked experience operating as a fleet).

Nevertheless, it was the instrument to hand. As Somerville said, 'there's many a new tune played on an old fiddle', and he would simply have to make the best of it. And so, he prepared to meet the Japanese in battle.

> Somerville thought that the Japanese aircraft would probably attack at moonlight – there was a full moon on 1 April – and arrive back over their carriers at dawn, at approximately 0600 hours. To accomplish this, Nagumo would have to reach his launch point by about 0200 hours. Somerville decided to ambush him. If his radar-equipped force found radar-deficient Nagumo during the night, he could launch a torpedo aircraft strike with a fair prospect of inflicting damage. Until last light on 31 March, he kept well to the west, out

3 Hugh Popham, *Sea Flight: The Wartime Memoirs of a Fleet Air Arm Pilot*, p. 100.
4 Hugh Denham, chapter 27, 'Bedford-Bletchley-Kilindini-Colombo', in F. H. Hinsley and Alan Stripp, *Codebreakers: The Inside Story of Bletchley Park* (Oxford: Oxford University Press, 2001), p. 275.
5 Simpson (ed.), *The Somerville Papers*, pocket diary, 29/3/42, p. 397.

of range of Nagumo's search aircraft, and then headed straight for the anticipated Japanese launch point, which he reached at 0230 hours.[6]

This was the strategy that was to dictate British naval movements for the next few days.

With the threat to Ceylon real and immediate, Arbuthnot, as Commander-in-Chief East Indies responsible for the ports and coastal waters of Ceylon, had to consider the safety of scores of British and Allied merchant vessels waiting to unload or to collect cargoes from Ceylon's ports. They needed to disperse, as tightly-packed in harbour they would have little chance against air attack, and if sufficient were sunk, could render the ports inoperable for months. Eighty-odd ships alone left Colombo on 30 and 31 March, the navy's 'Battle Summary' recording that the dispersal on 31 March saw 36 ships sailed in small groups, another 23 particularly important vessels sent to Cochin in south-west India.[7] The order was also given to clear India's eastern harbours. Arbuthnot wrote that

> Towards the end of March evidence was received of a probable enemy attack on Ceylon, and on the 30th March a dispersal of shipping was effected, all ships which had no immediate prospect of working cargo being sent to various anchorages around the south coast of India, to be recalled when the threat was less imminent.[8]

In Colombo, wrote Captain Agar, Arbuthnot made 'herculean efforts with a team of British tugs and pilots, to get this motley array of shipping clear of the port'.[9]

The RAF also made ready, and on 31 March pilots were issued with an operational order, stating that:

> There are indications that the Japanese intend to carry out an air attack on Ceylon on or about 1st April, 1942. It is likely that aircraft will be Carrier borne … Whilst there is no definite information regarding the composition of the enemy forces, it is probable that they will include two or more Aircraft Carriers, two or more first class Cruisers, two or more Second Class Cruisers and a Destroyer force. [The enemy will] probably attack from SE and aim at harbour shipping, aerodrome and oil installations.[10]

An appendix summarized the order of battle for 'our air forces' and their location on the island:

> <u>Land based:</u>
> 11 Bomber (Blenheim) Racecourse
> 30 Fighter (Hurricane) Ratmalana

6 Stuart, 'Leonard Birchall', pp. 67-8.
7 Battle Summary, Naval operations of Ceylon, 29 March to 10 April 1942, p. 5 note 2. This document contains excellent maps of the manoeuvres at sea of the British and Japanese fleets. Thanks to the work of the author of the 'Armoured Carriers' website, it is available online at http://www.navy.gov.au/sites/default/files/documents/Battle_Summary_No_15_and_16.pdf
8 'Admiralty War Diaries of World War II', Arbuthnot secret despatch, Colombo, 18/6/42.
9 Agar, *Footprints in the Sea*, p. 175.
10 Rex Morgan, *The* Hermes *Adventure* (Manly, Australia: The Runciman Press, 1985), p. 132, photograph of 'Operation order number 42', 31/3/42.

205 Catalina Koggala
258 Fighter (Hurricane) Racecourse
261 Fighter (Hurricane) China Bay
273 Fighter (Fulmar) China Bay
788 Torpedo-bomber (Swordfish) China Bay
803 Fighter (Fulmar) Ratmalana
806 Fighter (Fulmar) Ratmalana

Carrier borne:
Indomitable: 11 Sea Hurricanes; 10 Fulmars; 24 Albacores; 2 Swordfish
Formidable: 21 Albacores; 12 Martlets
Hermes: 12 Swordfish.[11]

Japanese submarines were active in the last days of March and first days of April, deployed to provide intelligence for the surface fleet ahead of its attack. Stuart writes that:

> *I-2* had sailed from Penang on 22 March to reconnoitre Trincomalee, becoming the first unit to deploy for Operation C. It arrived on 31 March, but could get no closer than 10 miles from the harbour, due to the patrol boat activity. Apart from weather reports, *I-2* reported little of intelligence value ... A second submarine, *I-7*, left Penag on 28 March, with orders to use its E9W11 floatplane to conduct aerial reconnaissance of Colombo and Trincomalee. However, it was attacked by a Catalina from Ceylon on 1 April and also encountered several patrol vessels, and the CO, Lieutenant Commander Koizumi, cancelled the aerial reconnaissance. *I-3*, tasked to reconnoitre Colombo, likewise accomplished very little, due to enemy patrolling.[12]

Somerville, commanding the fleet from aboard *Warspite*, along with Arbuthnot, D'Albiac, Layton, Pownall and all their staff officers, glued to desks or pacing up and down in their Colombo headquarters, knew that the Japanese were in the vicinity, and in force. The problem was that they couldn't find them, as much as the warships and the aircraft of the Fleet Air Arm and the RAF searched. Failing to locate Nagumo on the night of 31 March-1 April, Somerville withdrew southwest, then headed back to the anticipated Japanese launch site on the following

11 Morgan, *The* Hermes *Adventure*, p. 134 copy of 'Operation order number 42', 'Appendix B, 'Own air forces'. Stuart writes that On 4 April Ceylon had 7 Catalinas (4 British, 2 Canadian, one Dutch; an additional two RAF and three Dutch Catalinas were unserviceable, most or all of them in the process of being overhauled at Bangalore. Two more RCAF Catalinas arrived on 6 and 7 April). Rob Stuart, 'Air Raid Colombo, 5 April 1942: The Fully Expected Surprise Attack', *The Royal Canadian Air Force Journal*, 3, 4 (2014), p. 44, note 6. There were also 67 Hurricanes, eight flown from Karachi on 23 February, 60 from *Indomitable* on 6 and 7 March, one being lost by 30 Squadron on 3 April, crashing into sea after getting into a spin and killing Flight Sergeant Lawrence. (Ibid., p 44 note 7.) There were also 44 Fulmars, 14 Blenheims, 12 Swordfish, 144 anti-aircraft guns, and a radar station at each port.

12 Rob Stuart, '91 Bombs: The Japanese Attack on Trincomalee', at www.combinedfleet.com/Stuart-91%20bombs-at-Trincomalee.docx, no page numbers in document. Layton reported that on 1 April British aircraft attacked an enemy submarine 150 miles south east of Koggala, which must have been *I-7*. BL, Layton Papers, 74802, RAF China Bay: Enemy air raid on China Bay 9 May 1942.

night, withdrawing again before daylight on 2 April. 'Still no news of the enemy', he wrote on 2 April.[13] 'As dusk fell, Somerville was forced to make a decision'; after three days fruitlessly combing the ocean, 'anxiously awaiting sighting reports' and with the chances of detection increasing and his unmodernised 'R' class battleships running low on water, he decided to break off the hunt.[14] In fact, Nagumo had only just entered the Indian Ocean, via the Sunda Strait, on 2-3 April. At 9pm on 3 April Somerville set course for Addu Atoll, which Force A sighted at 8:15am on 4 April, in order to refuel and take stock in conference with his captains, sending the light carrier *Hermes* and the heavy cruisers *Cornwall* and *Dorsetshire* to Colombo and Trincomalee to resume refits or other duties. Force A entered the enormous lagoon of Addu Atoll at midday on 4 April, Force B arriving at 3pm.[15]

On 3 April Squadron Leader Leonard Birchall and his Catalina crew, just landed in Ceylon the previous day, had unloaded their aircraft. As the commanding officer of 413 Squadron, Birchall inspected the Koggala RAF station and the accommodation provided for his officers at a Galle hotel and for the crew at a commandeered girls' school, Richmond Hill, at Kumbalwella near Galle.[16] But settling in was not a luxury afforded Birchall and his eight-man crew: given the Eastern Fleet's abortive search for Nagumo's armada, Catalinas had been ordered to keep on looking for the Japanese. Layton and Somerville could afford to take no chances, even if the first warning of an impending attack had been a false alarm. In actual fact, it had not been, British intelligence officers merely getting the date wrong by a couple of days; Nagumo was indeed approaching the island from the south-east, as Birchall was soon to discover. The Japanese admiral was proceeding at 'fuel-efficient pace', having decided to delay his attack from April 4 to Easter Sunday, April 5. 'He felt that – just as the Americans at Pearl Harbor – the British would be less alert and attending church'.[17] Birchall wrote that on 3 April:

> we arrived just around noon and I was taken into the operations room where we were briefed, interrogated, and the crew were sent to the rest house. The next day we went back to the aircraft and started to unload our supplies. It was at this time that I was informed that they suspected the Japanese might be somewhere in the vicinity of Ceylon ... They asked if I would take off first thing in the morning before dawn [Saturday 4 April].[18]

13 Simpson (ed.), *The Somerville Papers*, p. 398.

14 'Britain's Midway: The Royal Navy versus the Imperial Japanese Navy: The 'Easter Sunday' Raid', at http://www.armouredcarriers.com/battle-for-ceylon-hms-indomitable-formidable/

15 Battle Summary, p. 5.

16 One hopes Birchall found Koggala more amenable than James Thompson of the Royal Marines, who wrote of 'the important flying-boat base in Ceylon where sanitary conditions were on the level of the first desert camp, the wet round seats, the filthy, stinking buckets, the dirty beds. But their officers and ranks were content and either uninterested or too lazy to make improvement; prepared to accept and prepared to inflict. As once I waited for a 'plane to Singapore I could suffer only one day and night of R. A. F. dirt hospitality in Kogalla [sic] Base and hurriedly departed to a hotel in Galle. When discomfort can be easily avoided it is foolish to remain'. Thompson, *Only the Sun Remembers*, p. 68.

17 'Britain's Midway'.

18 Leonard Birchall, 'The Japanese Ceylon Attack and Afterwards', in *The Empire Club of Canada Speeches, 1945-1946* (Toronto: The Empire Club Foundation, 1946).

In this manner Birchall and his crew, on 'a wonderful day, nice and clear', were dispatched to make their single but telling contribution to the war against Japan. They were taken to the jetty on the lake to prepare for a 24 hour flight. Because there had been no time to practice night landings on Lake Koggala's hazardous surface, the Catalina would have to stay aloft all night in order to land in daylight the following morning.

> Everything was going along merrily. We had just finished a little snack and were getting ready to go home – this was four o'clock in the afternoon – when somewhere out in the horizon we suddenly saw some specks which appeared as if they were a convoy. We had had no notification of convoys in that area, so we immediately went in that direction to investigate. As we got in the area where the convoy could be identified we ran into the outer screen of the Japanese fleet. As they attacked us we identified the ships and immediately started out on our first signing point. This had to constitute the position, course, and speed, the actual composition of the forces, and also we gave our position. The normal procedure was that we repeated this three times. We got through twice, and half way through the third time, when an explosive shell came in and knocked the wireless set out and also laid the wireless operator *hors de combat* at that time. In the meantime, about forty Zeroes were buzzing around us. The first casualty was our port gunner who had his leg practically knocked off at that time. It was necessary to put him inside the aircraft on the crew bunks. The engineer then got into that position and the fight was on. We got as low as we could to stop attacks from underneath us, but they started coming in from the top and the next thing we knew they had punctured the gas tank and the gasoline was on fire and flowing down inside the aircraft. We managed to get that out. At the same time we were blazing away with all we had in the vicinity of the attackers and the machine started to break up.[19]

The flying-boat crashed into the sea where it was attacked from the air, two airmen killed and the other six being picked up by the Japanese destroyer *Isokaze* and promptly interrogated. The Japanese knew that their presence had been detected, so preparations were made for an attack on Ceylon the following morning.

Crucially, from the British point of view, Birchall's message reporting a large enemy formation off Ceylon got through to Naval Headquarters in Colombo at 4:05pm that Saturday afternoon, and was soon passed to Somerville at Addu Atoll, furious that he had been caught out. 'Damn and *blast*', he wrote: 'it looks as if I've been had because a Catalina has just reported a large enemy force 350 miles SE of Ceylon – evidently the party I've been waiting for and here I am [600] miles away and unable to strike'.[20] Immediately, he ordered his ships to get ready to put to sea again, and *Cornwall* and *Dorsetshire* were ordered to rendezvous with the fleet south of Ceylon. 'That Saturday afternoon another urgent message summoned me again to the Operations Room' at Arbuthnot's headquarters, wrote Agar. 'Our Catalina aircraft had reported, and was shadowing, a large force of enemy carriers accompanied by battleships and cruisers steering west from the Malacca Straits. It was Nagumo's force, and the attack on Colombo was obviously on'.[21]

19 Ibid.
20 Simpson (ed.), *Somerville Papers*, to wife, 4/4/42, p. 399.
21 Agar, *Footprints in the Sea*, p. 179.

Cipher Clark T. W. Baker of 2/1 Australian Field Regiment, on a cipher course in the Secretariat Building in Colombo, remembers Birchall's message coming through. 'I can well remember the trucks rushing through Colombo with red flags flying, they had loads of ammunition on board for the ships in harbour'.[22] Within an hour of receiving Birchall's report, Air Vice Marshal D'Albiac was in conference at his headquarters, briefing his subordinates about the likelihood of a dawn attack.[23] At 5:45pm on 4 April a 205 Squadron Catalina piloted by Flight Lieutenant 'Jock' Graham took off to take over shadowing the Japanese fleet now that Birchall's boat had been shot down, using his information to locate the enemy.[24] At 10:37pm Graham reported sighting a destroyer.

The warning meant that more shipping needed to be cleared out of Colombo harbour; six of those previously ordered away had now returned, meaning that there were 46 ships in harbour when Birchall's report came in.[25] More vessels were therefore despatched on the afternoon of 4 April, wrote Arbuthnot: 'an early attack being expected, a further 25 ships were sailed from Colombo to the westward, with orders to return the following afternoon'.[26] Observed from the air and sailing at intervals of a few miles, the ships looked 'like beads on a necklace'.[27] They were accompanied by the Royal Indian Navy sloop *Clive*, the corvette *Marguerite*, and the sloop *Shoreham* as an anti-submarine escort.[28] Other vessels were moved out too, Arbuthnot reporting that the Dutch depot ship 'COLOMBIA with three Dutch submarines which were unfit for operational service was also sailed to Mannar, on the northwest coast of Ceylon'.[29] All of this activity meant that there were 21 merchant vessels still in Colombo harbour along with eight fleet auxiliaries and five Royal Navy vessels – the armed merchant cruiser *Hector*, the submarine depot ship *Lucia*, the destroyers *Decoy* and *Tenedos*, and the submarine *Trusty*, all deemed unfit for sea owing to defects.[30]

On the evening of Saturday 4 April a big inter-service dance was held in Colombo, along with the usual weekend parties and social events. Cecil Callis of 34th Indian Division wandered from his room in Echelon Barracks, right by the seafront with Galle Face Green on one side and the harbour on the other, to the lounge bar of the Colombo Swimming Club, a regular haunt since his arrival in the capital in February. The bar was 'usually crowded with Royal Navy and a few Merchant Navy Officers, and Airmen. On the evening of April 4th there was not a sailor or airman in sight. The place was almost deserted, just a few lonely-looking girlfriends. We wondered why this was, perhaps they were on combined exercise? The next morning we knew the real reason'.[31] What had happened, wrote Sergeant Pilot G. C. Bate of 30 Squadron, was that

22 Morgan, *Tho* Hermec *Adventuro*, p. 133.
23 Stuart, 'Air Raid Colombo', pp. 37-8.
24 Ibid., p. 37.
25 Battle Summary, p. 5.
26 Clancy, '*The Most Dangerous Moment*', p. 65.
27 Ibid.
28 Battle Summary, p. 5.
29 'Admiralty War Diaries of World War II', Arbuthnot secret Colombo, 18/6/42.
30 Battle Summary, p. 5. It appears that the summary was wrong, as *Decoy*'s ship's summary has her searching with fleet and at Addu on 6 April.
31 BBC World War Two People's War oral history archive, Cecil Callis, 'Eastern Travels', chapter 7, 'Unwelcome Visitors', A4428083.

> An inter-service dance was held on the Saturday evening, 4 April 1942, in Colombo. During this function all personnel were ordered to return to their units immediately. Upon return to the station the pilots were briefed that a Jap carrier force had been sighted by 413 Squadron at Kogalla and '30' was to go to full readiness prior to first light.[32]

The Easter Sunday raid, 5 April

At 12:45am on 5 April Graham's Catalina, still in the air seven hours after taking off, reported seeing six destroyers, and at 6:15am a battleship, cruiser, and other vessels 110 miles from Dondra Head. About 90 minutes later the aircraft was shot down, killing all the crew.[33] At 5:34am a third Catalina was sent up, this one piloted by 240 Squadron's Flight Lieutenant Bill Bradshaw. Though this aircraft survived, it did not report what it saw – six aircraft that looked like Fulmars at 6:40am, and later four that looked like Seafires – assuming them to be British as they were so close to Ceylon. They were, in fact, the Japanese aircraft coming to attack Colombo.[34] Shortly after first light on Easter Sunday, 5 April, a force of 125 aircraft had taken off from the carriers, led by Commander Mitsuo Fuchida of *Akagi*, the man who had led the attack on Pearl Harbor. His force comprised 36 Val dive bombers, 53 Kate attack bombers, and an escort of 36 Zero fighters. Nagumo kept the rest of his force, approximately 180 aircraft, as a second wave to be launched once Fuchida had confirmed the location of the main target, the Eastern Fleet.[35]

Meanwhile Layton had the island's defenders on high alert. At Ratmalana airbase most of 30 Squadron's personnel

> were up by 0400, and the aircraft were at immediate readiness by first light, which came at about 0600. A routine patrol by 2 of 30 Squadron's Hurricanes reported 8/10ths storm clouds over most of the island. The RAF were unaware of the range of the Zero, or that they could carry drop tanks, so it was generally thought by Fighter Operations in Colombo that an attack was most likely to be the following day, but the crews watched and waited.[36]

Sergeant Pilot Bate of 30 recounted that 'all pilots manned their aircraft and began a full readiness … We sat in our aircraft until approximately 0645 to 0700, at which time the Squadron was ordered to stand down and go for breakfast'.[37]

Ceylon at this stage had only modest radar cover, the radar stations linked by telephone to Fighter Operations Headquarters. The personnel of Air Ministry Experimental Station 254 had

32 David Dick compilation, 30 Squadron newsletter (February 1986).
33 Stuart, 'Air Raid Colombo', pp. 37-8.
34 Ibid., p. 38.
35 Smith, *Fist from the Sky*.
36 Barrass, 'The Battle of Ceylon – 1942 – Part 2'. Researching this topic for some years, I have used some sources that either no longer appear on the internet, or that I cannot find. John Barrass, '30 Squadron and the Battle of Ceylon' (HQ Strike Command: Command Media Services, n. d.), a version appearing later as '30 Squadron and the Air Battle Over Colombo 5 April 1942', at 30 Squadron Association website, http://www.30squadronassociation.com/history/ceylon.html
37 David Dick compilation, 30 Squadron newsletter (February 1986).

arrived in Colombo on 18 March, its equipment four days later. The unit had established its base at Colombo Golf Course in the suburb of Ridgeway and worked around the clock to erect the masts and set up the equipment, and was declared operational on 25 March.[38] Yet the station failed to detect the Japanese formations as they crossed the south coast heading up country for Colombo. Though some have attributed this to maintenance work or a leisurely shift change, Stuart refutes such notions, his exhaustive research leading him to conclude that the station's location, six miles north of Ratmalana airbase, hindered its efficacy, along with possible interference from nearby hills, while also acknowledging that operators had probably been at their consoles for too long and were therefore less alert than they should have been. The limitations of the station were already known, D'Albiac having reported at the Commanders' Meeting on 31 March that the station had only been able to pick up single aircraft at a maximum range of 30 to 40 miles.[39] The Japanese also avoided the ground warning system 'by flying well off the coast during their approach flight'.[40]

This meant that although intelligence intercepts and the sightings of Birchall's and Graham's Catalinas had given the island's defenders long-range warning of the enemy fleet's whereabouts and course, the early warning system for the actual attack had failed, meaning that Ceylon's RAF defenders, already outnumbered, were at a distinct disadvantage from the start.[41] 'I shall *never* get over this', D'Albiac is reported to have said.[42] The Japanese aircraft arrived over Ceylon shortly before 8am and flew up the coast in full view of people on the ground. At 7:40am 'four "vic" formations each of six or seven navy type 99 dive bombers escorted by navy Zero fighters approached Ratmalana'. They passed over it and 'stepped up' from 6,000 to 8,000 feet, turned towards the harbour and out to sea, and then turned back, ready for their bombing run.[43]

At 7:50am 30 Squadron's aircrew at Ratmalana airbase 'were horrified to see formations of enemy aircraft overhead. The alarm was given and the startled pilots rushed to take off. The Japanese were aware of the Ratmalana base and a small force of dive-bombers was detailed to attack it', doing so as the British aircraft attempted to get off the ground.[44] Some measure of relief for 30 Squadron's pilots as they struggled to get airborne was provided by the presence of an unserviceable B-17 Flying Fortress which had overshot the runway and crashed, and which attracted a lot of Japanese attention. 'Apparently every Jap that attacked the field shot at the B-17. After, we wondered how many B-17's were claimed as destroyed when the Japs got back'.[45]

At low level the Zero was much more manoeuvrable and, armed with cannon, more effective than the machine-gun armed Hurricane. The Hurricanes also suffered from a lack of tracer ammunition as it had started to explode in the intense heat.[46] The only advantage the

38 Stuart, 'Air Raid Colombo', p. 39.
39 TNA, ADM 199/663, Commanders' Meeting minutes, 31/3/42.
40 Stuart, 'Air Raid Colombo', p. 43.
41 BL, Layton Papers, 74802, 'Japanese air raids and operations off Ceylon 5-9 April 1942', 9 /6/42 and Japanese air attack on Colombo 5 April, Air Staff Commander-in-Chief Ceylon.
42 Tomlinson, *The Most Dangerous Moment*, p. 99.
43 BL, Layton Papers.
44 Barrass, 'The Battle of Ceylon – 1942 – Part 2'.
45 Barrass, 'The Battle of Ceylon – 1942 – Part 3', 'Eyewitness Recollections of 5 April 1942 at Ratmalana by D. A. McDonald, then a Pilot Officer on 30 Squadron', at https://www.raf.mod/history/ceylon3.html
46 Barrass, 'The Battle of Ceylon – 1942 – Part 2'.

Hurricanes had 'was their robustness, as the Zero was quite flimsy and would not take much damage'.[47] 'Unable to operate as a wing, 30 Squadron's Hurricanes took off in ones and twos and fought very much as singletons.[48] Pilots without aircraft fired Thompson sub-machine guns from the ground, and Bofors guns

> did grand work, only on two occasions were enemy aircraft seen to dive over the runway chasing low flying aircraft, one a Hurricane; he appeared to get away, the other a low flying Fulmar attempting to land was less fortunate and got shot down by a Navy '0' in spite of 3 Bofors giving him all they had. Airmen stationed at the Blind Institute [a requisitioned school for the deaf and blind in a colonnaded building at Ratmalana] were subjected to unpleasant attention from low flying enemy aircraft, and a few bombs, but soon reached cover in the trees, where they took up their posts for paratroop invaders.[49]

The 2nd Battalion The Ceylon Light Infantry formed part of the Ratmalana defence scheme, providing static defence both here and at the racecourse against parachutists and other threats, armed with rifles and light machine guns, its men also helping to clear debris and rescue injured people in the Ratmalana workshops.[50]

Sergeant Pilot Bate reported that:

> At the time of the raid, our aircraft were parked around the perimeter of the field – no blast bays – the ack ack units had arrived just prior to the raid and were not dug in but just sand-bagged and located on the field in the open ... The aircraft were scrambled by the firing of a verey cartridge from the control tower.
>
> It was an overcast day with broken rain clouds with a ceiling of approximately 1,000 feet. As it was starting to drizzle my 'erk' and I climbed onto the wing of my aircraft to close the cockpit. As we were doing this we heard the sound of aircraft and looking up through the broken cloud saw formations of aircraft passing over heading in the direction of Colombo.
>
> My airman said, 'Look at the Spits. They must be reinforcements!'. I looked and said, 'Those are Japs'. I jumped into my aircraft and along with Flight Lieutenant Davidson started up and headed for the end of the strip for take off. At the same time the lorry carrying the other pilots headed back to the aircraft. We were caught on the ground with no warning. Dave and I started our take-off as the first bombs hit the field, and we became the first airborne. Still no verey light!
>
> As soon as we were airborne we were in cloud and lost each other – I was on my own. When I broke on top I was jumped and I headed back into cloud. It seemed to me that every time I came out of the cloud the Jap aircraft were waiting. It was impossible to gain

47 Ibid.
48 Ibid.
49 Operations Record Book 'Summary of events'. Where?
50 TNA, WO 172/1558, 2nd Battalion the Ceylon Light Infantry, war diary, April 1942. This file contains a map of Ratmalana and the surrounding suburb, a diagram of the layout of the airbase, and maps of the coastal defences from Grand Pass to Mount Lavinia. The file also contains a CLI report on the raids, which noted the very high spirits of the troops. The unit's strength was 750 officers and men.

> any height to get above them. I decided to head out to sea and climb back into the area. I was fortunate to gain some height and came back to attack a formation of single engine aircraft flying in a 'V' formation. I attacked the formation and shot down two aircraft on the starboard side ... From then on it was a real hornets nest. Thinking back on it I cannot remember seeing any of our aircraft during this time. Everyone had their own private go. Because we were caught on the ground any squadron tactics we had were not available to us.
>
> When I arrived back at the field – no circuit – over the trees and on the ground, maybe even downwind – to refuel and rearm, the ground crews had the bowser out in the open, so I taxied straight up to it. The armourers hit the wings, the refuelling crews began refuelling – all this out in the open. As this was going on the Japs again strafed the airfield. I jumped off the wing heading for a ditch not far away; one of the armourers threw me his rifle and suggested in no uncertain terms to shoot at the B******s!
>
> As I looked out from the ditch, after the strafing attack, not one airman had left his job; all were carrying on rearming and refuelling as if everything were normal ... The last action I saw on the field was three naval Swordfish in a tight 'V' come over the field and a Jap fighter take them all down.[51]

These unfortunate aircraft, a flight of six Swordfish from 788 Squadron armed with torpedoes, arrived over Ratmalana as the fight was in progress, sent there from China Bay at first light to refuel before attempting to locate and attack the enemy fleet. Tragically, approaching along a designated air corridor, the Swordfish mistook the six approaching Zeros for British aircraft, even firing recognition flares and flashing the code letter for the day. 'Burdened by their torpedoes, the biplanes were unable to take meaningful evasive action. All six were sent into the ground or sea', the Japanese returning to gun the survivors, five of the 14 airmen killed.[52] 'I had half my face blown off and we ended upside down in a paddy field', wrote S. M. De L. Longsdon, the squadron's commanding officer. 'A sorry tale'.[53]

Pilot Officer D. A. McDonald said: 'Why the Japs did not keep us on the ground I will never know. We took off in sections of two and never did have an opportunity to operate as a squadron unit'. Once airborne, McDonald attacked a line of Val dive bombers.

> All our aircraft were loaded with straight ball type ammunition because a couple of weeks before, the 4E incendiary started to explode in one of our aircraft due to the intense heat [when] sitting uncovered in the sun. I was not able to see whether I was hitting the Jap or not, but finally noticed some liquid pouring out from under his wing. I then looked around and saw two very nasty looking aircraft above me, rolling to attack. I figured that they would likely out-turn me so I dived for the deck hoping to outdistance them. I saw tracers going by each side of me and I was almost immediately covered with oil and glycol. By this time I was quite low and was heading across the harbour, which was full of ships. Some of them – possibly all of them – took pot shots at me. I knew I would have to crash land and the Galle Face Green appeared to be my best bet.[54]

51 David Dick compilation, 30 Squadron newsletter (February 1986).
52 'Britain's Midway'.
53 Tomlinson, *The Most Dangerous Moment*, p. 104.
54 Barrass, 'The Battle of Ceylon – 1942 – Part 3'.

McDonald came down on the seafront outside the Galle Face Hotel, from where members of staff emerged and rushed him inside.

> 'I expect you could use a drink', said an officer from headquarters. A waiter duly arrived with a tumbler of amber liquid, which Don gulped down only to discover with typical RAF horror that it was iced tea rather than whisky. It was only 8.30 in the morning! By 8.35 all enemy aircraft had left the scene, and half an hour later fourteen Blenheim bombers took off to try and attack the Japanese fleet.[55]

From his bed in the City General Hospital, suffering from severe burns after a Zero attacked his Hurricane, Flight Sergeant Thomas Paxton confirmed that McDonald had downed the aircraft. George Chater, 30 Squadron's commanding officer, visited him in hospital and took him the bottle of scotch he had requested. McDonald recalled later that

> our communications system was very inadequate. The signal for the Squadron to scramble was for the control tower personnel to fire a Verey pistol. That morning whoever was to fire the pistol was so excited that he forgot that he was in the tower under the roof when he fired. Apparently it was pretty exciting for *them* dodging the flare. I believe the only casualty among the ground crew was a chap standing under a palm tree being hit by a coconut shaken lose by a bomb blast.[56]

Regarding his own experience, the critically-ill Paxton said that 'although it was getting hot in the cockpit and the throttle became too hot to hold' he had continued firing before abandoning his aircraft at 1,600 feet. Local people had rescued him from a tree, where he had landed by parachute, and took him to hospital.

Despite being surprised, the cloud cover enabled 21 of 30 Squadron's Hurricanes to get airborne and seek cover. 'Few of the ground staff witnessed the combats as the clouds obscured their view, occasionally an aircraft would dive out of cloud being chased by another, the rattle of 12 machine guns being easily distinguished from the enemies fire of cannon or dual machine gun effort'.[57] Chater took a Hurricane and flew to the racecourse airbase to see if any of his men had landed there, as the telephones weren't working. Flying Officer H. K. Cartwright was safe in hospital in Colombo with slight injuries, the Kenyan Flying Officer R. Allison was reported safe in hospital with a bullet wound in his neck. A captain in the Ceylon Light Infantry (CLI) arrived with the body of Sergeant O. Browne.

> This captain witnessed the combat between our pilot and a Japanese aircraft. Sergeant Browne shot down his quarry but was attacked from astern by a Navy "O". His aircraft dived into a paddy field in flames, but for the quick action of the CLI forces in the vicinity his body would not have been recovered. He was taken from the wreckage but he had been killed on impact.[58]

55 Ibid.
56 Ibid.
57 David Dick compilation, 30 Squadron newsletter (February 1986).
58 Ibid.

Pilot Officer J. A Whalen, a 30 Squadron pilot from Canada, recalls seeing 'seven Jap bombers in perfect 'V' formation heading for the aerodrome. I picked off the two right hand rear planes without much trouble, just like shooting geese. As I climbed back up for another drag at them I saw a Zero chasing a pal of mine, Bishop. So I went after him and got him'. Squadron Leader Arnold Roberts of the Royal New Zealand Air Force stated that

> word was passed to me that the pilots had no transportation and could not get to the airfield from their quarters which were in the nearby Golf Course Clubhouse. Just at that moment a local gentleman (Ceylonese) came down the airfield road in a large saloon car. I tried to convince him that his car was needed but it became obvious that he was not going to part with his pride and joy, and the only way to get fast action was to push my pistol in his face with one hand and pull him out with the other. Then it was full speed ahead to collect the pilots. I cannot recall much of the trip back except that the vehicle was badly overloaded and people seemed to drop off without any reduction in speed as we came alongside individual aircraft.
>
> The Japanese in some cases were flying so low that from the ground we could clearly see the crew members. We could hear bombs falling in the direction of the Railway Workshops and the Blind School and wondered if our living quarters and the Squadron's HQ were on the receiving end. By this time, with one exception, we were in slit trenches firing rifles, which was all the armament we could muster, in the general direction of the Japanese aircraft.[59]

Assessing 30 Squadron's action, Stuart writes that:

> The 27 fighters taking off from Ratmalana got caught up in defending their own airfield. In this they were successful. Aided by heavy cloud cover, the first few Hurricanes to get airborne managed to bounce the 14 Vals before their bombs were dropped, shooting down 5 of them and damaging up to 6, as well as destroying one Zero. Distracted by the defending fighters and hampered by cloud cover, the remaining Vals did little damage to Ratmalana.[60]

The pilots of the other Colombo based Hurricane squadron, 258, had been able to take to the air unmolested, as the Japanese were unaware of the new airbase at the racecourse. The squadron had 14 fighters in the air by 7:35am. Landing after a harrowing series of air combats, the squadron's commanding officer, Squadron Leader Peter Fletcher, told the Station Intelligence Officer that

> Having received no warning and finding the enemy aircraft overhead we took off and climbed for the harbour being the most likely point of enemy attack. When we arrived we found the bombers had already commenced the attack. There was a very strong force of enemy fighters as top cover, and considerably above my formation. I decided to attack the bombers in the hope it would impair the efficiency of the attack, realizing this would put

59 Ibid.
60 Stuart, 'Air Raid Colombo', p. 42.

> the enemy fighters in a strong position. Continued attack as long as possible though heavy losses. AA [anti-aircraft] continued even when we were overhead.[61]

258's Operational Record Book records that:

> The nine Hurricane II's scrambled as a Squadron and the five Hurricane Is as an independent flight. One or two enemy aircraft were encountered overhead but the main body, approximately 75 aircraft were then concentrated over the harbour with approximately 35 Navy 0s a few thousand feet above acting as cover. As 258 Squadron approached the Harbour the enemy bombers were preparing to attack. When the Squadron arrived in the harbour it was on a level with the enemy bombers and below the Navy 0s. Squadron Leader Fletcher attacked the bombers with the Hurricane IIs. He continued to attack for as long a period as possible.[62]

Flight Lieutenant Edwards, Fletcher's number two, had followed his commander's aircraft, and confirmed that one bomber had been destroyed, 'one Zero probable'. He stated: 'Peel off after dive bombers and caught one down at sea level going away west. This I gave a six second burst quarters stern attack. I saw the enemy aircraft dive straight into the sea'. Then Edwards found Zeros on his tail, which he evaded in cloud cover. When he came out of the cloud he was 'pounced on' by four more. A series of dogfights ensued, in which he shot down a Zero, at one point during the combat narrowly pulling out of a spin as his aircraft plunged towards a paddy field.[63] Edwards crashed and was found by CLI troops, Bugler McLeod conveying him, with the help of ARP men, on the bar of his bicycle to a place where his wounds could be tended before he was sent to hospital.[64]

Fletcher reckoned he had been hit by shell burst from British anti-aircraft guns, and bailed out with oil entering the cockpit. With the Japanese attempting to machine-gun him as he parachuted to earth, he played dead and landed in a coconut plantation. The Vals attacked by 258 Squadron were the 19 from the carrier *Shokaku*. Stuart writes that:

> 258 Squadron pretty much shot its bolt attacking *Shokaku*'s Vals. The 5 Vals from *Zuikaku* which attacked the harbour and were probably responsible for the damage inflicted on the British tanker *San Cirilo* escaped fighter attack, as did the 53 'Kate' torpedo bombers which attacked after the Vals. Each of the Kates acting as level bombers, carried one 800-kilogram bomb, and all of them attacked the harbour area.[65]

Thunder clouds hung over Colombo and intermittent showers of heavy rain fell, accompanied by strong gusts of wind. St Thomas's College at Mount Lavinia near Colombo was a school for

61 BL, Layton Papers, 74802, 'Japanese air raids and operations off Ceylon 5-9 April 1942', 9/6/42, and Japanese air attack on Colombo 5 April, Air Staff Commander-in-Chief Ceylon, Fletcher report to Station Intelligence Officer 258 Squadron.
62 From 258 Squadron's Operational Record Book, quoted in Kelly, *Hurricanes Over the Jungle*, p. 15.
63 Ibid.
64 TNA, WO 172/1558, 2nd Battalion The Ceylon Light Infantry.
65 Stuart, 'Air Raid Colombo', p. 42.

over 700 boys. A few weeks before the raid, the State Council had decided to close all schools in the city because of the threat of attack and the need to take over buildings for military purposes. Headmasters were ordered to begin vacating their premises on 1 March, most taken over for use as barracks by incoming service personnel, and as military hospitals, required in anticipation of casualties following an attack. Out-of-work teachers were told to join the ARP or were transferred to inland schools or temporarily found other employment.

On 4 April a 'very polite officer' had called on St Thomas's warden, Reginald de Saram, and requested 'vacant possession within 24 hours'.[66] That evening a CLI detachment arrived and took over the college telephone while a military deputation inspected the buildings before handing them over to 35th British General Hospital, which had arrived from Baghdad the month before.[67] A few days earlier an anti-aircraft battery had been erected by the nearby Mount Lavinia Hotel, and practice firings were conducted out to sea. This recent development meant that when, on 5 April, the 'ack-ack' report of anti-aircraft guns was heard, it was at first believed to be another practice, until the unfamiliar sound of a dog fight broke over the college chapel. De Saram recalls that

> as we went to chapel there were rather more aeroplanes than usual in the air and they continued to fly around while service was going on. The service was over and the congregation had just gone out when there came a burst of firing from the AA gun near the hotel ... A second or two later machine-gun fire broke out above the chapel. Then we knew. It was the real thing. Several dull thumps were heard in the distance to the south. These were Japanese bombs bursting over the aerodrome and the railway workshops at Ratmalana. Then came a much louder thump nearby and clouds of smoke and the smell of burning from the direction of the big club [the sports field area]. This was a Japanese aeroplane which crashed on the edge of the big club knocking a hole in the barrel drain and coming to rest about five yards from what is now the Lower 3A classroom ... When we came out of the chapel the plane was burning fiercely and the ammunition popping off. Both the Japanese in the plane were dead and their bodies were buried by the College servants just by the lower school classroom.[68]

Dr William Hayman, the sub-warden, left the chapel to see a large formation of aircraft heading at a great height from the south towards Colombo.

> There was no firing, so we assumed the planes belonged to the RAF. I returned to breakfast on the verandah and was halfway through my first egg when I heard planes low down and heading in the direction of the Mount out to sea. Shells were bursting some distance behind the first plane and I looked in vain for the towed target. Then a second plane dived through the bursting shells and fired a vicious machine-gun volley against the first plane. It was then I realized that this was a raid. There was a tremendous crash and then a loud explosion followed by many smaller ones. Leaning over the verandah wall I saw clouds of brown smoke rising

66 N. M. P. Billimoria, *Seventy-Five Years at Mount: A History of St Thomas' College Mount Lavinia, 1918–1993* (Colombo: The College, 1993), p. 128.

67 It was destined to remain here in Mount Lavinia until January 1946, when it moved to Singapore.

68 Billimoria, *Seventy-Five Years at Mount*, p. 129. Troops of the CLI arrived to guard the crashed aircraft.

> from behinds the botany lab. I waited no longer but went to the air raid shelter. There were still splinters of shrapnel falling on the quadrangle and roofs but no damage was done. I saw a small boy running towards the smoke [caused by the crash of a Japanese aircraft], so I had to run and fetch him into the shelter ... The Japanese plane had cleared the roof of Thalassa and crashed near the barrel drain. It passed over the head of Mrs de Vos the Warden's cousin who was crossing the big Club to join the Matron in Winchester [one of St Thomas's English public school-modelled 'houses']. The plane passed low over her head and she had thought to herself 'Why do they allow these silly young pilot to show off?'. In Winchester Sgt. Penny of the Signals got the Matron – Mrs Gunawardene – to lie under her bed for protection from flack.[69]

Many other people had their morning worship interrupted by the raid too, including the parishioners of St Luke's Church in the Borella district of Colombo, packed with locals and military personnel for Easter Sunday service when dog fights began overhead.[70] Cynthia Samuel was 'living in a house very near to Colombo Racecourse, which had been converted in a very few days into a runway':

> As usual, the ayah had taken our seven month old baby for their early morning walk, but on this morning they came back very soon. The ayah said that 'one soldier-master' had told her that she should take the baby home as some Japanese planes were coming. Therefore we decided that we had better not go to church, but stay with the baby. Soon after we heard the noise of planes and went out onto the verandah. We had never seen so many planes. They were very high and in perfect formation, and went towards Colombo.[71]

Bubbles Mullins, who lived in the Cinnamon Gardens district, also thought that the anti-aircraft gunfire was a practice, but soon saw Japanese aircraft from her garden.[72] Corporal B. A. Sadar, a non-commissioned officer in the Ceylon Army Medical Corps, 'was hunkered down in a building opposite the Racecourse Barracks in a house-turned-into-camp called The Maligawa – Sir James Obeyeswekera's stately mansion'.[73] Badar recalled that

> The siren wail commenced once the enemy planes were observed in the horizon. Once that started, we jumped into trenches thinking it was a drill. The basic practice in barracks was to take to the trenches at the sound of the sirens regardless of it being a drill or not. When we jumped into the trenches only did we witness the planes flying overhead. They were passing the Racecourse and heading towards Galle Face. Once the planes passed us, the bombs started falling. The raid lasted around half an hour. Once the sirens stopped, we

69 Ibid., p. 130.
70 Clancy, '*The Most Dangerous Moment*', p. 82. Also in Kris Thomas, 'A War Story: Ceylon During World War II' (2017), Roar Media, at https://roar.media/english/life/history/a-war-story-ceylon-during-world-war-ii/.
71 Cynthia Samuel, letters to author, 2/3/99 and 8/3/99.
72 Bubbles Mullins, letter to author, 1/3/99.
73 Thomas, 'A War Story'.

> knew it was safe to come out of the trenches. The sight was utterly horrifying to witness. We came out of the trenches crying and shocked.[74]

Assigned to an ambulance unit, Sadar then helped rescue casualties. Joan Gottelier had been on duty at HMS *Lanka*, the Colombo naval headquarters, until 3am that morning before the transport took her home to her quarters.

> I had just got off to sleep when the raid sounds went and actually where I was in Turret Road we had a trench outside and I got cramp and stood up and then that shrapnel [indicating a lump of metal] fell beside me. But the plane came up passed by the lake and shot two Tamil or Sinhalese kids and it came up Turret Road over the policeman's box there and our digs there and it let off these bombs. Over the road some Army chaps were there and they sort of got on their bikes straight away and found these two kids and took them to hospital. I went back to work in case there was anything extra to be done.[75]

As dog fights developed in the skies above Colombo, the harbour was taking a pounding from Japanese bombs and machine-gun fire. The guns defending the port responded, firing 527 light anti-aircraft and 1,027 heavy anti-aircraft shells and 22 rounds from naval 12-pounders.[76] In the harbour, undergoing a refit, the luck of the destroyer *Tenedos* finally ran out. She had been one of *Prince of Wales* and *Repulse*'s escorts on the day they went down, at one time being mistaken for a heavier ship and straddled by Japanese bombs. She had then survived service with ABDA Command in and around the Dutch East Indies, ferrying evacuees from Sumatra. John Bennett was an engineer at the firm of Walker Sons and Company, working at the firm's Colombo harbour premises:

> When the raid occurred we were completing the refit of the Destroyer HMS *Tenedos* which was lying at the end of our jetty. A stick of bombs fell, some on the jetty and the remainder on the stern of the destroyer setting off the after magazine and torpedo warheads. The resulting explosion was of considerable force and forty feet of our very solid reinforced concrete jetty disappeared entirely and the destroyer was sunk. Parts of the destroyer actually fell in our works machine shop area some 150 yards from the Jetty.[77]

One of the 33 men who died on board *Tenedos* was Sir Robert Peel, son of the actress Beatrice Lillie.[78] Sixth baronet and an only child, shortly before his death Peel had been socializing with some of the tea planters' children, who realized who he was when they made him show a piece of jewellery bearing the family crest. The explosion on *Tenedos* was particularly severe because

74 Ibid.
75 Gottelier interview, April 1999.
76 BL, Layton Papers, 74800, Narrative of operations by the Japanese fleet against Ceylon area April 1942.
77 D. Bennett, 'Walker Sons and Company War Record' (1945), unpublished manuscript sent to Ashley Jackson by Gill Bennet in 1999. For a detailed account drawn from the company's war narrative, see Jackson, 'Refitting the Fleet in Ceylon'.
78 Star of *On Approval* and *Thoroughly Modern Millie*; the salvage ship *Salviking* removed the wreckage in February 1944.

the ordnance detonated, and the blast damaged the neighbouring merchantman *Benledi*, also hit by a bomb as she was unloading military vehicles and ordnance. Another victim of the attack was the Armed Merchant Cruiser *Hector*, which was hit, set ablaze, and settled on the bottom, where she burned for a fortnight after the flames had reached her oil fuel.[79] The reservists of the Ceylon Naval Volunteer Force (CNVF) took part in the action around Colombo that day. Lieutenant Simpson, 'a figure of awe' in the CNVF known 'for his powers of colourful nautical vocabulary, moved the armed trawler *Overdale Wyke* close to HMS *Hector*, anchored next to the Island Breakwater to try to help put its fires out, when a stick of bombs fell on the moorings he had just left'.[80]

At the time of the raid the submarine depot ship *Lucia* was preparing to load torpedoes onto the submarine *Trusty* moored alongside. Lieutenant Commander Bill King, *Trusty*'s commanding officer, was having breakfast when the alarm sounded, and on reaching the submarine's bridge 'saw a stream of enemy aircraft burst out of a cloud off the harbour mouth and seemingly come straight at him. The submarine's signalman had manned a Bren gun and was firing without success at the enemy as they flew low over the depot ship's masts. King could actually see the enemy pilots huddled in their cockpits'.[81] All the bombs dropped about 20 yards short except one, which went through the deck of *Lucia* and out again through the bottom without exploding. 'Some of the *Trusty*'s crew were in the depot ship … and were trapped by a watertight door which had become jammed; they had to squeeze out through a porthole and swim to the submarine'.[82]

Following his evening at the swimming club, on the morning of 5th April, it being Easter Sunday, Cecil Callis and his colleagues 'had a "lie in"':

> At 8am I was sitting on my charpoy having a cup of tea when we heard the sound of air-raid sirens. 'Funny time for a practice' we thought. Suddenly all hell was let loose! Our peaceful Sunday morning was torn apart by the sound of exploding bombs, the thunder of hundreds of heavy guns, the scream and roar of diving aircraft and the rattle of machine guns and cannon. Dashing out on to our first-floor veranda we had a grandstand view of a Japanese dive-bombing on the Harbour, a quarter of a mile away, beyond the town centre.
>
> Aircraft were diving and climbing, twisting and turning low over the harbour. Clouds of smoke went up, and columns of water rose above the houses, tall and white from exploding bombs. Hurricane fighters came weaving in, diving after the bombers, trying to shoot them down before they could release their bombs. One Jap plane blew up in a flash of flame over the centre of the harbour. Jap Zero fighters joined the fray. The din was terrific! While all this was going on I was up on the veranda with my camera, trying to photograph the spectacle, every few minutes jumping out of my skin when a Bofors gun 20 yards away went

79 She was in the process of being decommissioned from military duties, having spent two and a half years escorting convoys from the Middle East, India and Australia, serving on the East Indies and South-West Pacific stations, helping to round up German raiders, and on her last voyage bringing some of the Hurricane pilots to Ceylon who successfully engaged the Japanese over Colombo on the day that she was sunk.

80 'Investigator', 'Some Account of Ceylon's "Wavy Navy" between 1939-1942', copy of article from *Royal Indian Navy Association*, sent to Ashley Jackson by Peter Beauchamp, 31/3/99.

81 Wilson, *A Submariners' War*, p. 113.

82 Ibid. See William King, *Dive and Attack: A Submariner's Story* (London: William Kimber, 1983).

> off, crash-bang! Then, looking to my left towards the sea, I suddenly saw a plane diving straight at us. I shot down to the ground floor and dived under the stairs like a rabbit down a bolthole! That was the fastest I had moved for a long time.
>
> Fortunately the bombs dropped short and did little damage. I was soon out of the bolt-hole and back upstairs, but by now the Zero fighters and Val dive-bombers were scooting away chased by Hurricanes. Instead, high bombers appeared out of the clouds, in perfect formation, released their bombs and wheeled away.
>
> It was all over in less than an hour, leaving masses of black smoke rising from burning ships, warehouses, stores, workshops and jetties.[83]

Staying at the Mount Lavinia Hotel, Tom Simkins, who had escaped both Singapore and the Dutch East Indies and was now enjoying a relaxing reprieve in Ceylon, remembers the appearance of the Japanese aircraft:

> Just a short train ride from Colombo, on a rocky outcrop on the sea shore with the beach framed on one side with the white surf rollers of the Indian Ocean, and on the other, coconut palms prolifically endowed. If there was anything else that could make us forget that there was a war on, it was the millionaire style existence which we enjoyed. On 5 April I had awakened quite early to the sound of lashing rain and thunder and had dozed off again, but became conscious again later, thinking that the storm was really developing into a heavy one. Then, 'Hells bells', that's not still the storm, it's gunfire – lots of it. Looking through the French window door, I could see that the dark sky was riddled with flack. That didn't bother me immediately because I felt there was something else more important to be concerned about. It was those loud rumblings that seemed to be coming across the water, the low flying aircraft, and the long and short bursts of gunfire from different directions, together with two large explosions behind me.
>
> 'Invasion'. In thirty seconds I was ready for the road. I had travelled about 3,000 miles to get away from danger; I wasn't going to get caught on another island. By the time I had got to the bedroom door I was more awake and thinking sanely. A beleaguered Singapore situation just could not have developed overnight … or could it? Out on the verandah I did a quick look-see, but scanning the whole beach left to right and then out to sea, there wasn't a single landing craft or ship to be seen. What was all the noise about, and where were those aircraft coming from?
>
> I went out into the corridor and banged on George's door and nearly banged him in the face as he opened it and came out. I then made a quick dash back to my room and grabbed my skin-out bag and joined George outside. Flights of Japanese aircraft were sailing over the hotel from the direction of the sea without any apparent opposition and so low that I could see the figures in the cockpits. It seemed that their only target was the RAF base at Ratmalana in the distance somewhere behind the hotel.
>
> Ack-ack guns were now barking with greater intensity and it was getting really noisy. One aircraft crashed down in the garden behind the hotel and one plopped down in the sea at the front. Smoke could be seen rising in the direction of the city resulting from a separate

83 BBC World War Two People's War oral history archive, Callis, 'Unwelcome Visitors'.

> flight of aircraft which I learned later also attacked ships in the harbour. It really did seem as if the battle for Colombo had started. Then suddenly at 0915, all the activity stopped, the raid sirens wailed the 'all clear' and then the quietness sounded so quiet. Later that day whilst looking around we came across the aircraft that had come down. It was a burnt out shell so amazingly intact, with the two men inside looking like two skeletons with a few parts missing.[84]

Another crashed near the Buddhist Kelaniya Raja Maha Vihara Temple seven miles from the capital.[85]

Vice Admiral Arbuthnot, in Colombo during the raid, wrote in his official report that:

> The attack duly developed on the morning of Sunday, 5th April, when Colombo was raided by some 70 Japanese carrier borne aircraft, mostly two seater dive bombers. A heavy and accurate attack was directed on the harbour and examination anchorage, and there can be no doubt that the policy of dispersal saved what would have been a serious loss of tonnage, and in all probability, the loss of Colombo as a port until the wrecks had been removed. H.M.S. HECTOR, then in the process of conversion back to trade, was hit, set on fire, and is probably a total loss. H.M.S. TENEDOS – unable to move from defects – was hit and sunk but may be salvable [she wasn't]. H.M.S. LUCIA was hit, but the hole was patched up locally: a permanent repair has since been effected at Bombay. The only merchant ship hit was the S.S. BENLEDI, which was set on fire. As the BENLEDI was laden with explosives, this might have been disastrous; fortunately the fire was extinguished by gallant work on the part of the ship's officers and officers from the nearby tanker BRITISH SERGEANT.[86]

The action by 30 Squadron had lasted for one hour and fifteen minutes and in this time most of the squadron's aircraft completed two sorties. Of the 21 aircraft it launched, eight were lost with a further eight damaged, five pilots killed and two seriously injured. 258 Squadron at the racecourse launched 14 Hurricanes, losing five with five pilots killed. 803 Squadron FAA launched six Fulmars from Ratmalana, losing four with eight crewmen killed. 806 Squadron FAA launched three, and lost three. The Hurricane squadrons claimed 18 kills and seven probables.[87] Slowly 30 Squadron's commanding officer, George Chater, pieced together the day's events. Flight Sergeant Paxton, in hospital with serious burns, died two days later. Sergeant C. J. Browne was dead after his aircraft was shot down, as were pilot officers Caswell of the Royal Australian Air Force and Geffene, an American. Flight Sergeant Tony Ovens' body was found in his aircraft crashed in a reservoir near the Kandy road. By the end of the day only seven of 30 Squadron's Hurricanes were fit to fly.[88] The day after the raid, 6 April, 30 Squadron repaired

84 BBC World War Two People's War oral history archive, Tom Simkins, 'Another Door', part 8, 'Colombo and UK', A1118495.
85 H. G. P. Jayasekera, 'How Japan Bombed Tiny Ceylon'. Jayasekera was President of the Ceylon War Veteran's Association.
86 'Admiralty War Diaries of World War II', Arbuthnot secret despatch, Colombo, 18/6/42.
87 The Battle Summary states a claim of 19 certain, seven probables, and at least seven damaged.
88 Barrass, 'The Battle of Ceylon – 1942 – Part 2'.

its damaged aircraft and inspected those that had crashed. Dawn Patrol was mounted, and all available units were at a state of readiness by 6:37am. The squadron's medical officer, Flight Lieutenant C. S. Grossmark, visited the mortuary to identify bodies. Sergeant Browne was buried with full military honours in Kanatte cemetery, Borella, and Chater and two of his fellow officers represented their squadron at the burial of four pilots from 258 Squadron.

Installations had been damaged, and at least a hundred civilians killed by shrapnel and falling masonry, deaths including those of 15 civilians killed when a bomb hit the Angoda mental hospital six miles east of Colombo harbour, the building not bearing a visible Red Cross.[89] Others died at the naval dockyard and the Ratmalana airbase. During the raid, in addition to the harbour and the Ratamalana airbase, railway workshops and the army petrol dump at Kolonnawa were also hit. The Colombo harbour workshops were seriously damaged, though with relatively few ships in harbour, damage to shipping was slight. According to the Chairman of the Colombo Port Commission, A. N. Strong, the low casualty figures were due to 'the excellence of Ceylon's ARP preparations'.[90]

The raid on Colombo was a major shock to the people of Ceylon as well as those charged with its defence. The panic engendered by the raid caused thousands of people to flee inland, leading to steep rent rises. Many people left for India. On the day of the Colombo raid Gerard Robinson cycled to Galle Face Green to see a Hurricane that had been shot down, and found himself travelling against a 'stampede' of people heading for the hills.[91] The raid disrupted food supplies because so many people fled, and food distribution arrangements broke down. The Storekeeper of Captain's Garden in the Maradana district heard the raid and crossed the Victoria Bridge over the Kelani river against a stream of traffic as people left Colombo and headed inland. Food stocks were abandoned and people looted what they could, the Captain's Garden store area 'covered a foot or more deep in rotting potatoes and onions'.[92] The Essential Services Labour Corps was called up to work under military direction to help make good the labour deficiency, including helping to run shops. As the Commander-in-Chief Ceylon's war diary recorded, a 'very high proportion of the small Indian boutique keepers left Colombo, and in order to distribute food to the populace it was necessary for their shops to be re-opened under Government control'.[93]

There was no good reason, known to any normal Indian or Sinhalese person, as to why Ceylon should not become the next Singapore or Rangoon, so the decision to flee was an entirely logical one. At the premises of Walker Sons and Company in the Fort area of Colombo harbour, of 3,000 workers on the books on the day of the raid, only 123 turned up for work on the Monday morning. Six months or weeks?? after the raid, only 700 people were working for Walker Sons

89 Clancy writes that the bombs that hit the Angoda hospital were intended for the nearby Kolonnawa fuel dump. Clancy, *'The Most Dangerous Moment'*, p. 91.

90 BL, Layton Papers, 74802, Japanese air raids and operations off Ceylon 5-9 April 1942.

91 Robinson, *Fading Edge of Empire*, p. 70. See Chapter 5, 'The Bombing of Colombo'. Robinson lived on Jawatte Avenue near the racecourse, and had a secret hide by the runway from which he could watch the activity on the airbase. He saw McDonald's Hurricane, which had 'gouged its way' along Galle Face Green on its belly.

92 SNLA, Lot 5/439, Dispatches 1942-1-12, 12/170, R. H. Bassett, *Administrative Report of the Commissioner for Development and Agricultural Marketing from January 1940 to December 1945* (Colombo: Government Press, 1945).

93 TNA, ADM 199/663, war diary, 5 April to 31 May 1942.

in Colombo docks, and it took a full year for a figure of 2,000 employees to be reached.[94] For months, the population of Colombo and other coastal towns was far lower than normal. Tom Simkins remembers that after the raid the Governor made a radio broadcast in which he praised the brave behaviour of the population,

> but by the following day they were not so brave as to remain in the city, for there was a grand scale of exodus ... The trains which dwindled to just a few passing through Mount Lavinia station, were packed and bulging with bodies half out of windows, or sitting on the buffers between carriages; there were some perched even more dangerously on top of them.[95]

With the Eastern Fleet having failed to find Nagumo, striking back at the enemy came down to shore-based aircraft. The half dozen Swordfish ignominiously shot down had been one attempt; the other was an attack by the Blenheim bombers of 11 Squadron. They took off at 8:30am to hunt for the enemy carriers, loaded with 500 pound semi-armour piercing bombs and 'hoping to catch Nagumo's carriers in the midst of landing-on his returning strike force'.[96] Alas, Wing Commander A. J. M. Smyth and his crews could not find the fleet due to heavy cloud, and the squadron returned to base. Despite the valiant efforts of the Blenheim and Swordfish crews, Somerville's conviction that the island's air strike force would be 'practically useless' had been justified. Layton wrote that the Fleet Air Arm aircraft in particular 'were more of an embarrassment than a help. They cannot operate by day in the presence of Jap fighters and only tend to congest aerodromes'.[97]

The principal Japanese target had been Colombo harbour, and Fuchida was dismayed to find the Eastern Fleet absent. While engaged over Ceylon he received a report about the sighting of *Cornwall* and *Dorsetshire* to the south, spotted by a floatplane from the cruiser *Tone* at about 12pm. Concerned that an attack was about to be launched on his own fleet, he ordered the recall of his bombers, while a number of Zeros stayed to continue the fight against the Hurricanes. Zigzagging desperately, the cruisers were attacked by a wave of 88 Japanese Vals dispatched by Nagumo, sunk within 20 minutes 230 miles southwest of Dondra Head in one of the war's most efficient carrier air strikes.

Though he was not to know it, and despite these losses, by sunset on 5 April Somerville was 'in a surprisingly favourable position' to deliver an attack on the Japanese fleet. 'He had closed to within 200 miles of Nagumo during the afternoon [and] ... remained undetected'.[98]

> There was now every prospect that he could launch a night torpedo attack with his *Albacores*. As Japanese carrier aircraft did not operate at night, their task force would be defended only by anti-aircraft guns ... Unfortunately, Somerville did not receive accurate intelligence on Nagumo's movements ... Somerville continued to search for Nagumo to the southwest of Ceylon until he re-entered Addu Atoll on 8 April. After a conference there with his senior

94 Bennett, 'Walker Sons and Company War Record'.
95 BBC World War Two People's War oral history archive, Simkins, 'Another Door'.
96 'Britain's Midway'.
97 Tomlinson, *The Most Dangerous Moment*, p. 110.
98 Stuart, 'Leonard Birchall', p. 71.

> officers, among them the rescued captains of *Cornwall* and *Dorsetshire*, Somerville finally realized how seriously outmatched he was. It was now clear that his fighters would not be able to ward off large-scale attacks like the ones that sank his heavy cruisers, that the R-class battleships were liabilities, and that Colombo, Trincomalee, and Addu Atoll were not secure bases.[99]

Despite the drama of the day and the losses incurred, most notably the two heavy cruisers, the British strategic position – dependent on Ceylon's survival along with that of the Eastern Fleet – remained intact when night fell. It could have been so much worse, especially if Nagumo had found Somerville's fleet, or vice-versa. What would have ensued would have been the largest fleet action since the Battle of Jutland in 1916, and it is very difficult to see, given the great superiority in aircraft numbers, quality, and tactics that the Japanese enjoyed over their British opponents, how Somerville could have avoided disaster. But the fact was that the enormous enemy fleet was still at large searching for the Eastern Fleet. The manner in which the British cruisers had been dispatched was a great shock, which left Somerville wracking his brains as to what to do next, convinced that there should be no further attempt to engage a fleet that he now knew to be far superior to his own – but aware, as were Layton and the commanders in Ceylon, that it was likely to attack again.

99 Ibid., p. 72.

5

The raid on Trincomalee

Ceylon remained on high alert in the days following the Colombo raid, and by 7 April an attack was expected on Trincomalee. But this time, there was to be no Eastern Fleet combing the waters around the island intent upon intercepting the Japanese armada. Somerville had decided that to do so would be to court disaster, and his ships were already on their way to sanctuary, Force A at Addu Atoll about to seek temporary shelter in Bombay, Force B departing for Mombasa. A bitter pill to swallow, it was a choice based on the cardinal requirement to keep the fleet in being, reinforced by a signal from the First Sea Lord just before he put to sea strongly advising him not to become engaged with anything except inferior forces.[1]

On 8 April Somerville signalled the Admiralty to agree that moving the Eastern Fleet away from Ceylon was both sensible and necessary:

> He was in no doubt of the probable consequences of continuing to operate near Ceylon. Our shore-based and carrier-borne air strength was quite inadequate to deal with such numbers as Nagumo was able to throw in. The battle fleet could not at present be protected in those waters, and in such circumstances was only a liability. In the Ceylon bases his ships could find little security against air attacks; in Addu Atoll none at all. Accordingly he was sending his slow division to Kilindini in East Africa to guard the WS convoy route, but would keep the fast division in Indian waters, to be ready to deal with any attempt by the enemy to command those waters with light forces only. But he would stay clear of Ceylon. Until modern reinforcements reached him, Somerville wrote, he could only 'create diversions and false scents, since I am now the poor fox'.
>
> In London the crisis which had suddenly, though not unexpectedly, blown up in the Indian Ocean aroused the gravest anxieties. On the 7th of April, Mr. Churchill told President Roosevelt that it seemed that the Japanese might be contemplating the invasion of Ceylon, and asked whether the Pacific Fleet could take such action as would compel the Japanese striking forces to return to the Pacific.[2]

At 2am on 8 April a 240 Squadron Catalina piloted by Pilot Officer Round took off from Koggala in the hope of locating Nagumo's fleet and providing Ceylon's defenders with precious

1 Agar, *Footprints in the Sea*, p. 177.
2 Roskill, *The War at Sea*, volume 2, p. 29.

early warning. At 3:07pm he reported sighting battleships and a carrier 475 east-south-east of the island. Four warships, three tankers, and four armament stores issuing ships were subsequently sailed out of Trincomalee, judged to be the most valuable ships present. The only vessels left behind were the Dutch light cruiser *Sumatra*, the monitor *Erebus*, the minesweeping trawler *Balta*, the boom defence vessel *Barbour*, eight merchantmen, and a naval stores issuing ship.[3]

On the evening of 8 April, the crew of the light carrier *Hermes* and her escort, the Australian destroyer *Vampire*, were enjoying a well-earned run ashore in Trincomalee. It was their first port visit for quite some time, and, with a month's pay in their pockets, the sailors went off to establishments such as the fleet canteen and the Elephant and Castle pub.[4] While they were there, however, the black flag was hoisted and roundup patrols started ushering the men back to their ships, which had been ordered to clear the port and seek safety at sea. By first light on 9 April, the Japanese fleet was 200 miles off Trincomalee.

Defending the harbour were the 18 Hurricanes of 261 Squadron, commanded by Squadron Leader A. G. Lewis, the 16 Fulmars of 273 Squadron, and a pair of Martlets from *Indomitable*. Ground defences comprised 196 Heavy Anti-Aircraft (HAA) Battery Royal Artillery, with four 3.7-inch guns; 1 HAA Regiment Royal Marines, with sixteen 3.7-inch guns; 163 Light Anti-Aircraft (LAA) Battery Royal Artillery, with 12 Bofors; 264 LAA Battery Royal Artillery, with 10 Bofors; 22 LAA Battery Royal Marines, with 12 Bofors; and a Gun Operation Room to coordinate their fire. The radar of Air Ministry Experimental Station 272 was located at Elizabeth Point just north of Trincomalee, and a screen of 50 barrage balloons was provided by 990 Balloon Squadron.[5] The main airbase was at China Bay but there was a satellite at Kokkilai 35 miles northwest, which the Japanese were unaware of, sparing it their attention. At least six of the Hurricanes and most of the Fulmars were located there, as, probably, were the Swordfish of 788 and 814 squadrons.[6]

Approaching Trincomalee, Nagumo sent seven floatplanes to search for British ships and to scout the harbour. The Trincomalee air strike group then began taking off at about 6am, 41 fighters accompanying 91 bombers, all of them employed as level bombers and each armed with a single 800 kilogram bomb, the Japanese admiral electing to send all of his torpedo bombers while withholding all of his dive bombers.[7] According to the official RAF report, the attacking aircraft were first seen on radar plots at 5:20am.[8] Stuart writes that the Trincomalee radar station picked up the incoming Japanese force at a range of 91 miles.[9] The red alert went up at 5:25am, the 'raiders passed' sounding at 6:45am.[10] More plots were subsequently picked up by radar, and China Bay sounded the red warning at 7:15am and Trincomalee at 7:20am.[11] Flight Lieutenant Rae Thomas's 413 Squadron Catalina had left Koggala at 2:56am and reported a large force at 7:16am before his aircraft was shot down, lost with all hands.[12] 261 Squadron's

3 Stuart, '91 Bombs'. This article contains an excellent table listing all vessels present, nearby, or sailed.
4 Morgan, *The* Hermes *Adventure*, Chapter 7 'The Last night of *Hermes*', p. 137.
5 Stuart, '91 Bombs'.
6 Ibid.
7 Ibid.
8 BL, Layton Papers, 74802, RAF China Bay: Enemy air raid on China Bay 9 May 1942.
9 Stuart, 'Air Raid Colombo', p 40.
10 Stuart, '91 Bombs'.
11 Ibid.
12 Ibid.

dawn patrol, led by Flight Lieutenant David Fulford, took off at 6:35am and orbited the China Bay airfield at 15,000 feet. 'A section of three Hurricanes on Dawn Patrol vectored to meet the raiders'.[13] They were sent forward to intercept at 7:06am, sighting them 30 miles from the coast and shooting down two Zeros for the loss of one of their own.[14] A dozen more 261 Squadron Hurricanes were scrambled, six each from China Bay and Kokkilai. Stuart has found no record of any 273 Squadron Fulmars being put up, though six were later scrambled to defend *Hermes* when she came under attack. China Bay was bombed at 7:25am by 50-plus bombers and fighters, the remainder concentrating on Trincomalee harbour.[15]

Ivor Ferdinands father was a railwayman. Railways 'being an essential service', he was 'mobilized but otherwise continued to do his normal work. We took up residence in a Railway Bungalow close to the station in Trincomalee. We found a shallow 'L' shaped trench in the garden and my brother and I dug it deeper'.[16] On the 9 April the Ferdinands family:

> were at home in our house just across the width of the road from the railway yards (an inviting target) when the enemy came. From the slit-trench in our front garden we had a wonderful view – the Japanese flying steadily across our house to China Bay and the aerodrome, the fall of the bombs like silver fish floating down, the barrage balloons, the fire of the AA guns barely a quarter of a mile away, and later the sinking of a bombed ship in the harbour.
>
> Early on 9 April 1942, while my father was away at work, the sirens sounded. My mother, brother, and the two domestics, and the dog went into the 'L' shaped trench. Rodney and I should have kept our heads down, for that was the purpose of the trench, but being curious and not aware of the danger we stood and watched and experienced one of the most exciting episodes in our young lives.
>
> Shortly after the siren sounded, we heard the buzzing sound of Japanese bombers and their fighter escort. There were about seventy planes flying overhead in formation. They were on their way to knock out the airfield at China Bay. They kept to their courses despite the 'boom, boom, bang, bang' of the anti-aircraft batteries. The planes were surrounded by puffs of grey smoke from the light AA guns and black smoke from the heavy AA guns but did not seem to be affected. They were flying above the barrage balloons and out of reach of the guns. Suddenly we saw what looked like large and beautiful silver fish floating down silently in the cloudless morning. They were bombs and soon there was the thunderous sound of explosions. We wondered where the RAF Hurricanes were because they had engaged the Zeros over Colombo. They arrived late when everything was almost over … The planes at China Bay were trapped on the airfield and unable to take off. Late in the raid we had the spectacle of a few thrilling dogfights but that was after the enemy had completed their bombing mission.[17]

13 BL, Layton Papers, 74802, RAF China Bay: Enemy air raid on China Bay 9 May 1942.
14 Stuart, '91 Bombs'.
15 BL, Layton Papers, 74802, RAF China Bay: Enemy air raid on China Bay 9 May 1942.
16 Ivor Ferdinands, 'Ivor and the Air Raid on Trincomalee', quoted in Ferdinands, *Proud and Prejudiced*, p. 177.
17 Ibid.

During the raid 17 Hurricanes and eight Fulmars got airborne, eight of the former and three of the latter being shot down. Trincomalee's anti-aircraft defences put up a spirited resistance, 784 heavy anti-aircraft and 953 light anti-aircraft rounds being fired during the action, along with support from the guns of *Erebus*.[18] A 7,200-ton First World War monitor mounting two 15-inch guns, *Erebus* had been retained in harbour because of her anti-aircraft armaments, and was hit, killing nine and wounding 22, of whom four later died. A. A. Loveridge writes that she 'escaped with a peppering thanks to her efficient HA armament'.[19] The merchant ship *Sagaing*, which was holding a military cargo that included ammunition and four aircraft (a Walrus and three disassembled Albatrosses, all lost) and, apparently, lots of beer and whisky, was also hit. Badly damaged, she was abandoned and drifted into Malay Cove (where she was later sunk by British shellfire aimed below the waterline to prevent the hulk becoming a hazard to shipping).[20]

According to Admiral Layton, the raid 'did considerable damage to the dockyard involving much labour in rebuilding'. The elegant and historic Admiralty House remained unscathed, but the Naval Yard houses nearby were rendered uninhabitable and Admiralty House became a communal mess for the Dockyard officers and their families. Loveridge writes that 'the Air Station at China Bay, the Dockyard, and the Naval Armament Depot received a terrific hammering, and it was only by sheer good fortune that the latter was not blown up; the Japanese were pattern-bombing, and their bombs landed consistently between the bays instead of on them'.[21] In what was afterwards thought to have been perhaps the first kamikaze-style actions of the war, a Japanese pilot appeared to deliberately fly his aircraft into one of the many naval oil tanks that were part of the Trincomalee naval complex. A Kate torpedo bomber from the carrier *Hiryu*, it crashed into tank 91, Stuart suggesting that it was possibly shot down by Trincomalee's defending guns.[22] If it was a kamikaze attack, the pilot was spoilt for choice, because the oil farm comprised 101 tanks of 12,000 tons capacity each, 'more than twice the 563,000 tons capacity of the 54 tanks at Pearl Harbor'.[23] The flames from this burning tank, recalls Ferdinands, 'were so fierce that at night we could read the newspapers standing in the garden'.[24]

Captain Fuchida wrote that despite RAF opposition 'our dive bombers found numerous carrier-type aircraft lined up on the apron of the field and quickly set them ablaze. Low level bombers carrying 800 kilogram bombs concentrated on airfield installations and naval base facilities. One of the targets, a munitions depot, went up in a spectacular display of fireworks'.[25] Ferdinands wrote that 'there was an eerie silence when the raid ended. Trincomalee had many open spaces, much bird life, and was surrounded by jungle, but the terrible sounds made by the

18 BL, Layton Papers, 74802, Air Staff Commander-in-Chief Ceylon 'Japanese attack on Trincomalee', 24/7/42.
19 Liddell Hart Military Archives (LHMA), King's College London, Correspondence of Sir Arthur Bryant, 1919-1984, Bryant, F7-15/2, Loveridge to Arthur Bryant, November 1957. Thanks to Andrew Stewart for this material.
20 Stuart, '91 Bombs'. As reported by the BBC, the ship was raised in 2018 and moved to be re-sunk.
21 LHMA, Loveridge to Bryant.
22 Stuart, '91 Bombs'.
23 Ibid.
24 Ivor Ferdinands quoted in (his brother) Rodney Ferdinands, *Proud and Prejudiced*, p. 178.
25 Janaka Perera, 'Air Raids 1942: No One Was Asked to Resign', *Asian Tribune*, 5/4/04.

bombs and guns had caused the birds to flee ... In the sky was a plume of thick black smoke from the direction of China Bay'.[26]

Arbuthnot's report to the Admiralty on the day's events stated that:

> The enemy's bombing was accurate and a considerable amount of structural damage was done to the Dockyard; a quantity of Naval Air Stores was also lost at the R.A.F. Station, China Bay. H.M.S. EREBUS was hit, but not seriously, and the S.S. SAGAING was hit, set on fire, and had to be beached. One Japanese aircraft crashed into an oil tank, setting it afire. The Armament Depot had some narrow escapes but suffered no damage.[27]

261 Squadron's report recorded the damage inflicted on the China Bay airbase.[28] The officers' mess was badly damaged and the squadron orderly room blown down by a bomb and all office equipment lost. The south hangar, the pyrotechnic store, the motor transport yard, and the main stores were completely destroyed by fire. Sixteen people were killed at China Bay and a number wounded. Two Fulmars were machine-gunned on the ground, a petrol bowser containing 700 gallons of fuel was hit and burnt out, and an oil tank and four vehicles destroyed. Thirteen aircraft under repair or being assembled were destroyed on the ground, along with seven Swordfish, four Fulmars, and an Albacore. The bomb dump near the north hangar was hit, the bombs continuing to explode throughout the morning. Three airmen were also killed on the ground.

On the day of the Trincomalee raid, the Blenheims of 11 Squadron sought once again to attack the Japanese fleet, concentrating on the carriers, particularly Nagumo's flagship, *Akagi*. They were ordered up at 7:40am, just as the attack on the port was broken off by the enemy aircraft. Eleven took off, two having to turn back. It took over two hours flying to reach the Japanese fleet, and the appearance of the British bombers surprised the Japanese. But it didn't take long for defending Zeros to get airborne, and they had soon accounted for three of the Blenheims for the loss of one of their own. The surviving Blenheims then set out for the return journey, though were unfortunate to encounter enemy Vals and Zeros returning from an attack on *Hermes*. Another Blenheim was shot down and crashed on a beach, in return for another Zero. Five of the original nine Blenheims made it home at Colombo racecourse, all badly damaged and unserviceable. Though their attack had been unsuccessful, they had come very close to hitting some of the carriers having penetrated the fleet's airspace, a fact that should have given the increasingly confident Japanese pause for thought. It was the first time Allied eyes had even seen Nagumo's task force at sea since the Japanese war had started, and the first time it had been attacked.[29]

As during the Colombo raid four day earlier, the damage to naval installations was belied by the destruction of ships at sea. Within sight of Ceylon's shoreline, *Hermes* was located shortly after the Blenheims had located Nagumo's carriers. The venerable carrier, steaming at over 25 knots as she tried to avoid their bombs, was attacked by 80 Japanese aircraft. After she had been dispatched, descending at an angle beneath the waves, her funnel still bellowing smoke, 590

26 Ivor Ferdinands quoted in Ferdinands, *Proud and Prejudiced*, p. 178
27 'Admiralty War Diaries of World War II', Arbuthnot secret despatch, Colombo, 18/6/42.
28 Stuart, '91 Bombs'.
29 A point made by Smith in *Fist from the Sky*, p. 196.

survivors were rescued by the hospital ship *Vita*. Captain Richard Onslow, 18 of his officers, and 288 of his men did not survive. The Japanese had then turned their attention to *Vampire*, both carrier and escort being dispatched inside 20 minutes. The attackers then found and sunk the corvette *Hollyhock* and the fleet auxiliary *Athelstane*, the tanker *British Sergeant*, and the cargo ship *Norviken*. Four Vals were shot down by Fulmars, which arrived too late to save *Hermes*.[30] Arbuthnot reported that:

> Most unfortunately, two Japanese aircraft which had been reconnoitering Colombo, on their return flight sighted and reported H.M. Ships HERMES and HOLLYHOCK and H.M.A.S. VAMPIRE which, with tankers BRITISH SERGEANT and ATHELSTANE had been sailed from Trincomalee before the attack and were then 70 miles south of it. The enemy's sighting report was intercepted and H.M.S. HERMES ordered to return to Trincomalee immediately. The R.A.F. were asked to send immediate fighter support from China Bay and available fighter support were despatched from Ratmalana. For various reasons – air raid damage to communications and a false RED alarm at Trincomalee – no aircraft arrived in time to help HERMES, which had to face alone a most determined attack by some 60 or 70 aircraft and was sunk after a 15 minute engagement. The enemy then turned on to the other ships, the HOLLYHOCK, VAMPIRE, and the two tankers, sinking them also. The Hospital ship VITA, on passage from Trincomalee to Colombo, was in the vicinity and was able to save over 600 officers and men. Others were rescued by local craft or swam ashore, receiving great assistance (which I acknowledged to the Government Agent) from locally organized relief parties.[31]

Vita brought the survivors to Colombo, arriving alongside at 7:30pm that evening. The men rescued from the water, many clad only in pants or towels, were issued with a fortnight's pay and given tropical shifts, gym shoes, pyjamas, pullovers, and socks, some of the clothing provided by the Australian Red Cross. J. W. Schneider-Loos writes that:

> I was the Headquarter Inspector Ceylon Government Railways in 1942 when the *Hermes* was sunk off the coast of Ceylon. The men who were picked up were brought to Colombo docks, given baths, food, new clothes, socks, shoes, etc. they were then entrained and taken by a special train which was brought to the docks by the side of the Caisson. One party was detained at Kandy, and the other at Diyatalawa, and taken to military camps. I was in charge of the special and travelled to the destinations. Colombo had a total black out and when the men were brought to the docks it was the same, we had to work with a few shaded lights.[32]

30 Stuart, 'Leonard Birchall', p. 73.

31 'Admiralty War Diaries of World War II', Arbuthnot secret despatch, Colombo, 18/6/42. The point regarding the failure of aircraft to reach *Hermes* in time to intervene is borne out in the Battle Summary, which states that damage to telephone circuits at Trincomalee stopped the message getting through to China Bay, a despatch rider being sent instead, p. 15, note 2.

32 Morgan, *The* Hermes *Adventure*, chapter 8 'Ashore at Last', p. 217.

Admiral Layton came to inspect the train as it waited at the dockyard station, and when the following day dawned it was chugging away through rubber and tea plantations as it made its way into the Central Highlands. Some of the men disembarked at Nuwara Eliya for hotels such as the Grand and the St Andrew's, some at the Diyatalawa military rest camp and the Lanka Barracks, others at Kandy, where they were taken to establishments such as the Queen's Hotel. Petty Officer Gill and 20 others arrived at the Grand Hotel by lorry, 'and what a state to arrive at a posh hotel in unshaven, filthy, still with obvious traces of oil fuel'.[33] Those too seriously wounded to make the train journey were taken to hospitals in Colombo. One of them, L. Evans, was horrified to see that instead of ambulances they were to be transported from the docks by stretchers loaded on to bullock carts, enduring a bumpy and uncomfortable ride to places such as St Thomas's College at Mount Lavinia. Here they were obliged to lie outside for a while as the college was in the process of being converted into a military hospital, beds still being moved into the buildings. Once inside, they were soon out again when a new air raid warning went up.[34] Joan Gottelier visited survivors in Colombo's hospitals, taking magazines, sweets, and other small gifts. She remembers the refrain 'bloody butcher Layton' on the lips of sailors who blamed the admiral for what had happened, especially the fact that *Hermes* had gone to sea without her complement of aircraft embarked.[35]

Fleeing from Colombo and Trincomalee

Both raids caused people to flee in panic. In Colombo, Michael Tomlinson arrived aboard the troopship *Devonshire* shortly after the raid, *Hector* still burning: 'By now it seemed that the Japanese were far away. But no one really knew. However the docks were still devoid of labour and a large element of Colombo's population was gone ... The newly-arrived troops had to row themselves ashore in the ship's boats'.[36] In Trincomalee, many civilians crowded on to the 8:30am train without tickets, others leaving for India aboard the Talaimannar ferry. Loveridge writes that the attack 'caused serious panic – the Cingalese [sic] behaved extremely well throughout, but the Tamils panicked badly and returned to India in bulk (there were, I believe, ugly scenes at the Talaimannar Ferry)'.[37]

33 Ibid., p. 215.
34 Ibid., p. 217.
35 Gottelier interview, April 1999. A charge against which Layton was keen to defend himself. Smith, *Fist from the Sky*, note 157: Layton's report puts the blame squarely on Arbuthnot. Layton wrote: 'Apart from the decision to clear the harbours of merchant shipping, naval movements during the period of the Japanese attacks were under the control of Admiral Somerville as Commander-in-Chief, Eastern Fleet, with Admiral Arbuthnot acting as his deputy at Colombo while *Warspite* was at sea. This applied to the movements, for example, of *Cornwall, Dorsetshire, Hermes*, and *Vampire*, though in the case of the two first-mentioned I advised Arbuthnot to sail them on a course which would have taken them to the west of the Maldives and clear of the Japanese naval aircraft which sank them. As to the *Hermes* and *Vampire*, I was not aware that these vessels had been sailed until they had already gone'. Layton Papers, TNA, ADM 1472A and B. Also BL, Correspondence and papers of Sir Geoffrey Layton relating to the naval war in the Pacific, 1940-45, catalogue numbers 74796-74806.
36 Tomlinson, *The Most Dangerous Moment*, p. 154.
37 LHMA, Loveridge to Bryant.

> Almost directly in front of our house were the hospital trains with the big red crosses on the top and sides. The ambulances soon arrived to fill them up with the casualties. Within a few hours Trincomalee began to empty. The civilians fled where they could. The only way out was the train line so civilians arrived at the station in their thousands with those belongings most precious to them. Few could get on a train, or wait for the next one, so they walked away along the railway line to put as much space as possible between themselves and the horrors of another air attack or invasion … Within a day, Trinco was almost completely deserted. We too would have to depart … Within a few days all of the boutiques and kaddais [small grocery shops] had closed and there was nothing to eat.[38]

In his report to the Admiralty, Arbuthnot described the 'effects of the raids':

> Locally, there was a general exodus of labour from Colombo and Trincomalee, severely hampering all work in the harbours. Trincomalee suffered particularly severely, all domestic labour leaving and both the food supply and sanitary services breaking down. At the time of writing [two months later] labour has not returned to the Dockyard area at Trincomalee, and although other areas are less affected, the general return of Indian labour to India has set a difficult problem since the Ceylonese themselves do not as a race engage in manual labour. In an attempt at a solution, labour battalions are being formed in Ceylon and others drafted from India.
>
> At Colombo, the difficulties in the harbour were acute for a time. As already stated, sufficient Naval personnel were available to take over essential harbour craft. A Docks Operating Company arrived from Rangoon, and this, with a battalion of Australian stevedores and a partial return of native labour, gradually enabled the harbour to get into full operation again.[39]

Trincomalee naval base was brought to a standstill, while in the absence of dock labourers ships in Colombo were unloaded by members of the armed services and British civilians acting as volunteer stevedores. Fortunately for defensive operations and the working of the port and the naval base, there was alternative labour to hand in the form of the many sailors and other service personnel who had recently arrived in Ceylon, some of them former crewmen of *Prince of Wales* and *Repulse*, some escapees from the Dutch East Indies, others landed direct from Britain and the Middle East. Arbuthnot wrote that their:

> presence in Ceylon turned out fortunately, as when native labour decamped after the air raids of the 5th and 9th April, Naval ratings were available to man tugs and lighters in Colombo Harbour, while at Trincomalee they took over practically all the duties in the Dockyard and port. Had they not been available all work in Colombo harbour would have been stopped for weeks and Trincomalee Dockyard would still be out of commission.

38 Ivor Ferdinands quoted in Ferdinands, *Proud and Prejudiced*, p. 178.
39 'Admiralty War Diaries of World War II', Arbuthnot secret despatch, Colombo, 18/6/42.

> In view of the certainty that native labour will disperse after any further attack, it is considered that the number of Naval ratings in Ceylon must be maintained at a level which will enable the Navy to take over essential harbour craft in emergency.[40]

But there were negative aspects too, the vice admiral adding that 'it is regrettable that both seaman and soldiers employed in the harbour were guilty of looting on a considerable scale. They were not the only offenders, but I was sorry to see really good work so marred'.[41]

Panic reigned ashore among the civilian population, and the evacuation of European civilians to South Africa and elsewhere was given fresh impetus. The day after the Trincomalee raid the Chief Secretary, the Governor's deputy, told heads of government departments to inform their staff that absence from work, save for sickness, constituted grounds for dismissal. Nevertheless, most of the people who had failed to report for duty after the Colombo raid continued to stay away, resisting all blandishments and threats. Therefore the Governor made a broadcast on 12 April in which he said that a current medical certificate, unless received prior to 15 April, would not be a valid exemption from duty (there was one reported case of a doctor signing hundreds of people off sick): if a government employee was absent thereafter, this would constitute a breach in the terms of employment, and dismissal without pension or gratuity rights would follow.

The Governor made his feelings clear in a radio broadcast on 13 April:

> In their recent attacks on our ports at Colombo and Trincomalee the Japanese received a sound drubbing and suffered more than they gained. Our casualties were, compared with those of many other blitzed towns, very light. That was because our defenders in the air were backed by a well prepared and well drilled Civil Defence. We had reason to be proud and still more reason to be self-assured. We had been tested and we had been proved. Our RAF men could *give it* and our civilians could *take* it. All seemed right. Since then all has gone all wrong. The ports of Colombo and Trincomalee today are playing at suicide. I went around the [Colombo] harbour last evening and found nothing doing. Not only the harbour, but the whole of the internal communications were not functioning. Between the Fort Station and Dematagoda no less than 700 railwaymen were absent (including 78 guards and 68 drivers) ... The labourers are following the rotten example of the men to whom they looked for a lead ... In the Colombo Post Office there are 43 telegraphists and 30 mail room absentees; at Trincomalee the Postmaster has been left with only two out of his staff of 13.[42]

On 14 April the Chief Secretary sent another circular to heads of departments authorizing them to dismiss people on the spot. Following through on his threat and heeding Whitehall's unequivocal instructions, the Governor told his superior in London that 'as a consequence of these measures, approximately 1,166 persons have ceased to be public servants'.[43]

40 Ibid.
41 Ibid.
42 SNLA, Lot 5/439, Dispatches 1942-1-12, Caldecott to Cranborne, 1710/42.
43 Ibid.

Official figures showed that the net excess of departures of Indian labourers over arrivals for April and May stood at 43,000.[44] Of greater significance was the very marked 'disinclination' to work in harbour and airbase areas following the raids, and the labour disorganization caused by the departure of the Indian contractors who normally supplied labour.[45] In an attempt at mitigation, bonuses were now offered to all employees who turned up for work on the day after a raid, and free midday meals were to be provided for all people working in threatened areas.[46] Measures were also taken to address a serious increase in incidents of theft and the pilfering of stores. Public announcements declared the death penalty for looting and whipping for pilfering, which were reported to have had a good effect.[47]

Losses and reaction

During the two raids the Japanese lost a handful of pilots and aircrew, while the British lost over a thousand civilians and military personnel. Around 85 civilians died during the Colombo raids and 20-40 in around Trincomalee.[48] Men were also killed aboard warships and other vessels hit in both harbours. The vast majority of deaths, however, occurred during and after the attacks on British warships at sea, 425 men from the cruisers and 325 from *Hermes* and *Vampire*. Tomlinson's tariff of losses has 65 pilots and aircrew killed during the combats, the Catalina reconnaissance flights, and the failed 9 April Blenheim attack on Nagumo's carriers.[49]

In terms of shipping, Nagumo's attacks on Colombo and Trincomalee and the stray ships of the Eastern Fleet, along with the coordinated raid of Ozawa's Malaya Force along the Indian coastline, led to the loss of two cruisers, an aircraft carrier, two destroyers, a corvette, an armed merchant cruiser, and 23 merchant vessels sunk, with a small number of naval vessels damaged. In terms of air assets, during the raid on Colombo 23 RAF and FAA aircraft had been lost. At Trincomalee four days later, according to Stuart's research, 28 aircraft were destroyed in the air, on the ground, or aboard *Sagaing*, including nine 261 Squadron Hurricanes (though this figure excludes the five Blenheims lost, which would put the total at 55).[50]

While the figures for British losses can be taken as fairly accurate, the Japanese kills claimed by the British have been the subject of debate, and naturally, at the time, the Japanese were not keen to publicize their losses. Contemporary British claims were certainly too high, if initially originating from faithful attempts to gather post-battle statistics. For example, while acknowledging that their was inevitably some inflation of the figures due to overlapping claims from the pilots involved, the Commander-in-Chief Ceylon recording 56 enemy destroyed, 25 probables, and 17+ damaged.[51] It is interesting to note that British commanders were using such figures

44 TNA, ADM 199/663, war diary, 5 April to 31 May 1942.
45 Ibid.
46 Ibid.
47 Ibid.
48 The war diary claims that no bombs fell on Trincomalee town but that 38 civilians were killed during the raid. TNA, ADM 199/633, war diary, 5 April 1942 to 31 May 1942.
49 Tomlinson, *The Most Dangerous Moment*, pp. 176-77.
50 Stuart, '91 Bombs'.
51 TNA, ADM 199/633, 'Narrative of operations by Japanese fleet against Colombo area, April 1942, appendix 1 to war diary 2, 5 April to 31 May 1942.

in their assessments, which included feeding them up the chain of command, and it is unlikely that they would have done so if they had not believed in their veracity. Alanbrooke – as Chief of the Imperial General Staff and chairman of the Chiefs of Staff Committee, the British Empire's most senior active military officer – wrote the day after the Colombo raid: 'At any rate the air action over Ceylon was successful yesterday and we downed 27 Japs'.[52] There would surely have been little point in deliberately deceiving the leadership back in London in the figures transmitted overnight. Alan Moorehead, writing in 1942, recorded a figure of 100 Japanese aircraft destroyed, and it is easier to discount such incredible claims.

Inflated contemporary claims were then taken into the historical literature, including both accounts written by those involved at the time and those penned by later historians. In his *History of the Second World War*, Churchill had the figure at 21 Japanese aircraft destroyed at Colombo (and 19 British), and 15 at Trincomalee (and 11 British) – and one would have thought that Churchill would have had access to good sources of data, and would not have deliberately cooked the books.[53] Tomlinson surmises that 17 enemy aircraft were lost in total.[54] Arthur Marder, in his classic history of the Royal Navy's struggle against the Imperial Japanese Navy, claims that the Japanese lost 33 aircraft, in total a figure representing nearly 10 per cent of the aircraft aboard Nagumo's carriers, which would have represented a fearful loss.[55] The authoritative historian of the naval war against Japan, H. P. Willmott, meanwhile, claims that in both actions the Japanese lost 29, the British 37.[56] Boyd has the figure at 18 Japanese aircraft destroyed and about 31 damaged.[57] The recent research of Robert Stuart shrinks these figures considerably, indicating that the Japanese lost seven aircraft over Colombo (the Japanese fleet's highest losses to date, it is worth noting), and five during the Trincomalee raid. He states that the Japanese admitted to having lost 19 aircraft in total during the entire Indian Ocean operation.[58] What made the British battle damage assessment that much more difficult was that so few Japanese wrecks were recovered in Ceylon; the figure was only about three or four, meaning that other downed fighters or bombers claimed must have crashed into the sea, and it is almost impossible to ascertain how many more failed to make it back to the carriers.

At the end of the day, frankly, losses on both sides – including pilots and aircrew – were of little significance, tragic though the loss of life was. For the British, the destruction of the cruisers represented the biggest dent in capabilities. But the Eastern Fleet was in the midst of a reinforcement programme, and they were soon replaced. Likewise, aircraft losses represented little more than tactical level impediments; the Hurricanes were soon replaced, and further reinforcements were arriving. The Hurricane squadrons were back up to full strength by the end of April, and by the end of May there were 72 Hurricanes in Ceylon, equivalent to three and a

52 Danchev and Todman (eds), *War Diaries*, p. 245.
53 Churchill, *The Second World War*, volume 4, p. 158.
54 Tomlinson, *The Most Dangerous Moment*, p. 176.
55 Arthur Marder, *Old Friends, New Enemies: The Royal Navy and the Imperial Japanese Navy*, volume 2 (Oxford: Oxford University Press, 1990), pp. 134-36.
56 H. P. Willmott, *Empires in the Balance: Japanese and Allied Pacific Strategies to April 1942* (Annapolis, MD: Naval Institute Press, 1982). p. 445.
57 Boyd, *The Royal Navy in Eastern Waters*, p. 384.
58 Stuart, '91 Bombs'.

half squadrons.[59] Clearly, in terms of losses, it is obvious that the Japanese attackers did far more damage than the British defenders.

But of course, it was not all about statistics, and it is difficult, on different levels, to assess who 'won' and who 'lost'. This was one of those cases in which the perception of the actions that took place were just as important as the reality – indeed, were an integral part of defining it. Perceptions of the attacks and ensuing combats were important for those who took part and those informed by news broadcasts and newspapers thereafter. Looking back from the distance of over three decades, 258 Squadron's commanding officer Peter Fletcher – by the 1970s, a knighted air chief marshal – recalled his belief at the time, 'shared by many when the battles were over',

> that the Japanese would return and because of the state of our defences my anxiety that the island would prove an easy prey. Yet another, again shared by many of whom some were in very high places, was my belief that the Japanese had suffered a reverse and on this I think there is still some room for debate.
>
> As far as the air battles were concerned, judgement on whether to claim victory or admit defeat is not simply a matter of arithmetic in comparing the losses suffered by both sides. Apart from the fact that there remains some doubt as to what the Japanese losses actually were, the widely held view that the Ceylon operations had deflected the enemy from continuing with his original strategic plans gave a boost to the Allied cause at a time when one was sorely needed.[60]

While morale among the Ceylonese population suffered a setback, the stout defence of the island was cause for some elation amongst the Europeans and the service personnel, and provided a tonic back in London too. After disasters against the Japanese elsewhere, they could be forgiven for seeing this as something of a success, not unlike the sentiments elicited by the evacuations from Dunkirk in May-June 1940. Certainly it was in Britain's interests to portray it as such and to try and put a good spin on the results. Here, the inflated claims regarding Japanese losses, earnestly believed to be accurate by many people at the time, came into play. Propaganda was important for an Allied cause that at that time seemed to be on the back foot everywhere, for the consumption of audiences including service personnel on the ground in Ceylon and the wider Indian Ocean region, as well as people in Britain, Ceylon, India, and distant (but now belligerent) America. No one knew what the future held, and presenting this as at least a plucky draw against the odds, the first Japanese setback, made eminent sense – and might well still stand as a perfectly admissible assessment of the two encounters. An analogy for the result of the raids on Ceylon might be a by-election in which a sitting member of parliament (the British) retains his or her seat with a reduced majority in the face of a spirited challenge from a rival candidate (the Japanese); when the dust had settled, and the smoke cleared from burning hulks and oil tanks, the fact was that Ceylon was still a British 'hold'.

59 TNA, ADM, 199/663, Layton's general summary for the period 10 April to 31 May 1942.
60 Air Chief Marshal Sir Peter Fletcher, 'Foreword' in Tomlinson, *The Most Dangerous Moment*, p. 12.

Alan Moorehead, dispatched to Ceylon shortly after the raid to report on this morale-boosting British 'victory', was convinced that that is what it was, even if this was not immediately apparent.

> The real significance of the raid on Ceylon was nowhere realized at once. It was believed to be the prelude to the invasion of the island, and my paper naturally ordered me to Colombo at once. Invasion or no invasion, it seemed to me that here was a wonderful chance for British propaganda. The attack had come at the end of a long list of British reverses and right in the middle of the Cripps negotiations. Half of India was in a state of nervous tension. Many believed that India would become a battleground within the next few weeks. Surely here, if ever, was a chance to restore confidence. Pictures of the wrecked enemy planes should be rushed to the mainland and distributed to every newspaper. Some of the wrecks themselves should be crated and sent over at once to be displayed to the jittering crowds in Bombay, Madras, and Calcutta. Newsreels should carry the story to the millions who attended India's vast number of cinemas. The successful British pilots should be interviewed and put on the air. Any captured Japanese should likewise be photographed and displayed. The people should hear of this victory and hear of it fully.[61]

One positive and slightly bizarre effect of the Japanese raids – and a very interesting barometer of the mood among certain sections of the population – was to stimulate a recovery in investor confidence. The Governor told the Colonial Secretary that prior to the raid a

> decline in deposits with the Bank from 1939 to 1942 was due to the uncertainties created in the minds of depositors by the varying fortunes of the war. Reverses on the part of the United Nations caused an increase in withdrawals and a decline in deposits ... The setback received by the Japanese in their air raid on Colombo and the arrest of their westward expansion however finally restored confidence and the ensuing excess of deposits over withdrawals has continued up to the present.[62]

Notwithstanding the arcane predictive properties of investor behaviour, many ordinary people in Ceylon were left wondering what the Japanese had in store for them next. Furthermore, many British servicemen were left bewildered and frustrated by the proceedings. Despite the advantages of radar and ULTRA intelligence (which of course only a tiny handful of people knew about), the arrival of the Japanese bombers and fighters on 5 April had taken Ceylon's defenders by surprise and early warning measures had failed. As one browned off pilot put it, 'it was a carbon copy of what 258 [Squadron] and other squadrons had more or less become accustomed to in Singapore, Sumatra and Java – insufficient early warning and an enemy force outnumbering the defenders eight or more to one'.[63] Others echoed this assessment. An eyewitness in Colombo said, 'you've never seen anything like it. An absolute shambles – planes on fire, ships on fire, buildings on fire, the guns crashing away at some high bombers

61 Alan Moorehead, *A Year of Battle* (London: Hamish Hamilton, 1943), chapter 10, 'April in Ceylon', p. 147.
62 SNLA, Dispatches 442, Caldecott to Stanley, 4/2/44.
63 Kelly, *Hurricanes Over the Jungle*.

which had broken out of the cloud in perfect formation, just like a Hendon Air Show'.[64] Furthermore, despite the presence of sizeable British air and maritime forces, the enemy had not been engaged at sea.

Aboard the ships of the Eastern Fleet, there was consternation. During the naval manoeuvres from 31 March to 5 April, men were unaware of the odds against them, but even had they known, some would have opted for a fight anyway. Men such as the pilots of the Fleet Air Arm were warriors, chomping at the bit for a taste of action and frustrated that it had not come their way. Hugh Popham, a pilot aboard *Indomitable*, articulates this sentiment well. Since entering the Indian Ocean, *Indomitable* – 'the warhead of a potential Eastern Fleet' – had been acting as little more than a ferry, rather than a fighting carrier, dumping her own aircraft ashore in the Sudan and transporting Hurricane's to the Dutch East Indies and Ceylon.[65] But when Somerville had formed his fleet up on the last day of March and begun the search for the enemy, 'it seemed like action was upon us ... the ship was electric with rumour'.[66]

> That night, as we steamed north, a striking force of Albacores, armed with torpedoes, was ranged, with their crews at readiness. As dusk deepened swiftly into darkness, the ship herself seemed to tremble with a strumming nerve of anticipation. Not many people slept. The knowledge persisted past the brink of waking: a Jap carrier-force was approaching Ceylon: we were on our way to intercept. Our chance had come at last.
>
> We were at Action Stations before dawn, hurrying up to the flight-deck almost as if the enemy might be hull-up ahead, almost as if we might be missing something. There was no news, nothing to be seen. We rushed down to breakfast in ones and twos, lifebelts and anti-flash gear near at hand, and hurried back on deck. All was still and expectant. Pilots, observers, air-gunners, with their Mae Wests unbuttoned and their helmets hanging round their necks, moved restlessly about the deck.
>
> 'For Christ's sake, let's get at the little yellow bastards', Jock said. 'What are we waiting for?'.
>
> What were we waiting for? Instead of driving northwards at full speed, we were dawdling about on the leisurely swells. We began to get edgy with impatience.[67]

When Popham and his fellow pilots learned of the attack on *Cornwall* and *Dorsetshire*, their bewilderment and frustration grew, and we 'raged and blasphemed with frustration: Why weren't we airborne and on our way? For Christ's sake, why?'.[68]

> All day it was the same, the sour anger of enforced inaction, of a sapping impotence. Rumours filtered through. Colombo had been bombed. Then why, and again why, weren't we there? For forty-eight hours longer we steamed in desultory circles, in a state of readiness that had long since become a mockery. Just our luck, we said bitterly, to belong to

64 Quoted in Alan Warren, *Burma 1942: The Road from Rangoon to Mandalay* (London: Continuum, 2011), p. 190. See chapter 15, 'Admiral Nagumo's Raid on Ceylon'.
65 Popham, *Sea Flight*, p. 100.
66 Ibid., p. 101.
67 Ibid., p. 103.
68 Ibid.

> the fighter-squadrons that never fought. The T. B. R. [torpedo, bomber, reconnaissance aircraft] boys were equally galled. The thought of an enemy fleet just over the horizon, simply waiting to be torpedoed, was too tantalizing to be borne.[69]

For some time, not even Admiral Somerville understood the odds against him, underestimating not only the enemy's strength, but also its will to fight. Unaware of anything more than basic details, many of his men, relishing the chance of a fight, were confused by his decision to retire in the face of the enemy, wondering why they were 'running away' rather than engaging. In his account Popham goes on to acknowledge that while it was entirely natural that 'we should be angry at seeing our first chance of action in six months go by default', they did not of course know the strength of the enemy and were not privy to the information that dictated Somerville's choices, and that discretion had had to be the better part of valour. The enemy, Popham later learned, 'had a superiority in sheer numbers that would almost certainly have made any battle a foregone conclusion. For the second time in six months, our Eastern Fleet might have suffered obliteration, leaving India, Ceylon and the whole Indian Ocean an open hunting-ground'.[70]

Somerville was just as frustrated as his men, and shocked. The 'experiences of 5 to 9 April 1942 shook him more than any other in his flag career'.[71] On 6 April he wrote to his wife: 'I hope I shan't have to pass another Easter day like yesterday. It certainly was a black one'.[72] Two days later he told the Admiralty that the 'enemy has complete control of Bay of Bengal and can, at his selected moment, obtain local command of the waters S and SW of Ceylon'.[73]

> Our present naval and land-based forces are quite inadequate to dispute this command. The Battlefleet is slow, out-gunned and of short endurance. Its available carrier-borne air protection would be of little use against repeated air attack of the scale used against the 8" cruisers. There is little security against air or surface attack at our naval bases in Ceylon and none at Addu.
>
> ... there seems little to prevent the enemy establishing himself on the East Coast of India and eventually occupying Ceylon.[74]

Reluctantly, Churchill concurred, writing that 'the experiences of the last few days left no doubt in anyone's mind that for the time being Admiral Somerville had not the strength to fight a general action'.[75]

On 8 April Force A had gone to Addu Atoll, conducting 'very heavy' air searches of the base first, as Force B proceeded to Mombasa. Layton agreed with Somerville's assessment of the situation, telling him on 9 April that 'it is now quite clear that the Eastern Fleet will not be able to afford any appreciable protection to Ceylon or the East Coast of India for some considerable

69 Ibid., p. 104.
70 Ibid.
71 Simpson (ed.), *The Somerville Papers*, p. 361.
72 Ibid., p. 400.
73 Ibid., p. 403.
74 Ibid., Somerville to Admiralty, 8/4/42, p. 403.
75 Churchill, *The Second World War*, volume 4, p. 160.

time. It follows therefore that Ceylon requires much more powerful Air Forces than now exist'.[76] On 10 April, Somerville told his deputy commander-in-chief that 'Ceylon is practically invested and is, therefore, quite unsuitable as my headquarters'.[77] Now on the back foot in the Indian Ocean, the Eastern Fleet retreated to Bombay and Mombasa, where its headquarters were transported a matter of days after the Trincomalee raid. It was already on its way even as the attacks on Trincomalee went in, painfully illustrating the fact that the navy was unable to do anything to prevent the Japanese raids. While it would continue to visit Colombo and Trincomalee, these ports were now considered too dangerous as permanent fleet bases, which from now on – and for the best part of the next 18 months – would have to be provided by Addu Atoll and Mombasa. Though Churchill had been adamant that Ceylon was needed as the fleet's main base, all agreed that, for the time being at least, it could not operate as such.

There was also discussion as to whether the Commander-in-Chief East Indies should quit Ceylon too. Vice Admiral Arbuthnot wrote:

> On the naval side, the Commander in Chief, Eastern Fleet, decided that, in view of the Naval superiority possessed by the Japanese (and, in particular, their superiority, both in numbers and performance, in Naval aircraft), Ceylon must be abandoned as a Fleet base until sufficient shore based aircraft were available to repel an attack. He therefore signaled his intention (signal timed 0716 of the 8th April) to divide the Fleet into two forces, of which Force B, consisting of the R class battleships, C and D class cruisers, and six destroyers would operated on the East African coast, and Force A, the (faster) remainder of the Fleet, would operate in the eastern Indian Ocean. Their Lordships, in a signal timed 1414 of the 16th April, confirmed that the Government's policy was to defend Ceylon but agreed that the primary object was to maintain the Eastern Fleet in being. They added that Colombo was to be the main Fleet base as soon as Ceylon was secure.[78]
>
> In addition, the Commander in Chief, Eastern Fleet, suggested (signal 1023 of 9th and 0320 of 10th April) that I should move to Bombay. I had myself less fear of a Japanese invasion, and in view of the complete confusion into which merchant shipping would be thrown during and after an unprepared move of my headquarters and the disastrous effect such a move would have on Ceylonese morale, I thought it would be better from all aspects that I should remain in Ceylon. At the same time, I agreed that it would be wise to prepare for a move should it become necessary. I also gave it as my opinion that the alternative headquarters should not be in Bombay owing to the danger of civil disorder if the Japanese landed in India: Kilindini, I suggested would be better. Admiral Somerville agreed and directed (signal times 0415 of the 14th April) that his staff at Colombo should be transferred to Kilindini as soon as convenient.[79]

Of course, the fact that the Japanese would not return, and that their capacity to do so would soon be drastically reduced, was unknown at this time, and the British spent the remainder of the spring of 1942 recovering from the shock of recent events while enacting their extensive

76 Simpson (ed.), *The Somerville Papers*, Layton to Somerville, p. 404.
77 CAC, Edwards papers, REWD 2/13.
78 'Admiralty War Diaries of World War II', Arbuthnot secret despatch, Colombo, 18/6/42.
79 Ibid.

Indian Ocean reinforcement programme. On 15 April, in a message to Roosevelt, Churchill returned to the 'ominous theme' of the Indian Ocean sitation:

> 'With so much of the weight of Japan thrown upon us we have', wrote Mr. Churchill, 'more than we can bear'. He asked whether the American Pacific Fleet could at once move back to Pearl Harbor, whether United States naval reinforcements could be sent direct to Somerville or, alternatively, whether they could come to Scapa to enable us to release powerful modern ships to the Indian Ocean. In the Prime Minister's view, we needed eight or nine weeks' respite, at the end of which we should have ample forces (including the *Illustrious*, *Valiant*, *Nelson* and *Rodney*) available to reinforce the Eastern Fleet. On the 17th the President replied declining to send American warships into the Indian Ocean, but he offered temporarily to replace some of the Home Fleet's battleships if they were sent east. He also said that measures were in hand in the Pacific which 'we hope you will find effective when they can be made known to you shortly'. The President may have been referring to the carrier-borne air raid on Tokyo or to the despatch of the task force which was soon to fight the Battle of the Coral Sea.[80]

Churchill continued to keep a watch on events in the region, anxious to see the timetable of reinforcements adhered to. On 14 April, he told the Chiefs of Staff that 'We must make every effort and run great risks to hold Ceylon'.[81] In the House of Commons on 23 April the prime minister described the need to defend Ceylon now that it was on the front line:

> This cannot be done without adequate shore-based aircraft and ample anti-aircraft artillery. Our resources were limited and there are, as I have said, many clamant calls upon them. However, casting aside a great many other needs, we did manage to give considerable measure of protection to Colombo and Trincomalee, and also to place in Ceylon military forces sufficient to require a substantial invading army to overcome them.[82]

On 25 April he told the Chiefs of Staff: 'Let me know exactly what improvements have been made in the garrison, Air Force, and defences of Ceylon since the Japanese attack'. What, he wanted to know, would be the situation by the end of May, and by the end of June?.[83]

The RAF striking force was soon boosted by the arrival of the Beauforts of 22 Squadron which reached Ceylon on 28 April having staged through Gibraltar, Malta, and Egypt before landing at Ratmalana. More air defence equipment was also en route, including more radar equipment, 50 more barrage balloons, and anti-torpedo booms, and by 13 May 1942 there were 64 heavy and 100 light-anti-aircraft guns defending Colombo and more at Trincomalee.[84] The members of Layton's Commanders' Committee were told on 23 April, at a meeting attended by Wavell, that there would be a Liberator squadron by the end of June, two Blenheim squadrons

80 Roskill, *The War at Sea*, volume 2, p. 29-30.
81 Churchill, *The Second World War*, volume 4, to Ismay for Chiefs of Staff, 14/4/42, p. 161.
82 Eade, *Secret Session Speeches*, 23 April 1942.
83 TNA, ADM 20/2410, Defence of Ceylon, 3/3/42 to 2/9/42, prime minister's personal minute to Ismay for Chiefs of Staff.
84 BL, Layton Papers, 74802, Reports and proceedings of the Eastern Fleet, 2 May to 10 May 1942.

operational by the end of April, and two more by the end of May, and that a Wellington squadron had now arrived.[85] At the start of 1943, there were 25 squadrons in Ceylon or shortly to arrive.[86] At sea, the strength of the Eastern Fleet continued to build and its air arm was gradually upgraded with more capable aircraft, and Somerville's training programme improved its capacity to fight as a fleet at sea.

A Japanese failure?

On one level (as Peter Smith puts it) the British 'got a mauling'.[87] But what had the Ceylon raids achieved for the Japanese? Certainly, they had not won the hoped-for strategic victory, which would only have occurred had they removed the capital units of the Eastern Fleet from the order of battle. They had also failed to knock out the British port facilities and airbases, all of which remained operational. The Japanese pilots who attacked Ceylon were surprised on three accounts. First, that the harbours had not been sheltering the Eastern Fleet, to be devastated like the American fleet at Pearl Harbor. Secondly, that they had encountered accurate and heavy fire from anti-aircraft guns. Third, that they had come under attack from modern fighters for the first time in their brief history of conquest. The first loss of Japanese aircraft in the face of modern fighters manned by experienced pilots dented the spell of invincibility which they had enjoyed over the last four months. But this was hardly a major setback for the Japanese, and the Eastern Fleet had been lucky to get away with some not inconsiderable losses, as opposed to calamitous destruction. At relatively little expense, Nagumo had ensured that there would be no British counterattacks in the region of the Malay barrier for two years, and had secured the south-western flank of the Greater East Asian Co-Prosperity Sphere, for the time being at least. But would such a British counterattack have occurred anyway – especially given the fact that, regardless of the results of the Ceylon raids, the British were in no position to mount attacks to regain the lost Allied colonies anyway? Furthermore, the Japanese western perimeter was already as secure as it could be, and this situation would not change until the Allies had more offensive depth in the region later in the war. The attacks made the British cautious, and that was, for the time being at least, a very good thing from their point of view.

85 TNA, ADM 199/633, Commanders' Meeting minutes, 23/4/42, Wavell in attendance. At slight variance, the Chiefs of Staff told Somerville in May that by the end of August the reinforcement of Ceylon's air forces should be complete. The island's air force would then comprise three fighter squadrons comprising 72 Hurricanes, one light bomber squadron of 16 Blenheims, half a torpedo bomber squadron of eight Beauforts from 217 Squadron, and two flying-boat squadrons amounting to 18 Catalinas. TNA, ADM 20/2410, Defence of Ceylon, 3 March 1942 to 2/9/42, Chiefs of Staff meeting (42), 158th meeting, 22/5/42, to Somerville.

86 TNA, AIR 23/4887, Defence arrangements Ceylon. In the Trincomalee area there were three fighter squadrons at Minneriya, a general reconnaissance squadron at Sigiriya, three FAA squadrons and a fighter squadron at China Bay, and two torpedo bomber squadrons at Vavuniya, with an advanced landing ground at Dambulla. In the Colombo area, there was a fighter and two torpedo bomber squadrons at Ratmalana, a fighter squadron at the racecourse, and six FAA squadrons at Katukurunda, and four flying-boat squadrons at Koggala. Air HQ 222 Group to Air Headquarters India, 16/2/43. There were also at this time 42 barrage balloons at Colombo and 15 at Trincomalee.

87 Smith, *Fist from the Sky*, p. 196.

As it so happened no further Japanese attacks on anything like this scale were to come, and some claimed that this was as a result of the surprising level of resistance that the Japanese encountered in the skies above Ceylon, though it is more likely that this was only ever intended as a raid, and that Nagumo now headed home, pleased with this latest escapade in a long line of success to date, even if disappointed not to have found Somerville's fleet. Events that were to occur shortly after the raids, to be explained in the next chapter, ensured that – even if the Japanese had wanted to – a repeat performance was extremely unlikely, even if it were not beyond Japan's increasingly straitened capability. Despite the further whittling down of the operational strength of the Eastern Fleet and the loss of precious but replaceable aircraft, the raids on Ceylon can be counted as a failure for the Japanese in a number of respects, especially as it was the first and last time that they attacked in the Indian Ocean in such strength. Stuart writes that the results for the Japanese were 'meagre'; in the second raid, 'were it not for the ships sunk by the dive bombers, the commitment of KdB [Kido Butai, the 1st Air Fleet] to attack Trincomalee would not have been worth the trip'.[88] The same can confidently be said of the Colombo raid. Fighting against their will and from a defensive posture, the British had achieved, by default as much as anything, their strategic objectives – Ceylon remained inviolate, and the fleet intact. Without the resolve to press home the attacks and given their limited results, the raids had been little more than a storm in a Ceylonese teacup.

88 Stuart, '91 Bombs'.

6

Mountbatten, Kandy, and South East Asia Command

After all this, the emergency passed; the strategic threat to Ceylon and the Indian Ocean sea lanes dissipated with surprising speed in the weeks following the raids. Though enemy submarines along with a few auxiliary raiders and cruisers were to forage across the Indian Ocean for the rest of the war, Nagumo had sailed for home as soon as the strike on Trincomalee had been completed, the Japanese never to return in such strength. For the next two years, while the enemy retained mastery of the waters of the eastern Bay of Bengal and the Malacca Strait, the threat posed by Axis forces in the wider Indian Ocean was limited and successfully contained. The Allies' capacity to use the sea lanes to access the Middle East, the Persian Gulf, India, and Australasia was hindered but never again threatened so seriously as had been the case in the early months of 1942.[1] But of course, this was not known at the time, and the two months following the raids saw Britain's preparations for Indian Ocean defence reach their peak.

Strategically, following up the attacks would have been the sensible thing for the Japanese to have done; knock out the Royal Navy, take Ceylon, and make a concerted effort to sever the sea lanes of the western Indian Ocean. It was clearly a course of action that commended itself to significant elements of the Japanese military leadership. On 13 April the foreign minister told the German ambassador in Tokyo that Japan was thrusting towards Ceylon and the area north of it, and that the thrust would extend step by step into the western Indian Ocean.[2] Hitler and Mussolini were delighted with the Ceylon raids and the prospect of Japanese power helping them fulfil their own ambitions in the western Indian Ocean and Persian Gulf, as well as allowing them access to the treasure trove of strategic raw materials that the Japanese had captured thus far.

The 'Revised defence plan for Ceylon', prepared immediately after the Colombo and Trincomalee raids, obliged the British to plan their defence against a Japanese scale of attack amounting to 250 aircraft, bombardment by capital ships, and the landing of a large invasion force.[3] But with British reinforcements continuing to arrive, the odds on Japanese success in the event of such an attack shortened by the week, their window of opportunity swinging shut. To take the island, they would need to win air superiority against a strengthening RAF, and

1 A much more detailed account of what happened in the Indian Ocean in the remainder of 1942, as well as in 1943, 1944, and 1945, is provided in Jackson, *Of Islands, Ports, and Sea Lanes.*

2 Boyd, *The Royal Navy in Eastern Waters*, p. 385.

3 Ibid., p. 391.

then, if they did manage to get troops ashore, overcome more than two divisions of imperial troops. And all of that would depend upon overcoming the Eastern Fleet now being prepared to meet the Imperial Japanese Navy in battle. Churchill grew in confidence regarding not only Britain's ability to defend its strategic bottom line in the Indian Ocean, but also Japan's capacity, or, indeed, intention, to launch another major raid. Furthermore, though the Americans had stopped short of actually deploying naval units to the Indian Ocean to strengthen the British position during the gap between the Japanese raids and the completion of Britain's reinforcement programme – scheduled to occur in June – they had basically told Churchill that if push came to shove, they would find the wherewithal to do so, or at least cover the Royal Navy in other theatres in order to release warships for deployment east of Suez. Churchill's mood improved further following the successful British capture of Diego Suarez in Madagascar in early May, forestalling a possible Axis bid to base forces there for Indian Ocean operations. In a dexterous example of the management of stretched strategic resources, the British had also warned their naval commander in chief in the Mediterranean, Admiral Sir Andrew Cunningham, that he might at short notice have to sail all his capital units through the Suez Canal to reinforce Somerville's Eastern Fleet.[4] The British government would do whatever was necessary to protect the sea lanes of the Indian Ocean, considered to be an 'inescapable commitment'.

Accounting for Churchill's increasingly sanguine mood regarding Indian Ocean security following the shocks of 5-9 April, several other contributing factors can be discerned. The prime minister clearly had access to the very best secret intelligence regarding the enemy, and this made him aware of potential Japanese limitations, while everyone else, naturally, was fixated on Japanese strengths. It is clear that he was increasingly of the opinion that the Japanese were operating at the end of their tether in the Indian Ocean, and beginning to feel the pinch of strategic overstretch. Just as the British couldn't defend everywhere at once, so too the Japanese couldn't threaten everywhere at once.[5] In addition, Churchill exhibited here as in other theatres a strategic sixth sense and the capacity to accept risk, an essential faculty given his unique role as British warlord, the sole individual capable of seeing all across the scene, the sole individual responsible for acting in it. Finally, he believed that British reinforcements were sufficient to block the Japanese, perhaps exhibiting more faith in the effectiveness of British forces and less faith in those of the Japanese than the situation warranted. The American 'Doolittle' raid on Japanese soil on 18 April also provided a psychological boost to the Allies while delivering a concomitant blow to the Japanese. Nagumo and other naval leaders were censured for having allowed an American task force to get so close to the home islands, and now set off in search of it.

Then, at the beginning of June, something happened that completely deescalated the situation and effectively removed the likelihood of significant Japanese operations in the Indian Ocean all together; the Americans hammered the Imperial Japanese Navy at the Battle of Midway, destroying four fleet carriers in the space of four days.[6] It was a catastrophic blow. Following this signal defeat, though there was no room for complacency, it was pretty clear to an informed observer that the enemy threat had greatly diminished.

4 Ibid., p. 385.
5 See his upbeat assessment in correspondence with Admiral Neville Syfret, commander of the Madagascaar expedition.
6 Three of the four carriers sunk at Midway had been part of Nagumo's force during the Indian Ocean raid of 4-9 April.

The Indian Ocean would now be a far more difficult place in which to pursue operations for the Japanese given their grievous losses and the need to concentrate resources closer to home in order to meet the mounting threat posed by the US Navy. The Italians were no longer any threat at all east of Suez, and the Germans could do little more than deploy the odd U-boat group. While not counting his chickens, Somerville was aware of the change in the latent balance of power here, as were the top brass in Ceylon. As Lieutenant General Pownall confided to his diary in August, reflecting how much things had changed with regard to Ceylon since his arrival in February:

> My chances of getting away from this place into something more useful look anything but rosy. I strongly suspect that, having got me on to this shelf, I shall be left here. It wasn't a shelf when I came here; Ceylon was regarded as the next place to be attacked and it was no insult to be put here, anything but.[7]

Further indicating the diminution of the enemy threat, the Australian brigades were released in July and allowed to continue their interrupted journey home, replaced by the 20th Indian Division.[8] In the following month, Wavell sent two divisions to the Iran-Iraq command given the heightened German threat in the region – and therefore to India and the Indian Ocean too. These included the 5th British Division, that four months before he had kicked and screamed to get to India, its transfer to Iran indicating the extent to which the threat to India and Ceylon had diminished, even if it had not entirely disappeared.

The war in the Indian Ocean, as 1942 slid into 1943, became becalmed, resolving into a pattern that would last until the second half of 1944. Japanese expansion had reached high tide with the final conquest of Burma and the Philippines in May, and an unsuccessful British counterattack in the Arakan had run out of steam. The enemies now dug in on the defensive, exhausted and with little choice but to glower at each other across India's eastern border and across the waters of the Bay of Bengal. For the Japanese, the the window had slammed shut on the opportunity to gain control of the Indian Ocean's pivotal sea lanes. For their part, the British marked time, unable to eject the enemy from the conquered territories of the eastern Indian Ocean rim or regain command of the sea, concentrating instead on the essentials of sea lane protection. Its reinforcement programme completing in June-July, thereafter the Eastern Fleet almost immediately began to be stripped back to allow for the concentration of warships in the Mediterranean as important battles and invasions took place there, the British demonstrating skilful management of straitened resources as the pulse of war shifted across multiple theatres.

Moan and groan though he might, Somerville was left with sufficient resources to protect the most vital British interests in the Indian Ocean – the sea lanes and the convoys that passed along them – though was to spend the next two years unable to launch strikes at Japanese-held

7 Bond, *Chief of Staff*, p. 101.

8 See TNA, WO 106/4486, Ceylon reinforcement, for correspondence regarding the return of these brigades. Also, WO 106/3716, Australian troops in Ceylon. For army forces in Ceylon in 1943, see WO 33/1909, Ceylon order of battle 1942, and WO 160/4588, Ceylon order of battle 1943. Includes excellent maps showing divisional, brigade, and battalion lay downs and areas of defensive responsibility assigned to army units.

territory, his fleet weak enough in terms of capital ships to cause him to remain worried lest the enemy return in strength. There were several scares; in January 1943 a 'generally reliable' source emanating from the British consul in Macao warned that the Japanese were preparing a surprise attack on Ceylon with a concentration of warships at Singapore.[9] Because of this, Ceylon needed to remain strongly defended, as late as September 1943 the Defence Bases Committee of the Chiefs of Staff Committee endorsing Somerville's view that an attack on the island remained more than a remote possibility, and that, therefore, it needed to keep its guard up and not significantly reduce its scale of defences.[10] In February 1944 the main strength of the Imperial Japanese Navy concentrated on Singapore, resurrecting fears of a new Japanese raid which Somerville feared the Eastern Fleet would be ill prepared to meet, and flustering Churchill.[11] Fortunately, it transpired that the enemy had no such intent and that the arrival of the main fleet at Singapore was a measure of weakness, not strength; it mustered there in order to undertake a docking programme now that their main base at Truk in the Pacific was within range of American bombers.

South East Asia Command (SEAC) and the turn to the offensive

The Indian Ocean theatre would have to wait until events elsewhere allowed for its reinforcement, a process that was to see Ceylon transformed into a launch-pad for operations and high-level planning as the Allies slowly quit the defensive posture they had been obliged to assume in the early months of 1942 and turned to the offensive. A new command apparatus for Allied war-making in the Indian Ocean region, South East Asia Command, was created in August 1943 and resources freed by victories in the Atlantic and the Mediterranean enabled a slow strategic swing to the east, meaning that air, land, and maritime forces would be built up in India and Ceylon. By this time the Japanese were a spent force in the region: arriving in Ceylon for a stint at headquarters in September, James Thompson, who had first visited on the day Pearl Harbor was attacked, entered 'a securer, gayer Colombo'.[12] In the same month, Somerville returned the Eastern Fleet's headquarters to Ceylon following its enforced sojourn in Mombasa, indicating the turning of the tide in the Allies' favour.

The formation of SEAC was intended to bring new cohesion and impetus to the war in the Indian Ocean region, and to relieve India Command of responsibility for Britain's war against Japan while unifying command of air, land, and maritime forces. The new command was designed to improve the direction of the ramshackle Allied war effort in the zone between the Middle East and the Pacific, and to draw Japanese forces away from the Pacific to the China-Burma-India theatre. It provided a level of strategic direction above that of 'field' commanders such as General George Giffard, commanding the 11th Army Group in Burma, Lieutenant General (later General) Sir William Slim, commanding its subordinate Fourteenth Army, and

9 TNA, WO 208/924, Ceylon: Possible Japanese invasion, February 1942 to January 1943, British Military attaché Chungking to Commander-in-Chief India and War Office, 15/1/43.

10 De Silva (ed.), *Sri Lanka*, WO 203/5174, COS (43), Report by the Defence Bases Committee on the importance of Ceylon for future operations in South East Asia, 6/9/43.

11 See Jackson, *Of Islands, Ports, and Sea Lanes*, chapter 12.

12 Thompson, *Only the Sun Remember*, p. 204.

Somerville, commanding the Eastern Fleet in support of operations against the Japanese across the wider Indian Ocean.

Winston Churchill was SEAC's main architect, as he had been of Persia and Iraq Command the previous year.[13] 'I circulated to the War Cabinet my proposals for the organization of Command in South East Asia', he wrote on 21 June 1943. 'The vigorous and effective prosecution of large-scale operations against Japan in South-East Asia and the rapid development of the air route through Burma to China necessitate the reorganization of the High Command in the Indian theatre'.[14] underpinning Churchill's reasoning was his belief that India Command was conservative and slow, though he expressed his thoughts more diplomatically in his official communique. Describing the traditional role of the Commander-in-Chief India, he wrote that 'the functions of Supreme Operational Command, combined with those of War Member of the Government of India and Commander-in-Chief, India, responsible for all military administration, training and internal security, are more than one man can discharge. It has therefore been decided that the statutory command in India shall be divided from the Operational Command in South-East Asia'.[15] The position that Wavell had occupied as Commander-in-Chief India, air-land warlord for a vast theatre, was being split in two.

What this meant was that the administration of India as a base for the forces in the wider region would remain under the Commander-in-Chief India, now General Sir Claude Auchinleck following Wavell's appointment as Viceroy of India in September 1943, and to whom, along with the Government of India, Auchinleck would be responsible. As Commander-in-Chief India he would remain in charge of the defence and internal security of India and would continue 'to exercise his present responsibility in respect of the East Persia Supply Route', a supply line sending British aid to the Soviet Union as a supplement to the Anglo-American route that employed Persian Gulf ports and the rail and road infrastructure of Iran.[16] But prosecuting operations against the Japanese would be removed from his purview:

> From a study of the Command systems in other theatres, particularly those where Allied as well as British forces are operating, the conclusion has been reached that the appointment of a Supreme Allied Commander, responsible for the conduct of operations against Japan in South-East Asia and for the development of the air route to China, is the best arrangement. Subordinate to him will be a Deputy and a Naval Commander in Chief, Army Commander-in-Chief, and Air Commander-in-Chief.[17]

The American general Joseph Stilwell was to be Deputy Commander-in-Chief South East Asia and 'in that capacity will command the Chinese troops operating in Burma and all the US air and ground forces in theatre'. The new command meant that its 'supremo', Mountbatten, was responsible for Allied operations from the borderlands of Burma, China, and India to Singapore

13 Churchill forced through his decision to split Middle East Command and create the new Persia and Iraq Command at a critical moment in the region in August 1942. See Jackson, *Persian Gulf Command*, chapter 12, 'Churchill's New Command'.

14 TNA, CAB 66/41/14, The reorganization of command in India South East Asia, 22/9/43.

15 Ibid.

16 Covered in detail in Jackson, *Persian Gulf Command.*

17 TNA, CAB 66/41/14.

and Java in the south, and from the Cargados Carajos islands north-east of Mauritius in the west to Borneo and Indo-China in the east. It now fell to him to take the war to the Japanese in Burma and the occupied territories of South-east Asia and the East Indies, coordinating a sprawling collection of Allied forces.

In his early forties, promoted from captain to acting admiral almost overnight, related to royalty, handsome, and alive to the importance of publicity, Mountbatten inevitably attracted criticism.[18] He had gained experience of the Empire and the wider world by dint of his royal connections and his naval career. During the First World War he served aboard Admiral Beatty's flagship in the North Sea, and in the early 1920s accompanied the Prince of Wales on his imperial tours aboard the battlecruiser *Renown*. The two had been peers at Cambridge, and the 'Playboy Prince' was Mountbatten's best man when he married Edwina Ashley in 1922. During the 'battleship tours' Mountbatten had developed a fascination with India that was to be given full rein when he became Britain's last viceroy in 1947. He had already experienced high command in the war as Chief of Combined Operations, and now set out for New Delhi to establish his headquarters.

At the beginning of November 1943 Mountbatten had his first taste of Delhi as a military nerve centre, forming impressions of the city's torpor that reinforced his desire to move SEAC's headquarters to Ceylon as soon as possible. Even before SEAC's creation, the Chiefs of Staff had opined that its headquarters should ideally be away from India, possibly in Ceylon. Mountbatten believed that he would struggle to enact SEAC's plans from Delhi; India Command had been starved of war essentials for the prosecution of decisive operations, and now they were becoming available, like a starving man confronted with a banquet it didn't know what to do with them. He also thought that

> the climate and antiquated and slow methods used in India have their effect on the keenness of officers after a year or two, and so I have found that the plans made by the India Staff are somewhat pessimistic and unenterprising. My team of British and American planners, who have come bursting with enthusiasm and desperately keen for aggressive plans, find that the lines of communication which run up the Bengal and Assam railway and the Brahmaputra River are not capable of carrying supplies for the type of operations which they would like to carry out.[19]

Inevitably, clashes between an extant headquarters and a new one that had effectively been created to replace it in a major function – fighting the Japanese – caused friction. While the 'new boys'' accusations of lassitude and operational timidity on the part of the old dog, India Command, were not without foundation, the latter was bound to find the tone adopted by SEAC galling. On a visit to Delhi in October 1943, Somerville wrote that

> Unfortunately one or two of D's ['Dickie' Mountbatten's] staff started off on the tack that India, as usual, was all adrift, that India wanted waking up, and so on. This struck an

18 See Bond's *Chief of Staff* for Pownall's criticisms, and more generally, Andrew Roberts's coruscating essay, 'Lord Mountbatten and the Perils of Adrenalin' in Roberts, *Eminent Churchillians* (London: Phoenix, 1995).

19 Ziegler (ed.), *Personal Diary*, p. 22.

> extremely low note, and made a very poor opening chorus for the party. However, I was able to intervene at an early stage and get D to make a special point of thanking A[uchinleck?] for all that had been done.[20]

The logistical issue was critical, and was one of the first areas identified as requiring immediate action. As SEAC's new Chief of Staff, Lieutenant General Pownall – who hadn't been left on the shelf in Ceylon after all – put it:

> The whole problem of operations in Burma is dependent on what the Americans call logistics – in fact the capacity of the Bengal-Assam railway. The authorities said that the railway could only handle 'X' tons a month. It's pretty clear that they've never really been hustled to produce 'X+Y'. Like any other Indian organization they are pretty lethargic, and GHQ, also affected by the Indian mental atmosphere, have never pushed them hard enough. They've had a shock now. Not only from Mountbatten who will not take 'no' for an answer, but, more important, from General Somervell, the U. S. P. A. O. [Principal Administrative Officer] from Washington who offered them U. S. railway units to run the Assam metre gauge and practically guaranteed to improve capacity by 50 per cent .... And all our Burma operations, what is possible and what is not, are conditioned by the tonnage capacity to initiate and maintain them.[21]

Supporting China was very important to the British in this theatre because it was very important to the Americans, and Mountbatten, as a supreme *Allied* commander, had to do more than pay lip service to supporting the Chinese. The Quebec conference in August 1943, where the decision to create SEAC had been endorsed, 'laid down quite clearly that our task was to open up road communications with China and to improve facilities for the air route'.[22] This headline task was indicative of American power in the alliance; Churchill would far rather have left China well alone and concentrate instead on a triumphant return to the lost colonies of the eastern Empire, but SEAC's remit went far beyond colonial reconquest.[23] Though Americans

20 Simpson (ed.), *The Somerville Papers*, to Cunningham, 27/10/43, p. 478.
21 Bond (ed.), *Chief of Staff*, pp. 112-13.
22 Ibid., p. 113.
23 The well-known and long-running disputes between Churchill and the Chiefs of Staff regarding British strategy versus Japan are considered in Jackson, *Of Islands, Ports, and Sea Lanes*. The Chiefs of Staff believed that putting the weight of Britain's effort against Japan under American command in the Pacific was the right thing to do, as this would end the war soonest by defeating Japan in its own backyard and the skies above its own cities. Footling around in the jungles of Burma, on the other hand, would not fundamentally contribute to the conquest and surrender of Japan. 'The first mortal thrust will be the Pacific thrust, upon which the Americans have already embarked. We should not be excluded from a part in this thrust'. Nicholas Sarantakes, *Allies Against the Rising Sun: The United States, the British Nations, and the Defeat of Imperial Japan* (Lawrence, KS: University Press of Kansas, 2009), p. 37. While Churchill was not deaf to the need to contribute forces to the Pacific, he was loathe to see the Indian Ocean ignored, and wanted British forces to lead the reconquest of the lost colonies here, and cash in on the investment Britain had made in building up its forces in the Middle East and South Asia. If the British were simply to be an adjunct in an American crusade in the Pacific, it would be 'no exaggeration to say that the solidarity of the British Commonwealth and its influences in the maintenance of peace in the Far East will be irretrievably damaged'. Ibid., p. 35.

might quip that SEAC stood for 'Save England's Asian Colonies', Washington's interests in the theatre were sizeable and would have to be catered for. The Americans weren't interested in regaining lost British colonies; they wanted Mountbatten to concentrate on Burma – and therefore China – not the invasion of Malaya and recapture of Singapore. Washington's overriding concern was keeping China in the war because it was tying down the bulk of the Imperial Japanese Army. Britain thus maintained high level contact with Chiang Kai-shek and his representatives, and Mountbatten had other Allies to work with too, including the Dutch, who had subordinated their forces in the east to Britain.

SEAC encompassed some of the knottiest problems of imperial and intra-Allied politics and strategy: it was responsible for regaining territory lost in an embarrassing manner to the Japanese; it presided over a major Anglo-American alliance interface; it had to operate in cooperation with the prickly Chinese; it was starved of sufficient resources in key areas such as the landing craft vital for amphibious assaults of the type envisaged for the liberation of occupied territory because it fell far behind the European, Mediterranean, and Pacific theatres in the strategic order of priorities; and it was charged with supervising the surrender and reoccupation not only of Burma and Malaya but also of the Dutch East Indies and French Indo-China, maelstroms of nationalist discontent, post-occupation trauma, and opposition to the return of the colonial powers that SEAC would represent when it deployed Indian divisions as armed peacekeepers at the end of the war. As Pownall put it, 'the hard fact is that the Americans have got us by the short hairs ... We can't do anything in this theatre, amphibious or otherwise, without material assistance from them'.[24]

Given the situation, Mountbatten's skills were perhaps uniquely matched to the challenges of SEAC, the only British-led supreme Allied command of the war. Despite the reservations of some senior political and military figures, Mountbatten was a popular leader among the servicemen and women at large and made great efforts to see and be seen by those serving under him and to communicate confidence and a sense of purpose in what, compared to Europe, the Mediterranean, and the Pacific, was a backwater theatre. There was no doubt that he could be extremely charming. David Jacobs, a Seaman Petty Officer, had a sign on his desk in Colombo which read 'Admiral D. Jacobs'. One day Mountbatten paid a surprise visit to his office, and was upon him before the sign could be concealed. Mountbatten paused, and looked from the sign to Jacobs. 'I'm not quite sure', he said, 'whether I salute you or you salute me'. 'Then he completely won my heart by picking up a rather glamorous picture of my mother and asking with a smile, 'Who's this? Your girlfriend?'.[25]

Touring and meeting the men and women under his command was central to Mountbatten's interpretation of his role. When not on the road, his days were dominated by military headquarters

This is from chapter 2 of the book, 'Churchill versus the Chiefs'. In arguing his corner, Churchill would emphasize that the American top brass didn't really seem to want substantial British forces deployed to the Pacific, and Roosevelt's view was that unless things went seriously awry there, British forces were of more value remaining in the Indian Ocean. As Churchill marshalled such opinion to try and get round the Chiefs of Staff, they did their best to circumvent his Bay of Bengal/South-east Asia strategy. Mountbatten, unsurprisingly, shared Churchill's outlook. As Alanbrooke put it, 'after creating Dickie and his command he is loath to see its wings clipped and reduced to a creature crawling about in Burma'. Ibid., p. 50.

24 Bond (ed.), *Chief of Staff*, p. 164.

25 David Jacobs, *Jacobs' Ladder* (London: Peter Davies, 1963), p. 63.

meetings as well as those of a political and diplomatic nature, entertaining people such as the governor of Burma, the foreign minister of Thailand, the commander of Dutch forces in the east, and the head of the American army in Asia. At the heart of Mountbatten's work as Supreme Allied Commander South East Asia was the need to 'get on' with all sorts of different people, who, while on the same side, were pursuing different objectives – British, Indian, American, Australian, Dutch, French, Thai, Burmese as well as military, naval, political, imperialist and nationalist. It was a political, as much as a military, appointment. Demonstrating his initiative and desire to push on in the SEAC theatre, overcoming problems associated with climate, terrain, and lack of transport aircraft and landing craft, Mountbatten took measures to increase the carrying capacity of the Bengal and Assam lines of communication so that his busy staff could realistically apply their plans.

The logic of moving to Ceylon

Right from the off, Mountbatten was determined to get his headquarters moved to Ceylon. In mid-November 1943 his chief signals officer, Micky Hodges

> came back from the reconnaissance party I sent down to Ceylon. I intend to move my headquarter to the ancient capital Kandy, [a hill station in Ceylon's Central Province] which is at the height of about 2,000 feet, so the temperature never rises above 85 degrees, whereas Delhi reaches 115 … at present we are almost entirely dependent upon GHQ India for our Intelligence, Public Relations, Administration, etc, and I want to make sure that my staff can stand on their own two feet.[26]

Pownall backed his boss and 'favoured a move at the earliest opportunity because he deplored the lethargic "non possumus" attitude that prevailed at the Delhi headquarters'.[27] Epitomizing Delhi's sluggish and bloated characteristics, Pownall reckoned that there were more generals than stenographers at GHQ.[28] Somerville encouraged the move to Ceylon too, because it would bring SEAC closer to his own headquarters in Colombo, recently returned from Mombasa, and because he loathed war-time Delhi. As he wrote on 27 October that

> the whole atmosphere of this place both official and social, is wrong. Very slowly and very reluctantly, Delhi has been brought to realize that there is a war on, but the inertia and resistance to quick action seems fundamental in the place, and unlikely to be overcome by Dickie or anyone else. I was therefore not surprised when D[ickie] informed us yesterday of his intention to move to Ceylon before the next hot weather.[29]

The move was opposed by the Americans and was viewed with some scepticism by the Commander-in-Chief India, Auchinleck, as well as by the regional air commander. Mountbatten

26 Ziegler (ed.), *Personal Diary*, p. 27.
27 Bond (ed.), *Chief of Staff*.
28 Ibid., p. 117.
29 Simpson (ed.), *The Somerville Papers*, to Cunningham, 27/10/43, p. 480.

wrote of his first meeting with him that he 'seemed already to have built up an icy barrier between us'.[30] Pownall wrote that

> it doesn't sound as if Mountbatten had got on too well with the Auk [Auchinleck]. The former effervescent and dynamic, the latter very mulish at times … I wouldn't say his nose is out of joint but he cannot exactly relish a Supreme Commander coming to sit down in what is so very much his parish. Fortunately I do know him and all the senior Staff of GHQ very well. They may be feeling that we have been sent out here to take on a job, a part of which they failed (pretty noticeably) to do themselves last year.[31]

Although Ceylon was 500 miles further away from the Burmese battlefields than Delhi, Mountbatten's decision to move reflected his desire to adopt a maritime strategy in defeating the Japanese, rather than simply pursuing them overland through the inhospitable and disease-ridden terrain of Burma. His centrepiece plans revolved around amphibious invasions of both Burma and Malaya. It was hoped that relocation to Ceylon would enable the fledgling command to escape the stifling immobility that seemed to afflict India Command's headquarters and the seat of government in New Delhi, and because Mountbatten believed that Europeans worked better in a cool climate like that found in Kandy. Nevertheless, SEAC was to create a 'hectic inactivity' all of its very own.[32]

The move to Ceylon required a massive transfer of personnel. 'I have asked my four Commanders-in-Chief, Somerville, Peirse, Giffard, and Stilwell, to keep their staffs that they bring down with them to the smallest possible number, and I find that the minimum total with which we can move to Kandy is 4,100!'.[33] The estimated figure rose towards 10,000, a scale inevitably frowned upon by the Chiefs of Staff in London, who sent a telegram in January 1944 asking for it to be cut down. Layton wrote to Cunningham in the Mediterranean the following month:

> In these days when manpower is the vital thing it does make one wonder if it is right that one Commander should collect together seven thousand able-bodied men and women to plan and supervise operations the scale of which … is likely to be distinctly less than was contemplated when the staff was estimated at four thousand.[34]

Somerville told his wife that SEAC headquarters risked becoming a 'colossal staff doing nothing', citing its strength in December 1943 as 5,500.[35]

SEAC's headquarters gained a reputation for luxury and high living, compounded by the presence of a 30-piece band, a nine-hole golf course (pre-existing, not cut especially for staff

30 Phillip Ziegler, *Mountbatten: The Official Biography* (London: HarperCollins, 1985), p. 229.
31 Bond (ed.), *Chief of Staff*, p. 110.
32 Ziegler, *Mountbatten*, p. 268.
33 Ziegler (ed.), *Personal Diary*, p. 27. Mountbatten added that 'In case anyone should think this number is excessive I am told that when Eisenhower moves to Rome the party will be something like 26,000!'. Ibid. Ziegler claims that the Kandy headquarters soon rose to 10,000. Ziegler, *Mountbatten*, p. 279.
34 Ziegler, *Mountbatten*, p. 279.
35 Simpson (ed.), *The Somerville Papers*, 6/12/43, p. 497, and letter to Tennant, Ibid., 22/1/44, p. 505.

officers!), and a Cadillac for the supreme commander, complete with sirens and motorcycle outriders. Mountbatten also attracted criticism for ordering an unreliable airstrip to be carved out of the mountains near Kandy, and for procuring a little-used caravan built by workshops in Colombo. Kandy was certainly 'remote from the sordid business of battle'.[36] SEAC headquarters became a 'byword for elegance and luxury'. Peter Fleming called it a fête champêtre, while Lieutenant General Adrian Carton de Wiart, Churchill's special representative to China, was reminded of the court of Napoleon.[37] His biographer, however, makes the (perhaps unconvincing) point that all of this came with the Mountbatten phenomenon – 'Mountbattens do not come on the cheap'. SEAC headquarters was 'a superbly effective piece of public relations; and though it irritated some it encouraged others. Kandy was an efficient headquarters, but it was also an expertly contrived theatrical entertainment'.[38] This was important, because inter-Allied diplomacy and cooperation were crucial aspects of SEAC's purpose. Struggling to amass the resources necessary to mount large-scale amphibious attacks in Malaya or even smaller locations such as the Andamans and Phuket Island, and with things moving slowly on land in the China-Burma-India theatre, a key role for Mountbatten was to sustain morale, explain what was going on to the men and women serving under him, and to foster and maintain diplomatic relations. Mountbatten's job, it turned out, was to keep the show on the road in a challenging theatre in which the war could not be won and that, consequently, was always a Cinderella as far as resources were concerned.

Many of SEAC's plans to rid the Andaman and Nicobar Islands, Burma, French Indo-China, Java, Malaya, Singapore, Sumatra, and Thailand of the Japanese were destined to founder because, as had been the case in the months following the Ceylon raids, resources continued to be denied – or were taken away – given the demands of other theatres.[39] The Indian Ocean region remained behind Europe and the Mediterranean in the order of priorities as far as the British government was concerned. For the Americans, it was an even lower priority, focused as they were upon 'Europe first' (with a somewhat reluctant extension into the Mediterranean) and with the Pacific always vying for primacy. The simple fact was that the Indian Ocean was a crucial theatre for reasons of logistics and the provision of resources that in early 1942 had momentarily been afforded the highest possible defensive priority as the Japanese threat waxed and these functions were seriously threatened. But now that the threat had passed, it was never going to become a theatre of offensive priority and, therefore, was denied the resources deemed necessary to rid the theatre of the Japanese.

SEAC's staff began to arrive in Kandy in early April 1944, Ceylon developing as a major Allied decision-making and command nerve centre as plans to recapture Rangoon and invade Malaya were developed, and as the Eastern Fleet turned to the offensive in order to push the Japanese out of the waters of the eastern Indian Ocean. On 15 April Mountbatten left Faridkot House, his home in Delhi, for the last time, bidding farewell to the 55 servants and then flying to Ceylon. 'On entering the South East Asia Command territory I was met by six Spitfires who escorted us down to Ratmalana airfield. Here a vast concourse was awaiting us, headed by the

36 Ziegler, *Mountbatten*, p. 279.
37 Ibid.
38 Ibid., p. 280.
39 See Chapter 20, 'The War of the Codewords', in Ziegler, *Mountbatten.*

Commander-in-Chief Ceylon, Admiral Layton, and the Commander-in-Chief Eastern Fleet, Admiral Somerville'.[40] 'Here we are', wrote Pownall:

> Very much of a change from Delhi and an improvement in many ways. The conduct of affairs from here will not be so easy but we should be able to detach ourselves from interfering in other people's affairs. Mountbatten's temperament being what it is, it's a good thing to get him away from the hurly burly of detail that tempted him in Delhi. Here we are pretty well forced to stand back. We ought to be able to work here more happily as a family party.[41]

Mountbatten described the set up in Kandy, SEAC's new home town:

> The new SEAC Headquarters consists of the Supreme Allied Command HQ in Peradeniya Botanical Gardens, the Army Group HQ and the Air Command HQ, all three of which are on different roads leading from Kandy, and each about four miles from the centre of town. The Eastern Fleet HQ (SEAC Section) are in Kandy itself and are much smaller than in Delhi, since we have the main Eastern Fleet HQ only a short distance away in Colombo.
>
> I am living with my personal staff at the King's Pavilion in Kandy. The most senior officers are living at the Suisse Hotel. Officers of Colonel's and Brigadier's rank are also living at the Suisse Hotel. Officers of Brigadier General's and Major General's rank and officers of the Wrens, Wacs [Women's Army Corps], Cwacs [Ceylon Women's Army Corps], and women civil officers are living at the Queen's [Hotel] ... The Wrennery, in which all the British and American female ratings and enlisted women live, has been built on the 8th and 9th holes of the golf course. Admiral Layton decided that, since he had had to requisition the Botanical Gardens for us, thus interfering with the pleasure of the natives, he should also requisition a part of the golf course, in order to interfere equally with the pleasure of the Europeans!.[42]

Kandy underwent a massive transformation. Wireless and signals facilities were established as a matter of priority, as communications were essential in a theatre defined by great distances between headquarters establishments and battlefronts.

> [W]e are erecting British and American Hospitals, cinemas, officers' clubs, NAAFI, etc. Our communications flight, however, has to be some distance from Kandy, as we cannot put up an airfield among the mountains. It will be realized that SEAC has become the principal, if not the only, industry of Kandy, and a lot of buildings have had to be put up. The only brick buildings, however, are the War Room and my own office block. All the remainder are either built out of wood or plaited bamboo, known as bashas or cadjan huts.

40 Ziegler (ed.), *Personal Diary*, p. 98.
41 Bond (ed.), *Chief of Staff*, pp. 162-63.
42 Ziegler (ed.), *Personal Diary*, p. 99.

> All the various organizations (of which there are a surprising number) which work under my orders have established liaison missions in my HQ and one way and another we have a very large and motley collection of people in Kandy …
>
> My own office block at Peradeniya has rooms for my personal staff, secretaries, typists etc., on one side and the Chief of Staff and Assistant Chief of Staff with their personal assistants and secretaries sit on the other side of the main entrance. Round this are grouped a series of huts housing Wedemeyer and his staff, Wheeler and his staff, Jerram and his staff, Micky and his signals organization.
>
> All the various roads have been given suitable names. The press live in Fleet Street with the Public Relations Departments and the censors. Irving Asher [an American officer with a background in the film industry] and his photographic laboratories are in Hollywood Boulevard. The Medical Advisory Division are in Harley Street. The dentist has set up his shop in Welbeck Street, etc.[43]

Mountbatten made use of local facilities too, worshipping in the chapel of Trinity College, Kandy, presenting it with a captured Japanese machine-gun at the end of the war. His personal quarters were more than satisfactory, comprising the King's Pavilion and a rest bungalow.

> The King's Pavilion was built in 1829 on the site of the house of the Prime Ministers of the old Kings of Kandy. It stands in extremely beautiful gardens, which although small are so surrounded by beautiful trees that the town is completely hidden … By the King's direction the King's Pavilion was put at my disposal and it certainly makes the whole difference having such a lovely house to live in.[44]

He first visited the rest bungalow at Ellatota near Nuwara Eliya on 22 April:

> We drove up in the afternoon, stopping for tea at the Hill Club in Nuwara Eliya. This is 6,000 feet up and it was quite cold … Although the distance is only eighty miles it took us just over three and a half hours so twisting and winding is the road. I do not know when I have seen more beautiful country, with waterfalls, tea gardens, jungle, moorland, and every possible variety of scenery … The bungalow itself is very dashing and modern, having only been completed three years ago for a rich planter.[45]

Mountbatten's perigrinations from SEAC HQ Kandy

From his new headquarters, the Supreme Allied Commander South East Asia moved at pace around his vast command. Mountbatten's schedule was crowded with official duties and constant visits to India Command's headquarters and various operational headquarters at or near the

43 Ibid., p. 100.

44 Ziegler (ed.), *Personal Diary*, pp. 100-01. He had visited the house in 1922 when travelling with the Prince of Wales on his Empire Tour. It almost certainly wasn't by the 'King's direction' that the King's Pavilion was made available to him, but by the direction of the Government of Ceylon.

45 Ibid., p. 102.

front line. The pace was intense. On 25 April 1944 he wrote in his diary that he had been 'invaded by the Dutch Minister for Colonies and Acting Governor General of the Netherlands East Indies, Dr Van Mook, the Dutch Commander-in-Chief, Admiral Helfrich, commander of the Netherlands Indies Navy serving as part of the Eastern Fleet, the Dutch Ambassador to China, Dr Lovink, who are all staying in the King's Pavilion for three or four days'.[46] Four days later he drove to Colombo to visit the carrier USS *Saratoga*, on loan to the Eastern Fleet, accompanied by Rear Admiral Clem Moody, commanding the Eastern Fleet's aircraft carriers. Following this visit, Mountbatten returned to the King's Pavilion.

> I came back in the SEAC Special which leaves Colombo each night at 1830 and gets into Kandy at 2145. It has a conference room and a private car attached in which I gave high tea to eight of our officers ... This train runs down at 0805 every morning getting in at 1115. It takes the many people who are going on by air or rail or sea from Colombo.[47]

On 6 May Mountbatten visited the Army Group Camp at Kondesalle near Kandy. 'General Playfair [the deputy commander] received me at the Army Group Commander-in-Chief's beautiful bungalow ... It has a magnificent view with the mountain ranges in the distance and cocoa and rubber plantations all around it'.[48] Interspersed with the many visits in Ceylon and frequent flights to disparate locations in Britain, Burma, China, India, and the Middle East, were innumerable commanders-in-chief conferences in Kandy to discuss the higher direction of the war. Mountbatten had sometimes to be the bearer of bad tidings, for example telling 'my Army Group Commander-in-Chief, General Sir George Giffard, that I had lost confidence in him, and was asking for his replacement'.[49] Giffard's fault was that, like Somerville, he was little disposed to view Mountbatten as his direct superior, and refused to obey Mountbatten's order to continue fighting through the monsoon season. Understandably Pownall, as Mountbatten's right-hand man, had little sympathy for Giffard or Somerville, both of whom thought that Mountbatten's role should be that of the chairman of a committee, not a supreme commander. But as Pownall wrote in his diary:

> Supreme Allied Commander is a supreme commander with a superior staff ... [and] though we are preparing to take into account C's-in-C's views (and have done our damndest to create the machinery to do so) there is no doubt who is in *command* of the whole show. 'Supreme Commander' means just that – he is not just the chairman of a committee.[50]

46 Ibid., p. 103.
47 Ibid., p. 104.
48 Ibid., p. 105.
49 Ibid., p. 106. This was in May 1944, Giffard eventually being replaced by General Sir Oliver Leese in October.
50 Bond (ed.), *Chief of Staff*, p. 117. The many pages devoted to letters and signals from Somerville to the Admiralty, naval colleagues, and Mountbatten himself regarding their disagreements bear testament to the unedifying disputes over command boundaries that came to scarred SEAC.

On 17 May 1944 Mountbatten began a two-day tour of RAF stations in Ceylon, including an inspection of the flying-boats, air crew, and ground crew of 231 Squadron of the Royal Netherlands Air Force at China Bay. He also visited the flying-boat base at Koggala, 'a newly built Flying-boat Station making use of a large lake whose height is now artificially controlled by a sill [a timber controlling the entrance to a lock or dry dock] leading to the sea. I counted some twenty flying-boats at anchor on the lake. The remainder of course were all out on patrol' (the figure indicates the great augmentation of Ceylon's flying-boat strength since the Japanese raids, when only six or seven had been available to hunt for the enemy fleet).[51] On 18 May, wrote Mountbatten, 'I drove to the Queen's Pavilion, where I was met by the Governor, Sir Andrew Caldecott, and Geoffrey Layton. I then had the unusual experience of taking the chair at a meeting with the Governor and the Commander-in-Chief in their own Government House'.[52]

Later in the month he entertained Noël Coward, who had arrived in a destroyer from Africa at Mountbatten's behest to perform for the troops in Burma, Ceylon, and India. On 31 May Mountbatten took the SEAC Special to Colombo and 'from the harbour took Admiral Somerville's barge and visited the French battleship *Richelieu*. 'She is the most lovely looking ship imaginable and quite colossal, being of some 46,000 tons displacement'.[53] Mountbatten was able to cheer the crew considerably by reporting that their wine ration was soon to be reinstated. The following day he lunched at Government House with Caldecott. 'I find him very charming and am very sorry for him as he has a crippled leg and a weak heart and his wife recently committed suicide by throwing herself out of their residence (Queen's Cottage) in Nuwara Eliya'.[54]

On 9 June Mountbatten went to Sigiriya airfield near Kandy where 'we boarded my flying wireless station, the Mercury'. Sigiriya was to all intents and purposes Mountbatten's private airport, also housing the 'Hapgift' (a Dakota given to him by Hap Arnold), a second Dakota named 'Sister Anne', and an Avro York. From Sigiriya Mountbatten flew to China Bay 'and drove down to the jetty where Clem Moody's barge met me. I got on board the *Illustrious* and addressed the 2,000 sailors on board'.[55] He then proceeded to visit the escort carrier *Atheling*, the cruiser *Phoebe*, and the Dutch destroyer *Van Galen*. After this he had lunch in the dining cabin of *Illustrious*, which he himself had designed in Norfolk Navy Yard, Virginia (he had been chosen to command the ship, though promotion supervened).

In late June Mountbatten was prevailed upon by his staff to take some leave. He retreated to his bungalow in the highlands, half an hour's journey by jeep and in easy reach of dispatch riders bringing work to him, and connected to headquarters by a scrambler telephone. Respite over, on 27 June he flew from Sigiriya to Delhi, where he stayed at Viceroy's House. From here he visited Burma at a time when the fighting around Myitkyina was at its heaviest. On 1 July he flew to Dimapur, and 'then started off without delay in a convoy of jeeps down the

51 Ziegler (ed.), *Personal Diary*, p. 107. Excellent shots of the base can be seen on the November 1944 Air Ministry film 'Ceylon flying-boat base', Imperial War Museum (IWM), London, ABY 61.

52 Ziegler (ed.), *Personal Diary*, p. 107.

53 Ibid., p. 109.

54 *The Argus* of 3/1/44 records that Lady Olive Caldecott died after a 'fall' from a window of Queen's Cottage, the Governor's hill station residence in Nuwara Eliya. A Reuters report said that it was 'officially stated' that the 'fall occurred while she was in a state of temporary mental depression due to insomnia and neurosis'. Intriguing ...

55 Ziegler (ed.), *Personal Diary* p. 111.

famous Manipur road for Kohima', where his party spent three hours going over the battlefield, including the Naga village, Church Knoll, the district commissioner's tennis court and bungalow, and Garrison Hill.[56] The Battle of Kohima in Nagaland, north-east India, had ended on 22 June and led to the relief of Imphal, actions that stemmed the Japanese U Go offensive and marked a decisive turning point in the war in this theatre.

On 4 July he returned to Ceylon. His travels next took him to London, departing Sigiriya on 2 August following meetings with his commanders-in-chief to discuss plans for an amphibious assault on Rangoon in order to link with the Fourteenth Army's advance on Mandalay. On 8 September he was back in Delhi before visiting Cox's Bazaar, where he was met by the new Air Commodore Commanding 224 Group, the Earl of Bandon ('Paddy Bandon … a delightful chap whom I knew in Delhi').[57] They left by jeep for Ramu, encountering monsoon rain in the Arakan as they drove to Imphal. On 11 September Mountbatten arrived at Myitkyina in the Sister Anne, landing in a queue with about 20 Dakotas of the Air Supply Squadron, having lost their fighter escort. It was home again after this latest foray to the Burma front. 'We flew direct across the Bay of Bengal to Ceylon and landed at Ratmalana at 1700'.[58] He arrived at Kandy station at 9:45pm and drove to the King's Pavilion, where he found waiting for him urgent telegrams from Churchill, who was in Canada. Immediate SEAC representation was required at the Quebec conference – Quadrant, as it would become known – which necessitated pulling a brigadier out of a bridge party and dispatching him to Canada at 3am.[59]

In Kandy Mountbatten and his staff busied themselves with planning for Burma and the offensive to regain Malaya. In the process he 'gave a dinner party confined to generals, admirals, and air marshals, excluding brigadiers, air commodores, and commodores, and still had thirty guests', the type of detail regarding the size of his command and the numbers of people who served under him that Mountbatten revelled in.[60] During this period Mountbatten discovered that he had been allocated the resources necessary for Operation Dracula, the amphibious and airborne attack Rangoon. The news, wrote Pownall, put him 'in the seventh Heaven of delight'.[61]

Back in Kandy on 9 October 1944 after a visit to a range of destinations in India, Mountbatten received a telegram from Churchill requesting a face-to-face meeting in Cairo. Arriving there on 15 October ('Ceylon to Cairo in 19 hours'), he was put up at the villa of the Resident Minister, Lord Moyne (less than a month before Moyne was assassinated on the steps of the building by the Stern Gang).[62] On 20 October Mountbatten went to the airport to meet the prime minister's party, numbering over 50 and including Anthony Eden, Field Marshal Sir Alan Brooke, and General Sir Hastings Ismay. Mountbatten had breakfast with the PM, and afterwards 'went through the usual business of being told that I opened my mouth too wide, asked for too

56 Ibid., p. 116.
57 Ibid., p. 129.
58 Ibid., p. 133.
59 Ibid., p. 133.
60 Ibid., p. 134.
61 Bond (ed.), *Chief of Staff*, p. 187. Pownall noted that while the British wanted Rangoon as a stepping stone to the reconquest of Burma, the Americans were only interested in it as a route for channelling aid to China.
62 Ziegler (ed.), *Personal Diary*, p. 141.

many resources, and that my Army had too big a tail'.[63] After this routine Churchillian admonishment, Mountbatten was pleased when Eden revealed that Churchill had said:

> I give Dickie full marks; we gave him a lousy job, and we have given him absolutely no help or assistance ever since he has been there, in fact the reverse; but nevertheless he has kept the show running and always turns up smiling whatever we do to him. We really must try and help him all we can in future.[64]

Four days later the Supreme Commander was back in India, attending a parade in front of the Red Fort in Old Delhi during which Viceroy Wavell presented four Victoria Crosses and one George Cross. The following day he landed in Ceylon at Ratmalana. At Kandy, the Governor of Burma, Sir Reginald Dorman-Smith, arrived with General Giffard, and stayed with Mountbatten. Adding to the menagerie lodged at King's Pavilion, the Free French Mission to SEAC, under General Roger Blaizot, arrived soon after. On 4 November Mountbatten flew to Vavuniya airfield in northern Ceylon and then travelled by jeep to visit the 28th East African Brigade. Later, Lieutenant-General Leese arrived to replace Giffard.

In August Admiral Sir Bruce Fraser had succeeded Somerville at the helm of the Eastern Fleet. The fleet had by this stage build up to a great strength, for it was soon to be split in two, the more powerful portion becoming the British Pacific Fleet, deployed to the Pacific to aid the Americans against the Japanese. 'On 12 November', Mountbatten wrote, 'Bruce Fraser came up for a farewell before taking the British Pacific Fleet to Australia'.[65] As Fraser took this newly-formed fleet eastwards, the naval forces that remained in Ceylon were designated the East Indies Fleet, commanded by Admiral Sir Arthur Power. Four days later Mountbatten flew from Ratmalana to 'the great naval and air base at Addu Atoll' in an American B-25 Mitchell bomber. On 17 November he took off from Koggala lagoon and flew to the new RAF station at Kankesanturai in Ceylon's extreme north. He was then driven with Colonel Sir Humphry Tollemache of the Royal Marines to Hammenhiel Camp, on a small island between Kayts and Karaitivu islands on the Jaffna peninsula, 'the base which I have started for the Small Operations Group', one of the many special operations units now massing in Ceylon.[66]

In early December Mountbatten went back to Imphal, where he witnessed the investiture of a clutch of British generals: 'I heard for the first time in my life the remarkable order, "Lieutenant-Generals – Quick March!", as Bill Slim and his three Corps Commanders stepped off smartly ... The King had given special permission for the Viceroy to knight these generals on the field of battle'.[67] On 16 December Mountbatten was at Kalewa with the 11th East African Division, and crossed the Chindwin over a Bailey bridge 1,152 feet long. He then went to the headquarters of the 82nd West African Division, and visited territory that had been under Japanese occupation only the day before, as the Allied advance in Burma gathered pace.[68]

63 Ibid., p. 143
64 Ibid., p. 145.
65 Ibid., pp. 150-51.
66 Ibid., 154.
67 Ibid., p. 156.
68 Ibid., p. 157.

On 22 December 1944 Mountbatten was back in Kandy. Whilst there, Prince Philip arrived on leave and Mountbatten took him and Lieutenant General Sir Frederick 'Boy' Browning, Pownall's replacement as SEAC Chief of Staff, to a small Christmas Eve party. Browning was staying with Mountbatten at the King's Pavilion, and the party was a 'chaotic occasion', partly because the cook got drunk and served the meal backwards.[69] Browning needed to get to know all of the command's personalities as quickly as possible, including the numerous Chinese, French and Dutch generals whom he met ('but what they do', he wrote to his wife Daphne du Maurier, 'I really don't know').[70] Eventually he managed to find his own accommodation at Malabar House, located on a hill overlooking the beautiful Kandy lake, early mornings alive with the sound of drumming from the Temple of the Tooth. Browning described SEAC as 'a very curious set up':

> By the end of 1944 it had become a large and complex structure and dealt with a multiplicity of issues, interservice, inter-allied and inter-theatre. It was the ultimate planning authority for military campaigns and was deeply concerned with political questions, particularly in liberated territories ... Some of those visited Kandy and attended meetings regarded it as an extraordinary circus, but it was necessary to satisfy Mountbatten that progress was being made on all fronts and to keep him fully briefed, although at arms length on everything except matters of strategy and principle.[71]

Mountbatten spent Christmas Day going around one mess after another making speeches. Every mess he went to seemed to have at least one large elephant outside and one small elephant inside, and at the Wrennery he went for a ride on one surrounded by Wrens. As the New Year of 1945 dawned, Mountbatten was lunching at the King's Pavilion with the outgoing Commander-in-Chief Ceylon, Admiral Layton, and his successor, Lieutenant General Sir Harry Wetherall. On 10 January he took the train to Colombo, changing during the journey into white tunic, 'and on arrival I went straight to the Queen's House, where I met Harry and Alice Gloucester', the Duke of Gloucester and his wife who were on their way to Australia where he was to become Governor-General. They spent a day in Colombo at the Queen's House, and there was an official sherry party at midday for Ceylonese dignitaries. 'Several of them said, rather sourly', Mountbatten wrote: '"We had begun to think you were a myth, as none of us ever met you", to which I replied: "Socially you can continue to regard me as a myth, as I am only out here on a war job"'.[72] While clearly not at all interested in becoming involved in Ceylon's social scene, Mountbatten remained devoted to touring among the men and women serving under him, also on 'war jobs' in the east. On 11 January he went round ship after ship in Tricomalee harbour, dining aboard *Illustrious* with all the flag officers and captains of the British Pacific Fleet, about to depart for waters further east, and he made a special effort to visit Prince Philip's ship, the

69 Richard Mead, *General 'Boy': The Life of Lieutenant General Sir Frederick Browning GCVO, KBE, DSO, DL* (Barnsley: Pen and Sword, 2010), chapter 23, 'Kandy (December 1944-May 1945)', location 4038 Kindle version.
70 Ibid., location 4050.
71 Ibid., location 4073.
72 Ziegler (ed.), *Personal Diary*, p. 166.

destroyer *Whelp*. 'I must have talked to over 12,000 sailors in the course of the day and shaken hands with hundreds of officers and selected men', he wrote.[73]

Two days later Mountbatten was in New Delhi. 'I was driven straight to the Viceroy's House, where I found Edwina, who had arrived the night before from England, via Karachi, where she had spent a couple of days visiting hospitals' in her role as Superintendent-in-Chief of the St John Ambulance Brigade.[74] The back and forth between Ceylon, Burma, and India continued. On 30 January Mountbatten left Kandy for Colombo and later in the day landed at Poona where Edwina was waiting with the Governor of Bombay. They 'drove straight to Government House, where we had been given the rooms originally used by David (Prince of Wales) when he and I were out there in 1921'.[75] The following day they watched George Formby's opening show for the troops, attended by over 5,000 people. On 3 February he was back in Ceylon for an appointment with the dentist, watched through the window by a Ceylonese gardener and six American GIs. He was about to protest at this impertinent audience 'when one of the Americans threw a log, aimed at an eight foot snake near the window'. On 15 February he 'worked all day at high pressure until 1840, when I drove to Colombo. At 2200 I went to Radio SEAC studios to make a recording to be broadcast to the troops on the occasion of the fall of Mandalay' (though imperial forces were on the outskirts of the famous town at this point, it was to take more than a month before the Japanese exited it and the British could formally claim its capture with the occupation of Fort Dufferin).[76]

The frenetic pace of activity continued during a prolonged period in India. On 12 March Mountbatten flew back to Ceylon after addressing 80 officers of brigadier rank upwards at GHQ India, thanking India Command for all it had done for SEAC. The following day Lord Roger and Lady Keyes, on a goodwill tour of the Empire, arrived to spend a few days on their way back from Australia.[77] Mountbatten was then off for more conferences in Burma, and on 22 March walked up Mandalay Hill and the covered stairway of the Buddhist colony. He drove to Fort Dufferin, 'the walls of which had withstood all British artillery fire and had only been breached by a 2,000-pound RAF bomb'.[78]

Back in Ceylon, on 29 March he was taken by barge to inspect the headquarters of the Ceylon Royal Naval Volunteer Reserve in Colombo.

> On way back stopped off aboard HMS *Renown*. The captain, Basil Brook, was a watch-keeper in the *Queen Elizabeth* with me in the last war. The last big ship I had served in in Colombo harbour curiously enough was the *Renown* in 1922 [when on the Prince of Wales' Empire Tour]... Then on to Queen's House where I got involved in a colossal lunch party which the Governor and Lady Moore were giving for the Red Cross and St John lady workers in Colombo. Then on to make a recording at the Colombo Broadcasting Station,

73 Ibid., p. 168.
74 Ibid., p. 168.
75 Ibid., p. 177.
76 Ibid., p. 180.
77 Ibid., p. 195.
78 Ibid., p. 196.

> then on to visit HMS *Mayina*, the naval transit camp, then on to visit the naval barracks at HMS *Lanka* during a severe tropical rain storm.[79]

The following day he continued his busy tour of military installations in Colombo, going all over the headquarters of Force 136, SOE's eastern branch now headquartered in Ceylon, before flying from Ratmalana to Koggala, from where he 'drove to the lovely old town of Galle where I met Edwina at the conclusion of her St John inspection. We drove all round the fascinating old Dutch town and went shopping, finally ending up at Klosenberg Bay where we bathed and had a picnic lunch'.[80] On 5 April he 'gave a lunch party for all the Flag, General, and Air Officers in Kandy, British, American, Chinese, Dutch, and French, to meet Edwina'.[81] Then it was off to Burma for more meetings.

On 1 June Mountbatten landed at the new SEAC airstrip in the mountains 19 miles from Kandy, the first aircraft officially to do so, hundreds of workmen lining the runway and cheering. On 14 June he had meetings with his air and naval commanders-in-chief, Sir Keith Park and Sir Arthur Power, and then took off for Rangoon, occupied by imperial forces the previous month, where he attended a parade with Burmese people lining the streets.[82] At the Parade Ground there was a 17-gun salute from the Royal Field Artillery, and a huge march past that took over half an hour in columns of six to pass the saluting base. There was then a naval review with the cruisers *Cumberland* and *Ceylon* at the head. Back in Kandy on 25 June, Mountbatten's 45th birthday, the 'Americans gave a colossal party' at the Kandy Officers' Club. 'I had no idea I had so many Americans in Kandy, as there must have been between two and three hundred' in attendance.[83] On 12 July 1945 Mountbatten flew to the Philippines, landing in Manila to meet General MacArthur and Admiral Kincaid. Again demonstrating his capacity to get on with people whom others loathed, he wrote that MacArthur was 'one of the most charming and remarkable characters I have ever met, and so sympathetic and friendly towards SEAC'.

The war against Japan was entering its final weeks, though at this time, of course, it was not known that the atomic bombs would bring about a precipitous conclusion to hostilities, and a huge built up of British arms was anticipated in the east to assist the Americans in their assault on the Japanese home islands, while Mountbatten's long-awaited assault on Malaya prepared to get underway.

79 Ibid., p. 197.
80 Ibid., p. 198.
81 Ibid., p. 199.
82 Park, like Browning, was another well-known name in the European theatre now being deployed east for the 'final push' in the war against Japan. With his wife, Dol, he flew from Northolt in a Dakota via Malta, Cairo, and Calcutta in February 1945. As soon as he arrived in Ceylon, he had a major decision to make, agreeing to supply General Slim's Fourteenth Army in Burma by air throughout its advance on Rangoon. This involved sustaining over 300,000 men, the air force supplying the army with 2,000 tons of supplies per day. Slim's army was almost entirely supplied by the American Combat Cargo Task Force, whilst the RAF's 221 Group provided artillery support. Park made a speech to his staff at his Kandy headquarters on 2 March, then spent a week touring his enormous new command, travelling over 17,000 miles before the month was out.
83 Ziegler (ed.), *Personal Diary*, p. 218.

Ceylon, island of headquarters

Many of the British servicemen and women sent to Ceylon were involved in the world of intelligence-gathering and covert operations. Donald Horton, for example, worked at Far East Combined Bureau at HMS *Anderson* near Colombo, where staff operated around 100 wireless sets listening in to the Japanese.[84] Graham Rouse, meanwhile, belonged to a Deceptive Warfare Unit sent to Ceylon in advance of the anticipated landings in Japanese-occupied territory. The unit's job was to go into bays away from the actual landing beaches and play the sound of activity through special loudspeakers, and to deploy searchlights to confuse the enemy, all under the cover of smokescreens.[85]

In addition to its role as a base for air and maritime forces conducting operations across the region, and a training and rest and recuperation base for land forces involved in the Burma campaign, Ceylon was a major British and Allied nerve centre boasting significant administrative, planning, and intelligence-gathering facilities as well as a range of military bases and foreign military delegations. Orbiting SEAC headquarters in Kandy were a host of subordinate headquarters including those of the Eastern Fleet and the RAF's 222 Group with responsibilities stretching across the Indian Ocean from Africa to Asia. It was also home to Far East Combined Bureau which, along with Wireless Experimental Station (WEC) Delhi, was Britain's major regional Bletchley Park outstation. Ceylon also hosted a range of special forces outfits involved in the war behind enemy lines, the gathering of information ahead of the long-anticipated Allied reconquest, and good old-fashioned spying, by the latter stages of the war focused more on one's allies than one's enemies.

Ceylon was home to so many headquarters establishments for a number of reasons. One was the strategic significance the island had attained following the fall of Singapore, when by default it became home to the Eastern Fleet. Its geographical location also meant that it was a sensible setting for forces involved in sea lane protection across the Indian Ocean, located nicely enough to warrant, for example, its own air group command. Its location also made it a good base for troops heading to or seeking relief from the war in Burma, for reasons of transport and political considerations in many ways a less troublesome spot than India. The move of SEAC's headquarters to the island in April 1944 then caused a range of subordinate headquarters and outfits to gravitate to the island, in order to be as close to the regional decision-making centre as possible.

Tussles for control of resources among military commanders responsible for operations in places such as Ceylon, East Africa, and India led to a centralization of command, and this process witnessed an accretion of authority to headquarters establishments in Ceylon. One example was Admiral Somerville's battle to gain control over the region's flying-boat resources. Another was the creation of the Indian Ocean General Reconnaissance Operations, which went by the ungainly acronym IOGROPS. Up until its creation, there were parcels of anti-submarine aircraft spread out all round the Indian Ocean but no central control. For instance the South African Air Force operated land-based aircraft from places such as Walvis Bay and Cape Town, RAF flying-boats worked from St Lucia, Madagascar, Pamanzi in the Comoro Islands,

84 BBC World War Two People's War oral history archive, Donald Horton, 'My Naval Service in World War Two', A4377936.

85 BBC World War Two People's War oral history archive, Graham Rouse, 'Working with the German Navy', A3536651.

Dar-es-Salaam, and Mombasa under Air Headquarters East Africa in Nairobi; Wellingtons flew from Aden and Mogadishu under Air Headquarters Aden; flying-boats all round India came under the command of Air Headquarters Bangalore; and other flying-boats operated under Air Headquarters 222 Group Ceylon with advanced bases across the Indian Ocean in places as far away as Diego Garcia, their work supplemented by land-based aircraft flying from places such as Kankesanturai.[86]

All of these forces were doing the same thing – protecting convoys, hunting for enemy vessels, mounting general reconnaissance patrols, searching for survivors. There was clearly a case to be made for better coordination of the combined efforts of these disparate forces, and so IOGROPS was formed. Air Marshal Durstan, commanding 222 Group Ceylon, decided that as a first step all merchant shipping should be routed in lanes which could be patrolled, and the navy agreed. Joint naval-air operations rooms were set up in Colombo (C-in-C Eastern Fleet and AOC 222 Group), Bangalore, Bombay, Karachi, Aden, Mombasa, Durban, with Colombo exercising overall control.

Intelligence-gathering and covert operations outfits proliferated because of the importance ascribed to intelligence, and the many and sophisticated ways in which it was gathered and processed. Special forces and 'behind enemy lines' outfits sprouted because this was a region where the enemy occupied vast swathes of territory that the Allies intended to reclaim. They planned to do so by air and land operations in Burma, along with amphibious and maritime operations as they advanced through the Arakan, assaulted Rangoon, and invaded Malaya and the Dutch East Indies. All such operations would benefit from, indeed demanded, prior penetration, the fostering of resistance movements, and the gathering of data on a range of topics including enemy strengths and unit locations, inshore waterways, tidal currents, and the material composition of beaches (was beach 'X' firm enough to take a Bren gun carrier or a tank, for instance?) in order to assess their accessibility for men and vehicles who would need to get ashore safely and then move off beach heads and begin advancing inland.

While not quite 'fortress Europe' ahead of D-Day, this represented an enormous challenge, involving the build up of sufficient air, land, and maritime forces and the procurement of requisite backing for plans from the Anglo-American political-military leadership.[87] Meanwhile, special operations behind enemy lines could provide intelligence on the enemy, prepare sabotage operations for when the moment of invasion arrived, and train, arm, and help organize indigenous resistance movements. Special 'beach assault' style forces could be trained and prepared, specialist teams inserted, and covert missions run by the type of people who gathered data on tides, beach conditions, and all the vital information required before the Allies started sending men in landing craft towards enemy-held shores.

One of these outfits was the Special Boat Unit, renamed the Small Operations Group (SOG) in January 1944, based at Camp Hammenhiel. One of its units was Detachment 385, trained by Lieutenant Colonel H. G. Hasler, who had been appointed by Mountbatten as Officer Commanding Special Operations Group, SEAC. It was formed in July 1944 when over 100 officers and men of the marines arrived in Colombo having passed a selection programme in Britain, responding to notices calling for volunteers for 'hazardous duties' and specifying that

86 Banks, *Wings of the Dawning*, p. 287.

87 See H. P. Willmott, *Grave of a Dozen Schemes: British Naval Planning and the War Against Japan, 1943-1945* (Shrewsbury: Airlife, 1996).

they needed to be strong swimmers.[88] At Hammenhiel the men lived in tents, and their numbers were further whittled down through arduous training and tests, including courses in jungle warfare, small boat handling and seamanship, snorkels and oxygen cylinders, simulated attacks on ships, and demolitions. Specially staged battles were followed by trips to Trincomalee harbour and a climb up 7,360-foot Adam's Peak. The detachment was transferred to Burma in February 1945. Known as Mountbatten's 'private navy', SOG also included Combined Operations Pilotage Parties (COPP), specifically trained to gather information on beaches and waterways. In mid-April 1944 COPP 8 sailed in the submarine *Stoic* to survey prospective invasion beaches.[89]

Ceylon was a major base for Force 136, the name adopted for SOE in the east in April 1944, its personnel operating in Burma, Malay, Sumatra, and Thailand. In September 1942 Christopher Hudson had visited Ceylon to organize a branch of SOE's India Mission. There he found that Lieutenant Colonel Frederick Innes Tremlett had already begun preparations. Originally run from Meerut, Force 136's headquarters transferred to Ceylon in late 1944. Its headquarters was established at Kandy in a purpose-built compound and a training facility was opened in a commandeered beach-side mansion at Mount Lavinia originally built as a gubernatorial residence by Lieutenant General Sir Edward Barnes, the road-building governor of Ceylon in the early nineteenth century. It provided a 'far more convenient and secret place from which to direct operations and in which to brief agents, than had been the Colombo Galle Face Hotel'.[90] Holding camps were opened at Horana for men destined for Burma, with an Advanced Operations School located on an island in China Bay. Here there were two huts on a coconut estate, one for sleeping, the other used as a mess, where gin and coconut milk was a favourite. There was a beach right in front of the camp, where training with folboats (a type of collapsible kayak) took place.[91] In January 1944 three bungalows were acquired for the use of Force 136 men destined for Malaya. A bungalow buried deep in a tea plantation at Yawalatene was also acquired. Operatives were inserted behind enemy lines by British and Dutch submarines and Liberator squadrons.

The first Force 136 operation launched from Ceylon was Operation Bunkum, a reconnaissance of the Andaman Islands in which agents were inserted by submarine. A great deal of work was also undertaken to support armed resistance in Thailand. For example, a group of Thai students from Britain was sent to Ceylon, from where they boarded the submarine *Tactician* and were taken to a rendezvous off the coast of Thailand. By August 1945 Force 136 had armed several thousand Thai people. Ceylon was also used to train agents for Mountbatten's abortive ? assault on the island of Phuket off the coast of Thailand. Force 136's Ceylon-based Anglo-Dutch country section focused its attention on Sumatra and included members of the Dutch

88 Peter Haining, *The Banzai Hunters: The Forgotten Armada of Little Ships that Defeated the Japanese, 1944-1945* (London: Robson Books, 2006), p. 155. See Bruce Wright, *Frogmen of Burma: The Story of the Sea Reconnaissance Unit* (London: Kimber, 1970). It is interesting to note how many of these 'memoir' type books written in the 1950s, 60s, and 70s have forewords by Mountbatten, a reflection of his willingness to retain 'leadership' of the South East Asia Command theatre in the historical record, his willingness to undertake such tasks, and the desire of those who served under him to have his imprimatur on their work.

89 Trenowden, *Operations Most Secret*, p. 139. In this book see chapter 4, 'Singapore, Ceylon, and the Andaman Interlude' and chapter 5, 'Ceylon Headquarters Established'.

90 Ibid., p. 77.

91 Ibid., p. 118.

Corps Insulinde. RAF Special Duties squadrons, usually flying long-range Liberators, were used to parachute agents and supplies into occupied territory, and most sorties were flown from Ceylon bases. Freddy Spencer Chapman's Force 136 team in occupied Malaya were in contact with headquarters in Ceylon and air supplies from the island supported the 3,500-plus Malayans trained to harass the Japanese when the British mounted their amphibious assault late in the war. Liberators of 357 Squadron from Minneriya flew 249 sorties in June and July 1945 in support of these forces.

Ceylon was a base for other clandestine organizations too. The Secret Intelligence Service (MI6), under the guise of the Inter-Services Liaison Department (ISLD), mounted missions in occupied territory, for example transferring agents to Penang Island from the submarine *Tactician*. The American Office of Strategic Services (OSS) was granted permission by Mountbatten to establish itself in Ceylon and provided with training camps in Galle, Clodagh and Trincomalee, with headquarters at Kandy and a supply depot at Colombo.[92] OSS was active in the China-Burma-India theatre, even though General William Donavan, Director of OSS and forefather of the CIA, could not persuade MacArthur or Nimitz to allow it to operate in the Pacific.[93] 101 Detachment was based in Burma and 404 Detachment in Ceylon, accommodated in a large bungalow next to St Peter's College near Colombo. It had facilities for waterborne training at Galle and for jungle training at Clodagh and Dambulla. OSS Operational Groups conducted irregular warfare directly against the enemy and worked with resistance groups, and also gathered military intelligence. A 'morale operations' section started a radio station near Chittagong that imitated Thai-language Radio Tokyo broadcasts in Thailand. OSS operatives radioed from Bangkok to Ceylon, and Free Thai agents set up network across Thailand to radio intelligence back to the island. OSS Maritime Unit swimmer units in Ceylon were used to test new breathing apparatus. OSS's Arakan Field Unit was based in Ceylon, composed of Detachment 404 specialists. Its work included surveying beaches and rivers along the Burmese coast, inserting agents, and supporting British landings in spring 1945. OSS was also collecting political intelligence regarding the intentions of its allies in the post-war world. A joint SEAC Translation and Interrogation Centre was based in a purpose-built camp at Mahara, eight miles from Ceylon. Among other things, it served as a holding tank for potential agents, some of whom had been snatched from junks off the coast of Japanese-held territory. In the space of a few weeks in the summer of 1944 the centre also received 100 enemy prisoners, divided into Japanese and non-Japanese wings.[94]

Ceylon was also one of the British Empire's main intelligence-gathering hubs, even before the war the site of a wireless transmitting station at Naval Headquarters Colombo, which covered the area north to India and Burma, east to Malaya, south to Antarctica, and west to Madagascar.[95] There was a corresponding transmitting station in each of the Empire's main regions and these stations sent out hundreds of thousands of messages every month, with the

92 See Richard Aldrich, *Intelligence and the War Against Japan: Britain, America, and the Politics of Secret Service* (Cambridge: Cambridge University Press, 2000), pp. 174-75.

93 Eugene Liptak, *Office of Strategic Services, 1942-45: The World War II Origins of the CIA* (Oxford: Osprey, 2009).

94 Aldrich, *Intelligence and the War against Japan*.

95 See map in Brian Lavery, *Churchill's Navy: The Ships, Men, and Organization, 1939-1945* (London: Conway, 2006), Admiralty radio broadcasting areas 1942, p. 35.

latest Admiralty orders and information to ships at sea, 'the Area Broadcast, which all ships listened to'.[96]

In this vast theatre ULTRA intelligence was used to locate and destroy enemy forces, particularly useful in the search for enemy submarines and their supply vessels. The naval element of Far East Combined Bureau, an inter-service intelligence facility, had moved from Hong Kong to Singapore in August 1939, and soon after the attack on Pearl Harbor was relocated to Colombo. Under this dispersal, some army and RAF codebreakers were sent to WEC in Delhi, and the navy codebreakers were sent to Ceylon, to be established in Pembroke College, an Indian boys' school near Colombo. The codebreakers arrived here on 14 January 1942, and the Wrens were billeted in a Wrennery in Galle Road, Colpetty, near Colombo, in what had been a girls school and was informally known as the 'Looney Bin'.[97] The Colombo outfit was responsible for all British SIGINT and cryptanalytic activities in East and Southeast Asia, from Singapore to Ceylon.

The station was operational in Colombo by the end of January 1942 and decrypted Japanese naval messages and encrypted the JN 25 code (the main Imperial Japanese Navy code). The intercepted messages concerned the movement of Japanese submarines, major surface combatants, and convoys. Its radio intelligence facilities included radio fingerprinting, direction-finding stations, a 'Y' service station, and a naval and military cryptanalysis section. When Ceylon was threatened, it was moved to Mombasa along with Eastern Fleet headquarters.[98] Here it took over an Indian boys' school a mile outside of Mombasa that became the shore base HMS *Alidina*. The civilian wireless operators were left behind in Colombo with codebreakers in an attempt to keep continuity on the JN 25 operation, and they were able to make a major contribution by decrypting JN 25 messages revealing Japanese movements in the Pacific before the Battle of the Coral Sea. Returning to Colombo in September 1943 when the Eastern Fleet headquarters relocated, HMS *Anderson* developed as 'the first purpose-built sigint facility in the Far East and was conceived on a huge scale', its key purpose to work on JN 25.

> The intercept station and codebreaking operation had to be set up on the only available site at the Anderson Golf Course, just six miles from the Colombo [naval] HQ… This was hardly an ideal site for intercepting radio traffic, stuck between the railway line and a main road, directly under the flight path of aircraft flying into the Racecourse Aerodrome and far too close to a 33,000-volt high-tension electricity supply.
>
> *Anderson* was spaciously laid out on a level, open site surrounded by jungle. Dozens of single-storey huts with shallow verandahs lined the roads, with beds of shrubs softening their rectangular shapes. Some of the buildings had tiled roofs, but most were clad in rattan, which was cooler. The all-important direction-finding hut stood alone, bristling with aerials, in a clear, round space 200 yards in diameter, with no other structures near it.
>
> The main reception area had some 100 receiver bays which monitored the medium-frequency bands most used by the Japanese. Each bay was operated by one or two operators, who were allotted a single Japanese radio channel to monitor: their job was to record all signals, and to alert their superiors if they detected transmissions from an enemy vessel …

96 Ibid.
97 Aldrich, *Intelligence and the War Against Japan*.
98 When it moved from Hong Kong, the army and RAF returned to their respective services.

> Anderson was able to decipher Purple, the code used by the Japanese for diplomatic messages ... and the station also received Ultra decrypts from Bletchley Park; but its principal strength was its ability to read the 'fingerprints' of individual Japanese ships' transmissions.[99]

HMS *Anderson*

> was primarily concerned with Japanese naval signals, and served as an outstation of the Japanese Naval Section of the GCCS [Government Code and Cypher School] at Bletchley Park. It also served as a DF [Direction Finding] station for the Royal Navy. The third station was at Powder Island, just south-west of Trincomalee ... It was equipped with both HF [High Frequency] and MF [Medium Frequency] DF facilities. The fourth site was at Hambantota, which served as a direction-finding station.[100]

By 1944 *Anderson*'s main section, working on the JN 25 code, was handling 150 to 200 messages a day. Other sections looked at JN 11 (another naval code) and JN 40 (a merchant shipping code), and Japanese naval air codes. 'Colombo was one of three major Allied SIGINT centres that worked on Japanese naval traffic – the others being the US Navy's OP-20G in Washington DC, and the Fleet Radio Unit, Melbourne (FRUMEL)'.[101] The main receiving room held about one hundred receiver bays, and 'radio communications between all the main Japanese bases in South-East Asia were covered continuously at *Anderson*'. Originating in the need to keep in touch with Australian military establishments, for intelligence and other purposes, a regular air service to and from Ceylon was inaugurated. The first flight took off from Koggala lake on 10 July 1943, arriving on the Swan River in Perth 28 hours latter. Liberators flying from Ratmalana soon joined the service, and the airbase at Negombo was also employed as it expanded.[102]

Many female service personnel arrived in Ceylon as members of the Wrens to perform the manifold tasks associated with intercepting and breaking codes, *Anderson*'s staff reaching over 1,200 in 1944 with plans to rise further to over 1,700.[103] From late 1943 the Colombo code-breakers experienced enhanced results because of improved reception, a dramatic increase in staff and equipment, and the promise of direct access to American intercepted code recoveries. This was as part of the British-USA (BRUSA) Agreement reached between Bletchley Park and the American army, and by June 1944 Colombo was linked to the Hawaii and Melbourne code-breaking outfits.[104]

99 Duff Hart-Davis, *Man of War: Officer, Adventurer, Agent* (London: Arrow, 2003), p. 267-68.

100 Desmond Ball, *Signals Intelligence (SIGINT) in South Asia: India, Pakistan, Sri Lanka (Ceylon)* (Canberra: The Australian National University, 1996), p. 8.

101 Ibid., p. 69.

102 Roger Thiedeman, 'Koggala, Catalinas, and the Double Sunrise', *Sri Lanka Sunday Times*, 27/2/00.

103 Aldrich, *Intelligence and the War Against Japan*, p. 244. In his section 'HMS *Anderson*: Sigint in SEAC, 1943-1944', Aldrich details Admiral Somerville's battles with the Admiralty and Bletchley Park over resources for *Anderson*, which formed part of his command, leading to a direct appeal to the Chiefs of Staff. More generally, see chapter 10, 'Secret Service and Mountbatten's South East Asia Command'.

104 Intelligence breaks were not a one-way street. In May 1942 the Australian steamer *Nankin* was captured by the German auxiliary cruiser *Thor* off Western Australia. It was carrying mail for Ceylon, including top secret summaries of the combined operations intelligence centre in Wellington. It

Along with Allied codebreaking bases in Melbourne and Hawaii, Colombo also correctly identified Midway as a major Japanese target over two months before the defining naval engagement. Breaking the JN 25 cipher led to effective interceptions of Japanese forces, some of them in the Indian Ocean. The heavy cruiser *Haguro*, destroyed after a large force of East Indies Station warships left Trincomalee following intelligence reports, was one of its victims:

> The sinking of the *Haguro*, and the contributions played by [HMS] *Anderson* [the Ceylon code-breaking unit] in providing intelligence on the Japanese navy's movements and intentions during the attacks on the Philippines, Okinawa, and Rangoon, led to a congratulatory telegram from Bletchley Park and a morale-boosting visit to the station from Mountbatten himself, during which the Supreme Allied Commander South-East Asia told the Royal Navy codebreakers they were worth 'ten divisions'.[105]

Warships operating from Ceylon extended the Allies' intelligence-gathering reach. Enemy signals in and around Sumatra and Java were monitored by vessels taking part in offensive operations east and south-east of Ceylon, 'an enormous tract of water which was particularly hard to cover by normal intercept arrangements'.[106] RAF Wireless Units based at HMS *Anderson* provided personnel for 'Float' parties, which were RAF Y sections installed on capital ships to give warning of air attacks. 357 Wireless Unit had a strength in the summer of 1944 of 190 officers and men. The first RAF Y Float party served on *Renown* during Operation Millet in October 1944.[107] Another party served aboard the carrier *Illustrious* off the north coast of Sumatra in December 1944 and monitored all Japanese air activity in the target area. This continued to be the norm, and during Operation Stacey, an East Indies Fleet photographic reconnaissance mission over Penang and the Kra Isthmus in February 1945, the Y party supported the operation by providing tactical information on air movements and information on enemy reactions.[108]

The SIGINT site at Peradeniya directly serviced Mountbatten's SEAC headquarters and the subordinate air and ground headquarters for the theatre – Air Command SEA and Allied Land Forces SEA. It operated as a joint or Allied activity, with close links to the facilities in Brisbane and Delhi. 'It was primarily concerned with compilation of order-of-battle intelligence from SIGINT produced by allied SIGINT activities elsewhere, and the dissemination of "authoritative estimates of Japanese order of battle, dispositions, and capabilities" to the various theatre headquarters'.[109]

WEC concentrated on Japanese army and air force codes and cyphers. Operational control was exercised through Indian Wireless Intelligence Service, controlled by GHQ India in Delhi, in turn subordinate to SEAC in Kandy. WEC served as the coordination centre for all British

referred to ULTRA intelligence, though, very luckily, the material was not passed to the Japanese (who would have seen that their naval cipher had been broken). This intelligence lapse, however, could have had catastrophic consequences, and was kept secret by British governments for decades after the war.

105 Michael Smith, *The Emperor's Codes: Bletchley Park and the Breaking of Japan's Secret Ciphers* (London: Bantam, 2000), p. 130.

106 Alan Stripp, *Codebreaker in the Far East* (Oxford: Oxford University Press, 1995), p. 94.

107 Ibid., p. 76.

108 Ibid., p. 77.

109 Ibid.

Army SIGINT activities in the India-Burma theatre, with two principal sub-centres, one at Bangalore, the other at Barrackpore, and more than a dozen other intercept and direction finding stations.

> The network provided strategic and operational SIGINT to Lord Mountbatten's SEAC, and operational and tactical SIGINT directly to field commanders in eastern India and Burma. In July 1943, a new radio station was installed at the WEC to link up the Special Communications Units stretching from London to Delhi with Mountbatten's Signal HQ in Colombo and [Central Bureau in] Australia so that, for example, Bletchley Park could receive Japanese ciphers from the office of the Commander-in-Chief, South East Asia and for a two-way traffic in ciphers and decrypted intelligence.[110]

The SIGINT activities at Peradeniya involved a Special Liaison Unit responsible for the dissemination of ULTRA SIGINT from Bletchley and WEC to Mountbatten and his senior commanders; US Special Security Officers responsible for SIGINT received from the War Department in Washington; and a joint SIGINT team, which at the end of the war included an officer from Central Bureau in Brisbane to coordinate the exchange of SIGINT with the South West Pacific Area command and SEAC.[111]

Ceylon's evolution as a major Allied base brought thousands of service personnel to the island in the second half of the war, joining the forces still stationed there for its defence and the men and women operating the shore establishments and platforms of the RAF and the Royal Navy. The following two chapters turn to a description of their experiences on the island, and the efforts made to accommodate and entertain them.

110 Ibid., p. 78.

111 F. W. Winterbotham (author of *The Ultra Secret: The Inside Story of Operation Ultra, Bletchley Park, and Enigma* (London: Weidenfeld and Nicolson, 1974)) was responsible for establishing the SLU at Peradeniya, and visited in October 1944 to assess its performance and ensure that Mountbatten and his headquarters was receiving all the ULTRA SIGINT concerning them. Geoffrey Ballard, author of *On Ultra Active Service*, was the Central Bureau Liaison Officer at Kandy.

7

Plain tales from Ceylon: Part I

The following chapters offers a flavour of the experiences of British servicemen and women stationed in Ceylon during the war, hence the reference to Charles Allen's famous collection of colonial reminiscences, *Plain Tales from the Raj*, itself a nod in the direction of Rudyard Kipling's *Plain Tales from the Hills*.[1] Through published diaries and memoirs written by 'those who were there', the BBC's superb 'World War Two People's War' oral history archive, and a series of letters and memoirs sent to the author by old Ceylon hands in the 1990s, the chapters explores the world of the temporary military migrants deposited in Ceylon by the tides of war, as well as some of its residents. In collating such material one is minded of the vogue in recent years for 'forgotten voices' books, usually emanating from the trenches of the First World War though occasionally coming from the eastern theatre of the Second World War, as in Richard Aldrich's landmark *The Faraway War* and a handful of oral histories from the Burma campaign.[2]

Servicemen and women deposited in Ceylon were part of a broader movement involving millions of people dispersed about the globe in order to prosecute imperial and Allied war aims, the pursuit of which depended on bases established in an array of overseas locations, many of them British colonies. Throughout the war Ceylon teemed with multinational servicemen and women, civilians, and officials, forming a tense and vibrant community charged initially by the proximity of danger and the possibility of defeat, later with the anticipation of large scale attacks against Japanese-occupied territory around the Bay of Bengal and the Malay Barrier.

As a major centre of wartime activity Ceylon is yet to register in the historical record in the way that other imperial redoubts such as Cairo, Malta, and Singapore have done, perhaps because it was not directly under enemy threat for as long as those places, certainly because the war in the Mediterranean and North Africa has received far more attention than the war further east,

1 Charles Allen, *Plain Tales from the Raj: Images of British India in the Twentieth Century* (London: Futura, 1976) and Rudyard Kipling, *Plain Tales from the Hills* (Calcutta: Thacker, Spink, and Company, 1888).

2 Richard Aldrich, *The Faraway War: Personal Diaries of the Second World War in Asia and the Pacific* (London: Corgi, 2010). As examples of the genre more generally, see Max Arthur, *Forgotten Voices of the Second World War: An New History of World War Two in the Words of the Men and Women Who Were There* (London: Ebury Press, 2004); Julian Thompson, *Forgotten Voices of Burma: The Second World War's Forgotten Conflict* (London: Ebury Press, 2009); and Kazuo Tamayama and John Nunneley, *Tales by Japanese Soldiers of the Burma Campaign* (London: Cassell, 2000). There is also an excellent oral history of the British Empire during the war, Christopher Somerville's *Our War: How the British Commonwealth Fought the Second World War* (London: Weidenfeld and Nicolson, 1998).

bar the short campaign in Malaya and Singapore and the more drawn out struggle in Burma.[3] Indubitably, aside from the first six months or so of the eastern war, Ceylon was not at any significant risk of enemy conquest and, other than in Burma, there was little prolonged fighting on land in the South-east Asia theatre. Indeed, as the memoirs and reminiscences encountered here testify, Ceylon was regarded as something of an island paradise by many of those based there, and could seem frustratingly remote from the 'real' war taking place in Europe, the Mediterranean, and the Pacific.[4] But these factors do not make its wartime history less worthy of record, for the experience of those dispatched to the island to guard it, to mount bomber, submarine, or destroyer patrols from its ports, to prepare for combat in Burma, and to staff its headquarters establishments, form part of the rich tapestry of the story of men and women from Britain and other lands sent hither and tither by the demands of an extraordinary global conflict.

This tour of wartime Ceylon begins with an account written by the celebrated Australian journalist and sometime historian Alan Moorehead. His record of a visit in April 1942, shortly after the Japanese attacks, contextualizes the island's place in an expanding and interconnected war and gives a contemporary flavour of the country and its inhabitants through the eyes of one itinerant European visitor. As a war correspondent Moorehead had followed the action across the Western Desert and eastern Mediterranean, chased the tail of Iran's British invaders as they streamed towards Tehran in August 1941, carrying on out into the Indian Ocean as war expanded in the east, composing vivid pen portraits for the British press along the way. Now, with the Japanese raiding Ceylon and India, he travelled east to see what was going on:

> [The Japanese now] sent out the first raids on to Indian soil. Cocanada and one or two other places on the east coast were bombed, not seriously, but badly enough to panic the frightened people. From Madras there was a wholesale evacuation, and while refugees packed the roads inland and the railways were strained to the point of disorganization the ordinary life of Madras itself was almost at a standstill. For a few days food was difficult to get and even transport was disrupted in the city. Shops closed their doors and the wildest rumours of parachutists and bombing raids spread up and down the peninsula. From top to bottom the Japanese dominated the Bay of Bengal. The stage was set for invasion, fast, deadly and violent.[5]

'Then', he wrote:

> abruptly, from out of the blue sky, a great and good thing happened for the Allied cause. The Japanese raided Ceylon. They fell upon the fuelling depot of Colombo in the west of

3 There are many books giving a rich flavour of Singapore. For Cairo, see Artemis Cooper's memorable *Cairo in the War, 1939-1945* (London: Penguin, 1995), and for Malta, see James Holland, *Fortress Malta: An Island Under Siege, 1940-1943* (London: Orion, 2003). Another wartime imperial nerve centre that would benefit from treatment is Delhi, home of India Command and the Government of India.

4 Winton writes that 'In the first months of 1945 the East Indies Fleet's sense that they were in an operational backwater increased. In Ceylon the fleet was in the war, but not of it'. Winton, *Sink the* Haguro*!*, p. 22. Some excellent contemporary Ceylonese scenery, including the Royal Botanical Gardens where SEAC headquarters were, can be seen in the famous film *Bridge on the River Kwai*, which was entirely shot in Ceylon.

5 Moorehead, *A Year of Battle*, p. 146.

> the island and the naval base of Trincomalee in the east. Nearly one hundred Japanese aircraft were blown out of the sky. They were blown up so thoroughly that not a single Japanese airman was recovered in Ceylon. Very few of the raiders got back to their ships, and that meant that at least two enemy carriers had quite insufficient aircraft with which to carry on. For the first time in months here was victory, clear, sharp and conclusive. It was the first time that the Japanese had begun to reach the limits of their dynamic series of conquests, that here at last was force to arrest them, that the rot in the British lines was stopped. In its very minor way, this was as important to the Far East as the Battle of Britain had been in Europe.[6]

Despite his journalistic hyperbole and outrageously optimistic figures regarding Japanese losses during the Colombo and Trincomalee raids, Moorehead's assessment was credible, and, though it was not apparent at the time, accurate in so far as the Japanese never sortied west in such strength again. Given the developing situation, Moorehead wanted to get to Ceylon as quickly as possible as he saw great propaganda value in the events unfolding there. But he was delayed in Bombay waiting for passage on one of the crowded bombers being rushed to the island, his time in the port city spent impatiently in clubs and bars before finally he got a flight. 'Our pilot was a smart young Singhalese boy and he told us great tales of Ceylon' as the aircraft flew over Poona to Hyderabad, Madras, and Trichinopoly, then across the Palk Strait.[7] Flying over the island, heading south for Ratmalana

> [w]e went elephant hunting from the air. We had a wild chase then over the jungle. It glowed with a moist lush greenness, the quintessence of greenness. Here and there the undergrowth parted into a little clearing round a waterhole and then we would go zooming down a hundred feet above the treetops. Wild birds and deer leapt up screaming. Then at last we sighted an elephant, an enormous brute with two of its young. They were drinking as we swept down and in a daze of fear the mother elephant lifted her trunk and went thundering into the trees, the two little ones in hot pursuit behind her.
>
> We kept on a strict route over the palm trees, for another Japanese attack was expected at any time, and came down outside Colombo.[8]

After this unobtrusive entrance, and though he had visited Ceylon six years before, Moorehead wrote that

> it was still a shock to see the almost crazy fertility of the place – the natives carrying huge branches of bananas and sacks of pineapples. Coconuts, mangoes and pawpaws – they grew haphazardly anywhere, and the jungle reached down to the city streets as though it would suddenly engulf everything in a wave of green fleshy leaves … We went to the Galleface [Hotel] and for the first time since the war began I had the joy of sinking back into a really first-class hotel.[9]

6 Ibid.
7 Ibid., p. 151.
8 Ibid.
9 Ibid.

His window looked out 'on a great sweep of rolling breakers … Looking out of my window and seeing a line of vessels making southward for Australia, I experienced homesickness for the first time in many years'.

> One quick skirmish around Colombo for information convinced me that I need never have come. This was no second Singapore. The island was defended far more strongly than I could have believed. There were many old friends here, units from the Western Desert. There were Australians, Africans and Indians. There were the increasing Hurricanes of the RAF, as well as the Fleet Air Arm. The sense of confusion and delay I had in India fell away. Here in Ceylon they had really prepared, and given a little more time they would be secure.[10]

Moorehead had already encountered some of the island's prominent military figures in other theatres of war, meeting Air Vice Marshal D'Albiac, the RAF commander, for example, 'when he went to take command in Greece the year before'.

> Admiral Layton, the Commander-in-Chief, had come across from Singapore. He was a squat, slow, bush-eyebrowed man, a sailor who had been born, launched and sent into action like a battleship. He lacked subtlety perhaps, but he was a solid and sound man to talk to. One good thing was that the three services were getting together. D'Albiac had an Army lieutenant as ADC, Layton has an airman, and so on. As Richard and I went round GHQ, Hurricane after Hurricane went by until there were thirty or more overhead, and from the sea two cruisers were entering the harbour. It all looked healthy.
>
> If they had not yet got around to dealing with propaganda as a military instrument, at least they had made a start on the political and economic security of the island. Someone with more brains than were evident in Singapore was tackling the problem of native labour. On the docks a labour pool was being established and priority of unloading given to the most important cargoes … Natives running the vital services like railways were being organized into a sort of civilian army … A recruitment campaign was being organized throughout the island … The menace of a native uprising was always there, of course, but here at least we were strong enough to keep it in check and even induce a little enthusiasm for the British cause.
>
> The main thing was that this air victory had occurred, and in many ways the native was being shown that we had no intention of evacuating Ceylon. Many of the white women and children were remaining in the hill stations like Euralia [Nuwara Eliya]. Others were working in the army and navy offices. The moral seems to be that if you garrison a place with fresh troops and fresh arms and show you are in earnest over the defence, then the native population will begin to throw its weight behind you.
>
> Old airfields were being enlarged and new ones hewn out of the jungle. We drove out to one of these where elephants had been put to work knocking down the palms, some of them thirty feet in height, and dragging them off. The need for this expansion was clear enough for an American Flying Fortress lay partly wrecked on the edge of the Colombo field. It

10 Ibid., pp. 151-52.

had landed and run the full distance and the pilot had only just saved himself from crashing into the palm trees by jamming his brakes. The big machine had upended on its nose.

Just about this time Tokyo radio broadcast a flamboyant account of the Colombo raid. It was given by one of their pilots and he described how he had seen his flight commander, badly hit, deliberately raise his hand in salute to the emperor and then dive headlong to his death into a ship in Colombo harbour. Did the Japanese pilots commit suicide? Were they fanatical enough to glory in a death like this? The RAF pilots who had fought off the raid and many others in Malaya and Singapore were not decided ... They took me first to see the wreck of a Japanese Navy Nought enemy fighter. It was twisted beyond all recognition.[11]

He described the classic RAF 'types', with their special private language and their interest in beer, girls, and aerodynamics. He also visited some of the army units stationed on the island:

Buried there in the green jungle these men do not appear to me unhappy. They were working out the adventurous parts of their lives, and they felt they were living fully and completely. It was not quite so easy for the soldiers up-country. Apart from the routine work and the forced marches they were making through the jungle as part of their new training, they had nothing to do but wait. They were badly plagued with insects and the heat. They had not had the quick thrill of air fighting or the airmen's chance of getting up and out of the island, and many of them were discontented and bored. An invasion might have come as something of a relief.[12]

Pottering around Colombo when the monsoon began to break, Moorehead looked across the Indian Ocean for the next battle to cover, hopefully in person this time. 'A message arrived for me from Charles Foley, my foreign editor in London: "Any dog's chance of getting to Madagascar quickly?"'.[13] On 5 May, a British invasion force supported by Eastern Fleet warships had landed at Diego Suarez, and it was time to up stumps once again.

By the skin of our teeth [he reflected] we had held the Axis in the east on the Burmese border. Now the Axis was coming after us in the west. There seemed to be no rest anywhere. But then, looking back over the past two years, when had there been any real lull in this central sector of the world war? The old business of plugging and patching up the Empire here and there seemed to go on and on. As soon as the balloon held in one place, the pressure had to be rushed to some other spot where the balloon was sagging. And it was leaking all over the place. When were we going to get a real striking force and strike someone?.[14]

11 Ibid., pp. 152-53.
12 Ibid., p. 155-6.
13 Ibid., p. 157.
14 Ibid., p. 159.

Voyages east and arrival

Journeying across dangerous waters, servicemen and women arrived in Ceylon aboard troopships and warships, stopping off along the way at places such as Aden, Bombay, Cape Town, Mombasa, Port Said, and the Seychelles. Michael Tomlinson arrived aboard the trooper *Devonshire* shortly after the Japanese raids, the hulk of *Hector* still burning in Colombo harbour. He was destined for the Combined Naval and Air Operations Room:

> In much the same way as they had at Singapore, we found ourselves deposited at Colombo in a strange tropical land. Few of us had ever left Europe before. The climate was hot and humid and we had been over two months confined in troopships, only being released ashore twice. A new life, in almost every accepted sense of the word, was about to begin for us all. This time there seemed perhaps less of an emergency than there had been at Singapore but a return of the Japanese in the near future seemed highly probable.[15]

Troopships from Britain progressed around the Cape of Good Hope until the more direct route via the Mediterranean was reopened in 1943 following the Allied invasions of North Africa and Italy.[16] In September 1944 Tony Inman left Liverpool in a convoy on board the trooper *Orantes*, bound for Colombo. After traversing the Mediterranean, the convoy passed through the Suez Canal. 'From the upper deck you could see over the top across a sandy waste. Occasionally there were groups of Arabs who shouted and pointed and when the nurses were seen, exposed themselves and made obscene gestures. The nurses thought this a huge joke and replied with derogatory signals about the exposed manhood'.[17] The convoy crossed the Indian Ocean and docked at Bombay, where Inman was quartered at the cricket club. 'I expect this first contact with India was a shock to those of us who had never been outside the UK. The heat, the smells, the teeming people, the beggars, the betel juice on the pavements which looked like blood, the bazaars, the "pukka sahib" attitude of the white residents'. The final stage of the voyage to Ceylon was accomplished aboard the trooper *Nevassa*, an 'ancient ship running alive with cockroaches and red ants'.[18]

Others made the more indirect progression to Ceylon around the Cape, including Earnest Heap, tasked with taking the coal-burning boom defence vessel *Barbour* to Ceylon. She was armed with a single anti-aircraft gun and a three-inch gun for surface craft and harbour defences. 'The ship rolled like a bastard and before long most of the crew were sick as they ploughed through the Atlantic'.[19] *Barbour* called at the Azores to coal and water before waddling on to Freetown, Lagos, Walvis Bay (where they were welcomed by the British community), and

15 Tomlinson, *The Most Dangerous Moment*, p. 154.

16 Jackson, *Of Islands, Ports, and Sea Lanes* dwells on the nature of these voyages and the phenomenon of the global movement of convoys and, in particular, troopships.

17 BBC World War Two People's War oral history archive, Tony Inman, 'A View from the Back: The Recollections of a Fleet Air Arm Observer 1941-1946', part 9, chapter 9, 'Going Foreign', A8109119. This was the view of Egypt from on board a ship on the canal. Viewed from the desert, warships and liners passing through the narrow canal looked like steel castles moving through the sand.

18 Ibid.

19 BBC People's World War Two People's War oral history archive, Earnest 'Guy' Heap, 'Guy Heap's War', A6103766.

Cape Town, where some Australian troops had taken a car up the stairs of the best hotel. The ship called at Durban during Christmas 1941, then on to Mombasa where the crew broke into the rum locker and moved to attack the captain, requiring the dispatch of a patrol from the battleship *Royal Sovereign* to calm things down. *Barbour* then proceeded across the main belt of the Indian Ocean with refuelling stops at the Seychelles and the Maldives, finally arriving in Ceylon, where she was to take up defensive duties.

Kenneth Williams of *Carry On* fame joined up in 1944 and worked with the Border Regiment to improve his fitness before being posted to the Royal Engineers Survey Section. Like so many imperial servicemen, Williams's voyage to Ceylon began in ignorance in a northern British port. All he knew, as he left the Royal Engineers Survey Training Centre at Ruabon in Denbighshire, was that he had an 'overseas posting'. On 12 April 1945 he embarked on a troopship at Greenock, which proceeded to assemble in convoy with a destroyer escort. The convoy followed the usual route east – Gibraltar, Port Said – and 'on 29th we entered the Suez Canal. All the way, Egyptians lining the banks offered goods for sale to the troops. When one of them held up a hookah a soldier from the deck shouted, "Up your pipe" – and the pedlar repeated it gleefully, "Yes, up your pipe"'.[20]

By 7 May the ship was alongside in Bombay and lorries took the men to a transit camp at Kalyan. Then he 'exchanged the torpid heat of Kalyan for the verdant freshness of Dehra Dun, high in the foothills of the Himalayas'.[21] Later, Williams wrote, 'I was sent to Ceylon, where I served with the 62 Map Reproduction Section in Kurunegala until the maps were no longer required and the unit was disbanded'. In Ceylon, the unit lived in *bashas* – huts made of rush matting – in a coconut grove, with the commanding officer's headquarters and the British other ranks' mess at the centre of the collection of buildings, separated from the Indian other ranks' mess and barrack block.

Eighteen year old Alan Brundrett arrived in 1944, and the diary he kept for two years offers a splendid view of Ceylon from the vantage point of a young British sailor. His journey east was accomplished aboard *Silvio*, a Landing Ship Infantry. On 26 January it left Aden, 'passing through the boom defences and slipping into the Indian Ocean. Our next port of call, we learn, will be Bombay, a distance of about 1,600 miles'.[22] Hammerhead sharks were sighted as well as flying fish, and then 'a new experience for us this evening; we had a film show on deck under the stars. *Hit the Ice*, starring Abbott and Costello'.[23] Brundrett remarked upon the warm breeze and the beauty of the night as many of the men slept on deck for the first time, lying 'spellbound for some time, gazing up at the tropical stars, which shined with intensity. The swing of the ship was quiet; it seemed poised motionless while the stars themselves gave the impression of moving back and forth above the masthead'.[24] On 1 February *Silvio* left Bombay and the men were 'told that our final destination is Colombo, Ceylon, some 1,000 miles distant'. To see them on their way, on the following day there was a 'surprise announcement to say that a Japanese submarine was thought to be somewhere in the area'.[25]

20 Kenneth Williams, *Just Williams: An Autobiography* (London: HarperCollins, 1993), p. 26.
21 Ibid., p. 30.
22 Alan Brundrett, *Two Years in Ceylon: The diaries of a Naval Secretariat Member, 1944-1946* (Lewes, Sussex: The Book Guild, 1996), pp. 151-52.
23 Ibid., p.153.
24 Ibid.
25 Ibid., p. 154.

African troops, who had garrisoned Ceylon from the moment of its greatest peril in spring 1942, remained a prominent feature of the island's military population throughout the war as it became the base for the 11th East African Division's Burma campaign. In March 1944, for example, there were 2,720 soldiers from the Central African protectorate of Nyasaland alone stationed there.[26] Like their Australian and British counterparts, African troops arrived by sea, in their case after lengthy journeys from colonies of origin to East African ports of embarkation. The 3rd Battalion The Northern Rhodesia Regiment arrived from Kenya in July 1944, forming the 22nd East African Brigade along with the 1st Battalion The King's African Rifles and the 1st Battalion The Rhodesian African Rifles. The advanced party of this latter unit had left Salisbury in November 1943, followed shortly by the rest of the battalion, amounting to over 900 men. Their journey to Ceylon was a minor epic in itself. They travelled from Salisbury in Southern Rhodesia to Kamina in the Congo by train, to Kabolo, also in the Congo, by lorry, by train to Albertville on Lake Tanganyika, by ferry to Kigomo, by train to Mwanza on Lake Victoria, by ferry to Kisuma, and then by train to Nairobi.

Other Southern Rhodesian troops left Moshi near Mount Kilimanjaro on 20 June 1944, taking part in a 'nine-day exercise designed to screen the movement of the troops to the coast en route to Ceylon'.[27] During an 80 mile advance on Arusha, the troops attacked small parties of 'Japanese', provided by the Northern Rhodesia Regiment. The men travelled by rail from Nairobi to Mombasa where they boarded the troopship *Strathaven*, the askaris greatly excited by their first glimpse of the sea. They landed at Colombo on 14 September 1944 and were sent to Horana Camp, home of the 22nd East African Brigade, which formed a reserve supplying bulk reinforcements to the 11th East African Division in Burma. In one of the Indian Ocean's worst maritime disasters of the war, in February 1944 nearly 1,000 men of the East African artillery lost their lives when *Khedive Ismail*, taking them from Mombasa to Colombo, was sunk by a Japanese submarine.[28]

Early in January 1942 the 34th Indian Division moved at short notice from Jhansi to Ceylon. This involved a journey of 1,300 miles by train, the heat increasing and the speed decreasing as the cramped carriages moved south, and then a ferry ride across the Palk Strait. Landing in Ceylon at Mannar, the division again entrained. Cecil Callis was one of the division's soldiers:

> Through the carriage window on the opposite side was the lovely view of a perfect 'tropical island' beach; a line of foam creamed onto a white beach of sand, fringed by graceful palm trees swaying gently in the warm breeze ... Another first impression that stays in my memory is of travelling through jungle where we saw natives, brown and bare to the waist, who wore sarongs like long tight skirts almost to their ankles, their long black hair reaching down to their waists. They seemed to belong to the distant past.[29]

26 Timothy Parsons, *The African Rank and File: Social Implications of Colonial Military Service in the King's African Rifles, 1902-1964* (Oxford: James Currey, 1999), p. 166. Of that number, 750 were Lomwe, the largest Nyasaland group in the 11th East African Division.

27 Christopher Owen, *The Rhodesian African Rifles* (London: Leo Cooper, 1970), p. 27.

28 See Brian Crabb, *Passage to Destiny: The Sinking of the Troopship* Khedive Ismail *in the Sea War Against Japan* (Stamford, Lincolnshire: Paul Watkins, 1997).

29 BBC World War Two People's War oral history archive, Callis, Chapter 4, 'South to Ceylon', A4427985.

The train travelled down the west side of the island before heading inland for the hills and Kandy, 'a beautiful little town set in a river valley, within a ring of mountains'. After a seven day journey, wrote 'Fan Tan', one of the division's British officers

> [W]e arrived at our destination, incredibly dirty. To our horror, we found leading civilians, the GOC [General Officer Commanding], and many senior officers of the CDF [Ceylon Defence Force] waiting to give the 'Regular' unit a State reception! Silence was mainly due to the younger elements [among the troops] being in a complete haze. They had no idea where they were, they were seeing many strange things – such as the sea and they could not understand why the local Indians [i. e. the Ceylonese] did not respond to their questions, spoken in pure Punjabi!'.[30]

At Kandy, Callis recalls, signals headquarters was established with the men barracked on the outskirts of the town. The maintenance section and workshops and offices where he worked were located in a large requisitioned bungalow on Brownrigg Street, its extensive walled garden used as a lorry park.[31] From divisional signals HQ detachments were posted around the island, Callis joining the Colombo detachment in February to look after its lorries and motorbikes.

Imperial servicemen and women posted to Ceylon were offered a variety of literature to aid acclimatization and orientation, and to ensure that they lived as harmoniously as possible with the local population. The booklet *Ceylon and its People* was 'published for and issued free to all Ranks and Ratings of the Fighting Services in Ceylon'. Among other pieces of advice, it stated that Ceylon's European population was more interested in the defence of the island than the defence of the Empire, either an intentional or unknowing slur on their patriotism. Furthermore, it claimed that they were suspicious of 'superior' people, and 'must be treated with much more tact than, say, the inhabitants of Yorkshire or Wiltshire', an astounding reflection on metropolitan views of the British population, never mind that of 'colonials' in Ceylon.[32]

Air Command South East Asia issued its own special guide book. It offered airmen and women advice on 'what to bring' and, more importantly perhaps, what not to bring, cautioning against shipping out motor cars, polo ponies, or grand pianos, another amusing reflection of prevalent attitudes about what colonial life meant for Britons in the east. It warned against checking off a 'formidable list of tropical kit and accessories', as 'you may very successfully be led up the garden path' by unscrupulous shopkeepers urging the unsuspecting serviceman or woman heading east to get fully kitted out with sola topees, malaria belts, and canvas wash-stands. The booklet told people to 'travel as light as possible. There's nothing you can't get in India'. [33] It also advised readers to 'be careful what you buy [once in Asia] – what's okay in an Eastern atmosphere is often quite unsuitable and utterly ridiculous when transferred to a flat in London, a cottage in Hampshire or a country villa near Oxford'. Curios and other items bought in India and Ceylon would 'soon find themselves in the vicar's jumble sale'. The

30 Fan Tan, 'Soldiering in Ceylon', p. 66.
31 BBC World War Two People's War oral history archive, Callis, Chapter 5, 'Kandy and Colombo', A4428038.
32 IWM, K. 84.1437, *Ceylon and its People* (Colombo: *Ceylon Daily News*, 1944).
33 IWM, K. 02/1516 RAF Air Command South East Asia.

publication offered advice on which clubs to join, basic language translations, and the lowdown on unpleasant creatures.[34]

Special films were also produced for men and women destined for points east. The RAF Film Production Unit issued 'Life in Air Command South East Asia' for those posted to Burma, Ceylon, and India in what by 1944 was an expanding theatre of operations. The film detailed alluring opportunities offered by service in the east – betting on horses, gaining the suntan that could complete a man's handsomeness, meeting members of the women's auxiliary services, and experiencing exciting places. It condescendingly warned against local shopkeepers, 'all of them dirty, some of them even genuine', and proffered information about different 'types' of natives and how 'absurdly cheap' it was to procure the services of servants to cater for one's daily needs. The film showed airwomen shopping and sightseeing, people on leave in Calcutta and Darjeeling, and men working in Ceylon, 'where it is no hardship to live in tents' and where there was plentiful swimming and sailing.[35]

Landscape, flora and fauna, Colombo and Trincomalee

Following journeys east in convoys, for many thousands of British men and women Ceylon formed a backdrop for a period of their lives that would later furnish enchanted memories informed by youth, excitement, danger, and the 'exoticness' of the setting. Ceylon's flora, fauna, and scenery left strong impressions on the minds of these wartime immigrants, as did encounters with the capital city, Colombo. Perhaps the first thing to strike new arrivals, at least those from Britain, was the heat. James Thompson wrote that

> Colombo is always hot, nearly always humid, the city streets breathlessly sun heated, the pavements baked, the tar stickily bubbling. From January to April Colombo drips in a wet pall of damp, oppressive air; any slight exertion at even seven o'clock in the morning soddens clothing with perspiration. It can be unbearable. A fitful breeze winds tiredly across Galle Face Green, the frontage to the ocean.[36]

'Memories of Ceylon are still vivid amongst the men of the fleet', wrote John Winton.

> the runny butter, and the tiny pigeon-size eggs, and the curious paw-paw jam. There were the flowers, tobacco flowers and stocks, and frangiapani, and those with waxy petals strewn on the roadways ... There were the shrines to Buddha and the little shops in Colombo selling dubious gem-stones and carved ivory; there were the roads crowded with dust-raising lorries and the bullock carts, all festooned about with hanging earthenware pots; there were the muddy water buffaloes in the paddy fields, and the great crows croaking on

34 Ibid.

35 IWM, APY37. See the Colonial Film Database website for a link to the film and a textual description, at http://www.colonialfilm.org.uk/node/5430

36 Thompson, *Only the Sun Remembers*, p. 194. Thompson also writes of Christmas 1941, 'my first snow festival in the sunshine', p. 192.

> the rooftops, and the pale lizards crouching in corners, and the native villages, smelling of raw arrack spirit, and sweat and excrement and dried fish.[37]

Most servicemen and women arriving in Ceylon were exhilarated by its physical beauty.

> From the sea, the island was one of the most romantic sights in the east, rising from the horizon, like a blue wraith, like a mirage, with the smoky green crest of Adam's Peak above the bright green jungle which rolled right down to white beaches and the water's edge ... The exotic smells, the spices and flowers, of Ceylon floated miles out to sea to welcome the sea traveller.[38]

'The moment we reached Ceylon', wrote the Labour member of parliament Tom Driberg,

> there was a magical change. The hills and the woods were as green as England's with mountains grander than Scotland's rising above them ... From Colombo to Kandy we were lucky enough to get a lift from a superbly furnished Dakota, the SAC [Supreme Allied Commander]'s private aircraft ... There was warmth and hospitality in our welcome, from the airmen at the airstrip who told us of the joy with which the news of Labour's victory [in the 1945 General Election] had been received by the men out here to the 'boy' who made our beds in the excellently equipped camp.[39]

Approaching Ceylon from the sea on 4 February 1944, Alan Brundrett wrote:

> We caught our first glimpse of Ceylon through the mist early this morning in the shape of its majestic mountains, with Adam's Peak standing out conspicuously in the centre, a familiar silhouette to any philatelist as it is featured on the three-cent stamp ... Soon Colombo's interesting, low skyline becomes clear. The Secretariat, Town Hall, Cathedral and Galle Face Hotel can be picked out, and the sun's rays strike a slim white obelisk; a war memorial, no doubt. The island's mountains of green and purple, bathed in sunshine, provide a worthy backdrop to such a delightful scene. Westwards, along the coast beyond Colombo, lovely trees and feathery palms fringe the beach, and natives in quaint canoes can be seen ... As we near the fine breakwater one can see the spray thrown up by the breakers along the coast and hear the boom as they crash against the shore. The tides are responsible for what is known as the 'Colombo Roll' across the entrance to the harbour, where three distinct waves are discernible at times ... Colombo is one of the principal ports of the Indian Ocean and is thought of as the junction where East meets West. Many large ships are to be seen in port, as well as barges, tugs, sailing boats and Maldive 'buggaloes', an altogether busy and fascinating setting ... We were bewildered by a scene completely alien to us. Rickshaw coolies stripped to the waist, their brown bodies glistening with sweat; some quite skinny, old before their time; people shouting in strange tongues; constant hooting of car horns and jingling of bells. Strange odours mingle with the scent of flowers.[40]

37 Winton, *Sink the* Haguro*!*, pp. 24-25.
38 Ibid., pp. 22-23.
39 Brundrett, *Two Years in Ceylon*, p. 278.
40 Ibid., pp. 155-56.

After quitting the ship Brundrett was sent to HMS *Mayina*, a transit camp in the jungle about six miles out from Colombo.[41] Here he noted the 'heavy scent of flowers', fireflies darting about, 'their luminescent bodies easily seen', and a jungle road, 'dusty and unlit … It is a new experience to lie there and hear the weird noises of a tropical night, frogs croaking hoarsely, the sounds of bats and crickets, giving an overall continuous pulsating sound rather like that made by refrigerators'.[42] Like many before him, Brundrett had entered the world of mosquito nets and monsoon rain.

In Colombo, Brundrett was employed at Naval Headquarters on Upper Chatham Street near the sea front, and lived at the naval camp just outside the city, to and from which he would catch the bus each day. As he understood it, at this stage of the war 'the current task of the East Indies Station is to cut off the supply lines of the Japanese Army in Burma and attack their shipping. Here in naval HQ important behind-the-scenes planning goes on to ensure that these operations are successful'.[43] A friend serving aboard the destroyer *Rotherham* gave him detailed accounts of patrol sweeps and encounters with the enemy, and news filtered through of carrier strikes on the Nicobar Islands and hunts for Japanese vessels as the powerful naval forces based on Ceylon went on the offensive.

Like thousands of other imperial servicemen, Brundrett was soon out and about exploring the capital. Prudently obtaining a street guide prepared for the benefit of visiting service personnel, he toured the city's famous landmarks. These included the Clock Tower on Queen Street, the Noah's Ark-like building of the Colombo Club, and Galle Face Green, 'a very wide lawn over a mile in length with the fine Galle Face Hotel standing at the end'.[44] Here Sinhalese couples, families, and servicemen and women would promenade. There were also the zoological gardens and day trips to the nearby beaches of Bentota and the 'delightful' Mount Lavinia Hotel, its terrace bar and swimming pool overlooking the picturesque beaches that flanked the rocky promontory on which it stood.

Like most visitors to Colombo, Brundrett was struck by the city's sharply contrasting districts, the posh Cinnamon Gardens area contrasting sharply with Pettah, Colombo's 'native quarter', where the intensity and colour of crowded street markets and the taste of unusual fruit left a marked impression on young people fresh from rural and suburban Britain. Along with the routine of military office work, there were the inevitable obtrusions of the east; outbreaks of typhus and malaria, for example, and the contemplation of the strangeness of living as an elite alien in what was manifestly someone else's land, the riddle at the heart of the colonial condition. Like Brundrett and so many others, a young Fleet Air Arm (FAA) officer was struck by the beauty but also the poverty of the country, manifest in the form of beggars and people suffering from diseases such as elephantiasis and rickets.[45]

James Thomspon described the contrast between affluent Colombo – the 'European' quarter and civic district – and the 'native quarter' of Pettah:

41 For some rare film footage of *Mayina* see 'Navy in Ceylon', Title ID 9270, University of Brighton's Screen Archive South East, at http://screenarchive.brighton.ac.uk/detail/9270/

42 Brundrett, *Two Years in Ceylon*, pp. 157-58.

43 Ibid., p. 173.

44 Ibid.

45 Will Iredale, *The Kamikaze Hunters: Fighting for the Pacific, 1945* (London: Pan, 2015), p. 178.

> On one side of the small, overcrowded harbour spreads the honeycomb of Pettah, a slum maze of dirt, stench or gleaming silk in dim boutique shops and colourful, brilliantly figured Hindu temples; on the other side of the wharves, the wealthy sweep of the Galle Face Green, wide, white paved, palm fringed avenues, the spacious well kept Club grounds, smart bungalows and planned, ordered streets. In the city centre, large, high-ceilinged cool stores, Millers and Cargills, the Colombo Apothecaries, crowded junk and jewel littered Indian and Ceylonese shops, rings, silks, ivories, painted masks, native work. Many small, clean Chinese restaurants, the busy, ever full Free China, serving foo yung hai, sharksfin, egg and asparagus soup, bowls of birdsnest, crab and chicken, heavy, think enough to float a spoon, exquisite, varied noodles, prawns and curried lobsters, baked crabs and sunflower seeds. The war in the East; with succulent mandarin pork balls at the brightly lit Shanghai, half way down the Galle Road.[46]

Many service personnel not stationed in Colombo and its suburbs were based around Trincomalee. As a port it was popular with sailors, John Winton summarizing their memories thus:

> [T]here was the coming of Gracie Fields aboard, and the visiting ENSA performances, with their disquieting joking references to civilian hardships – not mentioned in the letters from home. There was swimming in the sea, with every now and again the jab in the stomach and boom of the small anti-saboteur-swimmer charges they detonated each time the harbour entrance was opened. There were the sand crabs on the beach who vanished in a flurry of movement until they left only two eyes on stalks, like wary periscopes. There were soldiers in the mess, just passing through, with stories of Burma, and its trees and its rain, both of which went on forever. There were open-air cinemas with performances for a thousand men under the tropical stars.[47]

Thomas Russell was stationed at Trincomalee aboard one of the 'R' class battleships. He recalls that it was 'great for swimming', and that 'hands to bathe' was nearly as popular a pipe as 'up spirits'.[48] 'Despite the shark risk', he continued, 'those clear blue waters were irresistible, especially after the heat of a battle wagon designed for the North Atlantic'. Though the harbour and its naval shore facilities didn't offer 'the same female attractions of a Durban' (it didn't have the civilian population of a Durban or a Colombo), shore leave did offer a really good beer in the little fleet canteen: 'McEwan's export beer was cold, dark and sumptuous, and after the South African lager a real treat'.[49] There was an anti-submarine boom protecting Trincomalee, and hands were permitted to bathe (though with fear of shark attacks) and play water polo. 'The result was that quite a number of the men became good swimmers', wrote Agar. 'How thankful I was later to have made this rule', he added, referring to the sinking of his ship, *Dorsetshire*, on

46 Thompson, *Only the Sun Remembers*, p. 194.
47 John Winton, *Sink the* Haguro*! The Last Destroyer Action of the Second World War* (London: Seeley, Service, & Co., 1979), pp. 24-25.
48 BBC World War Two People's War oral history archive, Thomas Russell, 'Approach of the Storm', chapter 18, A7358844.
49 Ibid.

5 April 1942 and the hours spent in the water by survivors before they were rescued.[50] For the sailors based at this major naval anchorage, writes Winton:

> there was the same time-honoured daily routine: scrub decks, gun drill, painting ship, cleaning during the long hot seemingly endless forenoons. With the sound of bugles, the motor-boat engines as they passed from one ship to the next, the cries of native bumboatmen, Trincomalee had all the sounds of continuing imperial confidence. Under the awnings, the sun at midday reflected off the still water with an intensity that hurt the eyes. At noon there was the sailor's tot of rum, and an English cooked dinner of roast meat and veg. Then, in the afternoons, head down, and sleep.[51]

Dennis Small, a Royal Marine, variously mounted guard at naval headquarters near Kandy, served at HMS *Ukassa*, a large FAA station that was home to over 3,000 sailors and Wrens, and worked at a remote radar station on the coast. He had arrived in Ceylon aboard the troopship *Athlone Castle* and after disembarking was taken with hundreds of other men on a train journey into central Ceylon. Alighting at night the men began to march along a dirt track 'winding through towering palm trees, passing through small palm leaf built villages with hurricane lamps hanging over verandahs. Occasionally one would hear the sound of Indian music drifting out from the huts, mingling with the croaking of toads, and the screeching sounds of the tropical forest'.[52] On arrival at the designated camp, stumbling over trenches dug to carry away the monsoon rains, Small was issued with a blanket and a mosquito net and shown to a derelict hut, in which he and the other occupants were 'too frightened to speak at night as two large pale eyes appeared and moved around the room'. These, the new arrivals were informed the following morning, belonged to wild dogs.[53]

John Mills remembers his time at Natcheecunda, a naval base near the main runway of HMS *Bambara* at China Bay. 'Accommodation took the form of wooden-framed huts with coconut palm roofs. The huts were full of insects, and rigging mosquito nets, checking boots for scorpions and the bed for snakes became second nature. Outside, monkeys, squirrels, mongooses, armadillos, chameleon lizards, and spiders of all sizes were constant companions, and during the monsoon season clothing quickly became mouldy'.[54] Wren officer Freda Wade wrote that 'Our washing stank of woodsmoke and the dhobey [Indian Army slang for laundry worker] used to starch our dresses, which were made of thick drill, so that they were like a board to open up before putting on'.[55] She recalls mongooses in the rafters and baboons swinging from the trees outside, and the risk of tarantulas in the loo.

Life for many servicemen and women could have a distinctly 'primitive' edge. In some camps, officers lived in wooden-framed cabins with thatched roofs, other ranks in dormitories. Food,

50 Agar, *Footprints in the Sea*, p. 173.
51 Winton, *Sink the* Haguro!, p. 23.
52 BBC World War Two People's War oral history archive, Dennis Small, 'The 1939-45 War: A Personal Experience', part 4, 'A Night to Remember', A8532489.
53 Ibid.
54 BBC World War Two People's War oral history archive, John Mills, 'Homeward Bound Some Where', A888815.
55 BBC World War Two People's War oral history archive, Freda Wade, 'A Posting to Ceylon', A7011802.

rationed, was often of the tinned and powdered variety, reducing to a 'warm sludge' in the heat.[56] Hot curries, fresh juices and exotic fruits such as pawpaw, mango, and watermelon broke the mealtime monotony. Of all his recollections of Ceylon, Tony Inman set apart the taste of 'fresh bananas straight off the tree and dishes of tea (Ceylon, naturally), no milk, but sugar and lime. My mouth waters at the memory'.[57]

> At night scented woodsmoke hung in the air, fireflies twinkled in the jungle blackness, frogs and insects croaked and chirruped. The humidity made it impossible to sleep under anything more than a mosquito net, which would thud intermittently as a flying insect lost its way. Morning habits were adapted to include a careful inspection of sweat-soaked flying gear hung up at the end of the previous day, as nocturnal visitors were common.[58]

There were snakes, lizards, scorpions, and monkeys chattering in the trees.

Paymaster Sub-Lieutenant R. V. Ward, who had been on board *Prince of Wales* when she was sunk and arrived in Ceylon with Admiral Layton after escaping from Java, wrote:

> I lived in the Grand Oriental Hotel, Colombo, still on the staff of Admiral Sir Geoffrey Layton, now C. in C. Ceylon. Then I moved to HMS *Rajaliya*, RN Station Puttalam, some 50-60 miles north of Colombo and by the side of a spectacular lagoon, though the station itself was merely a large hole cut out of the jungle, large enough to receive visiting aircraft from our own or foreign ships in the area needing repair or servicing. Accommodation was crude kadjan huts but life was very interesting because of the local wildlife – elephants, crocodiles, cobras, monkeys and many other small mammals. We could swim in the sea a few miles west of the camp.[59]

Cecil Callis of 34th Indian Division wrote that when the divisional detachments that had been sent to places such as Colombo were recalled to Kandy, things became overcrowded.

> All personnel except HQ Company had to move out of town, live under canvas and travel in to work each day. One of the roads going out of Kandy ran alongside the River Mahaweli, through a small village called Haragama, then through many miles of coconut plantations, a picturesque road. We made our camp among the coconut trees on the slope of the valley, overlooking the wide river ... Settled in bed at night, you could hear the palm trees whisper and rustle in the breeze, the cicadas calling to each other and the great bullfrogs honking away down by the river. Quite romantic it was![60]

56 Iredale, *The Kamikaze Hunters*, p. 178.
57 BBC World War Two People's War oral history archive, Inman.
58 Iredale, *Kamikaze Hunters*, p. 179.
59 BBC World War Two People's War oral history archive, R. V. Ward, 'The Sinking of HMS *Prince of Wales* and *Repulse*', A4217979.
60 BBC World War Two People's War oral history archive, Cecil Callis, 'Eastern Travels', part 6, chapter 8, 'Back to the Hills', A4428173.

'In the morning it was not uncommon to find that white ants had eaten your kitbag, or to notice blood coming from a leech puncture in the stomach, or a pair of scorpions squaring up to each other outside the tent flap, and the dull thud of coconuts being harvested in the background'. It would then be necessary, Callis recalled, to 'sit down to an alfresco breakfast wearing your tin helmet for safety'.[61] Rowland Button was a radar operator posted to a radar station at Galle. 'It must have been one of the finest sites in the world for an RAF station, overlooking Galle harbour, right on a hill, in super scenery with a view stretching right across the hills into central Ceylon. Down below us paths led to beaches where we could swim and laze about'.[62] He was then posted to Horton Plains, a plateau in the Central Highlands, where work was interspersed with pig hunting, curry-eating, long walks, and visits to tea plantations.

Philip Skelsey was an Aircraftsman 1st Class in an RAF control room linked to radar stations on the coast, from

> where we plotted the course of British and American aircraft setting out on patrol over the Bay of Bengal or returning to base ... From the top of a hill near our camp you could see Hurricane fighters on the airfield at China Bay far below, like small moths in the distance. In the evenings, the sun dropping towards the sea, the sky was a mass of colour: turquoise, salmon-pink, deep crimson. At night, when we walked towards the town past red-brick bungalows, fireflies flitting among the palm trees, twin-engine Catalina reconnaissance planes came in low over the harbour, their headlights knifing the darkness.[63]

Accommodation for Skelsey and his comrades

> consisted of huts in jungle made out of dried palm leaves, and when we were out chipmunks and rats came out of the trees to chew any clothes or soap they could find. It was fatal to leave a piece of chocolate on the tables by our beds. We tried putting each table leg in a round cigarette tin and filling it with paraffin. Even this didn't work. Suicide squads of ants dived into the paraffin and constructed bridges with their dead bodies. Their comrades marched across these, up the table legs, and ate the chocolate. There was a corrugated cinema in town, and a monotonous diet of bully beef, stew and dehydrated potatoes and a canteen where the men could eat sticky buns and drink sweet tea.[64]

In June 1943 Ken Potter and the rest of his East African division moved 300 miles to the Kenyan coast from where they embarked for Ceylon, arriving in Colombo after a 14 day voyage. The soldiers moved inland 'to Peredeniya where divisional headquarters were billeted under canvas in the Botanical Gardens, surrounded by a fantastic collection of trees and shrubs from around the world'.[65] Potter strung his tent under a tree growing six inch-long avocado pears. Here the

61 Ibid.
62 BBC World War Two People's War oral history archive, Rowland Button, 'Rowland Button's War Story', A7495293.
63 BBC World War Two People's War oral history archive, Philip Skelsey, 'Ceylon', A3790343.
64 Ibid.
65 BBC World War Two People's War oral history archive, Ken Potter, 'Jungle Training in Ceylon (June 1943-May 1944)', A7473963.

division spent a lazy fortnight 'while the 14th Army decided where we were to go for training'. They were then despatched to Bentota on the coast, where Potter strung his newly-issued ridge pole tent 30 yards from the sea. One day he was

> awoken by half a dozen enormous turtles thumping their way up from the sea to a spot just under the guy ropes. Their tracks in the sand were wider than those made by Bren Gun Carriers. Having laboriously got above any likely high water mark, with their rear flippers they scooped out a hole nearly two feet deep. They then deposited in the hole a mass of eggs that looked just like ping-pong balls.[66]

A few weeks later he watched as the hatchlings made their way to the sea, attacked by gulls as they did so.

In November 1944 the Australian ship *Tamworth* was sent to Colombo as part of the 22nd Minesweeping Flotilla, spending the next few months working convoys from Aden to Bombay and from Aden to Cochin. On 13 November, wrote Hugh Campbell, he and fellow *Tamworth* sailors went 'for a trip to a little holiday resort and fishing village about twenty miles out'.

> The road all the way [to Negombo] was flanked with palms, many of them planted out in rows just like Tasmanian orchards, with houses built of everything from plaited leaves to plastered brick nestling amongst them. We made progress to the continual tooting of horns, as the natives swarmed over the roads like flies. They all raised their hands in a modified V-sign. I'm not quite sure whether they were wishing our war effort well, or just begging for cigarettes. Probably the latter from what I've seen, for even boys of nine and ten smoke whenever they can get tobacco. There was a delightful rest house at the beach; we stopped there for tea, and to cool off. This seems to be the land of electric fans. There are two or three in every room you enter. The whole country seems to me to be over-ripe. The trees are very luxuriant, flowers are bright, and everything is exotic, but always that musty smell of decay persists. In the city, filth and squalor are everywhere. Yet the natives seem to be happy enough living as they do, in spite of foul smells, acute overcrowding and ceaseless noise.[67]

The crew enjoyed another period of shore leave in January 1945, and Campbell told his parents in a letter home that 'we've been living gloriously easy life during the last couple of weeks – tons of sun, swimming, and sport, and no night watches'.

Edward Young, commanding the submarine *Storm*, left a vivid portrait of life in Ceylon for submariners resting between operational patrols hunting Japanese vessels in the Bay of Bengal and the Malacca Strait:

> Between patrols we made the most of our leisure. We swam daily in the warm water, sometimes wearing goggles to gaze down at the brightly coloured fish darting among the coral formations. We organized swimming and sailing picnics with the Wrens from the

66 Ibid.

67 Hugh Campbell, *Notable Service to the Empire: Australian Corvettes and the British Pacific Fleet, 1944–1945* (Garden Island, New South Wales: Naval Historical Society, 1995), p. 65.

> cypher office ashore, and went surf-riding on the palm-edged beaches further up the coast. Swimming in the harbour had one minor drawback: as a deterrent to midget submarines, small depth-charges were dropped at the entrance to the boom whenever the gate was opened, and if you were in the water within a mile of one of these depth-charges the sound-wave hit you in the stomach like an electric shock. We had plenty of sailing. [The submarine depot ship HMS] *Maidstone* possessed four or five dinghies, and these were out on the water most days. We invented an exciting game of sailing battles, in which every resource of seamanship was needed to get up wind of your opponent and then soak him by scooping water over him with a bailer; we soon entered too vigorously into the game, and after we had a few collisions, grappled alongside, boarded, and hurled each other into the water to our hearts' content, we had to abandon the sport because of damage to the boats.
>
> I was at sea when the jeep-hunts began. Phil May (commander of HMS *Tantivy*) and two or three of the others thought it would be good fun to take a jeep into the jungle at night, carrying with them an aldis lamp which they hoped would mesmerize the game while they shot at it with their .303 rifles. They met with indifferent success, and one night the jeep was chased by an elephant. The sound of the great beast crashing after them in the dark was too much for them, and soon afterwards the new enthusiasm died a natural death … Sam Marriott, commanding HMS *Stoic*, and one of his officers, paddled a canoe from Kandy down the Makaweli River until they reached the sea at Trincomalee. In the course of their trip they negotiated rapids, saw herds of wild elephant, and even shot a crocodile, bringing back the skin to prove it.[68]

All crews were given ten days leave after every two patrols. Young spent his first two in Colombo, which was:

> amusing, hectic, and very expensive. On one such occasion I flew back to Trincomalee on the mail plane; as always in air travel, the height flattened out all the natural beauty of the land, diminishing the vast tracts of jungle and forest to nothing more than thickly-grown parsley. Circling over Trinco before coming in to land, we peered down at the harbour full of toy ships of an extraordinary neatness; *Maidstone* and *Adamant* were easy to spot because of the submarines nestling alongside, but the flight-deck of the aircraft carrier *Illustrious* looked like an elongated ping-pong table.[69]

Sometimes ships' crews had to make their own entertainment. Hugh Campbell wrote that:

> Entertainment ashore is strictly limited – pictures seem to be the only thing. White girls are in a decided minority. That means we must find all our entertainment in the ship. We play quite a lot of cards, mainly crib and poker, and several times we have parties on board. We have a loud speaker rigged up on the fo'c's'le for music while we work.[70]

68 Edward Young, *One of Our Submarines* (Barnsley: Pen and Sword, 2004), originally published in 1952. See chapter 13, 'Passage to Ceylon' and chapter 15, 'Between Patrols: Ceylon', pp. 227-228.
69 Ibid., p. 228.
70 Campbell, *Notable Service to the Empire*, p. 65.

The European community, plantations, rest camps, and training

For off duty entertainment Ceylon was a dream posting, a site of rest and recreation for forces fighting in Burma as well as ships' crews and air force personnel. Its highland rest camps and the estate plantations provided holidays for the service personnel stationed in Colombo, Kandy, Trincomalee and the island's many other bases. It was common practice for planters to put their homes at the disposal of service personnel on leave, one of the many ways in which Ceylon's home front supported the war effort. An officer serving with the 34th Indian Division wrote that the planters had been 'wonderful' and offered 'great hospitality ... They subscribe to every war charity, spend all their spare time and petrol in entertaining troops, and have kept open house for those that require rest or a few cool nights'.[71] James Thompson wrote that 'to all troops in the island the plantations gave their homes and hearts; their hospitality and kindness brought untold, unrecorded happiness, pleasure and treasured comfort to friend and stranger', particularly relishing a visit to Demodara, the 'finest, the loveliest, the greatest plantation in Ceylon'.[72]

William Cameron was brought up on the Moray estate in the Maskeliya district. His home was a classic colonial affair:

> a front verandah with balustrades, cane furniture and a circular ship's clock, where my father would sit in the evenings before the tropical darkness fell, looking down the long garden and listening to the evensong of birds, as we children played. Behind the verandah were the lounge or 'withdrawing room', and its adjacent smoking room, in which during the war Dad built a three-quarter size billiards table. In the garden there was a pond, a large lawn, palm trees, and a second pond with a punt and a summerhouse, all surrounded by a thick shrubbery from where the banded crakes sent out their rolling call, and the beautiful pitta, or 'six o'clock bird', would give a melancholy warning that the day was ending. There was a line of Kitul palms on which wild cats, palm civets, would feed on the berries at night below the fronds, their eyes glowing ruby red in the light of powerful torches.[73]

Cameron's mother liked to entertain, and house parties, Sunday curry lunches, and picnics at the bathing pool were regular features of life, as were weekly club nights at the Maskeliya Club.

> After tennis Dad would play snooker, and Mum play bridge, while we children played games in and around the club premises with the other European children of the district. During the war it was at this club that I first fell in love. She was in the WRNS, in her twenties and her name was Gloria Grace. I was about ten years old. I believe she was unaware of my existence.[74]

Cameron also shared vivid memories of the war's impact in Ceylon and the life of its planter community. Concerned about the enemy threat, he was reassured by his father as well as the

71 'Fan Tan', 'Soldiering in Ceylon', p. 68.
72 Thompson, *Only the Sun Remembers*, p. 211.
73 Cameron, 'Bits and Pieces' and a second typescript sent to the author, 'Earliest Recollections 5-7 Years'.
74 Cameron, 'Earliest Recollections, 5-7 Years'.

presence of large numbers of troops throughout the island. 'Life on the tea plantations', he recalls, 'changed little':

> There was no curfew or blackout. There was rationing, but managers and junior staff bungalows, and the labourers' quarters, had substantial vegetable gardens, and cowsheds, and free ranging chickens were everywhere. In a village in Ceylon from any distance the houses are virtually invisible as they are totally enclosed by produce-bearing trees, coconut, toddy palm, jak, breadfruit, mango, banana, papaya, sugar cane and many other varieties. In the town it must have been very different, especially for the poor. There was a flourishing black market – but only for those who could afford it.[75]

All in all, Ceylon was:

> A paradise for sport, big game, peafowl, jungle fowl, and pigeon shooting in the lowland forests; grey partridge on the coastal plains in the north; snipe and duck in the fallow paddy fields and reservoirs, big game fishing on the coast, fishing for mahseer and catfish in the low country rivers, and rainbow trout in the hill streams over 4,000 feet elevation. Because of petrol rationing travel was largely curtailed (I remember my father used to switch off and coast down all the downhill stretches on the way to the club) and many of these sporting pursuits were abandoned until after the war. But this was no great hardship as tennis, golf, snooker, and squash were still available in the upcountry clubs, as was trout fishing in the hill streams that ran through the planting districts, as the Planters' Fishing Club maintained a trout hatchery near Nuwara Eliya which was maintained throughout the war.[76]

Thousands of imperial troops were hosted in the homes of planters like the Camerons. Edward Young's last leave was spent on a tea plantation near Nuwara Eliya, leaving Trincolamee in a naval lorry on a morning of oppressive heat.

> At first the road was flanked by jungle on both sides, and monkeys swung in the branches arching high over our heads. We came out of the jungle and drove among bright green paddy-fields and through native villages swarming with wizened old men, bright-eyed women, and naked children, all very attractive until the smiled and showed teeth hideously discoloured by the blood-red juice of the betel nut. We saw oxen at plough, and from time to time a tame elephant hauling a log along the road … Presently the road began climbing more steeply among the foothills, and the vistas grew longer and more superb, and in spite of the August sun we found the air turning chilly and had to put on extra clothes.[77]

After spending most of summer 1941 escorting 'the Monsters' – the world's largest ocean liners, now serving as troopships – around the Indian Ocean, the cruiser *Cornwall* put into Colombo at the end of August. Here she was to go into dry dock to have her guns changed, which presented the captain, Percival Manwaring, with the opportunity to rotate his c. 800-strong

75 Cameron, 'Bits and Pieces'.
76 Banks, 'World War Two Memories – Ceylon'.
77 Young, *One of Our Submarines*, p. 229.

crew through a cycle of leave. Consequently 350 men of the starboard watch, including Ken Dimbleby, trooped down the gangway to a tug that conveyed them to a jetty. Some were taken off by bus to meet their hosts, others boarded a train for:

> an interesting journey through picturesque country with magnificent scenery, the train meandering through the lowlands with flowering trees, coconut and banana trees, bamboos and palms, among many others, past rice lands, canals, rivers and lakes into jungles. As the train climbed into the higher country, we came to the tea plantations that play such an important part in the country's economy.
>
> There were gay scenes at the many stations and sidings where the train stopped, men and youngsters enticing the sailors to buy beer, buns and bananas among other fruit and sweetmeats.[78]

Peeling off at the various stops in pairs or small groups, Dimbleby was taken to the 300 acre tea plantation of the Bond family. After six months living on a crowded mess deck, he revelled in the large house, each bedroom with its own bathroom, Ceylon tea, banana, and pawpaw brought first thing in the morning by a servant before breakfast an hour later.[79] The visit provided a welcome chance to relax before returning to the cruiser and its hectic schedule of duties, soon to become much more dangerous with Japan's entry into the war.

Joan Gottelier's was a typical planter family with multiple connections to the war. Her father played host to hundreds of service personnel on rest and recreation breaks, her fiancé had been in the Ceylon Planters Rifles Corps and now joined the RAF, her brother, who had a heart condition that prevented him from joining up, knitted for the war effort between planting, and Joan herself served in naval headquarters from 1940.[80] She recalls that

> rice was rationed, and so was petrol. But the Planters decided to continue with their one-afternoon-per-week club afternoon. This was mainly to keep in touch with everyone and everything, and not remain isolated. But they did stipulate that 'standing your friend a drink' was OUT. This weekly club afternoon kept them sane! In Colombo, the Tennis Clubs kept going. I would have a couple of sets after work at the Colombo Garden Club. In the Victory Tournament, I played a Colombo Agent's wife, in semi-finals. She was tipped to win, but I beat her and wasn't very popular – 'a mere chit of a girl' beating a Colombo Agent's wife!.[81]

In terms of clubs, 'the Navy had the BSSI [British Soldiers' and Sailors' Institute of Colombo], as well as the Fleet Club and the Junior Fleet Club, the latter for Ratings. And how many dances

78 Dimbleby, *Turns of Fate*, p. 111.

79 On returning to Colombo, '*Cornwall* was infested with workmen running around like a lot of cockroaches and stealing just about everything they could lay their hands on … [I] made my way to a large chestnut tree that stood beside the dry dock. When a warship is in dock a canteen was opened next to the tree and it was the custom for sailors to take their supper under the tree and wash it down with a bottle of beer.' Dimbleby, *Turns of Fate*, p. 112.

80 Gottelier interview, April 1999.

81 Ibid.

did I go to there!! Among my hospital visits was a Rating of just eighteen, who had lost a foot, caught up in the anchor chain. I eventually stopped visiting him, as he had a crush on me!!'.[82]

John Banks was a schoolboy living in Hatton, and recalls the hospitality extended by his parents to British servicemen and women. His father was the manager and part owner of Hatton Bank Limited, and they turned their home, Bank House

> into a holiday home for soldiers and sailors and the tennis court into a vegetable garden. I remember Piper Paterson. He had been wounded in the Desert and was recovering from his wounds. While with us, he played his pipes on a far hill overlooking the local club. There was Tim Aspinall of the Royal West African Frontier Force walking down the passage in a very starched pair of shorts, laid out for him by his African batman. He later went to Burma with his regiment and was killed in action. There was a sailor who had cut himself on coral at Addu Atoll and the wound refused to heal. It was hoped that a spell in the hills would help.[83]

At Hatton railway station the wives of tea planters served tea and buns to soldiers travelling up and down by the mid-day mail train. 'When my sister was twenty-one, one of her boy friends flew his Hurricane to Madras and brought back a flagon of Black Cat gin for her party'. Banks also remembers seeing the converted super-liners *Queen Elizabeth* and *Queen Mary* in Trincomalee harbour with thousands of Australians on board. There was strict petrol rationing, introduced in November 1941, which made his father, the local justice of the peace and therefore the distributing officer, very unpopular.[84]

The lack of variation in the temperature meant that rest camps were very important for the troops, as was the opportunity to visit Colombo for those based in remote areas. An officer of the 34th Indian Division wrote that those stationed in the jungle preferred town leave in Colombo, while those based in Colombo preferred the 'cool nights and country life of Diyatalawa … Above all, there is EFI [Expeditionary Forces Institutions – the NAAFI (Navy, Army, and Air Force Institute) element deployed in officially designated war zones], which ensures that beer, cigarettes and other essential items are available at reasonable prices'.[85] In the Central Highlands, numerous rest camps catered for off duty servicemen and women, their facilities supplementing the hospitality extended by the planter community. The hill country rest camps, together with the bungalows of accommodating planters where officers found billets, were visited by thousands of servicemen and women.

The hill station of Nuwara Eliya, established in 1825 as a sanatorium for British soldiers convalescing from malaria, was Ceylon's 'little England'. Here Europeans were refreshed by hilltop mist, cool air, and drizzle, the town becoming the island's 'outstanding resort for servicemen'.[86]

82 Ibid.
83 John Banks, letter to author, 7/2/99, and enclosed typescript, 'World War Two Memories – Ceylon'.
84 Ibid.
85 'Fan Tan', 'Soldiering in Ceylon', p. 68. James Thompson offers a description of a night on the town in and around Diyatalawa in *Only the Sun Remembers*, quoted at length in Jackson, *Of Islands, Ports, and Sea Lanes*, and memorable for being a night of drinking and mirth suddenly brought to a crashing end when, returning to the mess for dinner, he learned of the sinking of *Prince of Wales* and *Repulse*.
86 SNLA, *Times of Ceylon*, 13/6/44.

As well as the racecourse, Nuwara Eliya boasted a golf course, regular 'All Ceylon' tennis and golf tournaments, flower and vegetable shows, a circus, and gymkhanas. Alan Brundrett spent a week at the Craighton Village Rest Camp at Nuwara Eliya, surprised, like most people, by the temperate climate as well as the exhilarating road or rail journey required to reach it.

Cecil Callis made the journey to Nuwara Eliya along a torturous road snaking up the 6,000 feet to Nuwara Eliya, the road running 'along high ledges on mountainsides, and winds up "staircases" of hair-raising hairpin bends'.[87] The European area of the town was built like an English country town, with gabled roofs, bow windows, and cross-beamed walls. There were cottages with roses around the doors and herbaceous borders around the lawns. 'We even found a racecourse, with paddocks and some racehorses in the stables'.[88] Several miles away was World's End, one of the great scenic wonders of the island, a sheer drop of 5,000 feet with the sea 50 miles away in the distance. Nearby was was the well-known military rest camp at Diyatalawa, a mini-town of granite cottages and rows of tin huts with neatly painted windows and verandahs, used by the military since the Boer War and a main rest camp for other ranks (there was also an internment camp here for enemy aliens, and Italian prisoner-of-war camps in various locations). Nearby, and a site of recreation and physical fitness activities, was Fox Hill, named so because of the large white fox etched into the hillside above the legend 'HMS Fox 1913', a legacy of British sailors visiting before the last war. Diyatalawa also boasted a golf course with its own natural hazards, including leaches. 'To overcome them', recalled a member of the submarine *Tally-Ho*'s crew, 'one trick was to wear ladies' stockings which the leeches were not keen to climb. If they did, they were burned off with a lighted cigarette'.[89] A favoured variation of the game was taxi golf, which involved being accompanied around the course by two taxis loaded with drink. Win a putt, and a player would sink a beer, a birdie earned a double tot of spirits, and a bogey a single tot.

Another favourite destination in the highlands was the beautiful and historic town of Kandy. After mooring alongside the depot ship *Wuchang* in Colombo in November 1943 after their first war patrol in eastern waters, members of *Tally-Ho*'s crew went on leave to Kandy. They visited the Buddhist Temple of the Tooth in Kandy and the Peradeniya Botanical Gardens. One of the attractions in Kandy was the presence of American servicewomen, and some of the boat's officers installed themselves in the Grand Hotel, attending a Thanksgiving Ball at the American Club, their tropical white uniform standing out amid the American khaki. After letting off some Chinese crackers and causing a commotion, they were politely asked to leave the following day.[90] African troops stationed in Ceylon also enjoyed periods of leave featuring elephant rides and ngomas (drum and dance parties) as well as visits to Kandy lake and the Queen's Hotel, Nuwara Eliya, and tea plantations.[91]

87 BBC World War Two People's War oral history archive, Cecil Callis, 'Eastern Travels', part 6, chapter 8, 'Back to the Hills', A4428173.

88 Ibid.

89 Ian Trenowden, *The Hunting Submarine: The Fighting Life of HMS* Tally-Ho (London: William Kimber, 1974), p. 146.

90 Ibid., p. 48.

91 NAM, 1997-08-57, Photograph album of East African battalions in East Africa, Ceylon, Burma, and India.

Of course, it was by no means all about rest and recreation. Many of the service personnel stationed in Ceylon were there to train ahead of operational deployments. Some units were green and honing their battle skills for the first time before facing the enemy, others seasoned soldiers and undergoing a training and rest and recuperation break between operations. Troops stationed in the island for its defence also practiced their planned tactics should the invader come. Cecil Callis recalls the 34th Indian Division's 'manoeuvres for the defence of the island', which for him brought a very busy period maintaining and repairing the instruments, equipment, and vehicles of the Royal Signals, Callis himself concentrating on the motorbikes of the dispatch riders.[92] For soldiers such as George Shepperson, the prime experience of Ceylon was as a training venue. He spent three months there with his KAR battalion in 1944 preparing for the 11th East African Division's Kabaw valley campaign. Shepperson recalls several strange experiences in Ceylon, not least burying a British officer in Kandy; an askari policeman 'had wanted to kill an NCO but hit the officer instead!'.[93]

The recreational activities of the African troops were interspersed with periods of intense training, including practice assaults and watercraft (a photograph in the *Times of Ceylon* showed askaris floating jeeps across a wide river).[94] There was also live ammunition practice, artillery bombardment, and attacks on enemy emplacements with rifles, Bren guns, bayonets, and grenades. The film 'Askaris Training in Ceylon' offers an excellent impression of their activity. According to the film's description, it shows troops in

> light fighting order and armed with Lee Enfield No. 3 rifles and Bren light machine guns advance through thickly wooded terrain. They advance through close country and scramble up a steep slope. A soldier operates an Ordnance SBML 2-inch mortar to fire a smoke bomb. The bomb, trailing a white tail of smoke, hits the ground and spreads a smoke screen. The soldiers advance up the hillside. A sequence of footage in fading light. Close-up of two soldiers lying prone; the man nearest camera has an Enfield rifle and next to him is a Bren gunner. The rifleman, with his rifle already cocked, fits a magazine to the Bren gun. The Bren gun has an old-pattern drum sight, so possibly a Mark III. The soldiers raise their weapons. The rifleman fires his weapon through thick cover, giving the camera a good view of the rifle's action.[95]

On 15 November 1944 Mountbatten visited the 22nd East African Brigade at Horana, confirming rumours that it would soon be deployed to Burma alongside the 81st West African Division. The brigade duly moved to Colombo where the men boarded the troopship *Aronda*. The convoy carrying the brigade set sail for Chittagong, escorted across the Bay of Bengal by Eastern Fleet warships, destined for the third Arakan campaign.

In November 1944 Tony Inman was sent on an escape and evasion exercise in the jungle.

92 BBC World War Two People's War oral history archive, Callis, chapter 8, 'Back to the Hills'. One of the bikes he had to repair belonged to Ron Newell, who hit an elephant at speed, breaking his leg and damaging his bike.
93 George Shepperson letter to author, 9/4/99.
94 SNLA, *Times of Ceylon*, 3/5/44.
95 IWM, JFU 151, text from Colonial Film Database.

> Three or four crew went up into the jungle with an instructor, known, of course, as Jungle Jim. He was a rubber planter who had escaped with his family from Malaya and was rumoured that he and his wife liked the jungle so much that they spent weekends camping out ... Under his guidance we built a hut of palm fronds guaranteed to keep the rain out ... Food, my memory says, was mostly corned beef fried in palm oil, which is as revolting as it sounds. It was difficult to sleep, what with the monkeys howling, other creatures grunting, squeaking, snorting, and shrieking. We stayed awake and played cards, which did not please Jim, who eventually got up and went outside. He called us out to show us, he said, something we should beware of at night. He would not allow a torch so we could see a luminous snake and sure enough there was this luminous thing. We should be careful, he said, as this type of snake tended to jump at its prey. The words were hardly out of his mouth before the thing jumped up in the air. I fell over backwards and down a filthy muddy bank and there was a general thrashing about as we all tried to escape from this leaping object. Jim then turned on his torch so we could see the 'snake'. It was a dead branch that had become covered in a fungus that glowed in the dark and it 'jumped' at us when Jim picked it up, unseen in the darkness. I think he won that round.[96]

Sometimes imperial units trained with locally-raised Ceylonese forces in order to develop the skills of the latter through interaction with regulars (meaning full time professional soldiers), activity that thawed what could be frosty relations between them. The Ceylon Garrison Artillery and the Ceylon Light Infantry, wrote a 34th Indian Division officer, 'regarded the entry of Regular troops with great suspicion. This has largely disappeared as a result of training together. They did very well during the air raids, although this was the first time they had been under fire'.[97] He continued, lauding Ceylon's qualities as a training venue:

> Ceylon provides one of the finest training grounds in the world, for jungle warfare or combined operations. The North is open, with coconut plantations and paddy fields. The centre is dense jungle and undeveloped. The South is mountainous and split by six rivers. Right round the island, in the coastal belt there is a continuous line of coconut estates and the hilly districts are covered with tea. The joy of being able to train, without entering villages or damaging crops, can only be really appreciated by those who have had to prepare for war in cantonments such as Lucknow.
>
> The narrow roads of Ceylon have provided some fine traffic jams and have taught us the need for traffic control. Numerous jungle paths give opportunities for practising turning movements by cyclists or lightly clad infantry, and there are any number of places on the coast which provide ideal conditions for training in combined operations.
>
> The astounding mixture of races, has enabled us to learn a lot about and from each other. British troops arrived from the Western Desert, and had been at war for three years, so they brought experience and confidence. East African troops recruited from tribes which live in the bush soon taught us how to 'live in' the jungle. Indian troops have proved as

96 BBC World War Two People's War oral history archive, Inman.
97 'Fan Tan', 'Soldiering in Ceylon', p. 67.

> adaptable as ever and, being the young members of the team, are always out to show what they can do.[98]

On one occasion some of the division's Indian troops and their British non-commissioned officers were given a guided tour of a battleship, though the proximity to the water was not to everyone's liking. As one British soldier put it, 'I joined the army to fight for King and Country, not to provide a meal for that ******* crocodile'.[99]

Service personnel stationed on the island for long periods adopted standard working routines. 'Where possible', wrote a FAA pilot based in Ceylon,

> most units operated under tropical routine, flying hard from dawn with lighter work or 'make do and mend' in the afternoon, meaning they were free to do as they wished when the fierce sun reached its zenith. At the end of a hot day officers showered, donned their smart white tropical rig and visited the mess or went into Colombo, sipping cool drinks on the terrace of the Galle Face Hotel while watching the golden sun sink into the slate-grey Indian Ocean.[100]

Once landed in Ceylon Tony Inman, who had sailed out from Britain aboard the *Orantes* and observed Arabs exposing their genitals while passing through the Suez Canal, was sent to the Royal Naval Air Station at Katukurunda. This aerodrome was known as HMS *Ukussa*, and at the time housed a squadron of Avengers and 'was used by carrier squadrons, usually from passing escort carriers, to do some working up'.[101] Because of his previous experience working with Fairey Swordfish torpedo bombers, Inman was soon sent to Trincomalee when it became necessary to provide air cover for capital units in the waters around the island. 'There had been a submarine scare in the Bay of Bengal and it was decided that an air escort was needed for the *Victorious* and four destroyers until such time as they were clear of the coast and *Victorious* could operate her own aircraft'.[102]

Four famous visitors

A number of well-known personalities, or people who would later become well know, served in Ceylon during the war, including the broadcasters Derek Jacobs and Desmond Carrington, the *Carry On* actor Kenneth Williams, the novelist Ian Fleming, the actor, playwright, singer, and raconteur Noël Coward, the poet Charles Causley, who penned an ode to Trincomalee, and Prince Philip of Greece.[103] It was while serving in Ceylon that Kenneth Williams developed

98 Ibid.
99 Ibid.
100 Iredale, *The Kamikaze Hunters*, p. 179.
101 BBC World War Two People's War oral history archive, Inman.
102 Ibid.
103 Winton, *Sink the* Haguro!, pp. 25-6. See also the poem 'Trincomalee', by 'Lucy', published in the *Fleet Poetry Broadsheet* in August 1944, p. 24. Other wartime Ceylon-inspired poetry appears in the Fleet Air Arm pilot Hugh Popham's volume. See 'Evening in Colombo', Popham, *Against the Lightning* (London: The Bodley Head, 1944), p. 30.

his skills as an entertainer: 'we held an impromptu concert at which my impersonations won vigorous applause', he wrote. 'The Quartermaster Sergeant – who had written the scripts and put the show together – told me I should take up entertaining professionally'.[104] From here his acting career took root. When an area order was issued stating that soldiers could express a preference for alternative regiments, 'I persuaded the CO to sign my application for CSE [Combined Services Entertainments] which was a newly formed organization to succeed ENSA'. He failed his first audition, though his drawing skills were used for posters, and succeeded in passing a second audition. Williams remained in Ceylon until August 1946, when he left Colombo for Singapore where he was soon playing the detective in the melodramatic farce *Seven Keys to Baldpate* at the Victoria Theatre.

Prince Philip, future husband of Princess Elizabeth, spent some time in Ceylon in the early days of the war. He had passed out of the Royal Naval College Britannia at Dartmouth just before war began. Though he had three sisters married to Germans, he was unquestionably British-oriented but still a Greek subject. Any difficulties that this might have presented in terms of his career in the Royal Navy during a time of war were ironed out, largely through the influence of his friend Lord Mountbatten. Nevertheless the Admiralty, as well as the Home Office and the Foreign Office, were concerned about the potential embarrassment that the service of a foreign prince from a neutral country in the British forces might cause. The authorities had to take into account the fact that 'Greece was not yet at war and it would have been embarrassing to have had a Greek prince killed in action while serving in a British man-of-war'.[105]

The solution was to send the young prince to a theatre where there was minimal fighting, and this, in the early months of the war with Germany, was the Indian Ocean. In January 1940 Philip was duly appointed to the battleship *Ramillies* stationed at Colombo. His appointment was 'a reasonably conventional assignment because midshipman tended to go to large cruisers or battleships where there were enough good officers to ensure they were given sensible training and not allowed too much responsibility too early'.[106] Life aboard *Ramillies* proved a spartan experience; originally commissioned in 1917, she was over 20 years old and felt like it. She was so uncomfortable that no one ever turned in properly because she was darkened at night and '"every scuttle is shut with deadlights". The midshipmen preferred to sleep in the gun room where they crashed out on arm-chairs, sofas, and even tables'.[107]

Serving with *Ramillies*, Philip sailed on convoy escort duties across the Indian Ocean, trips that included escorting the first convoy of Australian and New Zealand soldiers to the Middle East. In May 1940 he joined the cruiser *Kent*, stationed elsewhere in the Indian Ocean region: 'I can honestly say that when we first saw this gangling youth, running all over the ship trying to obey instructions from a host of gold braid, smiling and cheerful to everyone, no matter what their rank, he immediately became endeared to us'.[108] In September 1940 he transferred to the cruiser *Shropshire* operating out of Durban, ever popular with sailors, 'a melee of parties, dances, jungle car excursions, and even sample nights on safari which Philip robustly enjoyed

104 Williams, *Just Williams*, p. 36.
105 Tim Heald, *The Duke: A Portrait of Prince Philip* (London: Hodder and Stoughton, 1991).
106 Ibid.
107 Ibid.
108 Denis Judd, *Prince Philip: A Biography* (London: Sphere Books, 1991), p. 103.

to the full'.[109] Phillip visited Aden, Bombay, Fremantle, and Mombasa. He also spent a period ashore at naval headquarters at HMS *Lanka*, living on Upper Chatham Street, Colombo. For £12 he acquired a small car, a Standard Nine, with which to run around the island (now on display in the Galle Face Hotel).[110] He drove through the jungle to Trincomalee, and went on a minesweeping patrol with the Ceylon Naval Volunteer Force. On one occasion, he borrowed the Commander-in-Chief's barge and went to see the festival of the Buddha's Tooth in Kandy.

Another famous visitor to Ceylon was Noël Coward, who arrived at the invitation of his friend Mountbatten. Always seeking useful war employment beyond singing, acting and 'morale boosting', early in the war Coward had undertaken some intelligence work though remained a prisoner of his own celebrity. His war tours had already taken him to Australia, Canton Island in the Pacific, Beirut, Bermuda, Egypt, France, Gibraltar, the Gold Coast, Iraq, Jamaica, Kenya, Malta, South Africa, Southern Rhodesia, and Trinidad. The South African tour, Coward wrote, had been a replica of those in Australia and New Zealand – 'major venues alternating with troop concerts, hospital visits, broadcasts, endless meetings both formal and informal'.[111]

Looking forward to returning home after an extended period touring overseas, a signal arrived from SEAC Headquarters on 16 February 1944. Mountbatten wrote that 'the one universal cry is for entertainment and visits from distinguished people … I am sure that a tour by you would be immensely appreciated out here and if you will let me know whether you can come, and if so between what dates, I will arrange to have a tour laid on for you which would include visits to British and American soldiers and airmen'.[112] From South Africa

> it had been arranged for us to fly to Bulawayo to Nairobi, give a few shows there and in Mombasa, then to fly on to Cairo and straight home to England. The last part of this plan was drastically changed by the arrival of a cable from Dickie Mountbatten in Ceylon, asking us to come out and entertain the Fourteenth Army in Assam and Burma. This cable was a bombshell I had been out of England for five months and was longing to get home.[113]

Yet he went, sailing from Mombasa aboard the Eastern Fleet destroyer *Rapid*.[114] The journey took 12 days, slower than the five it could have taken because the destroyer was escorting a convoy part of the way. Coward described the voyage across the Indian Ocean:

> For me, at any rate, the time was all too short; after the first three days, when the sea was so rough that I had to lash myself into my bunk at night, we slid out on to the bosom of the Indian Ocean into halcyon weather. I lunched *tête-à-tête* every day with the Captain, and spent the rest of the time lying on the fo'c'sle in the sun, or wandering about the ship and talking to whoever was interested. As is usually the case in small ships the atmosphere

109 H. M. Queen Alexandria of Yugoslavia, *Prince Philip: A Family Portrait* (London: Hodder and Stoughton, 1960), p. 68.
110 Galle Face Hotel Museum information.
111 Barry Day (ed.), *The Letters of Noël Coward* (London: Methuen, 2007), p. 498.
112 Ibid., p. 499.
113 Noël Coward, *Future Indefinite* (London: Methuen, 2004), p. 250.
114 Ibid., p. 251.

> was friendly and informal. There were terrific arguments in the ward-room after dinner on various subjects … Sometimes, after one of these intellectual free-for-alls, I felt disinclined for sleep and went up to the bridge to chat with the Officer of the Watch and have some ship's cocoa under the vivid stars … I also managed during the twelve days to write a short story called 'Mr and Mrs Edgehill' … I scribbled and typed for hours daily in the Captain's cabin until, two days before we were due to arrive at Colombo, the story was finished … At last the voyage was over and the island of Ceylon appeared on the horizon, its mountains blue and purple in the morning light.[115]

In Ceylon Coward was assigned one of Mountbatten's aides-de-camp, Mike Umfreville, who came aboard to take him off and drive with him to Kandy. 'On my first evening in the King's Pavilion in Kandy, which Dickie has made his GHQ, he and I dined quietly', Mountbatten outlining the arrangements he had made for the tour.[116] After five days in Ceylon Coward flew to Calcutta, and thence to Burma where, among other things, he observed stacks of rotting Japanese corpses. He gave a concert to a camp of 2,000 African soldiers who 'gave him the bird' – one really does wonder what non-English-speaking Africans were supposed to make of a Noël Coward set! – before returning to Kandy. Here he did a show for Mountbatten's headquarters staff, then three or four more in various camps which entailed some long drives. 'And then what I had been dreading for a long time happened. I collapsed finally and knew that I had come to the end of my rope. The collapse was unspectacular and devoid of drama. It began during a long drive home after a show at a newly built RAF base'. About a dozen further shows had to be cancelled. 'I hated doing this and compromised by giving three, a week later, in the Naval Base in Trincomalee, but they were forced and not very good'.[117] Returning to Colombo, Coward stayed for a few days at the Galle Face Hotel. 'Eventually I took off at dawn, a very overdone tropical dawn with scarlet clouds piled against a lemon and blue sky, and flew home to England in a succession of different aircraft via Karachi, Sharjah, Bahrein, Cairo, Tripoli, Rabat, and Casablanca'.[118]

Ian Fleming, employed during the war by the Admiralty's Department of Naval Intelligence, visited Ceylon in December 1944 to review the intelligence provisions for the newly created British Pacific Fleet, based at Trincomalee though about to leave for bases in Australia and the Pacific. Here he met his old friend Alan Hillgarth, Chief of British Naval Intelligence Eastern Theatre (CBNIET).

> As well as his official NID [Naval Intelligence Division] role, Hillgarth was Prime Minister Churchill's personal intelligence representative in Colombo … [He] did his own signals, with the help of his trusted Wren assistant, Clare Blanshard, an attractive and amusing woman in her late twenties, who joked that CBNIET stood for Chief Bloody Nuisance in the Eastern Theatre.[119]

115 Ibid., p. 252-3.
116 Ibid.
117 Ibid., p. 268-9.
118 For Coward's valedictory ditty 'To Admiral the Lord Louis Mountbatten', see Day, *The Letters of Noël Coward*, pp. 501-02.
119 Andrew Lycett, *Ian Fleming* (London: Weidenfeld and Nicolson, 1995), p. 154.

As soon as he arrived on 23 December, Ian struck up a close friendship with Clare, who was evidently swept off her feet by the handsome, educated naval officer in his tropical uniform. In a letter to her brother, Paul, she captured the essence of a whirlwind romance:

> Since I last wrote (and continuously, every day, but about to be lopped off at a moment's notice like Marlowe's Faustus), a beauteous being has swum into my ken – on an official visit – and I like him very very very much indeed … As the Wrens say, whose letters I censor so monotonously, he's absolutely It. It doesn't make any difference that I don't mean anything to him as he's so awfully nice … so that is why I haven't written. Next time I write he'll have gone for ever and ever and practically won't have existed. But, believe me, he's the right shape, size, height, has the right sort of hair, the right sort of laugh, is 36 and beautiful. I wish I were more glamorous.[120]

Fleming had arrived in Colombo at the height of the Christmas party season. Staying at the Galle Face Hotel, he invited Clare to a dance at the 'Septic Prawn', a nickname for the Silver Faun nightclub in the hotel's basement. She was pleased to find that he was 'a plodder dancer: I dislike men who dance well'. She wore a stunning long white silk dress, plugged with little pieces of real silver. Fleming was fascinated with the garment and, 17 years later, sent her a postcard of the ballroom of a Sussex hotel where he was recuperating following an illness. He marked the front with an X and wrote, '"I'm behind the palm tree on the right, watching you clearing the floor in the centre"'. Clare recalled, 'He couldn't get over that dress. He really minded about materials and such things'.

Fleming also expressed an interest in exploring the Ceylon countryside. When Clare told him about the jungle which straddled the railway on the way up to the hill-station of Kandy, he jumped at the opportunity to investigate. Then, after a flying visit to see his brother Peter at the Deception Centre in Delhi, in the company of Clare and Hillgarth he flew from Ceylon across the Indian Ocean to Australia on 22 January 1945. Here Blanshard and Fleming spent some carefree days before he returned to London and the Admiralty. Later that year in a letter he thanked her for a cake that she had sent from ration-free Australia. It 'was gobbled till the saliva ran down my chin'. Keeping up the sensual tone, he hoped that her trip to Kashmir 'has made you brown and swollen your curves. He pleaded with her not to 'get thin or there will be nothing for your paramours to hold on to on the black satin divan with the orange cushions'.[121] The two renewed their acquaintance when she returned to Britain after the war, Fleming helping her find a job at the BBC, and they remained friends for years afterwards.

With so many military migrants in Ceylon, efforts needed to be made to entertain them in order to maintain both efficiency and morale. They inevitably interacted with the local population as well as with each other, which could generate tensions relating to gender, race, and sex. It is to these thorny topics that the following chapter turns in order to further the exploration of the serviceman and woman's experience of wartime Ceylon.

120 Ibid.
121 Ibid.

8

Plain tales from Ceylon: Part II

This chapter extends the exploration of the experiences and activities of imperial servicemen and women in wartime Ceylon, looking in particular at issues relating to race, sex, and gender, and the efforts made to entertain men and women far from home. Beauty was not only to be found in Ceylon's landscape, Cecil Callis opining that 'the dusky Sinhalese girls were very attractive and the Burgher girls, of mixed Sinhalese and European blood, were beautiful'.[1] This was a common opinion among British servicemen. Thomas Russell of the battleship *Ramillies* claimed that shore leave in Colombo 'revealed more female beauty in one place than I'd ever seen in my life'.[2] Alan Brundrett noted that 'the Sinhalese and Tamil women have a fine carriage and glide along in regal fashion, looking cool and graceful in their bright sarongs. Their ears and noses sparkle with coloured jewellery. Many of the husbands too are clad airily in thin white muslin'.[3] Tom Driberg also remarked on the physical qualities of the Ceylonese people:

> We drove up to the camp at nightfall, past clusters of small shops painted in gay stripes and ablaze with light. The people of Ceylon, we noted, walk with the smooth grace of ballet dancers, upright and dignified; their sarongs, in green or mauve or saffron, hang always with the inevitable perfection of the drapery of Greek statues. There was an aroma compounded of wood-smoke and spices and sandalwood. Certainly none of the British forces in Asia are more fortunate than those stationed here.[4]

The surfeit of human beauty to be found in this 'island paradise', combined with the surfeit of young unattached servicemen thousands of miles from home, meant that many people wanted to do more than just observe the beauty of the local population. Ceylon had something of a reputation in colonial circles as an 'anything goes' colony, and had gained notoriety as a scene of sexual encounter in 1903 with the scandal surrounding the death of the then commander-in-chief Ceylon, General Hector Macdowell, who shot himself in a Paris hotel

1 BBC World War Two People's War oral history archive, Callis, 'Eastern Travels', chapter 8, 'Back to the Hills'.
2 BBC World War Two People's War oral history archive, Russell.
3 Brundrett, *Two Years in Ceylon*, p. 187.
4 Quoted in Brundrett, *Two Years in Ceylon*, p. 278.

room en route to Ceylon after being censured in London for alleged homosexual activity involving Sinhalese boys.[5]

In the inter-war years, the incidence of venereal disease among servicemen in Ceylon was among the highest recorded in the Empire. Ronald Hyam writes that the 'easy opportunities, the separation from family ties and moral pressures, the fact that syphilis was rife in foreign parts and the knowledge that diagnosis and treatment of venereal disease could be readily concealed from loved ones, make it hardly surprising that venereal disease was always more of a problem abroad than at home'.[6] Between 1921 and 1926 the incidence of venereal disease in the army at home was 40 per 1,000 men. The figure stood at 103 in Egypt, 110 in India, 169 in the South China Sea, and 184 in Ceylon. The 1928 figures for the Royal Navy were 82 per thousand at home, 156 for African, Mediterranean, and West Indian stations, 304 for the China Station, and 204 for Ceylon.[7]

One of the results of Ceylon's rising population of servicemen was an increase in the incidence of venereal disease and prostitution. New venereal disease regulations were adopted, though the number of cases continued to rise dramatically. In 1942 49,586 cases were treated, rising to 87,433 in 1943 and 92,542 in 1944.[8] A report by G. H. Bromley, Deputy Inspector-General of Police, on the 'Traffic of Women and Children' in April 1944 recorded instances of servicemen being solicited for 'an immoral purpose' as well as being caught in brothels. Sinhalese men solicited the servicemen, for example two sailors in Colombo who were taken to a house and charged 50 rupees for sex with 15 and 16 year old girls. The police employed undercover officers, dressed in military uniform, to catch those breaking the law.[9] British army officers complained that local men attempted to solicit trade for prostitutes among African servicemen, but that new 'anti-pimping' legislation was coming into effect.[10]

A celebrated case of alleged sexual misdemeanour concerned G. F. 'Dick' Green, who worked in the Public Relations Department of the Commander-in-Chief Ceylon. When Ronald George joined the department he became a close friend of the mercurial Green, who was responsible for producing a magazine for Ceylonese forces on the island entitled *Veera Lanka*, published in both Sinhalese and Tamil. When not at his day job, Green found plenty of time for what he euphemistically termed 'verandahism'. According to George, this was 'a compound of drink, sex, benzedrine, and cigarettes'.[11] The term 'verandahism' came from the fact that Green had colonized a section of the verandah opening from the main quarters of the officers' mess, 'and turned it into something special'.[12] While most officers lived in spartan quarters, Green had

5 See Trevor Royle, *Death Before Dishonour: The True Story of 'Fighting Mac'* (London: St Martin's Press, 1982).
6 Ronald Hyam, *Empire and Sexuality: The British Experience* (Manchester: Manchester University Press, 1990), p. 89.
7 Ibid.
8 SNLA, Administrative reports, 1944, volume 1. See also Dr S. F. Chellappah, *Administrative Report of the Director of Medical and Sanitary Services for 1944* (Colombo: Government Press, 1945).
9 SNLA, Lot 5/439, Dispatches 442, 29/4/44. See Thompson's description of being solicited for sex in Pettah, *Only the Sun Remembers*, pp. 196-98.
10 TNA, WO 172/3985.
11 C. Green and A. D. Maclean (eds), *A Skilled Hand: A Collection of Stories and Writings by G. F. Green, with Memoirs and Criticism* (London: Macmillan, 1980), p. 106.
12 Ibid.

turned his glory hole into a haven with a divan, easy chairs, Bokhara rugs, Hessian wall hangings, and pictures. There, he would have parties with anyone he liked, regardless of race or gender. Inevitably, this behaviour had got him noticed, and other officers vowed to 'get him' when the chance arose.

Green had, in the eyes of his friend, 'flung himself' into self-indulgence 'under the headiness of the East'.[13] His dénouement came in late 1944 when, returning home extremely drunk after one of his forays, he entertained a rickshaw puller while mess dinner was taking place nearby. He apparently had sex with a Sinhalese boy on the verandah of the officers' mess, and was caught in bed with another, and the military police were called by vindictive fellow officers'. He was 'found on his bed, all the lights on, in the wrong place, at the wrong time, with someone whose company, in the circumstances, could only be regarded by the military authorities as conduct unbecoming, to say the least'.[14] His discovery by the Sinhalese staff soon roused the attention of fellow officers, including those out to teach Green a lesson. As a result, he was cashiered from the army and imprisoned for two years, the sentence being completed back in Britain after the war.

As well as having a formative experience as an actor and entertainer in Ceylon, Kenneth Williams also had a rare sexual encounter. It took place in a coconut grove in Kurunegala with a young Sikh boy, a story that later in life Williams would recount when in his cups. The episode – 'a Barclays Bank, not the full thing' – appears to have been something of a sexual peak in a life of mental and spiritual, but rarely physical, homosexuality.[15] There were then the countless affairs and casual liaisons between members of the armed forces and local or itinerant women in Ceylon. Ken Ward remembers the Christmas 1944 mess party aboard the carrier *Indefatigable*; 'as the boys got drunker, so did the Wrens', there was plenty of licentious behaviour and 'glasses and pineapples flying around when the drink ran out'.[16] James Thompson wrote of the toll that affairs between male and female service personnel or local inhabitants could exact:

> Ceylon was rich in warm possibility. Many bungalows were hollowed by their small, personal tragedy of absence, divorce or acknowledged infidelities. And always and ever the yearning to leave, to go home to the rose-dream England, the house by the sea, to return and retire to Devon, Sussex or the country counties.[17]
>
> … [T]he invading officers brought and left sorrow, unhappiness and disruption. We joked at a new design for living; Mr. and Mrs. Smith and officer attached; the emotional, physical, social *ménage à trois*. Captain Jones, temporarily detached; serving Mrs. Robinson, victualled Mr. Robinson. Slum spots of war in the West side of Colombo.[18]

13 Ibid., p. 107.
14 Ibid., p. 108. See in Green book, 'George, 'A Disaster, 1944'; Green, 'Extracts from Ceylon Journal'; and Lieutenant Z (Green), 'Military Detention'. See also Robert Aldrich, *Colonialism and Homosexuality* (London: Routledge, 2002), sub-section, 'Scandal, Tragedy, and Literature: The Life and Work of G. F. Green'.
15 'Gyles Brandreth talks about KW', www.carryonline.com, accessed in 2006 and now also available as 'Remembering Kenneth Williams', at https://www.gylesbrandreth.net/blog/2018/4/14/remembering-kenneth-williams
16 Iredale, *The Kamikaze Hunters*.
17 Thompson, *Only the Sun Remembers*, p. 189.
18 Ibid., p. 195.

Having married shortly before leaving Britain, Thompson writes of numerous affairs or casual encounters in the various parts of the Indian Ocean to which he was posted, especially the Seychelles and Ceylon. Here, his great love was for Jeanette, whose husband was away, and his spellbinding memoir is in many ways a love letter to both her and to Ceylon: 'The stifling, torrid Colombo night. Jeanette alone in darkness, under the thirsting tree, my name a sad thought in her mind … Away from the warm, white side of the lovely girl in the Colombo bungalow, the restless voices of the surf murmuring through the open blinds, the soundless ceiling fan cooling our close bodies'.[19] Jeanette, he wrote in one of many other tender passages, 'moves closer to my body on the crowded Colombo dance floor and I bend my head to her fingers in the gloom of the Silver Faun, that painfully respectable, demurely closing night club'.[20]

Thompson partially ascribed such affairs to the detachment and loneliness felt by service personnel far from home or local residents whose spouses were away, together with the strictures of regimented military life:

> the problem of loneliness, distance, the fear of spiritual collapse in an atmosphere of utter personal unimportance and negation; the emotional surrender to the automatism of war, the obliteration of the individual, the ruin of the sanctity of man, the effect of the inability to control one's coming or going, the growth of the philosophy of caring no more.[21]

But a lot of it, of course, was simply down to human nature. Thompson describes things well in a reference to wartime Colombo:

> Over-populated, over-manned, hectic; Fleet ridden, Army jammed; the city's face flushed with nervous excitement, the bars crowded, desire loose-footed in the spilling, dress-essential ballroom. A life which attracted the stray, evacuated women; from Malaya, Java, Burma; many women of several colours. In great demand; seeking and providing both forgetfulness and pleasure. In a city invaded by the carelessly spending officers from England, callously, understandably seeking their pleasure; returned from extended sea months or arrogantly, timidly en route for Burma, the body-rotting jungles and the bayoneting Japanese. The time before even one heartening victory; originally in the years of yearning and struggle. Give them one more kiss before they go to the Araḳan.[22]

Race relations

Often linked to issues of sex, race relations were also prominent features of the wartime landscape as servicemen and women from different backgrounds mixed with each other and the local population. The arrival of tens of thousands of aliens in Ceylon created racial tensions and misunderstandings. As elsewhere in the Empire, the presence of Africans caused concern, usually based on racial stereotypes and furtive imaginations and frequently triggered by sexual

19 Ibid., p. 67.
20 Ibid., p. 192.
21 Ibid., p. 188.
22 Ibid., p. 195.

concerns, as often as not the figments of overactive and racially confused minds. It is likely that, as was the case elsewhere, the thought, as much as the fact, of Africans having sex with members of other races triggered concerns greater than the issue warranted.

Alfred Birkett moved to Horana near Colombo after his African regiment had completed its jungle training up country. Their first experience of the local population was 'when the headman of the village and some villagers came to watch the Africans bathing. Africans wore three-quarter-length trousers and the story had got around that the reason for this was because they were black they had tails and the trousers hid the tail'. Needless to say, the African soldiers were not at all impressed when they learned the reason for the locals' curiosity.[23] It appears that this was not an isolated incident; it was reported to the War Office that many people believed that 'Africans are cannibals, marry by capture, have tails, and are perpetually practicing black magic'.[24]

In September 1943 it was reported that East African troops stationed in camps at Kiribathgoda, seven miles outside of Colombo on the main road to Kandy, shot and wounded some Sinhalese women.[25] This provoked a flurry of angry debate in the State Council along with criticism of Governor Caldecott and the General Officer Commanding Troops, along with a display of the kind of racial prejudice that African troops often stimulated when deployed overseas. After the shooting incident bolts were removed from rifles in the offending camp. There had already been complaints about Africans 'roving about in search of women and drink'.[26] In the State Council, there was fierce debate about the presence of Africans in Ceylon. 'I must ask you, Sir, why on earth these African forces are in Ceylon? Why should there be any African forces in Ceylon? Ceylonese troops are in Africa!'.[27] The speaker went on to say that it was as ridiculous as Chinese troops appearing in Britain for local defence. Mr Abeywickrama recounted an experience he had had in Galle, a town in which East Africans were also billeted. 'One day I saw a procession of women going into the interior. I asked them where they were going; and they told me that they were leaving their homes because they were informed that the Africans eat children, that their best food was the flesh of infants'.[28]

Other speakers reported the common belief among villagers that 'these people are brought here to eat up the Japs when they land in Ceylon'; that they 'should be behind barbed wire'; and that it was 'difficult to convince the villagers that they are not cannibals'. A representative from the Anuradhapura region, where another African brigade was based, reported that African nakedness while bathing had annoyed Buddhists. ('Fan Tan' also records locals being startled by African troops bathing naked in a sacred pool).[29] One speaker referred to 'the broad-lipped

23 BBC World War Two People's War oral history archive, Alfred Birkett, 'With the East African Rifles in Ceylon', A8831874.

24 TNA, WO 172/3985, 11 (East African) Division progress report number 1, September-October 1943.

25 SNLA, 442, '"Misbehaviour" of East African Troops', *Ceylon Daily News*, 24/9/43.

26 Ibid.

27 SNLA, Excerpts from State Council proceedings, Governor's dispatch to the Colonial Office, September 1943.

28 Ibid.

29 'Fan Tan', 'Soldiering in Ceylon', p. 68.

Africans. They are a most ugly sight. It is awful to look at these fellows'.[30] Not all speakers agreed, and some argued that they were the best troops in Ceylon, others that racial stereotypes had no place in the debate. Such issues were naturally taken very seriously by the authorities, and other evidence seemed to support the concern surrounding the effects of stationing Africans in Ceylon. A censored letter sent by an army driver to his family in Uganda said that 'we are having enjoyment with white ladies. We pay seven and a half rupees to have a go with them'.[31] In October 1943 the General Officer Commanding Ceylon told the War Office in London that sexual assaults by Africans were causing a 'political backlash' in the Ceylon State Council.[32]

In an attempt to counter prejudiced views regarding African troops, British officers from African units, along with Ceylon government officials, gave talks to local civilians. Additionally, newspapers emphasized that African troops were 'our best defenders' and that projects undertaken by them, such as bridge construction, 'will also serve civilians'.[33] When African reinforcements were arriving in large numbers in spring 1942, the *Times of Ceylon* published an article entitled 'Swarthy giants here to defend us. Veterans from East Africa. Reminder of dim past'. (The fact that Africans were there as *defenders* was also emphasized in the Indian media, for example in the 'Indian Movietone News', later renamed 'Indian News Parade' films produced by the Government of India and shown in cinemas). The *Times of Ceylon* wrote that 'news can now be published' of the arrival of the first African troops: 'Citizens of Colombo were astounded when they saw askaris from East and Central Africa for the first time. One is reminded of the shock the Romans had when they with unbelieving eyes witnessed Hannibal's elephants on parade'. Another article exhorted the Ceylonese people to 'Say "jumbo" to them! African troops are friendly'.[34]

For their part, many African soldiers appear to have been unimpressed by the locals. The peculiar situation, a result of empire and global war, in which Africans were deposited in Ceylon to defend its people, stimulated some enterprising propaganda and information initiatives. The East African army newspaper *Heshima* (Kiswahili for 'honour', 'respect', or 'good reputation') attempted to address African concerns and queries regarding the local population. The authorities were especially keen to ensure that Africans understood that the Ceylonese were not Indians, as the small but well-to-do Indian community in East Africa, from where many of the Africans soldiers hailed, was viewed with suspicion by many of them. There was also the need to mitigate the fact that many African soldiers, who had heard about the martial prowess of the Indian Army, were perplexed as to why they themselves needed to come and defend 'India', the subcontinent being frequently conflated with the island off its southern tip. Articles in African army newspapers stressed that Ceylon was an entirely different country from India, and that the people were not Indian (though of course, many of them were!). Moreover, African troops were told that by defending Ceylon they were providing an advanced defence of their African

30 SNLA, Excerpts from State Council proceedings, Governor's dispatch to the Colonial Office, September 1943.
31 TNA, WO 172/39.
32 TNA, WO 106/4500, General Officer Commanding to War Office, 12/10/43. Also WO 172/9544.
33 SNLA, *Times of Ceylon*, 9/11/42.
34 NAM, 1997-08-57, Photograph album of East African battalions in East Africa, Ceylon, Burma, and India, press cuttings. Also NAM, 518-22, 'Swarthy giants here to defend us: Veterans from East Africa. Reminder of dim past', *Times of Ceylon*, 8/5/42 and 'Say "jumbo" [meaning 'jambo'] to them! African troops are friendly', *Times of Ceylon*, 8/5/42.

homelands. They were also exhorted to learn from the local population on subjects such as animal husbandry and agriculture, a standard colonial injunction.[35] A report observed that in his encounters with Ceylonese civilians 'the askari delights in his martial superiority'.[36] One KAR officer noted that the Ceylonese tended to treat Africans with the contempt that they themselves often encountered from Europeans. The apparent lack of interest in the war displayed by many Ceylonese people, led the askaris to 'look on them with the utmost contempt'.[37]

As far as Indian troops were concerned, there was some reservation and animosity on the part of Ceylonese people who remembered the role the Indian Army had played in suppressing the 1915 uprising:

> Relations with the people of Ceylon are improving. British and Empire troops have been popular all along. All our Indian troops come from the Punjab and the astounding rumours about how 'Punjabis' put down riots in the last war, still circulate [riots in 1915, beginning in Kandy and spreading to Colombo and other town, brought the declaration of martial law and robust suppression involving a Punjabi regiment of the Indian Army]. This was the main cause for continual accusations against Indian troops, when we first arrived.[38]

There were also, as with troops from all nations, incidents of disorder involving the local population. In May 1943, for example, men of an Indian pioneer unit had broken bounds and 'invaded' a nearby village, coming off worst in the incident as the villagers fought them off.[39]

Another way in which the war influenced racial attitudes in Ceylon was by showing Europeans to be less than invincible, particularly through the series of extraordinary defeats at the hands of the Japanese. Europeans were no longer seen as 'gods' by the indigenous population, writes Ivor Ferdinands, and their behaviour while in Ceylon challenged long-held views regarding the 'superiority' of white people and their status as paragons of morality and virtue. 'Invaded by hordes of WRNS [Women's Royal Naval Service], ATS [Auxiliary Territorial Service], WRAF [Women's Royal Air Force], it was not long before doormen at hotels in and around Colombo had names and numbers of girls of easy virtue for persons on leave ... At that time the Europeans in Ceylon were thought to be whiter than white'.[40]

As Leslie, a Burgher woman, writes:

> The attitude of the man in the street changed dramatically. The troops had swarmed everywhere and had thrown discretion to the four winds. They had fraternized with the locals, made love in the streets, got drunk in the hotels, and generally behaved in a most 'un-European' manner. There had been nothing of that British 'stiff upper lip' of the pre-war days. Ceylonese had been trained to look up to the British as paragons of everything that was

35 See Katrin Bromber, 'Do Not Destroy Our Honour: Wartime Propaganda Directed at East African Soldiers in Ceylon (1943-44)', in Ashwini Tambe and Harald Fischer-Tiné (eds), *The Limits of British Control in South Asia: Spaces of Disorder in the Indian Ocean Region* (London: Routledge, 2008).
36 TNA, WO 172/3985, 11 (East African) Division progress report, July-August 1943.
37 Ibid.
38 'Fan Tan', 'Soldiering in Ceylon', p. 68.
39 TNA, CO 968/12/7, Commander-in-Chief Ceylon, war diaries, April to June 1943, War Council minutes, 17/5/43.
40 John Banks to author, typescript, 'Second World War – Ceylon Continuation', 24/4/99.

> civilized and respectable. After the war the white man would never again be able to lord it over the locals. The veneration, the respect, and the fear had gone for ever.[41]

Ivor Ferdinands describes changing racial perspectives in the following terms:

> Before the war the British were a charmed race living apart from the ordinary citizens of Ceylon. They lived as an upper class, the rulers and masters in the administrative, commercial, and planting spheres. War caused a temporary hiatus in this racial separation which ultimately had to be abandoned. The administrative sector had already been Ceylonized. In planting the shortage of young Europeans led to the first Ceylonese being engaged and gradual Ceylonization of the planting sector began. Military disasters at the hands of the Japanese destroyed the notion of European superiority, and the spectacle of Tommies toiling and working in the sun, often bare-bodied, destroyed the assumption of pre-war days that Europeans were only masters and rulers.[42]

The invasion of foreign troops also had the power to change some hardy colonial practices in the cosseted world of the planters. The 'arrival of British troops and girls opened our eyes. Up until then we had to wear double-terrai hats [a double-felt variation of Gurkha slouch hats] with red linings or the topee if we went out in the sun but the military forces seldom wore anything on their heads and we colonials learned that we would not get heat stroke if we, too, went out without a hat!'.[43]

Another factor contributing to changing racial attitudes was the presence of working class Britons. Ivor Ferdinands writes that 'it was traditionally the public school types that went out to Ceylon, as administrators or planters. Now locals got to see all sorts, often engaged in very public activities, be it performing manual labour or getting drunk. There was also the regular sight of exuberant and drunken Europeans'.[44] John Banks, who as a boy collected military cap badges in Colombo, recalls a large drunken Australian holding Captain C. J. P. Martin at arms length over Colombo harbour. He dropped him in with the words 'Swim you bugger!'. Charles Martin, Banks observes, could not swim.[45] William Cameron was 'greatly entertained on a visit to Colombo to see a race down Galle Face Green by two Australian soldiers, who had got down from their rickshaws in which they were being pulled, placed their rickshaw coolies in the rickshaws, protesting loudly, and careered down the Green to the cheers of their companions'.[46]

Their encounter with Ceylon obliged European servicemen and women to confront prevalent attitudes regarding race. People such as Alan Brundrett came to distinguish themselves from the 'sahib' types, almost as alien to them as the Sinhalese and Tamil people among whom they moved each day. Though they might fall in with customs such as calling waiters 'boy', they often felt uncomfortable and detached from the world of the colonial settlers. A Fleet Air Arm pilot wrote that 'the people are so well disposed and good looking. Their clothes blend with the

41 Ferdinands, *Proud and Prejudiced*, p. 176.
42 Ivor Ferdinands to author, typescript 'Ceylon's Strategic Place in the War', 7/6/99.
43 Banks letter to author, 26/7/99.
44 Ferdinands, 'Ceylon's Strategic Place'.
45 Banks letter to author, 26/7/99.
46 Cameron, 'Bits and Pieces'.

countryside; they have a natural instinct for harmonious colour … I am only irritated by those who treat them automatically as inferiors. They only do it as a matter of form because they see other people doing it'.[47]

James Thompson best captures perspectives on racial divisions within Ceylon, and it is no surprise to discover that he had a more cosmopolitan, de-racialized view on matters than was likely to have been the norm. This was no doubt partly because he spent many months there, rather than just paying a brief visit on leave, but was also because of previous exposure to people from Ceylon, albeit members of the elite.

> In the further East Ceylon was our base, our anchorage, our home. Always we came back to this golden island and to the squalid and beautiful city of Colombo. There, after I had left the Regiment, and was luckily transferred to our Staff, I lived the typical staff city life of the warring British in their tropics.
>
> I grew to love this island, in which I ultimately carved a new way of living, a life which gained in depth and intensity and meaning as time passed. New friends, new influences and interests which gradually absorbed my mind into their pattern …
>
> In this I was fortunate; before I arrived I had friends in Ceylon and through them other friendships came, Tamils, Ceylonese, Burghers; and Raju Coomaraswamy, a friend from Oxford years, who welcomed my arrival and whose kindness I can never repay. Through his friendship I climbed the glass strewn walls of racial prejudice and the intricate barriers of our colonisation. I was interested in Ceylon, the peoples, the problems; I wondered at the beauties of mountain and flashing shoreline, drawn always to the red god in the sun.[48]

Thompson wrote scathingly of white colonials in a manner not uncommon among educated Britons encountering them in places such as India, Kenya, and South Africa:

> With rare exceptions, to the inhabitant English, this [the society of non-Europeans] formed a dead, unknown world, tedious and unimportant. Servant trouble, tea prices, coolie demands, the dull best-seller; the last or pregnant scandal, the recent or future leave. Essential perhaps, but a social and mental world of the half life; another gin and a new limerick; normally severed from the people of the island. Still colour bound, prejudiced, deliberately intolerant. And yet within the confines of their own rigid community life preserving snob-layered caste systems as devitalising and formidable as the ancient castes of the native peoples.[49]

Rather than socializing with such people, Thompson was happier in the non-European Lawn Club, reminiscing with Coomaraswamy, with his Centipede scarf knotted about his neck, talking of Oxford, 'picturing the quadrangle of All Souls, the Bodleian and the Camera against the soft skies of the Summer Term … Sitting in the cane chairs, out on the smooth lawn, until

47 Iredale, *The Kamikaze Hunter*, p. 178.
48 Thompson, *Only the Sun Remembers*, 186-87.
49 Ibid., pp. 190-91.

the brief twilight ended and the white marble palace of the Town Hall lay under a great, close moon'.[50]

Notwithstanding Thompson's penetrating assessment and powerful description of racial divisions afflicting Ceylon's society, it would be a mistake to over-generalize about the attitudes of British and imperial service personnel stationed there during the war. Some, no doubt, would have possessed and evinced racial prejudice or naivety, ingrained through prevalent cultural attitudes brought from home. But some, surely, would have had little problem accepting and adapting to life in a setting where different races mixed, and to have done so without any problems when encounters occurred. It would be nice to think that Cecil Callis's breezy summary is representative of the attitude of many foreigners stationed in the island during the war: 'We were always on good terms with the local Kandy population, both European and native. Football and cricket matches were arranged, we were invited to clubs and dances and other social events, and sometimes to parties at people's homes'.[51]

Social barriers, built up over centuries of European colonization and interracial aloofness, began to dissolve. As young male planters went off to war, gaps were left and people from beyond the European planter class began to fill them. There was a thawing, if not a breakdown, of social snobbery, though this was to be a lengthy process in a racially segregated society where, for example, there were no non-whites in the club and the members even looked down on white engineers from the local engineering firm as second class. Yet beyond such redoubts of imperial society, things most certainly were changing because of the war.

Women

Young Britons, whose previous experience had been confined to home village or town, encountered many new freedoms and challenges during their time in Ceylon, the same being true for some people from among Ceylon's different ethnic communities.[52] This was particularly the case for women, as they dealt with the regular importunities of men, often exhibiting distinctly sexist and chauvinistic attitudes, as well as an array of quite thrilling experiences in among the routine of office work and camp life. Twenty-year old Dorothy Entwistle was a Morse operator in the Wrens specializing in Japanese Morse code, and had the opportunity to stow away with an RAF pilot flying to Madras to pick up gin for a Christmas party, and she was by no means the only woman invited for a spin in an RAF or FAA aircraft.[53] Mary Pratt remembers the

50 Ibid., p. 191. The local people would also rib the British for being 'temporary colonizers' because of their habit of not settling in their colonies. Thompson, *Only the Sun Remembers*, pp. 189-90.

51 BBC World War Two People's War oral history archive, Callis, 'Eastern Travels', 8, 'Back to the Hills'.

52 IWM, ABY 58, 'Personnel of the Women's Auxiliary Air Force arrive by air at an RAF airfield in Ceylon'. Text from Colonial Film Database: 'Distant shot of RAF Douglas Dakota transport aircraft. The Dakota taxis to dispersal, directed by hand signals from an airman. The first WAAF, a Wing Officer wearing a pair of sunglasses, disemplanes. An RAF Sergeant helps other WAAFs down from the plane. Group shot of gathered WAAFs. Close-up of bemused-looking WAAF'. See also IWM, ABY 117, 'WAAFs at Work and Play in India', a July 1945 film showing footage on reel 3 of WAAFs at Ratmalana.

53 These rather dramatic booze runs seem to have been something of a common thing, as I've come across several references. Another one is recounted by Iredale: Major Ronnie Hay of the FAA, commander of

unbelievable welcome received in Durban as her convoy proceeded east. There was flag-waving and posies of flowers as they broke their journey at the naval shore base HMS *Assegai*. She then served at Eastern Fleet naval headquarters at Kilindini, 'a parched campsite with very basic quarters where the WRNS slept in bandas under mosquito nets in steaming heat'.[54] In the evening they danced, met friends for drinks, or were rowed in liberty boats to the warships in harbour. Transferring from Kenya to Ceylon, Mary made the voyage aboard the Armed Merchant Cruiser *Chitral*, and was shocked that she and the other women were treated as ordinary matelots, made to swab the deck, clean quarters and latrines, and sleep in hammocks. This unwelcome equality with their male peers did not extend to splicing the mainbrace, the daily ration of rum given to sailors.

Freda Wade volunteered to serve with the Wrens in Ceylon, leaving Britain in September 1943. Her home for the first six months of her stay was St Peter's College along the Galle Road where the Wrens were kept under guard the whole time, not to keep the inmates in but to keep amorous souls out. They were not allowed 'ashore' without a male escort, and then had to sign a book saying where they were going and who they were going to be with, and be back by ten. They were banned from sunbathing, and if they got burned were considered unfit for duty and could lose pay as a result. Wade worked at St Joseph's College, part of the Colombo shore base HMS *Lanka*, the Eastern Fleet's headquarters. Others remember the naval practice of having to 'sign out' Wrens for a date. Arthur Davis of 212 Squadron based in Karachi recalls that his squadron escorted the convoy carrying the first Wrens to serve in India into Bombay. Cashing in on this link, the airmen arranged to take the Wrens out. 'It wasn't quite like a normal date as one had to sign them out and in and explain what you intended to do and where you were going. This naturally caused the truth to be bent a little …'.[55] Joan Gottelier remembers Australian troops being particularly 'hectic', as she put it, and she would wear a fake wedding ring to dances in order to help deflect unwanted male attention.[56]

The military authorities took measures to 'protect' the female officers from male attention, welcome or otherwise. Mountbatten wrote that in Kandy, officers of brigadier general and major general rank were accommodated alongside female military and civilian officers at the Queen's Hotel.

> We were all puzzled why Admiral Jerram had arranged the billeting in this manner, until a bright American officer pointed out that it was the presence of female officers at the Queen's that had made it undesirable to allow the young Colonels or the very old officers now entering their second youth to be billeted at the same hotel. The Major Generals were considered to be belonging to the most staid level.[57]

47 Naval Fighter Wing on *Victorious*, flew from Ceylon to Ulundurpet in southern India to buy a four-gallon jar of Perry's Naval Strength Gin. He returned to base with his precious cargo wedged between the seat and the control column. In October 1944 he used it to celebrate his engagement to a Wren. Iredale, *Kamikaze Hunters*, p. 177. He also recalls doing a slow roll over *Victorious* following an all-night session getting 'fearfully plastered with all my squadron mates'. Ibid., p. 178.

54 BBC World War Two People's War oral history archive, Mary Pratt, 'Recollections of a War-Time WREN', A3436067.

55 Banks, *Wings of the Dawning*, p. 344.

56 Gottelier interview, April 1999.

57 Ziegler (ed.), *Personal Diary*, p. 99.

Trenowden writes that the camp of the First Aid Nursing Yeomanry (FANY), built by the Royal Engineers in Colombo, was well protected and guarded. FANY personnel were deployed to Ceylon to work as code clerks, telegraphists, and wireless telegraphy operators. The camp was

> surrounded by a high wire fence … there was a single gate, guarded day and night by a sentry and a second sentry patrolled the perimeter … No outsiders, officers or other ranks were allowed inside the camp without special permission. The FANY, after all, had to be guarded not only from the enemy but from our own troops as well.[58]

A popular story related to a telephone call received by Colonel Hudson, head of SOE:

> 'Hello Hudson. This is Brigadier X, Ceylon Army Comannd. Yesterday evening I went round to that Fany camp of yours, as I wanted to call on a girl there whose parents I know. The sentry on the gate refused to let me in or even take a message. I think you might do something about that. Make some arrangement or other; not just have an officer of my rank kept out by a sentry'.
>
> 'That's what the sentry is there for!'
>
> 'Yes, but I mean, can't something be done … ?'
>
> 'Certainly something will be done. I shall tell the sentry to continue to carry out my orders. Goodbye'.[59]

Freda Wade was one of the many women who met her future husband while serving overseas with the forces. In her case, she married a major in the Ceylon Army Service Corps, the ceremony conducted at Christchurch by the chaplain of the shore base HMS *Bherunda*, Gilbert Jessop, who before the war had been vicar of the church where Freda had been christened. Freda's husband's company of soldiers was responsible for feeding 13,000 troops a day, while she now worked at HMS *Highflyer* at Trincomalee. The nearest neighbours were Italian prisoners of war and East African soldiers. Their bungalow had no sanitation, 'just thunder boxes and a supply of wood shavings'.[60] Leslie writes that some Burgher women had relationships with foreign servicemen, perhaps even having children, though few became 'GI brides' on the conclusion of hostilities.

Leading Aircraftwoman Nancy Barnett, a member of the Women's Auxiliary Air Force (WAAF), had arrived in Ceylon aboard the Dutch troopship *Johan van Olden Barneveldt*. As was common, their gender made the WAAF service personnel aboard the ship both a novelty and a minority, and they were therefore accorded privileged treatment. 'This led a handful of WAAFs to a sumptuous style of life from the one we had left. Real food on real tables and so much we usually took gateau, wrapped in our serviettes, to the boys on board'.[61] In January 1945 Nancy volunteered with two friends to work on the teleprinters in the signals section at the Koggala flying-boat base. On their first day in camp amid the tall gloomy trees, they were frightened by a 15 foot-long monitor lizard called a kabaragoya.

58 Trenowden, *Operations Most Secret*, p. 114.
59 Ibid., p. 116.
60 BBC World War Two People's War oral history archive, Wade.
61 Banks, *Wings of the Dawning*, p. 345.

> Other WAAFs were in ciphers, or were WAAF nurses, even a WAAF hairdresser. As a small group of forty in a station of 2,000 men, there was a stern warning to the 'brutal and licentious soldiery' that these women were here to do a job – even 'wolf whistles' would not be acceptable. This was adhered to and the WAAF's got on with the job. Nancy and two colleagues had to maintain a three-shift cover on the teleprinter for twenty-four hours a day, seven days a week. They suffered from fevers with everyone else, and tended to get run down in the high humidity, but the main relaxation was keeping cool in the water at the beach nearby and the occasional run into Galle in the 'passion wagon' which belied its name. It was a relief to go on leave up into the hills at Nuwara Eliya, in a cool English-type atmosphere and enjoy the luxury of guest-houses run like a country house with log fires in the grate and other comforts. Then back to the damp heat of the palm plantations, the snakes and the minor dragons at Koggala, backing up the flying-boats out on patrol. The Sunderlands and Catalinas looked a fine sight on the lagoon.[62]

Peggy Wightman wrote that:

> [s]ome of the Wrens are getting very spoilt by the officers, they haven't been used to it and it is going to their heads. A lot of the worthier types don't get a look in, they couldn't possibly live up to what the girls are beginning to expect. It was exactly the same on the way out, the Wrens were treated like first class passengers, for example they were allowed on decks banned to the troops. Consequently many had romances on board with the officers, while the troops were just herded together and never saw a female; what a stupid life it is and what a dissatisfied one after the war is over.
>
> Shelagh is letting everyone know that lots of the things we are doing are not the job of a qualified signal officer! I sometimes wonder myself, especially when as today the yeoman came into my office and said, 'You are looking very lovely today DSO [Duty Signal Officer] if I might say so, I could fall for you', this from a petty officer mark you. I said, 'Well thank you very much, but hardly the thing to say to your signal officer'. The answer to that was, 'Oh, come off it. I can't be bothered with all this red tape, do you know I've been doing this job for thirteen years'. Which job he was referring to I didn't try to find out. I must say he is jolly good at his job and would do anything for me. The whole set up is priceless out here when your loggist turns up on watch in a sari speaking very little English and a nineteen year old sailor says he has never taken orders from a woman in his life![63]

Rodney Ferdinands records the changes that war brought to the Burgher community, and the manner in which it opened up new vistas to young women. After the fall of Singapore:

> we were now very much a part of the war ... The British wanted as many allies and friends as they could find. Burghers suddenly found they were very much in demand as allies and trusted friends of the British. Burgher boys found that they did not have to study, pass examinations and join the public service as clerks. They could instead join the army, wear a

62 Ibid., p. 347.
63 Aldrich, *The Faraway War*, pp. 676-677.

dashing khaki uniform with one or more 'pips' on their shoulders, a peaked cap at a jaunty angle, and ride in jeeps and army trucks ...

The Burgher girls enjoyed the war even more than the boys. Before the war, not too many Burgher girls went out to work after they finished school. There were those, ad they were not in the majority, who after they left school, trained as teachers, nurses and stenographers. Most Burgher girls, however, were forced to remain at home and occupy themselves with sewing, cooking, visiting and such lady-like activities as piano playing, painting, singing and church activities. The only boys the Burgher girls had contact with were cousins and friends the brothers brought home.

The war changed all that. Burgher girls were suddenly very much in demand as clerical assistants in the various army, navy and air force offices. They wore attractive khaki uniforms with jaunty caps or blue and white naval uniforms. They were picked up from home, driven to work, and brought back. They were paid well and met lots of lonely European servicemen, who were far away from home and desperately in need of female company ... The world of the Burgher girls had become more cosmopolitan and more exciting. They began to enjoy themselves doing all those things that were not permitted, not possible in the past.

It made it hard for the Burgher boy to continue with his studies. He could not compete with the 'white ants' (as we ungraciously called the European servicemen), the money, the transport, the NAAFI chocolates, the cigarettes and all the other unobtainable 'goodies' the servicemen showered on 'our' girls, their mothers, and the younger children. Cycling to the Fort for my studies in accountancy, peddling against the wind and almost blown off my my bicycle on reaching Galle Face, I would study the Burgher girls in their snazzy uniforms when the trucks overtook me. They ignored me. I would next be passed by Burgher boys in khaki uniforms, pips on their shoulders, peaked caps on their heads, confidently riding motor cycles or being driven in army transport. I often wondered whether an extra five years of study and examinations was worth the effort. The war might go on forever.[64]

Radio, newspapers, theatre, films, sport, and dances

Everyday entertainment in Ceylon might include chess with Sinhalese players on the streets of Colombo, attending one of the ubiquitous concert parties, or joining a bathing party, heading perhaps to Mount Lavinia with its picturesque hotel and pretty beaches, Bentota, or one of the other innumerable beaches and coves. There were dances and balls, such as the New Year 1943 Gala at the Galle Face Hotel, its upbeat theme 'the end of the beginning', a reference to Churchill's famous speech marking the victory at the Battle of Alamein, which he said marked not the beginning of the end of the war, but perhaps the end of its beginning.[65] A Fleet Air Arm officer wrote of evenings at the Silver Faun night club, followed by skinny-dipping in a secluded bay. Monica Hulme writes that Trincomalee was 'a town full of uniformed officers, and the

64 Ferdinands, *Proud and Prejudiced*, pp. 173-4. For a beautiful painting of a Ceylonese servicewoman, see the portrait by Leslie Cole of Company Quartermaster-Sergeant Van Omoheusen of the Auxiliary Territorial Service, at IWM, Art. IWM ART LD 5688.

65 SNLA, *Times of Ceylon*, 15/12/42.

social life was a whirl … I remember my older sister having a whale [sic] of a time! It was all parties, dances, and picnics'.[66]

Dances were all-important social events. Mary Pratt remembers the Galle Face Hotel, out of bounds to other ranks and barred to women unless accompanied by officers, and the Silver Faun nightclub. This was one of the classiest establishments in Ceylon, frequented by the great and good. Mountbatten wrote in his diary on 6 March 1945 that 'on Tuesday I left Kandy at 1730 by car, and drove to Admiral Power's Headquarters. Here we changed, and went with the C-in-C to the "Silver Faun" for dinner'.[67] James Thompson remembers the 'crowded, perspiring bars of the Galle Face Hotel, the sensuous gloom in the Silver Faun, the moon-white beaches at Lavinia'.[68] In many evocative ways, James Thompson describes the stifling heat and humidity of Colombo. 'But through the war years', he wrote,

> the crazy city still danced; in formal English evening dress or taut uniform. The English do not deign to make concessions to mere nature; one merely takes two extra collars; then peels the shapeless, sweat-stained garments to the floor in the privacy of the midnight bathroom.[69]

Wrens officer Peggy Wightman writes:

> Tonight we are having a dance in the Mess; great goings on, an army of sailors on the front lawn stringing up lights in the trees and laying a wooden floor for dancing. It will be very effective and rather like a film set. Gloom has just descended because the Superintendent WRNS has just informed us we have to wear uniform as it is in the Mess. Instead of long colourful dresses against the men's white, we will be gallumping around in our sailcloth dresses with large white flat feet. Some of our more glamorous members are furious as they always entertain their boyfriends in backless dinner gowns. Sue and I don't think we have the sort of escorts who would notice and at least our feet will be comfortable and will take any amount of trampling on.[70]

Leslie, the Burgher woman in the 'sleepy little town' of Kandy, eloquently captures the changes wrought by the war in her community, dancing, motorbikes, and all:

> Kandy, before the war, was a pleasant and peaceful existence. Dances were few and far between, night clubs were non-existent, and the main attraction was the cinema. It was, however, a gracious existence, where respect for parents and elders was the norm, where we bathed and dressed for dinner, and were served at table by white-coated, dark-skinned servants, where good manners were second nature dances were slow and sedate.[71]

66 Monica Hulme, letter to author, 21/5/99. The Hulmes lived in a bungalow in Trincomalee that looked across the Esplanade towards an Italian prisoner of war camp.
67 Ziegler (ed.), *Personal Diary*, p. 190.
68 Thompson, *Only the Sun Remembers*, p. 3.
69 Ibid., p. 195.
70 Aldrich, *The Faraway War*, p. 676.
71 Leslie quoted in Ferdinands, *Proud and Prejudiced*, p. 175.

Into all of this, she continues, came the war:

> After the war came to the East and the Japanese bombed our ports, we began to be infiltrated by British troops. To teenagers like myself it was rather a thrilling adventure. Homesick soldiers, who my mother patriotically entertained, added to the excitement. Sleepy Kandy suddenly became alive with dances, cinema shows, and live entertainment to keep up the morale of the troops. The soldiers buzzed around the girls like bees around a honeypot and well-paid jobs became readily available as stenographers, secretaries, and clerks in the RAF and NAAFI. The young Burgher girls who had languished when they finished school suddenly found they were very much in demand and not only for office work!
>
> If the British woke up Kandy, the Americans who followed took her by the throat and shook her violently. There were nattily dressed servicemen everywhere throwing their money around carelessly and dazzling everyone with their overbearing presence. Burly American military policemen whizzed around on their Harley Davidsons and the hotels throbbed to the music of the American dance bands. The jitterbug and the jive took over and the sedate waltz and fox-trot were forgotten. The Yanks had their own cinemas, canteens, dances, and transport. They even had ice-cream, chocolates, steaks and lots of other goodies especially flown in from the States. They lacked for nothing other than home cooked meals and female company. To the young girls in Kandy the war seemed remote and the excitement of the present was very real ... It is indecent, almost immoral, to realize that while other people in other places were suffering untold horror and death, we had such a wonderful time. Kandy, during the war, was the most exciting time of my life. I had a ball.[72]

The Europeans and mixed race Ceylonese communities weren't the only ones to dance, and African and Indian soldiers, often in a more formalized, military setting, were well known for their performances. As a member of the Ceylon civil service, John O'Regan's responsibilities included North Central Province, where the 34th Indian Division, now commanded by Major General Frank Moore, was based alongside British troops. In his capacity as liaison officer, he received the following intriguing invitation:

> The officers, sergeants, and all ranks 2nd Battalion The Leicestershire Regiment At Home in the jungle on 27 and 28 June 1942 on the occasion of the liaison visit of the 1/2 King's African Rifles and 1st Battalion the Northern Rhodesia Regiment. As the night 27-28 June is the night before full moon and it should weather permitting be bright moonlight from sunset, it is hoped to arrange for N'gomas (tribal dances) by different African tribesmen enlisted into the KAR [King's African Rifles] and NRR [Northern Rhodesia Regiment]. It is also hoped that a Cuttack dance will be performed by an Indian Unit, and a Devil dance of Ceylon as well as turns by the concert party and a band programme.[73]

72 Ibid., pp. 175-75.

73 In August 1942 Somerville sailed with Force A from Ceylon to Kenya. The admiral wrote that:

> Before sailing, 250 officers and men of the King's African Rifles were embarked for passage to Kilindini. This was done at the request of the Commander in Chief, Ceylon, who stated these men had been absent from their wives for a long period, and finding the native ladies of Ceylon

In the towns, there were many other entertainment and recreational options for people on leave. Colombo offered an array of theatres, cinemas, shops, and canteens and restaurants. There was the New Olympia cinema on McCallum Road, other picture houses including the Regal, Elphinstone, National, Empire, and Majestic. There was the RAF Theatre in Maitland Crescent, where among other things, Elgar's *Enigma Variations* was performed. The New Garrison Theatre opened in Racecourse Avenue, its first production being Terence Rattigan's *While the Sun Shines* starring Joy Allen and McDonald Hobley. Brundrett remembers a huge turnout for a George Formby concert on the recreation ground, a Royal Marines band providing pre-concert entertainment. The arrival of Formby and the ENSA party was captured on film as they disembarked from an RAF Dakota at Ratmalana, wearing plain service dress with ENSA shoulder flashes. Formby and his wife Beryl appear from the aircraft carrying ukuleles. Also present is the diminutive British pantomime and comedy actor 'Wee' Georgie Wood, wearing a pith helmet much too large for him, who is helped down from the aircraft, followed by his 'stage mother' Dolly Harmer.[74]

For eating out, there was the popular Soda Fountain Cafe on Chatham Street and the Sundae Tea Rooms opposite the Nanking Hotel near the Clock Tower, along with the countless small shops in districts such as Pettah and the street vendors selling their famous 'short eats'. In nearby Main Street there was a SWOC (Service's Welfare Organization Committee) Cafeteria and Services' Club. Situated in the Fort district behind the *Times of Ceylon* building was a canteen for all servicemen and merchant seamen. Also in the Fort district was a service women's canteen on Queen Street and a NAAFI canteen in McCallum Road, with two large bars, a recreation room, and cinema shows.[75]

Early in 1942 Cecil Callis of the 34th Indian Division resided at Echelon Barracks near Colombo town centre, a two-storey barrack block with wide verandahs around a compound large enough for several football and hockey pitches. Those living there only had to cross a road to the seafront and Galle Face Green, the harbour located on the other side of the complex.

> Although we lived within sight of the sea we could not bathe in it because the coast here was protected by anti-invasion defences and barbed wire. However, just beyond Galle Face hotel, Colombo Swimming Club and pool were free to members of the Forces. We made

inadequate, their condition gave rise to some concern. In view of their high reputation as fighting men I was satisfied that their powers in other aspects could be accepted and merited attention.

Whilst on passage I asked ILLUSTRIOUS if her contingent of 150 could be persuaded to give one of their native dances on her flight deck – the conventional lion hunt with the Captain's Persian cat as quarry was suggested.. I was informed that this could not be arranged, the reason being explained subsequently. It was to the effect that in these tribal dances it is the practice to chant disparagements of neighbouring tribes, frequent reference being made to a portion of female anatomy. Since the men in ILLUSTRIOUS were of different tribes, a free fight would inevitably have resulted. The fact that a similar form of disparagement is used by the Maltese is of interest and suggests that these great travelers the Phoenicians either had, or else contracted, somewhat bad manners'. 'Admiralty War Diaries of World War II', Reports of proceedings, 1 July to 18 August 1942.

74 IWM, ABY 89, 'George Formby's ENSA Party Ceylon 1945', text from Colonial Film Database.

75 SNLA, *Times of Ceylon*, 5/5/44.

> good use of these amenities ... For a swim in the sea we could go five miles down the coast to Mount Lavinia, one of the many stretches of unspoilt, sandy, palm fringed beaches.[76]

There were then the more upmarket facilities of places such as the Grand Oriental Hotel and the Dominion Hotel next door to naval headquarters, which had been taken over by the navy for accommodation, and a range of sporting and 'gentlemen's' style clubs. Cargill's, the well known department store, was on York Street, 'Cave's extensive bookshop' was located on Chatham Street, and there was a YMCA and reading and rest rooms run by members of the Caledonian Society of Ceylon. Entertainment was also offered in the naval camps and barracks, including ENSA shows, table tennis, billiards, badminton, outdoor cinema screenings, and reading rooms. HMS *Bambara* was headquarters of the whole circle of naval and FAA camps around Trincomalee and there was a camp in the grounds of Admiralty House. The naval town boasted the Fleet Canteen, the Nelson Cinema, the Chinese Globe Café, and the Elephant and Castle pub.[77]

Entertaining tens of thousands of foreign troops became a major test for the military and civilian authorities in Ceylon. In addition to rest and recreation facilities, newspapers and radio stations were considered vital for morale. Ceylon had been one of the first colonies to introduce radio broadcasting a few years after its inauguration in Europe, Governor Sir William Henry Manning making the first broadcast in South Asia on 27 June 1924. The Central Telegraphic Office soon began playing musical records over the air, and English music programmes on Radio Ceylon were a popular favourite for planters and service personnel alike. On the local radio there was also plenty of war information and general entertainment. The radio listing in the *Times of Ceylon* for 7 November 1942, for example, featured 'Arms for Russia', the 'Brain's Trust', a 'talk in Tamil', a Tamil concert, Sinhalese folk songs, Dvorak from the BBC, Sinhalese war commentary, and British Forces Radio. At the end of 1942 the Colombo Station (the Ceylon Broadcasting Corporation) was broadcasting a weekly programme for 'Ceylon lads overseas' aimed at Ceylonese military personnel serving away from the island, and bi-weekly broadcasts in Swahili 'and other vernaculars' for African troops.[78] Alan Brundrett remembers listening to Radio Colombo and shows presented by the Royal Naval Volunteer Reserve officer Alan Williams. More distant stations could also be picked up, and Philip Skelsey remembers tuning in to Free French broadcasts from Brazzaville, a Vichy station in Saigon, and Radio Jakarta.

Radio SEAC represented an advance in popular broadcasting brought about by the war. It employed Colombo-based British announcers, including Desmond Carrington and David Jacobs, both of whom went on to work for the BBC. Arriving in Ceylon in 1945 after a flying-boat voyage via Cairo, Bahrein, and Karachi, Jacobs was Radio SEAC's Chief Announcer

76 Ibid.

77 The cafe's 'English dishes' included tomato soup, bacon, eggs and chips, egg on toast, fish and chips, pork chops and chips, beef steak and chips, chicken and chips, sausage and chips, omelettes, and banana fritters. See John Lindop, *Reminiscences of a Radar Plotter: Life in the Royal Navy in Ceylon at the End of World War Two* (Wigton: Mercianotes, 2016), p. 103. The book describes the author's memories of bases such as HMS *Mayina*, HMS *Bambara*, Nachchikuda Camp, Malay Cove Camp, and Diyatalawa rest camp.

78 SNLA, *Times of Ceylon* listing, 2/12/42 and TNA, WO 172/3985, 11 (East African) Division war diaries.

between 1945 and 1947 and became Assistant Station Director.[79] He initially lived in a Moorish-style house on Turret Road, Colombo, and like so many other new arrivals, his first task was to get used to the mosquitoes, geckoes, and other creatures with which he shared his abode. He was soon being instructed by his superior, Captain Mac Hobley, in the art of live broadcasting, before first taking the air with the announcement, 'This is Radio See-ack, Ceylon, broadcasting on 6.075 megahertz'. The station went on air at 6:30am every morning, and broadcast until midnight. About ten hours of the daily programmes were flown out from London, though the remaining eight hours had to be planned and delivered by Jacobs and his team.

In his spare time Jacobs roared about the island on a 500cc Matchless motorbike, often accompanied by a friend who was a captain in the Fourteenth Army. He soon left the house on Turret Street, and after a brief spell in a chummery moved into a bungalow on the sea shore with another friend, Desmond Carrington, a lieutenant just starting off in Ceylon with British Forces Radio Broadcasting. Jacobs delighted in having his own room for the first time in his new bachelor establishment. 'Here was employed Supiah, the cook, who made memorable Welsh rarebit fingers for tea, and the boy, Joseph, who came when his masters' clapped their hands. But Jacobs's rather easy war in Ceylon was not to last. From a balcony above the garage there was a magnificent view of the sea shining in the moonlight and against the moonlit sea, the silhouetted palms moving softly in the evening breeze'.[80] It was on this balcony that Jacobs's eyes met those of a young newly-wed woman, recently arrived in Ceylon with her RAF husband. They soon began a reckless affair. When they were told in no uncertain terms to avoid a scandal and stop seeing each other, the lady marched into Jacobs' office and categorically told his boss that she would *not* stop seeing him. As a result of this affair, Jacobs was posted home after a memorable 21 months on the island.

Ceylon's newspapers, like their British counterparts, focused on the war, particularly the leading English-language daily, the *Times of Ceylon*. Each issue was dominated by war news from around the world as well as the island itself. On 2 November 1942, for example, there were photographs of 'Germany's new fighter, the FW 190', of the Commander-in-Chief Ceylon, Admiral Layton, 'examining a home-made air raid siren', and another showing bomb damage in Dusseldorf caused by the RAF. Headlines featured the 'New hitting power of the RAF'; 'Reds planning winter offensive, say Nazis'; 'Wearing down the Axis defences: Greatest Allied barrage ever known in Africa', covering the opening of the decisive Battle of Alamein; and an article on the 'Sinking of USS *Wasp*' in the Pacific. The war was also the subject of a daily cartoon, on that day depicting Turkey preventing German aircraft reaching the Middle East.[81] A series of newsletters and pamphlets called *Yudhaperamuna* ('The Frontline') was distributed to the local public for propaganda purposes.[82]

Newspapers came to proliferate as this media boom, inspired by the need to entertain and inform hundreds of thousands of imperial service personnel, took hold. Some service papers were also intended to exert control over colonial subjects serving in the military, and to manage their expectations, as in the case of the East African forces paper *Heshima*. Dedicated forces papers included the *Ceylon Review: Ceylon's Weekly Journal for the Royal Navy, Army, RAF,*

79 Jacobs, *Jacob's Ladder*.
80 Ibid., p. 70.
81 SNLA papers.
82 Thomas, 'A War Story' shows a picture of some of these publications.

Merchant Navy, and Civil Defence Services and the tabloid-sized South East Asia Command's *SEAC* (pronounced 'See-ack'). This was a newspaper that Mountbatten was very pleased with given the high priority he attached to the morale of the million-plus service personnel under his command. It started life on New Year's Day 1944, edited by the editor of the London *Evening Standard* (and, later, the *Daily Mail*), Frank Owen. It featured extensive news coverage and a pin-up girl, 'Jane', in each issue, as well as a fascinating column in which servicemen aired their views in letters to the editor.[83]

In Trincomalee, servicemen received the *Trinco Entertainments Bulletin*. There was then the *Fleet Poetry Broadsheet*, a sophisticated publication put out by Naval Headquarters Colombo and printed by the *Times of Ceylon*. 'All the poems in this broadsheet are original contributions by Naval Personnel on the East Indies Station', the editor proclaimed. The April and June 1945 editions included contributions from Wrens, a Royal Marines corporal, a Royal Navy lieutenant, a navy lieutenant of the submarine service, a coder, an able seaman, and a sub-lieutenant in the Royal Naval Volunteer Reserve. Poems, some of them really rather beautiful, took as their themes home, war, and experience in the tropics. Titles in these two issues included 'Interlude in Arakan', 'Cooks to the galley', 'Epitaph for a young sailor', 'Ella', a sonnet about Ceylon, 'To England', 'Fleet fighter', 'Tropic song', 'When he is flying', 'Leave poem', and the sonnet 'Thoughts at Suez'. They capture, brilliantly, the humanity of young men and women in a distant land during a time of war.[84]

Troops deployed throughout the vast SEAC theatre developed their own unit newspapers, such as *Atoll*, printed by the men garrisoning the Cocos-Keeling Islands, *The Chahpot: The Magazine of the Lost Squadron* – 36 Squadron flying maritime reconnaissance missions from India – and *Tropic Tusker Tales*, the magazine of 413 Squadron Royal Canadian Air Force (the 'Tuskers'), flying Catalinas across the Indian Ocean from Koggala in Ceylon. Lieutenant J. Batson of the 13th (East African) Field Information Platoon had worked on the army newspaper *Morning Pioneer*, set up for British forces serving in Madagascar, and in 1943 found himself in Ceylon. Here he helped produce *Rhino*, a newspaper catering for the thousands of East African troops on the island. It was produced under 'field conditions', the roof of the editor's office fashioned from tarpaulin taken from an army truck, the table inside made from a crate. Ants wrought havoc with the supplies of paper, as did the tropical heat with the ink, and jackals would vandalize the office if given the opportunity.[85]

In Bombay the men of the shore base HMS *Braganza III* published *The Weekly Dekko* 'to express the news and views of the camp', priced at three annas.[86] The inability to print sultry photographs didn't stop the editors from drawing bikini-clad, stiletto-wearing women in seductive poses. In one issue 'Babe says', a regular cartoon inside the front cover, featured 'Babe' in her underwear exercising with dumbbells. 'I must go easy on these exercises', she says, 'otherwise I'll

83 Ziegler, *Mountbatten*, p. 256. Securing the services of the much-heralded Owen was a coup for Mountbatten and the whole command. Nevertheless, he had to overcome opposition to the appointment from Churchill and the Secretary of State for War, P. J. Grigg.

84 NAM, 7410-159-1-3-8.

85 Batson to Imperial War Museum, 29 December 1943, Appendix B, G. M. Bayliss, *Union Jack, a Scrapbook: British Forces Newspapers* (London: HMSO/Imperial War Museum, 1989).

86 *The Weekly Dekko: HMS* Braganza III, 1, 9 (June 1945). From William Dempsey interview, Woodstock, 2007.

soon be able to resist the boys!!!'. This kind of thing wasn't to everyone's liking, and the 'Letters' page carried a communication from a sailor who wrote that some 'of the articles and cartoons used in the current editions are, to say the least, obscene … If this is the stuff to keep up morale in this Forgotten Land … then by all means publish it, but for the sake of the more timid among us, please censor it before it goes to print'. The editor's reply was spirited, to say the least: 'Is your sense of humour as lacking as your mind appears to be narrow? … I welcome criticism, but I object to having my character slighted'. In this lively magazine, the 'Gossip column' brought news of troop movements, and there were jokes, quizzes, and a sports column.

The Weekly Dekko also published stories addressing themes close to the hearts of most service personnel. The story 'Peacetime', for instance, anticipated the end of the war and the return home to Britain where snow, 'cider at the Three Tuns' and 'the old oak beams and the roaring log fire' awaited, along with the Sunday joint 'majestically reposing on a bed of roast potatoes'. There were odes to the open road and the English countryside, 'rabbiting in the early hours of a January morning', family, summertime, and motorcycling along country lanes. 'This is how I remember my home, all this and more – but the rest is between me and the little girl I taught to ride my "Scott" [a make of motorbike] and naturally, not for publication'.[87]

An August 1942 copy of the *Haitan Bulletin*, newspaper of the naval base at Addu Atoll in the Maldives, reveals a busy programme of activities. Fifteen teams were entered in the seven-a-side football league, and the Marines Base Depot Organization team had recently been walloped 6-1 by the Seamen. Angling 'off the blunt end' of the base ship, *Haitan*, was popular; the men were 'expecting a new supply of fish hooks from Colombo', and were reminded that ham bones and lemonade bottles did not make for good bait. A cricket pitch had been laid out between the two football pitches, an athletics and tug-of-war meet was in the offing, and tombola was proving popular. The final question of the *Haitan Bulletin*'s quiz was: 'Do you want to say Adieu to Addu?'.[88]

For many people, religion was an important comfort, as was music. N. A. M. Flegg, a British soldier, retained a copy of the American *Song and Service Book for Ship and Field*, an official army and navy publication, 'given to me by Sergeant W. E. Ward of the US Army. Besides being an artist and draughtsman William Ward played the organ at the Protestant Church, Kandy'.[89] Another major concern for the welfare of servicemen and women was the arrival and dispatch of efficient mails from home. As Alan Brundrett, working at Naval Headquarters, Colombo, wrote on 1 December 1945:

> Among the ships docked there was the cruiser HMS *Cumberland*, which we heard was due in today. The sailors on the quayside were busy manhandling some of her cargo, which was being lowered down to them. No doubt there will be mailbags amongst them, containing letters from home. An event eagerly looked forward to: our lifeblood. There is always the

87 Ibid.

88 See the scanned copy on the Royal Navy Research Network Forum at <http://www.royalnavyresearcharchive.org.uk/SMF/index.php?topic=662.0>.

89 The *Song and Service* book by Ivan L. Bennett was published by the Government Printing Office, Washington, in 1942. NAM, 740-159 (4).

> same thrill and expectation when our postman comes round in the office with any letters for us.[90]

Peggy Wightman recorded 'great excitement' upon receipt of parcels from the cosmetics company Elizabeth Arden. 'Sue's mother had written to them and asked to have them sent out to us – they do special packs for the troops – boxes of powder, lipsticks and creams for all occasions, all beautifully packed in a satin lined box'.[91]

As well as magazines, newspapers, and radio, stage productions and the cinema remained a popular form of entertainment for servicemen. Service personnel in camps were shown films and stage productions at open air showings. Newspapers advertised the films of the day, such as Noël Coward's naval drama *In Which We Serve*; 'In Technicolor, John Wayne in *Reap the Wild Wind*' at the New Olympia in November 1942; *Ships with Wings* starring the aircraft carrier *Ark Royal*; and Bob Hope's *Give Me a Sailor*. The amateur 1943 film 'A Day in Ceylon', shot by the Army Kinema Unit's Sergeant Roy Lister, shows long queues of people waiting to see Disney's *Fantasia*.[92] At the National Theatre, Maradana, the Ceylon Amateur Dramatics Society staged over 35 free shows in late 1942 for the benefit of servicemen and women. The RAF took over the neat buildings of St Bridget's Convent in the leafy centre of Colombo, and in December 1942 the RAF presented 'Pukka Gen' with the RAFollies Chorus bringing 'a feast for eye and ear'.[93] In 1944 the RAF Theatre Colombo was showing 'the Victorian chiller *Gaslight*'.[94]

For those in rural areas there were occasional showings of British war propaganda films as Mobile Cinemas put on productions such as 'London Can Take It', 'Desert Victory', 'Birth of a Tank', and 'Naval Operations'. The touring vans performed their shows in schools and open air venues.[95] All of the wartime favourites were broadcast in Ceylon's cinemas, which, like fleapits back in Britain, were alive with khaki, bell bottoms, and air force blue. Latest Hollywood releases, such as *The Major and the Minor*, played in Colombo's cinemas, as well as British offerings. Richard Martin had a very brief encounter with Noël Coward at the cinema:

> In December 1944 I was an orderly for Lord Louis Mountbatten in Kandy. On this particular evening *In Which We Serve* was being shown for the first time. During the evening someone came and sat beside me. It was Noël Coward. He had come to see his friend Lord Louis. He turned around and said, 'How did you like that film, dear boy?'. I said, 'I loved it – it was really good'. He said, 'Oh good', and left.[96]

Sport was a ubiquitous pastime for service personnel. To his surprise, Ken Potter found himself named twelfth man in a Division versus Planters cricket match. 'Several planters had played for Oxford, Cambridge, or their county and several of the Division were either current county

90 Brundrett, *Two Years in Ceylon*, p. 315.
91 Aldrich, *The Faraway War*, p. 675.
92 IWM, MGH 4916.
93 SNLA, *Times of Ceylon*, 5/12/42.
94 Ibid., 29/5/44.
95 SNLA, Dispatches 440, January-June 1943. Being more of a technical nature, it was noted that films like 'Birth of a Tank' and 'Naval Operations' were less popular with audiences.
96 BBC World War Two People's War oral history archive, Richard Martin, 'A Chance Meeting with Noel Coward', A7074164.

players or equivalent'.[97] There was a posh pavilion 'in keeping with the Raj tradition' and, not expecting to be called to play, Potter got stuck into the John Collins's and gin-and-tonics 'liberally dispensed by the Ceylonese stewards' at lunch. This meant double vision when he was called in to bat late on. Cricket was very popular on the island, and Alan Brundrett recalls an All-India XI touring Ceylon and playing at the Colombo oval against the Combined Colleges, then the Services XI, then an All-Ceylon XI. The Layton Cup was a boxing trophy competed for by men from all of the armed forces stationed in Ceylon, including those of the Ceylonese Essential Services Labour Corps.[98]

Football matches attracted large crowds. On 1 December 1942 the *Times of Ceylon* showed a piper leading two teams out to be introduced to the Commander-in-Chief Ceylon before an England versus Scotland match at the Galle Face Sports Club ground.[99] Later in the month, while Lady Wavell visited a hospital and the graves of Japanese airmen killed during the raids, General Wavell watched an East African army team play the RAF Rovers.[100] *The Weekly Dekko* paper reported fixtures such as Bulldozers 'A''s one-nil defeat to St Francis Goans and Bulldozers 'B''s goalless draw with Burmah Shell. The camp's water polo team were runners-up in the Services League, and the base's bantam weight champion, it was reported, had won two cups and been runner-up in the Western India Championship.

William Dempsey, a signaller in the Royal Navy, was a keen featherweight boxer and footballer. A letter of 21 June 1944 from the headquarters of the Commander-in-Chief Eastern Fleet informed him that he was requested to box against the team from *Vengeance* in the Layton Cup, the match to take place on the carrier's flight deck. Dempsey also played football against a touring side brought to Ceylon by the Arsenal and England footballer (and England cricketer) Denis Compton who was stationed in India with the army.[101] A contemporary film showed part of an England versus 'The Rest' football match. A large crowd had gathered, and Commander-in-Chief Admiral Sir Geoffrey Layton watched the match with other senior military and civilian dignitaries. The film shows footage of the game, then of the presentation of the cup to the victorious England team, which included six RAF men, one of them the captain of Wolverhampton Wanderers.[102]

Shifting his SEAC headquarters from Delhi to Kandy, in April 1944 Mountbatten flew to Ceylon. After landing at Ratmalana and meeting the assembled dignitaries headed by the Commander-in-Chief Ceylon, his first duty was to watch the final of the Inter-Services League Ceylon, involving a match between the Civil Defence Services and the RAF. 'Excitement was at fever heat', Mountbatten wrote:

> Although my arrival was supposed to have been kept a closely guarded secret I had an unexpectedly enthusiastic welcome from the crowd, particularly the servicemen, with shouts of 'Good old Louis!' ... The Ceylonese team astounded me by playing in bare feet.

97 BBC World War Two People's War oral history archive, Potter.
98 SNLA, *Times of Ceylon*, 13/11/42.
99 SNLA, *Times of Ceylon*, 1/12/42.
100 Ibid., 12/12/42.
101 William Dempsey interview, Woodstock 2007.
102 IWM, ABY 46, 'Procession, air show and football match at Colombo, 11/11/44', text from Colonial Film Database.

> After the RAF team scored two quick goals in extra time, the Ceylonese team lost their head and fouled after the last goal had been scored and on their being penalized by a free kick the Ceylonese spectators stormed the ground. Upon this the British Service spectators joined in and a glorious free fight occurred between literally hundreds of people on the football field. It was a perfect introduction to Ceylonese life!
>
> In India I am sure that the natives would never have dreamt of supporting that type of fight with the British but here the Ceylonese are quite uncowed and most friendly; even this scrimmage was conducted in a thoroughly friendly atmosphere![103]

The Honourable Lieutenant Colonel John Kotelawala was one of the island's senior politicians and a future prime minister. As well as commanding the Essential Services Labour Corps, a wartime military labour force, he was Minister for Communications and Works, and on 4 April 1942 established the Services Welfare Organizing Committee (SWOC), dedicated to providing support for visiting imperial forces. A SWOC poster published by the Department of Information was entitled 'The "Homely" Front'. It read: 'You can make the home front the Homely Front. Do all you can to entertain the Forces, every one of them thousands of miles from their own homes'.[104] The poster showed pictures of men playing football, ping pong, cricket, darts, snooker, having a sing-song around a piano, and reading the newspapers in comfortable armchairs. SWOC's mission was to provide funds and leisure items to enrich the lives of service personnel stationed throughout the island. It included representatives of the British Soldiers and Sailors Institute, the Hospital Supply Association, the Salvation Army, the Troops Entertainment Committee, the United Services Hospitality Scheme, the War Services League, and the YMCA. People were encouraged to give books and literature for service personnel. As Governor Caldecott said in a broadcast to the colony, 'keep our defenders fit in mind as well as in body. We have now in our Island men come from all four corners of the earth to defend it. You have only to pass along our roads, streets, and lanes to see the British Commonwealth of Nations in microcosm'.[105] The War Services League, a society of ex-servicemen who had served in imperial and local military forces in the past, supported the Governor's aims by making items to be sent to servicemen, producing 5,000 gifts and comforts in 1943 alone. Illustrating the range of different military forces stationed on the island, these items were sent out to seven British regiments, two Indian regiments, three regiments of the Royal Marines, 18 Ack-Ack units, 14 RAF units, two warships, four military hospitals, two convalescence camps, four East African units, and eight rest camps.[106]

The presence of tens of thousands of military personnel had many repercussions for the people of Ceylon, as did more general war-related phenomenon, such as food shortages, propaganda, and inflation, and it is to the war's impact on the home front that the following chapters turns.

103 Ziegler (ed.), *Personal Diary*, p. 98.
104 SNLA posters.
105 Rhodes House Library (RHL), Bodleian Library, Oxford, MSS Ind Ocn s. 235, 'Speeches of His Excellency the Governor of Ceylon Sir Andrew Caldecott'.
106 SNLA, *Times of Ceylon*, 25/5/44.

9

On the home front: Part I

Governor Sir Andrew Caldecott displayed leadership and courage in guiding the colony through the war years. Like other colonial governors, as the king's representative and the outward symbol of imperial authority, many of his duties were ceremonial and diplomatic. But unlike most of his fellow governors, his role was also extraordinarily political – as opposed to simply gubernatorial – given the fact that Ceylonese politicians occupied powerful political and administrative positions alongside the members of the colonial civil service. To add to the political complications of his wartime role, he was also subordinated to the military direction of Admiral Layton's Ceylon Command.

Caldecott's professional duties were gruelling, the innumerable public appearances recorded in his papers giving a flavour of his activity. Part of his public role as the king's representative was to attend functions and dinners, usually as guest of honour and chief speech maker. During the war he made speeches at the Oxford society dinner, the Empire Day dinner, the Irish dinner, the Medico-Legal Society dinner, the Comrades dinner, and the Ceylon Planters Association dinner, and regularly hosted military commanders and attended formal military parades and inspected military installations. He opened the new Bank of Ceylon, the new Ceylon Royal Naval Volunteer Force headquarters, the 'Harbour Lights' war fundraising carnival, and the Kandy Food Exhibition. As well as speeches at school and college prize day events, he spoke at the thirteenth anniversary of the Ceylon Broadcasting Service, the Buddhist Theosophical Society's diamond jubilee, the Dutch Reform Church's golden jubilee, an air raid precaution (ARP) event at Colombo racecourse, and laid the foundation stone at the headquarters of the 2nd Light Anti-Aircraft Regiment. He gave a speech entitled 'London, Coventry, Bristol calling' and opened the 'London calling' event sponsored by the Rotary Club. He also spoke at the Farm School and the Ceylon Society of Arts Exhibition. On the radio, he made many broadcasts including those to launch the Ceylon War Savings Scheme and the Ceylon War Loan, to open the Ceylon Food Week, to inaugurate the Ceylon Boy Scouts Messenger Service, and to urge support for the Services Welfare Organization Ceylon, established to welcome and entertain imperial servicemen and women sent to the island.[1] His wife, Olive, meanwhile, before her tragic death in 1944, spoke at events organized by the Red Cross, the Young Women's Christian Association, and the Nurses Training School.

1 RHL, MSS Ind Ocn s. 235, Speeches of His Excellency the Governor of Ceylon, Sir Andrew Caldecott. He was replaced as Governor by Sir Henry Monck-Mason Moore in October 1944.

The Governor's activities reflect some of the many ways in which the war impacted on the life of the island's people, and this chapter focuses on the home front, concentrating on the employment of local people, migration stimulated by conflict, economic and political effects, the struggle for food, and the manifold demands of civil defence. The effects of war were experienced by ordinary people in many different ways, for example through employment opportunities and labour exactions, military recruitment and construction, propaganda drives, inflation, rationing, and the fear of enemy attack. Suborinated to military command the colonial government mobilized the home front for war as the value of Ceylon's military bases and its raw materials increased exponentially following Allied defeats in South-east Asia and the East Indies.

Indigenous Ceylonese forces

A powerful government agency forged by war was the Civil Defence Department, and among its many duties was responsibility for stimulating military recruitment among the island's population.[2] Recruiting offices were opened, such as the one located at 399 Galle Road in Colombo's Colpetty district, and the department launched an impressive range of publicity initiatives, including a barrage of posters, some generic ones provided by the Ministry of Information in London, others designed by Ceylonese government employees and printed locally.[3] These latter – probably the author's most significant find in the Sri Lanka National Archives – made imaginative use of national sentiment and pride to enliven the 'defend your home', 'your country needs you', 'careless talk costs lives', and 'grow more food' exhortations familiar in the canon of British wartime propaganda. Young men were enticed to join the army by appeals to their sense of national pride, illustrated by an April 1942 poster showing a Ceylonese man in full military uniform. 'Lanka calling', read the caption:

> Young men of Ceylon your country needs you now.
> We want you and every one of you.
> Remember it is your own homes you guard.
> Join the Army now.
> We feed you.
> We clothe you.
> We make a new man of you.

2 For the department's records, see SNLA, 29/2, section 2, Civil Defence Commissioner's records, including file 5 ARP scheme, file 151 progress of civil defence: monthly reports, file 387 history of war Civil Defence section, draft history of Ceylon Civil Defence Department, and file 534 Ceylon Fire Fighting Committee.

3 The IWM holds many colonial propaganda posters issued by the Ministry of Information. They showed images with words altered for specific colonies, sometimes with specially tailored images. For example. PST 15801, 'Tap for victory' was designed to encourage increased rubber production, showing rubber trees being taped, tyres being made, and bombers, using those tyres, taking off.

A more strident version of the poster declared:

> Guard your homes.
> Defend Lanka.
> You young men must come forward.
> Our country calls.[4]

The war's most striking recruitment poster was a vibrantly colourful affair depicting the British lion, carrying the Union Jack, marching alongside lhe Lion of Lanka, which bore the Lanka flag. The caption read:

> Forward together!
> British Lion and Lion of Lanka.
> Man the defences of Lanka your home.
> Join the Army now'.[5]

The image of 'Mother Lanka' was employed to encourage greater agricultural production, a use of imagery to stimulate nationalist sentiment directed towards the war effort that would not have been allowed in most colonial territories, reflecting the fact that Ceylonese people were in commanding positions in government departments.

It is evident that these posters had an effect, because recruits came forward in their thousands to enlist in Ceylon's many different military and military-related organizations. The island had a long tradition as a martial colony and its locally-raised military strength rose from 3,500 in 1939 to 26,000 in 1945, around 30,000 other people serving in the Agricultural Corps and the Essential Services Labour Corps.[6] Thousands more undertook civil defence roles, including those associated with air raid precautions and first aid in the event of casualties following an attack. Ceylonese troops in British uniforms served as part of local defence formations, as garrison troops for other Indian Ocean islands, and as support soldiers for British and imperial fighting units in the Middle East. From 1941 the War Office and Admiralty took command of locally-raised military and naval units in the colonies, and began to meet their costs. In return the Ceylon government paid a fixed military contribution to the British treasury.

Of the 26,000 Ceylonese who enrolled in military formations, nearly 15,000 did so under the aegis of the Ceylon Defence Force (CDF).[7] The CDF was rapidly expanded after Japan entered the war and an attack on Ceylon seemed likely. It included the five battalions of the Ceylon Light Infantry (CLI) as its largest component as well as the Ceylon Garrison Artillery, medical detachments, an anti-aircraft regiment, coastal artillery, signallers, engineers, pioneers,

4 SNLA, Lot 29/1, 1/2, Posters, leaflets, pamphlets issued in connection with the National Food Campaign by the Propaganda Department of the Director of Food Supplies. For reproductions, see Jackson, 'Defend Lanka Your Home'.

5 SNLA, posters.

6 For this history, see Jackson, 'The Evolution of a Martial Colony: Ceylon'.

7 By 1945 the CDF comprised 645 officers and 14,247 other ranks. Sergei DeSilva-Ranasinghe, 'A Historical Account of the Ceylon Defence Force (1881-1949)', *Sabretache*, xlix, 2 (2008), p. 41.

and service corps formations.[8] The composition of the Ceylon Engineers offers an insight into the purpose and tasks associated with these locally-recruited formations. In 1939, the unit's strength had stood at 350 men, organized as a Fortress Company and a Field Company. By April 1944, there were 2,500 men on the strength, its units including 9 Inland Water Transport (Port) Operating Company (350 men), 40 Engineering Battalion (1,000 men), an Independent Garrison Company (250 men), and a Mechanical Excavation Company (250 men).[9] The Ceylon Supply and Transport Corps rose from a strength of 18 officers and 59 other ranks to 59 officers and 2,369 other ranks.[10]

A contingent of the Ceylon Garrison Artillery became the first local unit to leave the island when in April 1941 it departed for the Seychelles to defend potential landing places with rifles and Bren guns and man coastal defence guns. Another artillery contingent was sent to the Cocos-Keeling Islands to protect the cable and wireless station, a CLI detachment escorted Italian prisoners of war from the Middle East to internment in Ceylon, the CLI also furnished guards for Mountbatten's Kandy headquarters, and on the conclusion of hostilities, CLI troops escorted Japanese prisoners of war from Ceylon to India.[11] A separate unit, the Ceylon Royal Artillery, numbered 1,488 men by 1943 and was stationed at Trincomalee.[12]

Another locally-recruited military outfit was the Ceylon Railways Engineering Corps which among other duties operated an armoured train between Colombo and Mount Lavinia, armed with First World War vintage machine-guns. The corps was formed by the militarization of railway personnel and supplemented by the arrival of an Anglo-Indian Railway Personnel detachment, encamped close to Trincomalee station. There was also a military role for the employees of the customs and excise department, who organized a coast-watching system to report shipping movements and suspicious aircraft. The all-European Ceylon Planters Rifle Corps (CPRC) had been formed by an amalgamation of the Ceylon Rifle Corps and the Ceylon Mounted Rifles, first raised in 1892. This 'Dad's Army, colonial style' recruited largely from among the coconut, tea, and rubber planting communities.[13] Some of its personnel could not be called up because of the demand for tea and rubber, essentially 'reserved occupations', but it helped the CDF provide local defence and was assigned guard duties at vulnerable civilian installations after pressure had been put on the government to give the corps something constructive to do.[14] The CPRC furnished around 700 officers for the British and Indian armies, the men leaving Ceylon in small drafts to undergo officer training at Belgaum in India. The regiment's badge showed three tea leaves and the motto 'Unitas salus nostra', 'unity our salvation'. Commanded by Lieutenant Colonel F. O. Spinks, it joined the Royal Navy for exercises and undertook other useful tasks, including digging tactical defences around Trincomalee and furnishing guides for Australian troops during route marches. The regiment underwent weapons training on Galle

8 IWM, 37972, Oscar Abeyratna, *The History of the Ceylon Light Infantry* (Ceylon Daily News, 1945), written by a CLI captain.
9 TNA, WO 203/1006, Ceylon Engineers 1944.
10 DeSilva-Ranasinghe, 'A Historical Account of the Ceylon Defence Force', p. 41.
11 Ibid., p. 42.
12 TNA, 940.531 SHU, Shuckburgh, 'Colonial Civil History', part 1, 'Introductory', part 2, 'Military Services', 3, 'Eastern Areas', A. 'Ceylon', p. 55.
13 Cameron, 'Bits and Pieces'.
14 It is clear from the archives that Ceylonese members of the State Council had little love of this all-European outfit and were not keen to support it.

Face Green and field training at the Royal Colombo Golf Course. Though inevitably dogged by well-meaning or malicious criticisms because of its 'reservist' nature – Joan Gottelier, whose father was a member, referred to it as the 'Royal Boozeliers', while the tea planter 'Kelavan' wrote of 'khaki-clad planters nursing beers and gins' – the fact was that there was work for such a unit to perform.[15] It was also the case that, had the Japanese landed, the men of units like the CPRC and the CLI would have fought and possibly died alongside the regular imperial troops defending the country. Of Ceylon's total military mobilization, many joined the British Army, including 4,150 from the Ceylon Pioneers and others from the Ceylon engineers, artillery, and service corps. Approximately 6,800 volunteered for the Royal Army Service Corps, 'of whom 4,500 proceeded to the Middle East, others in Sicily, Greece, Italy, and France'.[16]

Ceylonese soldiers provided valuable if undramatic assistance to the British Empire's war effort. All of the tasks they performed were essential, even if they were mundane. For forces stationed at home, for example, Ceylon's complex of military headquarters and bases had to be linked by lines of communication and secure phone lines, underground wires, for example, connecting Army Command to Trincomalee, Kandy, Kekirawa, Kurunegala, and Bentota.[17] The Ceylon Signals Corps was responsible for conducting much of this communications work, as Ceylon became networked by radar, teleprinter, wireless, despatch riders, and even carrier pigeon.[18] Only one outbreak of insubordination was recorded, when on 8-9 May 1942 15 Ceylon Garrison Artillery soldiers, prompted by pro-Japanese and anti-European sentiment, mutinied and tried to take over their gun battery on Horsburgh Island in the Cocos-Keeling Islands. Instigated by Bombardier Gratien Fernando, the mutiny failed, but one loyal soldier was killed and a British officer wounded, and seven of the mutineers were sentenced to death. Three were eventually executed, the only soldiers of the Empire to meet their end in this way.[19]

Like many other young men, Rodney Ferdinands felt the call to join up, and also experienced tragedy brought about by Ceylon's involvement in the conflict:

> The younger British 'planters', mercantile and shop employees and junior bureaucrats joined up and left to go overseas. Trinity lost her British schoolteachers. Ceylonese took the place of the British who had departed and were found to do the jobs just as well. It was constantly brought to our attention that there was a war being fought for the freedom of the world and each and every one of us had to play our part. As a teenager, I was thrilled and excited at the prospect of wearing a fancy uniform, shooting down Nazi pilots in the air, and becoming an instant hero. I saw an advertisement for pilots to be trained for the RAF and applied. Grandma Ginger wrote to my parents saying she would commit suicide if I joined the Air Force and that stopped my plans for I was only sixteen years old. A year later, my

15 See 'Kelavan', *Two Leaves and a Bud: Tales of a Ceylon Tea Planter* (Colchester: Bloozoo Publishing, 2000).

16 TNA, 940.531 SHU, Shuckburgh, 'Colonial Civil History', part 1, 'Introductory', part 2, 'Military Services', 3, 'Eastern Areas', A. 'Ceylon', p. 55.

17 As in other countries where the military expanded its presence, the theft of wire was a significant problem in Ceylon.

18 H. G. P. Jayasekera, 'Japanese Raided Colombo this Day in '42', *Daily News*, 5/4/02.

19 Noel Crusz, *The Cocos Islands Mutiny* (Freemantle: Freemantle Arts Centre Press, 2000).

> grandmother had the misfortune to be killed by an army truck that did not even stop after the accident.[20]

After finishing his education in Colombo, the young Burgher Douglas was destined to understudy his father as an estate superintendent. But the April 1942 raids and the

> sudden realization that the whole world was reeling under the onslaught of the Germans and Japanese, made me seriously consider defending everything we held dear … Our home was crowded with relatives and friends who had fled Colombo after the Easter raid. Most of my father's planter friends had left to join the armed services. There was only one thing a fired-up twenty year old could do and that was to join up and do his share.[21]

Commissioned into Ceylon Engineers in November 1942, Douglas did a course in surveying, drafting, map reading, carpentry, motor mechanics, and blacksmiths' work. 'Our service was in the field and I spent the next five years in some of the remotest jungle areas of Ceylon'.[22] He was part of 3rd Field Company which worked closely with the Public Works Department, working on bridges, airstrips, and water supplies. 'We constructed the 75 metre span across the Kalu Ganga, the concrete "monkey bridge" at Kantalai on the Kandy-Trincomalee road, the massive earth dam, reservoir and filtration plant near Kantalai with a pipeline to Trincomalee naval base, and the huge RAF camp at Polgolla, near Kandy, to house the staffs of South East Asia Command'.[23] Later, Douglas answered a special call for volunteers to join the Royal Engineers, 13 officers and 600 other ranks from his unit doing so.

> Our work commenced with six months of training in the use of heavy equipment in the jungles of Habarana. We were next used in the construction of airstrips at Katunayake, Kankasanturai, Koggala, and the secret airstrip at Hingurathgoda near Minneriya … My platoon was next given responsibility for constructing Lord Mountbatten's personal secret airfield at Mawatagama, near Kandy. Lord Louis, Lady Edwina and I would sit on empty fuel drums and chat while waiting for flights.[24]

On the conclusion of hostilities Douglas was posted to the notorious internment camp at Changi in Singapore, responsible for the transportation of liberated prisoners of war to hospitals, rest centres, and back to their home countries.

There were other military and semi-military formations in Ceylon too. The Ceylon Boys Technical Training Corps, which comprised 500 16-18 year olds in a camp noted for its 'healthy moral atmosphere' prepared youths for service in the many technical branches of the military.[25] On 2 December 1942 the *Times of Ceylon* pictured a ride-past before the Governor of the

20 Ferdinands, *Proud and Prejudiced*, p. 173.
21 Ibid., p. 174.
22 Ibid.
23 Ibid.
24 Ibid., p. 175.
25 SNLA, sessional papers, 9 (1943), Weerasinghe, *Report of Assistant CDC in Charge of the Essential Services Labour Corps (Maharagama), March 1942–March 1943* (Colombo: Government Press, 1943).

Ceylon Boy Scouts Messenger Service, a new addition to the colony's uniformed services.[26] The Governor was keen to involve schoolchildren in the colony's war effort and in addition to his radio broadcast on the occasion of the inauguration of this adolescent service, wrote an article for the *Ceylon Daily News* entitled 'How schoolboys can help in war work'.[27]

For some Ceylonese men from the European and Burgher communities soldiering was very much a spare time vocation. An extreme example, offering a glimpse of the lifestyle of the well-to-do mixed race population of Ceylon, is provided by Mervyn Ondaatje, father of the writers Christopher and Michael. Belonging to a leisured class, as a young man he had been sent to study at Cambridge. The family spent most of the year in Colombo and during the hot months from April moved up to Nuwara Eliya, following the standard Indian pattern of retreating to 'hill stations' in the hottest periods of the year. 'Cars would leave Colombo and perform the tiring five-hour journey, the radiators steaming as they wound their way up into the mountains. Books and sweaters and golf clubs and rifles were packed into trunks, children were taken from school, dogs were bathed and made ready for the drive'.[28] In Nuwara Eliya, 'they danced in large living rooms to the music of a Bijuo-Moutrie piano while the log fires crackled in every room or on quiet evenings read books on the moonlit porch'.

Most of the men belonged to the Ceylon Light Infantry reserves and took guns when on vacation.

> This was Nuwara Eliya in the twenties and thirties. Everyone was vaguely related and had Sinhalese, Tamil, Dutch, British, and Burgher blood in them going back many generations. There was a large social gap between this circle and the Europeans and English who never were a part of the Ceylonese community. The English were seen as transients, snobs, and racists, and were quite separate from those who had intermarried and who lived here permanently.[29]

When war came, little changed for the wealthy. 'Even during the war the August races were not to be postponed. Ceylon could have been invaded during the late afternoon as most of the Light Infantry was at the race track during these hours ... There were races all year long. The Monsoon Meet in May, the Hakgalle Stakes in February, the Nuwara Eliya Cup in August'.[30] Major Ondaatje, stationed in Trincomalee, was probably more likely than most not to notice an invasion, because according to his son he was a rather heavy drinker prone to delusions and banned from travelling by rail in 1943 because of his habit of holding up trains at gunpoint. This, according to his son, had a lot to do with his fear of a Japanese attack, 'and he became obsessed with a possible invasion. In charge of Transport he would wake up whole battalions and rush them to various points of the harbour or coastline, absolutely certain that the Japanese would not come by plane but by ship'.[31]

26 SNLA, *Times of Ceylon*, 2/12/42.
27 RHL, Bodleian Library, Oxford, MSS Ind Ocn s. 235, *Ceylon Daily News*, 26/5/42.
28 Michael Ondaatje, *Running in the Family* (London: Picador, 1984), p. 39.
29 Ibid., p. 41.
30 Ibid., p. 49.
31 Ibid.

Because of his drinking, it was decided to send Ondaatje to a military hospital in Colombo, accompanied by Sir John Kotelawala, a prominent military and political figure and a future prime minister. But the resourceful Ondaatje managed to smuggle some bottles of gin aboard the train, and it wasn't long before he was up to his old tricks, knocking out his travelling companion and taking over the train. He made it shunt backwards and forwards so that all trains, some full of troops, were grounded in the south. Clearly intent on making a night of it, he succeeded in getting the driver of the train drunk as well. When moving about the train, they were careful not to disturb a carriage full of British officers, and so climbed over it. When Ondaatje was finally apprehended and the incident brought to a close, it transpired that he believed that the Japanese had mined the train, and he removed several pots of food from the carriages, that were then thrown over a bridge.

The war brought new opportunities for the men and women of Ceylon's Burgher and Sinhalese communities. Ivor Ferdinands was a member of the Ceylon Cadet Battalion, a military formation for teenage boys comprising platoons from all the big public schools, who drilled every week and had an annual camp at Diyatalawa in August when they competed for various trophies. When they were old enough many young public school men joined the CDF as subalterns. They served mainly in Ceylon as garrison troops, writes Ferdinands, a boarder at Trinity College Kandy until 1940 and then St Thomas's Mount Lavinia, 'with all the privileges of officer rank, including smart uniforms and NAAFI (Navy, Army, Air Force Institute) purchases – spirits, cigarettes (Players, Capstan, Navy Cut, Senior Service, 333, 555, and 77 were some of the popular brands of the time), and chocolates. We as impecunious students could not hope to match their attractions for the girls though after demobilization it was a different story'.[32]

Some of these youngsters joined units overseas, and Ferdinands recalls the announcement in school of the death in action of St Thomas's former head prefect, Dugald Amerasekera, killed over Germany, while his more fortunate brother Rohan also joined the RAF and was awarded the Distinguished Flying Cross. Pilot Officer Ananda Kularatne, son of an English mother and the principal of Ananda College, Ceylon's premier Buddhist educational establishment, was also killed in action when his Halifax bomber was conducting a mission over Germany. Shelton Flamer-Caldera, meanwhile, died when his Hurricane got into a spin and crashed during a training exercise flown from Minneriya.[33] Mervyn Rex de Silva won a Leverhulme Aviation Scholarship from St Peter's College, Colombo and trained with the RAF Volunteer Reserve in Britain. He flew missions over Germany and later in the war served with 17 Squadron in Ceylon, based at Minneriya to protect the Trincomalee Fortress Area before the squadron was deployed to the Imphal valley in support of ground offensives in Kalewa and Taukyan. Captain Robert Senanayake, son of the Minister for Agriculture and Lands, served with the 1st Coastal Regiment Ceylon Garrison Artillery.[34] Numerous Ceylonese men served with regular British units, many drawn from among the island's European community. Kandy-born Jack Thornhill joined the Royal Navy and ended up serving in his home region, sent initially as a junior gunnery officer aboard the cruiser *Glasgow* which performed convoy duties in the Indian Ocean. In the latter stages of the war he served aboard the escort carrier *Hunter*, based at Trincomalee. Thornhill flew Seafires, a specially developed Sptifire with strengthened undercarriage and folding wings, flying

32 Ivor Ferdinands, 'Ceylon's Strategic Place in the War'.
33 Ibid.
34 SNLA, *Times of Ceylon*, 2/6/42.

patrols as far afield as occupied Singapore. The carrier's main role was to support amphibious operations, and Thornhill shot down three enemy Zeros in the Malacca Strait.[35]

The largest colonial naval contingents outside of the dominions and India were to be found in Ceylon, Hong Kong, Malaya, Kenya and Trinidad. Established in 1937 by the Volunteer Naval Defence Force Ordinance No. 1, the Ceylon Naval Volunteer Force (CNVF) was led by Commander W. G. Beauchamp. Formerly a major in the CPRC and a man prominent in Colombo shipping circles, he was appointed its Honorary Commander. In December 1942 he made a radio broadcast entitled 'Minesweepers and patrols: Efficiency of our own navy'.[36] The force's strength rose from 150 officers and ratings in 1939 to over 1,200 by 1945. In January 1939, responding to an advert placed in the *Ceylon Gazette*, selected recruits mustered at the Navy Office to be inspected by Vice Admiral James Somerville, then serving as Commander-in-Chief East Indies.[37] By May 1939 there were 16 officers and 114 ratings, and the force's aim at the time was to man and operate three minesweeping vessels (of this number 28 ratings were to be trained as signallers and gunners, and the remainder were 'Lascars' from Jaffna and surrounding islands). The force used the boom defence trawler *Barnet*, the Port Commission tugs *Goliath* and *Hercules*, and the launch *Ready* for training. 'The actual sweep itself was streamed up to the hundred-fathom line, fifteen miles west of the Colombo harbour entrance'.[38] Early training under sea conditions was obtained by parties making dawn trips on the *Hercules* carrying out routine inspections of the fishery area at the Pearl Banks off Chilaw.[39] The seagoing experience of ex-Peninsular and Oriental line commodore Lieutenant Commander P. J. B. Oakley was utilized when minesweeping training began and the standards achieved helped convince the local naval authorities that formal defence duties could be assigned to the CNVF.

Once properly up and running the CNVF's objective was to keep Colombo open for business and provide adequate protection for merchant shipping, without calling on the assistance of the Royal Navy. A drill hall for the new force, together with offices, officers ante-room, and a 'Rule-of-the-Road Teacher' machine, were built and installed close to a harbour-front slipway at Kochchikade, which lay immediately under the great advertising sign which welcomed ships to Colombo with the words 'Ceylon for Good Tea'.[40] The Governor opened the new CNVF headquarters in June 1939, and a subsequent one in July 1941.

The force's capabilities were extended with the acquisition of the armed trawler *Overdale Wyke* (dubbed the 'Overdue Tyke'), collected from Port Said by its officers and men and used for minesweeping and escort patrols. Anti-submarine and mine-sweeping patrols were extended to Trincomalee, and the force undertook escort duties between Colombo and Addu Atoll, Cochin, Diego Garcia, Madras, Malé, and Trincomalee. It also checked out suspicious vessels in local ports and at Addu Atoll, and contingents manned the Port War Signal Station at Trincomalee, split between Chapel Hill and the dockyard. They also mounted guard at

35 Jack Thornhill, letter to author, 1/2/99.
36 SNLA, *Times of Ceylon*, 5/12/42. There are some interesting perspectives on the CNVF, and Ceylonese men working with the Indian National Army, in Carl Muller, *Spit and Polish* (New Delhi: Penguin, 2000).
37 'Investigator', 'Some Account of Ceylon's "Wavy Navy" between 1939-1942', copy of article from *Royal Indian Navy Association*, sent to Ashley Jackson by Peter Beauchamp, 31/3/99.
38 Ibid., p. 36.
39 Ibid., p. 37.
40 Ibid.

Admiralty House Trincomalee and HM Naval Office at Plantain Point, and manned a mine-sweeping watch station at Elephant Ridge. Local signals were augmented by a ship-to-shore carrier pigeon service.[41] The force also provided personnel for the Coding Office at Colombo, serviced thousands of military vehicles destined for Burma, provided mess stewards for SEAC headquarters, serviced the island's lighthouses, and manned boom defences and operated controlled minefields. The force acquired the *Balta*, *Hoxa*, *Okapi*, *Sambhur*, and *Simla* – all trawlers and Arctic whalers – and the tug *Samson* and operated several motor fishing vessels and other auxiliaries.

Another CNVF role was survivor rescue, and 248 victims of enemy attacks on shipping were fished out of the waters between Ceylon and the Maldives by its vessels.[42] The force provided support in the Burma region and took several Axis ships as prizes, including an Estonian flagged vessel, and was called upon to accept the surrender of the Italian sloop *Eritrea* following Italy's capitulation, escorting her into port with a prize crew on board.[43] During the Japanese raids of April 1942 CNVF ships engaged the enemy and were, in return, machine-gunned. In 1943 the Royal Navy assumed responsibility for the CNVF, and it became the Ceylon Royal Naval Volunteer Reserve. Its base was commissioned as HMS *Gemunu*, an establishment with 1,500 personnel by the end of the war. In early 1944 a Royal Navy Aircraft Ceylonese Training Establishment was created to train Ceylonese for work at the navy's air stations, thus releasing Fleet Air Arm personnel for service aboard the Eastern Fleet's carriers.

The CNVF is emblematic of the work performed by locally-raised colonial forces that almost always overlooked in histories of the war. The fighting units of the Empire – the Indian Army, the King's African Rifles, the Royal West African Frontier Force – are embedded in the historiography; some might rightly cavil that their significance is not sufficiently acknowledged, but at least their contribution is recorded in accounts of, say, the war in the Western Desert, the defence of Malaya, or the Burma campaign. But the smaller colonial units, the levies supporting the RAF in places such as Aden and Mauritius, the locally-raised defence forces, and the colonial naval units, rarely get even a mention. Governor Caldecott articulated their value in a speech to the Ceylon Planters Association on 21 March 1941: 'Our debt to the British Navy and British Merchant Marine is so vast one hesitates perhaps to mention the debt owed to our own little navy, the Ceylon Naval Volunteer Force, which day after day preserves our approaches from the danger of enemy mines. It is hard, unspectacular, but essential work that is being done'.[44] Reviewing the efforts to date, including the dispatch of three batches of the Ceylon Planters Rifles Corps and units of the Ceylon Garrison Artillery overseas and the 'essential' training of the Ceylon Defence Force, he said that the 'Empire requires of Ceylon,

41 Ibid.

42 In May 1944 Air Vice Marshal Albert Durston, Air Officer Commanding Ceylon, claimed that, in addition to those rescued by the CNVR and other naval and merchant marine vessels, flying-boats had saved over 500 people. SNLA, *Times of Ceylon*, 25/5/44. By the end of the war 222 Group RAF aircraft alone had rescued over 1,000 survivors from sunken vessels. An Officer of the RAF, 'A Resume of the Activities of 222 Group RAF', prepared for a radio broadcast in 1945, transcribed from TNA, AIR 23/4802, at http://www.rquirk.com/speech222gp.html

43 See Somasiri Devendra, 'Ceylon Navy's Prize "Catch"', *The Sunday Times* (Sri Lanka), 29/5/16.

44 RHL, MSS Ind Ocn s. 235, Governor's speeches.

as her first duty in war, that she should keep her own defences up to requirements and man them fully and efficiently'.[45]

Migration, inflation, and raw materials

As well as the demand to join the armed forces, war impacted the home front in many other ways, some quite unusual permutations among them. Weapons training for Ceylonese soldiers, for example, led to a spate of armed robberies necessitating the inception of a police Gang Robbery Unit, while the shortage of manufactured goods and scarcity of spare parts meant that Ceylon's rail network was run down and much of the rolling stock became dangerous and unusable. Other unusual permutations included the brief spy mania that flowered in the wake of the Japanese raids, leading to attacks on Buddhist monks, and the relocation of the elegant Edwin Lutyens-designed First World War memorial from its position on Galle Face Green inland to Victoria Park, in case the enemy used it as a target marker.

Through radio broadcasts, newspaper articles, public events, and extensive information publications the Government of Ceylon attempted to enlist the support of the people in all manner of ways, effectively asking them to change the way they lived and make sacrifices for the war effort. As one stentorian poster put it:

> Ceylon the alarm has sounded!
> Build Ceylon's war effort.
> Words will not stop the Japanese.
> Here's what will:
> Grow more food
> Work harder
> Beware of rumours
> Lend your money
> Assist Civil Defence
> Save electricity
> Travel less
> Save paper.[46]

The official British government report on the colonial empire's war contribution acknowledged that colonies with garrisons and heavy military footprints were placed under significant strain, and that Ceylon had been 'greatly affected by such developments'.[47]

All those old enough to remember the war have stories to tell, usually informed by where they lived, what they or their parents did, and their family's station in life. Hyacinth Mahendrarajah memories of the war are worth quoting at length, for they offer a succinct summary of the ways in which the war was experienced and remembered by ordinary people:

45 Ibid.
46 SNLA, poster and advert files.
47 Bodleian Library, Oxford, Official Papers, Command 7167, 'The Colonial Empire (1939-1947)' (London: HMSO, 1947), p. 8.

In 1939 when the war broke out on 3rd September, I was a schoolgirl in Ceylon and lived in a town about 22 miles from the capital Colombo.

Travel became rather hazardous, and going to school was getting dangerous as I had a train journey followed by a twenty-minute walk. The roads were not very wide and there were no pavements, so it was difficult to get by with the British military tanks and trucks constantly passing by.

At school they dug trenches for the children to go into, for protection during an air raid. We were given instructions on air raid precautions and whenever the siren sounded we had to observe them. These were carried out frequently to help us remember exactly what to do in the event of a genuine air raid. For example – if we were in the classrooms we had to put a pencil across the teeth, block our ears with cotton wool and lie down under our desks, but if we were outside we had to go into the trenches.

Commander-in-Chief, Geoffrey Layton, visited our School, Holy Family Convent [at Bambalapitiya in Colombo], and came in all the classrooms. It was a very important day for us as he held the highest post at the time.

Life went on for a couple of years with the war like atmosphere all around. There were a number of Prisoners of War camps around our homes. The prisoners were all Italians and lived in tents. Most of them were free to visit the neighbouring homes and were often treated to a cup of tea. They were quite friendly and spoke English fairly fluently. One Christmas I remember they re-created the scene at Bethlehem depicting the Birth of Christ, which was so vast it took up the whole right wing of our Catholic Church. Usually we had just the crib of Christ, but the Italians had built a replica of the town itself including every detail such as roads, shops and the Inn. It was really very beautiful and people flocked from near and far to see it.

As time went by in the hustle and bustle of military vehicles the cost of living rocketed sky-high. Food was scarce as no ships called in at the harbour in Colombo, which was normally an important Port of Call in the East. Ships were being bombed before they reached the various ports. This resulted in a struggle to exist on 'meal a day' that consisted mainly of yams and vegetables grown in the countryside. Scarcity of food caused immense problems chiefly because the young and energetic breadwinners were recruited to the army by conscription. Due to these problems most of the children were compelled to keep away from school, which hindered their education considerably. After about three years of dreadful warfare in the western world, Japan entered the war and one day, it was Easter Sunday, we were in church and to our surprise we heard the sound of bombs and a flight of planes overhead. It was the Japanese who had bombed Colombo and its closest suburbs. Our army navy and air force were well equipped and they were able to scare the Japs away before much damage was done. This dreadful incident took place on the 2nd of April 1942.

By this time I was in grade seven at School and as a project I had a large map of Europe on the wall. I had to indicate where towns and countries were captured. Because of this I still remember that Adolf Hitler's first success was capturing some of the countries by first bombing Kiel Canal, and taking over Poland. After he attempted the surrounding countries, he dropped a few bombs over England, which caused some damage to Buckingham Palace.

After some time an aura of calm prevailed which helped most children in Ceylon to get back to school after four years of disruption. I lost a year of schooling when things were so

> difficult I had to stay at home — but I returned later and took my exams in 1944, and I got my Certificate after I had got married![48]

War caused people to move into Ceylon, away from it, and within it, some as refugees, others as evacuees, some as service personnel and labourers. Young European administrators, merchants, and planters departed for the forces, thereby creating job opportunities for non-Europeans. As has been seen, the threat of Japanese bombing and invasion caused panic in the first half of 1942, particularly among the people of coastal towns, leading some to move inland or to simply depart for India. Many Indian businessmen, money-lenders, labour contractors, and traders returned to India fearing Japanese invasion, as did thousands of other Indians, contributing to general alarm as they poured into the Madras presidency. In 1942, 202,897 people left the island, up from 112,599 the previous year and 92,144 in 1940.[49] The wives and children of many Europeans left too, mostly destined for that common bolt-hole for Europeans escaping war zones, South Africa. In addition to the in-migration of British, Indian, African, and Australian troops, several thousand Italian prisoners of war also arrived to be interned at Trincomalee, as did young European women serving in the army, navy, and air force. American forces also staged through the island occasionally, such as the 3,300 troops on their way to India and Iran and Iraq in June 1943, who disembarked in Colombo and were accommodated at Bussa, a small town seven miles north of Galle.[50] Another significant in-migration involved Indian workers, like the 20,000 required by the Minister of Agriculture in 1943 to increase rubber production, and the 3,000 allowed to proceed to Ceylon by the Government of India in early 1943 following a request from the Commander-in-Chief because of the demands of aerodrome construction.[51]

There were some unusual migrations, including a convoluted variation on the 'school run'. John Banks attended school at Haddon Hill, Ceylon's only European primary school, a boarding institution situated in the hill station Nuwara Eliya. After finishing here he was sent to the Lawrence Memorial Royal Military School (LMRMS) near Ootacamund in India, a military establishment endowed by Sir Henry Lawrence of Indian Mutiny fame for the children of poorer Anglo-Indian or English people employed on the railways or in the army. It became home to numerous boys from Ceylon during the war because they were unable to proceed, as was the normal practice, to schools in Australia or Britain, and LMRMS set up a Special Emergency Department to cater for them. 'Whilst waiting for war to end', wrote Banks, 'Dad decided to send us to LMRMS at Lovedale near Ootacamund in the Nilgiri Hills in southern India'. The journey to the Nilgiris entailed a fascinating three day train journey.

> We would leave Colombo in the evening and arrive by morning at Talamanaar in north-west Ceylon. Here we would embark on a ferry for the fifty miles or so crossing of the Palk Strait to Southern India. Having made the crossing, we entrained again, after passing through the quarantine department at Mandapam Camp. Despite the heat and the steady

48 BBC World War Two People's War oral history archive, Hyacinth Mahendrarajah, 'Schoolgirl's Memories from Ceylon', A 2821943.

49 IWM, *Ferguson's Ceylon Directory 1945* (Colombo: Ceylon Observer Press, 1945), p. 18. This publication also noted a serious crime increase during the war.

50 TNA, CO 968/12/7, Commander-in-Chief Ceylon, war diaries, April to June 1943.

51 De Silva (ed.), *Sri Lanka*, CO 54/982/6.

> stream of soot and grime which poured through the carriage window, the day journey through the seemingly endless plain of Southern India, fascinating for me with glimpses, however fleeting, of strange birds, desert plains, and dusty villages. In the evening of the second day we reached Trinchinopoli, where we had dinner in the station restaurant. Some time next morning we would change trains at Metapolium for the long slow climb up into the Nilgiri Hills.[52]

Economically, the war was a boon for some people in Ceylon, the large military presence meaning that the market was almost inexhaustible. New money gave the Ceylonese Board of Ministers funds with which to pursue social welfare policies. Government sought to cushion the ill effects of inflation – such as discontent among white collar and urban workers – by raising wages and salaries and subsidizing some commodities, though increased pay failed to keep pace with inflation and the resulting problems, such as unrest among estate workers, caused serious concern.[53] From 1942 a special war allowance based on the cost of living index was paid. Cost of living figures were drawn from two indexes: that relating to 'the working class, Colombo town' and that relating to 'estate workers'. In the case of the former, if the average price in the period November 1938-April 1939 was 100, it had risen to 203 by December 1944. In the case of the latter, if the average price in the period July-September 1939 was 100, it had risen to 210 by December 1944.[54]

While the cost of living index rose by more than 100 per cent, the active money supply escalated by 69 per cent between 1942 and 1945, caused in part by massive defence expenditure. Military works across the island employed 83,500 people by 1945 (a figure that had been even higher in 1943-44), reducing the unemployment rate to 4 per cent of its 1939 level.[55] At its peak in 1944, military expenditure stood at approximately 435 million rupees, up from 264 million rupees the previous year (a rupee at the time was worth one shilling and six pence sterling).[56] The index of notes in circulation in December 1938 had been 98 active and 100.4 gross; by January 1945, the figures had risen to 741.9 active and 755.2 gross. Currency in circulation rose from 52,081,610 million rupees in December 1938 to 277,856,791 in September 1944.[57]

Recruitment for the armed forces and civilian staff and labourers on military bases 'provided a temporary solution to unemployment problems. With their closure and general demobilization unemployment increased though not to the extent of causing severe problems for the government. The social discontent that manifested itself stemmed from severe inflation arising mainly from the increase in the money supply from the massive defence expenditure'.[58] Government resorted to a policy of price control and rationed essential consumer goods, and from mid 1943

52 John Banks, letter to author, and typed memoir, 'World War Two Memories – Ceylon', 7/2/99.
53 TNA, 940.531 SHU, Shuckburgh, 'Colonial Civil History', volume 2, chapter 7, 'War Savings', chapter 1, 'Control of Prices Through Subsidization', 'Ceylon', p. 468.
54 TNA, CP (45) 138, Cabinet: Ceylon constitution, memorandum by the Secretary of State for Colonies, 31/8/45, *Report of the Commission on Constitutional Reform*, appendix 10.
55 Library of the National Museum of Sri Lanka (LNMSL), *Post-War Development Proposals* (Colombo; Government Printer, 1946).
56 Ibid.
57 TNA, CP (45) 138, Cabinet: Ceylon constitution, memorandum by the Secretary of State for Colonies, 31/8/45, *Report of the Commission on Constitutional Reform*, appendix 10.
58 De Silva (ed.), *Sri Lanka*, p. lvxxvii.

went a stage further by freezing the prices of several important food items while subsidizing others. Importing and distributing rice, wheat flour and sugar was taken over by the state in order to make price control and rationing more effective. It wasn't just the locals who were affected by wartime inflation; 'In a shop in Chatham Street, Colombo', wrote James Thompson, 'I argued, haggled over the price [of a pair of lacquered glasses]; when silks, embroideries, ivories were plentiful and cheap. Before the thoughtlessly spent dollars weighted every purchase and the rickshaw wallahs increased their human hire rate 300 per cent and the scowling British troops walked in the soaking heat'.[59]

Because of the demand for Ceylon's major export products, the island became an important dollar-earning territory of the Sterling Area, ending the war with sterling balances of 1,260 million rupees. War meant that almost any raw materials or foodstuffs that a colony produced could find a ready market, and maximum production was encouraged by the Colonial Office. Britain's possession of empire meant that it was able to control resources across the globe, and Ceylon, like other imperial territories, had bulk purchase agreements with Britain for exports in demand, notably tea and rubber. Naturally this led to tensions between Ceylon as producer, on the one hand, and the Treasury and supply departments in Britain as insatiable purchasers on the other, the Colonial Office acting as arbiter.[60] While bulk purchase arrangements prevented prices from reaching their free market level – as also did the lack of shipping – they helped limit inflation.

Ceylon's raw materials were very important for the Allies after the loss of Malaya, particularly its output of that essential war commodity, rubber. On his flying visit to the island in April 1942, Alan Moorehead observed that rubber 'was the big thing. With the fall of the Far East, Ceylon remains almost the last source of natural rubber to the Allies. The day I arrived the island announced a scheme for stepping up production by two hundred per cent'.[61] Everything was being done to stimulate extra production; as the *Times of Ceylon* stated, 'the enemy holds 90 per cent of the world's natural rubber'.[62] The island now produced 60 per cent of Allied rubber, and by 1944 practically all tyres and inner tubes used by American forces in the South Pacific were manufactured in Australia using Ceylonese supplies. In April 1944 the American consul in Ceylon, Robert Buell, wrote that

> natural rubber is the A-1 priority strategic material of which there is an insufficient supply to meet the requirements of the United Nations. An adequate supply of natural rubber is *vital* to *victory* … Ceylon at present produces about 60 per cent of *all* the natural rubber available to the United Nations. Supplies of natural rubber from other presently available sources *cannot* be materially increased during the war. Therefore the production of natural rubber is the A-1 responsibility and the chief contribution of Ceylon towards victory.[63]

59 Thompson, *Only the Sun Remembers*, p. 193. He then posted his purchases home to his wife in Yorkshire for Christmas 1941, 'a long, dangerous journey for the shining lacquer glasses'.
60 De Silva (ed.), *Sri Lanka*, p. xxxiii.
61 Moorehead, *A Year of Battle*, p. 153.
62 SNLA, *Times of Ceylon*, 13/11/42.
63 De Silva (ed.), *Sri Lanka*, CO 852/605/9, 4/4/44, p. 290 and 295. In the same volume see 'Ceylon and wartime supplies: The case of rubber production', pp. lix-lxi. See also *Report of the Commission on the Rubber Industry in Ceylon, October 1947* (Colombo: Government Printer, 1947), copy in the library of the London School of Economics, Government publications 5487 (55).

Given the Allies desperate need Ceylon's rubber restriction scheme was abandoned, and producers were encouraged to increase output to the maximum by 'slaughter tapping', harvesting rubber to a point at which the life of the tree was threatened. 'The present drastic schemes for increasing production of rubber estates', wrote a Colonial Office official, 'are definitely being undertaken by Ceylon under the aegis of the [British] Ministry of Agriculture not in Ceylon's own long-term interests – far from it – but in the interests of the United Nations' war effort, and particularly the interests of American production'.[64] The value of rubber exported from Ceylon increased from 1,724 lakhs rupees in 1938 to 2,692 lakhs in 1943.[65] In 1939 Ceylon had produced 135 million pounds weight of rubber, a figure that had nearly doubled to 251 million pounds by 1945.[66] Shuckburgh writes that in the six pre-war years the average rubber export was 54,000 tons per annum. This figure rose to 101,500 tons in 1942, 105,500 in 1943, and 98,500 in 1944.[67]

Tea was traditionally one of the island's major export crops, Ceylon producing over a quarter of the world's supply. In 1941 the British Ministry of Food bought 138,000,000 pounds weight of Ceylon tea.[68] During the war the British Ministry of Supply contracted to buy Ceylon's crop, and around 265 million pounds weight was exported.[69] Under the system of intra-imperial food exchange much of it was exported to Iraq, one of the few countries in the Middle East where tea was drunk more than coffee, and also to Aden. Efforts were made to increase tea consumption in Ceylon itself, undertaken by the Ceylon Tea Propaganda Board (its motto 'Tea for vigour, vitality, and victory').[70]

Ceylon also exported copra, the dried kernel of the coconut, and during the war became the Empire's most important source of graphite, a commodity used in munitions work and which had previously been sold mainly to Japan. Before the war, most British graphite had come from Austria, Ceylon, Czechoslovakia, Germany, Italy, Korea, and Madagascar. Soon after war commenced, only Ceylon, which had provided 14 per cent of British requirements in 1938, remained available as a source, causing a surge in demand from America as well as Britain, some companies prepared to pay 400 per cent above peacetime prices.[71]

Coir fibre, made from the outer husk of the coconut and used, among other things, for making doormats, and kapok, a cotton-like substance surrounding the seeds of tropical trees, was also in demand. It was used for stuffing cushions as well as the Mae West lifejackets worn by RAF pilots, benefiting from Ministry of Supply demand as it sought to provide emergency bedding in Britain in the aftermath of air raids. Finally, Ceylon developed a cinchona bark scheme in answer to the Colonial Secretary's request in December 1939 for increased quinine production

64 De Silva (ed.), *Sri Lanka*, CO 54/982/6, no. 34, Ceylon labour for rubber production, minute by G. E. J. Gent, January 1943, pp. 232-33.
65 *Report of the Commission on Constitutional Reform*, appendix 7.
66 LNMSL, *Post-War Development Proposals.*
67 TNA, 940.531 SHU, Shuckburgh, 'Colonial Civil History', volume 3, 'Major Political Developments Arising Out of the War', chapter 2, 'Agriculture, Animal Husbandry, and Forestry', p. 149.
68 LHMA, Embleton Papers, 1/6/2, *Ceylon for Victory* (1943).
69 LNMSL, *Post-War Development Proposals.*
70 TNA, CO 852/19/2, Ceylon tea.
71 RHL, Fabian Colonial Bureau Papers, Mss Brit. Emp. S365, box 151, Ceylon 1939-1965, Dr Alfred Neustatter, 'Graphite Problems in Wartime'.

throughout the Empire (until its conquest, the major source had been the Dutch East Indies). A government cinchona plantation opened at Massena in the Balangoda district in 1943.[72]

Wartime politics

In 1939 Ceylon already enjoyed a significant level of self-government, particularly in financial matters, and the war was to lead to major advances towards independence. It was constitutionally the most advanced territory in the colonial empire, having enjoyed universal suffrage since 1931 – only three years after its introduction in Britain. The 1931 constitution 'endowed the leading politicians with positions of authority unimaginable in most of Britain's colonial possessions'.[73] Under the constitution 'responsibility over large areas of government activity was transferred to the Board of Ministers and the executive committees'.[74] Unusual in the colonial empire, indigenous people held senior positions in the political and administrative structure, and during the war the Board of Ministers, with the encouragement of the Colonial Office, becoming a quasi-cabinet and forged a genuine political partnership with the British authorities.[75] The State Council comprised 61 members, 50 elected on universal suffrage, eight nominated by the Governor, and three Officers of State – the Legal Secretary, the Financial Secretary, and the Chief Secretary, non-voting *ex officio* members. The State Council was divided into seven executive committees, the chairman of each being deemed a minister and sitting on the Board of Ministers along with the three Officers of State.[76]

An astute move was the appointment of a future governor-general, Oliver Goonetilleke, to the important position of Civil Defence Commissioner, and the State Council leader and future prime minister Don Senanayake was given a prominent role in negotiating food supplies. Like most other colonies, and Britain itself, the war brought bigger government to Ceylon. The state became more intrusive (for example, all able-bodied men were listed on a Register of Manpower), new reports on social and economic issues flew off the press, and new government departments were created and others expanded. De Silva writes that 'wartime spending in Ceylon and a more buoyant economy placed greater resources than ever before at the disposal of the ministers and these they used to good effect in keeping members of the executive committees busy and happy with projects in which they were interested'.[77]

Ceylon's political elite was 'socially conservative, politically moderate, and tactically gradualist … [and] far more westernized than their counterparts in any part of India'.[78] 'From the

72 SNLA, Lot 5/439, Dispatches 1942-1-12, R. H. Bassett, *Administrative Report of the Commissioner for Development and Agricultural Marketing from January 1940 to December 1945* (Colombo: Government Press, 1946).
73 S. R. Ashton, 'Ceylon', in Judith Brown and William Roger Louis (eds), *The Oxford History of the British Empire*, volume iv, *The Twentieth Century* (Oxford: Oxford University Press, 1999), p. 454.
74 De Silva (ed.), *Sri Lanka*, p. xxxii.
75 Ibid., p. xxxi.
76 TNA, 940.531 SHU, Shuckburgh, 'Colonial Civil History', volume 3, part 4, 'Major Political Developments Arising Out of the War', 4, 'Ceylon', p. 40, and Shuckburgh, volume 2, part 3, section 4, 'Colonial Government Finance', chapter 6, 'Eastern Colonies', 'Ceylon', p. 406.
77 De Silva (ed.), *Sri Lanka*, p. xlviii.
78 Ashton, 'Ceylon', p. 449.

outset, the Ceylon National Congress was an overwhelmingly conservative body. It was not until 1942 that it put forward independence as its main political goal'.[79] Nevertheless, even in the early month of the war, the Governor was at pains to apprise Whitehall of the attitudes of the politicians, who while supportive, would not be deflected from their nationalist agenda. In order to deepen the support of the political elite and justify and explain the need for constant effort on the part of the people, military leaders interacted with local politicians. This occurred most notably in meetings of the the Commander-in-Chief Ceylon's War Council, of which the ministers were full members, as well as those of the Board of Ministers itself. In addition, imperial military units often hosted local dignitaries. There were also ad hoc occasions for interaction, such as when Admiral Somerville invited a delegation to visit one of his fleet carriers in June 1942:

> In the afternoon I entertained the Minister and the Speaker of the House of Assembly to tea onboard H.M.S. FORMIDABLE and afterwards took them round the ship. They were accompanied by the Commander in Chief, Ceylon, who informed me subsequently that his visit had been most successful and would undoubtedly stimulate the Ministers to increased war efforts. The ignorance displayed by the Ministers on naval matters was abysmal. Questions were asked whether merchant ships and tugs were cruisers and destroyers, and it was difficult to persuade one of these gentlemen that a lighter propelled by two of his countrymen in loin clothes was not a submarine. The proceedings were enlivened by an air raid warning Red which proved to be false but which afforded excellent opportunity for the display of subsequent heroics.[80]

Another occasion when military leaders met with local leaders was recorded on a Universal News film in 1942. It showed Admiral Layton and Lieutenant General Pownall conducted by local dignitaries on a tour of a Buddhist temple at Kelaniya and the fortress of Sigiriya, the British officers being garlanded with flowers, removing their shoes to enter the temple, the visits observed by local people and intended to show sympathy and understanding with local society and general harmony of purpose in the war effort.[81] There were also occasional visits from community leaders from other colonies whose soldiers were based in the island, such as the June 1945 visit of 16 East African chiefs visiting thier men serving with the 11th East African Division. They were received at Government House by Governor Sir Henry Monck-Mason Moore and Lady Moore, accompanied by the Commander-in-Chief Ceylon, now Lieutenant General Wetherall. The chiefs change from African costume into 'jungle green' battledress to visit soldiers, and also visited the Colombo zoological gardens.[82]

Understandably, Whitehall wanted to postpone any consideration of constitutional advance 'for the duration', here as elsewhere in the colonial empire.[83] But for various reasons, it was obliged to change its mind in the case of Ceylon. This was because of the pressure brought

79 Ibid., p. 453.
80 'Admiralty War Diaries of World War II', Reports and proceedings, 5 June-1 July 1942.
81 IWM, RY 79, 'News from Ceylon', text from Colonial Film Database.
82 IWM, JFU 271, 'East African Chiefs in Colombo', text from Colonial Film Database.
83 Churchill opposed calls for a State Council election: 'It would be a great folly to have an election in Ceylon in the next few years. They are making heaps of money out of us at the present time, and

to bear on the Colonial Office by the Ceylonese politicians and, crucially, by senior British military and civilian officials on the ground, who argued vociferously for a significant advance towards full self-government given the remarkable cooperation displayed by leading Ceylonese politicians in helping the British war effort, and the need to ensure that they kept on doing so. The Ceylonese leaders were well aware that collaboration augmented their bargaining position, and the Board of Ministers took every opportunity to emphasize the importance of the island's war contribution and to press Britain for reform towards dominion status – not outright independence outside of the Commonwealth, an important fact as far as Whitehall was concerned and a clever tactic on the part of the politicians. Thus Ceylon's war-time role as a major source of raw materials and as a strategic base worked to the advantage of the island's nationalists, who exploited the situation with consummate skill.[84] In their dispatches to Whitehall, the Governor as well as Layton as Commander-in-Chief Ceylon and, later, Mountbatten as Supreme Allied Commander South East Asia, emphasized the fact that without concrete moves towards constitutional reform, Britain ran the risk of seeing Ceylonese cooperation diminished or even withdrawn, with potentially severe ramifications for the war effort.

In contrast to India and Burma, the political leadership of Ceylon backed the war effort, not baulking at Britain's declaration of hostilities on behalf of the island in September 1939 and offering active support thereafter. Even the subordination of civil to military government with the appointment of Layton as Commander-in-Chief Ceylon in March 1942 was accepted with grace. The nationalists did not, however, let the British forget their position. Addressing the Governor, the president of the Ceylon National Congress wrote:

> We believed that the War in which England is now engaged in was being waged for the freedom of small nations throughout the world. The recent declarations appear to restrict that freedom to such nations of Europe as have lost their independence. The Congress considers it anomalous that the people of Ceylon, a subject people, should be participating in a War effort to restore freedom to European nations, while they themselves are to continue indefinitely in a state of subjection within the Empire.[85]

On 2 March 1943 the joint secretaries of the Ceylon National Congress forwarded to London a copy of a resolution of 19 December 1942 which read: 'The Ceylon National Congress is of the opinion that Ceylon's association in a War said to be for democratic freedom, is manifestly contradictory and necessarily ineffective, without a guarantee of that very freedom to her. This Sessions [sic] therefore calls upon the United Nations to make forthwith a declaration, guaranteeing to Ceylon, freedom immediately after the war'.[86]

the whole area must be regarded as a war zone'. De Silva (ed.), *Sri Lanka*, PREM 4/50/16, WSC to Ismay, 25/5/44, p. 311.

84 See De Silva (ed.), *Sri Lanka*.

85 4 September 1942 Memorandum on the Rights and Status of Indians in Ceylon, H. M. Desai and George R. Motha, Members of the Ceylon Indian Delegation.

86 De Silva (ed.), *Sri Lanka*, CO 54/980/11, no. 29, p. 239, note 1. See also De Silva, document 140 renewing the demand for dominion status in October 1942 (p. 221), document 148 conveying to London a message from the Board of Ministers requesting 'internal home rule' within the British Commonwealth in January 1943 (p. 227), and document 150 of the same month (p. 229).

In January 1943 Caldecott articulated the Ceylon National Congress's demand for national freedom in a report to the Colonial Office. Even though its call for a promise of post-war dominion status was backed by the Governor and the Commander-in-Chief, Whitehall was reticent; as Colonial Secretary Oliver Stanley replied, 'I find it difficult to reconcile full significance of dominion status for Ceylon in unforeseeable conditions of post-war world with Ceylon's obvious needs in matters of defence, commerce, and external relations generally. Further there are general Empire defence interests in the Indian Ocean which it must be the responsibility of HMG to secure in their relations with Ceylon'.[87] But the Governor argued that an assurance of 'full *responsible* Government and internal Home Rule *within the British Commonwealth of Nations*' would prevent the 'immediate and progressive loss of co-operations and decrease of war effort coupled with the deflection of the great bulk of now moderate opinion towards intransigent nationalism and demand for the right to secession'.[88] Reform in order to preserve, was Caldecott's *sotto voce* message.

Though not as keen as its local representatives, the Colonial Office was prepared to offer full responsible government in all internal matters, to be sorted out post-war, Britain retaining control of defence and foreign relations.[89] 'HMG have very fully appreciated and valued the contribution which Ceylon has made and is making to the war effort of the British Commonwealth and UNITED NATIONS'.[90] Among British leaders on the ground, even if not in London, the moderate approach of Ceylonese politicians built confidence in their leadership and loyalty, and garnered the support of Caldecott, Layton, and Mountbatten for constitutional progress. These powerful advocates petitioned the Colonial Office for constitutional advancement, and as a result of this, London was persuaded in 1944 to agree to the appointment of a commission to examine a new constitutional scheme. The Soulbury Commission on constitutional reform duly arrived in Ceylon in December 1944, and Ceylon was set on course for independence after the war.

The moderate movement that pressed Britain for political concessions was far more influential in winning them than the island's more radical elements. From 1939 the anti-war propaganda of the Marxist Lanka Sama Samajist Party (LSSP), founded in 1936, had alarmed the Colonial Office in London. The LSSP encouraged strikes, rattling the planter community and causing it to call for an end to all political activity. Such a marginal party could be ignored in the 'phoney war' phase, but with the fall of France the party was declared illegal and its leaders arrested, though they escaped from gaol in April 1942 between the Colombo and the Trincomalee raids, and went on the run. With the LSSP banned the Communists came more to the fore, especially among the working class of Colombo and its periphery, though they were not inclined to encourage strikes. Inflation increased working class and white collar discontent, though major strike activity was curbed by the lack of encouragement from political parties and the Defence Regulations and Avoidance of Strikes and Lockouts Act.

The LSSP made strident efforts to spread its message among imperial troops. A pamphlet dated 20 April 1942 addressed 'comrades in the Army, Navy, and Air Force' and captured the party's political viewpoint. 'The workers and peasants of Ceylon extend to you their warmest

87 De Silva (ed.), *Sri Lanka*, CO 54/980/5/1, no. 52, 21/1/43, p. 228.
88 Ibid., Emphasis in original.
89 SNLA, sessional papers, 18 (1943).
90 *Reform of Constitution* (July 1943), p. 4.

Revolutionary Greetings!', it began. The servicemen had been 'dragged' through the disasters of Dunkirk, Norway, Crete, Libya, and Singapore. 'And now you have been brought to this island of Ceylon far, far away from your own country and your homes, to lay down your lives for what your rulers call "Freedom". What freedom did you British workers enjoy at home?'. Now here they were in the east, asked to sacrifice their lives 'in the interests of your oppressors and exploiters at home', the 'parasites' who were their 'real enemies'.

> These parasites are our enemies as well. This war, we have said, *is not your war. It is not our war too.* You will have noticed the effects of the first air raid on Colombo. You know how the workers ran away from the workshops and the City and its suburbs. The shops, hotels, laundries and barber saloons [sic] have closed down. The train and bus services have been disorganized. The normal life of the city has been brought to a standstill. *Why*? Have you not asked yourselves *why* this has happened in Malaya, Singapore, Burma and India too? You have been brought all this way to die defending Ceylon when the Ceylonese masses themselves *refuse to lift a finger* in its defence. This is easily explained. We are not interested in defending a country *which does not belong to us.* This country does not belong to you either. It belongs to the Imperialist bosses who exploit us here just as they exploit you at home. *They are our common enemies.*
>
> DOWN WITH IMPERIALIST WAR! DOWN WITH ALL IMPERIALISM! DOWN WITH THE HIGH COMMAND AND THE OFFICER CASTE! COMPLETE FREEDOM OF SPEECH FOR SOLDIERS AND SAILORS![91]

Another strand of wartime political life related to the shifting international climate, in which old-fashioned colonial rule was coming under increasing pressure not only from local nationalists, but from the emerging superpowers. In the British case, this largely meant American pressure to respond positively to nationalist demands and move towards decolonization, getting in step with Washington's nascent vision of a new world order, a United Nations world of independent nation states all, naturally, looking towards America and the west for leadership and espousing similar political and economic ideas. Churchill famously clashed with Roosevelt over the future of India during the war, and in places as diverse as the Caribbean, West Africa, and the Persian Gulf, as America became more prominent on the ground, it became more likely to pronounce on political and economic affairs. This was almost always to the detriment of continued British rule, leading to strident efforts in Whitehall to address, temper, and deflect American criticism and pontification.

Given this background, Whitehall was keen to monitor Americans visiting or based in British colonial territories, to try to seek to influence them positively, and to keep an eye on what they reported to Washington. Itinerant generals, economic advisers, presidential envoys, and senators were usually viewed with dread by British colonial authorities and their masters in London, to be welcomed open armed (if through gritted teeth) and given every facility, but simultaneously watched like hawks and their visits stage managed, if possible, lest they spend too long viewing slums or

91 'Issued by the Lanka Sama Samaja Party section of the Bolshevik Workers' Party of India, Burma, and Ceylon', reproduced in Tomlinson, *The Most Dangerous Moment*, appendix A, pp. 201-04.

talking to notorious 'agitators'. Whitehall closely monitored the 'receptioning' of Americans in the colonies, more mindful of the potential impact of negative reports sent to Washington than the men on the spot tended to be. Nevertheless, those men were increasingly well drilled, every effort being made to impress upon local British officials that being rude to American visitors or letting them go off piste was frowned upon, and that they needed to play their part in the mammoth diplomatic effort to put the Empire's best foot forward in order to head off American criticism of imperialism and oil the works of the all-important Anglo-American alliance.

And so it was to be in Ceylon. Here a War Publicity Committee had been formed in March 1942, and the need to counter American propaganda was discerned.[92] Though not in the spotlight of American attention, nor a source of prime ministerial-presidential correspondence, the island was cast in its shadow when a troupe of perambulating American senators decided to invite themselves on a visit. Up until this point, the main American interest in the island had revolved around the provision of rubber, and not a lot else. Though there were always likely to be a few American service personnel on business in Ceylon, and though later in the war American bombers staged through Ceylonese airbases to extend their operational range, their numbers were limited at the time of the visit though set to grow into the hundreds soon after when Mountbatten brought South East Asia Command's headquarters to Kandy.

On 26 July 1943 the Government of Ceylon received information from American consul Buell regarding the proposed visit of a group of senators on a global fact-finding mission.[93] The Governor extended an invitation for the party to stay at the Queen's House, his official residence in Colombo. No reply accepting the offer was received, though on 28 August the British ambassador in Chungking telegraphed to say that the party was leaving for Calcutta on the following day en route to Colombo. The Government of Ceylon and the military authorities duly rolled out the red carpet: General Playfair, army chief of staff, Governor Caldecott, and other senior officials spent the afternoon of 1 September waiting for the Americans at Ratmalana airport, but their flight was delayed. They then spent three afternoons waiting to receive their guests at Queen's House. When they eventually arrived, the Americans breezily informed the British that two of their number did not wish to stay at Queen's House lest it impair their freedom to establish contact with Ceylonese notables. The senators were moved out to be replaced by Brigadier General Rankin of the US Army, 'whose wide experience of the concoction of mint juleps was revealed to an interested audience before the official dinner party'.[94]

The Governor's report on the visit offered rich pen portraits of the Americans.

> Senator Brewster, the hard-faced ex-Governor of Maine, appeared to be the most astute member of the party, while the conversation of Senator 'Happy' Chandler, a rich-voiced Southern Democrat who threatened to regale the party with Kentucky minstrelsy, and invited His Excellency to visit him in his old Kentucky home, was, when intelligible to the cisatlantic ear, largely on the subject of 'short-snorters'. The meaning of this agreeable expression was apparent only from a description of the Senatorial invasion of

92 TNA, 940.531 SHU, Shuckburgh, 'Colonial Civil History', volume 4, 'Other Normal Activities Under War-Time Conditions', chapter 8, 'Publicity Services', p. 195.

93 TNA, FO 371/38522, letter from Governor of Ceylon enclosing report of a visit to Ceylon by five American senators, 3-5 September 1943. Dated 15 May 1944.

94 Ibid.

> London recently received, from which it appeared that the Prime Minister was invited by ex-Governor Chandler, in the course of an important discussion at No 10 Downing Street, to join this ocean-hopping fraternity by autographing a five-buck note.[95]

During the visit, the absence of American military establishments in Ceylon reduced the opportunities for 'glad-handing' to a minimum. Caldecott took the visitors for a drive in Colombo, and they left for Australia aboard a Liberator.

> The Senatorial party arrived in Ceylon direct from Calcutta, where conditions were at that time appalling. It must have been particularly shocking to the Americans, with their high standard of living and especially of cleanliness to see people dead and dying of starvation in the streets. Colombo, always cleaner and better kept than Indian cities, must have made, by contrast, a very favourable impression.[96]

The British concluded that the party had been easy to entertain 'thanks to a complete absence of "starch", together with an unvarying geniality of manner. And that should have been that, the Governor metaphorically and probably quite literally waving them off at the airport with a hearty smile and a huge sigh of relief. But there was to be a sting in the tail, and the Government of Ceylon's final judgement on the visit was influenced by the 'highly coloured' report on their tour which the senators 'thought fit to present to the American electorate on their return to the United States', the dreaded 'bad report' circulated back home adding another layer to the mounting condemnation of British rule.

95 Ibid.
96 Ibid.

10

On the home front: Part II

This chapter continues the exploration of the wartime home front, focusing on the impact on the built and natural environments, the work of civil defence, efforts to ensure adequate food supplies, fund-raising activities, and the mobilization of labour. The manifestations of war affected people very directly; shortages of some essential commodities, such as cotton piece goods and cement, became acute; the price of rice rose 100 per cent over a 12 month period; the April 1942 raids led to a serious dislocation of education as schools were shut in the Colombo area and people kept their children away; school and public gardens were converted into vegetable plots; meat imports from Britain and Denmark ceased, causing shortages and 'meatless days'; and pre-school milk feeding centres were opened. In line with all other countries, 'evidence of the existence of a black market were plain everywhere'.[1]

Physical infrastructure and the natural environment

The unexpected demands placed upon the island following the string of Allied defeats culminating in Singapore's surrender and Allied ejection from the Dutch East Indies meant that a great deal of construction and conversion work was required to make Ceylon ready to host thousands of service personnel and act as a major Allied headquarters. This required manifold preparations, and the home front was transformed as the echoes of war moved closer and its presence encroached on people's lives, checkpoints, barbed wire, road blocks, and military areas becoming features of everyday life. An officer serving with the 34th Indian Division wrote that:

> This delightful island has changed from an atmosphere of pre-war peace and prosperity to the serious realism of war. That such a change was necessary, nobody can deny. All the original spade-work was done by the GOC [General Officer Commanding] and a small staff which arrived in November 1941. By tact and persuasion they managed to satisfy civilians that buildings and many other treasured amenities must be given up for the duration of

1 TNA, 940.531 SHU, Shuckburgh, 'Colonial Civil History', volume 2, 'Rationing', p. 479. He gives the example of meat rationing and the difficulty of ensuring that meat was only rationed to genuine meat-eaters: when meat rationing was introduced, in May consumption stood at 10,000 pounds weight a day, but had risen to 30,000 pounds by October.

> the war. We owe a lot to them and to the Ceylon Government, for the hearty cooperation we have received.[2]

The environmental impact was significant as land usage changed, new roads and airbases were developed, and servicemen and women arrived in large numbers. Both their work and their recreation were bound to have an impact on the environment; near Hambantota, for example, British Army 25-pounder artillery pieces practiced firing across Embilikala Lewelya into part of the Bundala Bird Sanctuary;[3] the submarine *Stoic* ran into and killed a slumbering whale in the approaches to Trincomalee, damaging its bows so badly it required dry dock repairs;[4] an anti-submarine net stretched from the mainland across Trincomalee harbour to Elephant Island allowed grey langur monkeys to cross from the one to the other and colonize it;[5] and a favoured recreational pastime, indulged in by, among others, Prince Philip, was fishing, 'which in practice meant blowing fish out of the water with small explosive charges and then presenting fifty or sixty of them to the Captain's table'.[6] More generally, the activities of Ceylonese fishermen were impeded as military activities took place around the coast, and minefields and other defences were installed. There was then the incalculable damage to marine life caused by fuel spills from damaged or sunken vessels in Ceylon's coastal waters.

Aerodromes were built all over the island, for its own defence when the Japanese threatened, for Indian Ocean reconnaissance, and in order to enable Ceylon to play its part in offensive operations. The airbase hastily improvized at the racecourse in the Cinnamon Gardens suburb of Colombo required houses, including that of the Chief Justice, to be demolished. Ratmalana civil airport was taken over by the military, its runway doubled in length, requiring the destruction of houses. Kandawala, the charming villa and spacious gardens belonging to Sir John Kotelawala, was commandeered as station HQ.[7]

> Coconut plantations surrounded the aerodrome which made excellent camouflage and cooling shade, and among these quarters for personnel were quickly put up. Most of the buildings, on cement floors, were merely of *kadjan*, the plaited fronds from the coconut palm, on rough round timber, but were comfortable enough for all that in the unfailing warmth and allowed the welcome sea breezes to blow through.[8]

The naval air station at China Bay was expanded along with other facilities around Trincomalee. China Bay, wrote Michael Tomlinson, 'became a hive of activity in March 1942':

2 'Fan Tan', 'Soldiering in Ceylon', p. 68.
3 Banks, 'World War Two Memories – Ceylon'.
4 Young, *One of Our Submarines*, p. 197.
5 Ibid.
6 Judd, *Prince Philip*, p. 106.
7 Tomlinson, *The Most Dangerous Moment*, p. 68. The chairman of the Ceylon Tea Propaganda Board wrote that he was living at 'the club' because his bungalow had been requisitioned. His family had gone to Grahamstown in South Africa, and he was looking for a new bungalow in Nuwara Eliya as 'bungalows are now impossible to obtain in Colombo'. CO 852/19/2, Ceylon tea, letter to Sir Clifford Figg, Colonial Office, 29/10/43.
8 Tomlinson, *The Most Dangerous Moment*, p. 68.

> The station had been well built and designed on an RAF peacetime basis, with airmen's barracks, messes, headquarters, hangars, etc., solidly constructed for permanence … The officers' mess and quarters were on a low hill, immediately south of the airfield, and commanded an excellent view all round, both inland across Tambalagam Bay and seawards. North of the aerodrome and partly concealed by the surrounding jungle are huge fuel storage tanks.[9]

By the end of 1942 a space measuring 6,000 by 600 feet had been cleared of jungle and destumped at Minneriya, representing about half of the area that would eventually be cleared for this new fighter base.[10] At Sigiriya near the ancient city of the Buddhist kings, Mountbatten wrote that 7,000 trees had been bulldozed in the first week of work as space was cleared for the new SEAC runway 'right in the heart of the mountains only 19 miles from Kandy'. Here a 2,000 yard-long Bithess all-weather strip with a 200 yard overrun at either end was laid down. The trees were felled at the beginning of March 1945, Mountbatten landing on it officially for the first time on 1 June.[11] Airbases required a huge amount of land because of the length of the runways and the need for hangars and associated buildings to be dispersed in order to conceal their whereabouts and make it harder for an enemy to score as many direct hits as would be possible if buildings and aircraft were massed close together. On a visit in March 1943, Admiral Somerville reported that the 'FAA aerodrome at Katukurunda [HMS *Ukussa*] is now practically completed, and is a model of how an aerodrome should be laid out. From the air it was practically impossible to detect the dispersal points for the aircraft, or the hangars and workshops hidden in the jungle'.[12]

While Colombo lost houses and golf courses and race-tracks to airbases, tennis courts were dug up for vegetable plots, hallowed ground at establishments such as the Colombo Cricket Club was requisitioned, and barracks, radar installations, and aircraft blast pens and the like were constructed throughout the island, even including dummy control towers, antennae, buildings, and Hurricanes made of wood to deceive Japanese aerial reconnaissance. War-related construction and installation took place across the island, including anti-aircraft guns, trenches, barrage balloons, telephone and wireless facilities, air raid shelters, cleared fields of fire, harbour improvements, port defences, flying-boat anchorages, beach defences, first aid posts, anti-torpedo booms, roads, airfields, and a floating dock capable of accommodating battleships. African, British, and Indian sappers built bridges and roads across the island.[13] People sometimes were obliged to leave their homes in order to make way for military installations. A village near China Bay was emptied, and a 'slum area' of Colombo was cleared to make way for a 5.25-inch naval battery. An influx of over a 1,000 Royal Marines in 1943 for coastal defence work threw up one of the innumerable War Council discussions about accommodation and the location of forces, and the proposal for the siting of a new base, to include a battle school, seven

9 Ibid., p. 70.
10 TNA, ADM 199/663, War Council minutes, 4/5/42.
11 Ziegler (ed.), *Personal Diary*, p. 209.
12 Simpson (ed.), *The Somerville Papers*, to Pound, 11/3/43, pp. 450-51.
13 For a map of Ceylon's military airbases at the end of the war see IWM, 66397, 'Military airfields India/Ceylon and satellites', issued by Statistics at HQ Base Forces South East Asia, November 1945.

miles north of Colombo, was estimated to require the removal of 3,857 civilians from their homes.[14]

Offices and schools were shut down, areas of jungle and offshore islands were declared 'out of bounds' for use as military practice grounds, along with beaches where imperial forces practiced landings and beach assaults. In Colombo, schools and colleges were closed and taken over by the military, including the classical-style quadrangle of St Thomas's College, Mount Lavinia, requisitioned to become a military hospital, and the Buddhist Maliyadeva College in Kurunegala, taken over by the army. Hotels were also prime targets for military requisition; Colombo establishments such as the Grand Oriental next to Naval Headquarters were commandeered, along with Trincomalee institutions such as the Welcome Hotel. The same was true in Kandy, where Mountbatten's staff took over any accommodation they could find and built extensive new accommodation and office facilities as it imported over 5,000 people into the town and its environs.

Some of the buildings were needed for hospitals, such as 58 Indian Army General Hospital at Kandy and 51 Indian Army General Hospital at Ragmara, dedicated to East African troops. With large number of service personnel remaining in Ceylon throughout the war – in May 1944, there were 9,000 RAF personnel present alone, likely to rise to 17,000 in the foreseeable future – medical facilities were required. As an example, in that month, May 1944, there were five active military hospitals, with two others in the process of forming. They provided beds for 1,200 British personnel, 1,500 Indians, 1,600 East Africans, and 1,300 Ceylonese.[15]

In Nuwara Eliya, as in other parts of the island, hotels were requisitioned by the military either as offices or rest facilities. One such hotel was the St Andrew's, modelled on the famous Scottish golf venue, used for military purposes from 1942. The names of visiting military personnel are still recorded in the hotel's visitors' books.[16] The first arrivals were survivors from *Hermes*, sunk during the Japanese raid of 9 April 1942. Many arrived in their oil-soaked clothes after having been plucked from the sea and landed ashore by the hospital ship *Vita*. For these and later servicemen a committee was formed by local people to provide clothing and other necessities. Provisions for the kitchen and pantry, along with liquor and cigarettes, were supplied from the NAAFI set up in Nuwara Eliya. 'It was often felt that the Hotel was in its former heyday during these years as it had a major part to play in the lives of so many local and foreign servicemen, visitors, and permanent guests'.[17] Ceylon played host to many establishments dedicated to the welfare of servicemen, such as NAAFIs, British soldiers and sailors institutes, merchant services clubs, fleet clubs, and junior fleet clubs for ratings. A new Royal Navy canteen opened in 1944 at McCallum Road Colombo, containing two large bars, a recreation room, and cinema facilities, and Admiralty House at Trincomalee was transformed into an officers' mess.[18] In 1944 Galle, the old port capital of Ceylon, was opened so as to increase facilities for the landing of naval stores.

14 TNA, CO 968/12/7, Commander-in-Chief Ceylon war diaries, April to June 1943, War Council minutes, 17/5/43 and War Council minutes, 21/6/43.
15 TNA, WO 203/4532, Hospitals in Ceylon.
16 St Andrew's Hotel Nuwara Eliya, information from a visit in 2007.
17 David and Percy De Zilwa, *The Spirit of St Andrew's* (2006), pp. 5-6.
18 Naval Historical Branch (NHB), J. H. Brown, 'Admiralty House and the Royal Navy at Trincomalee, 1810-1957', unpublished typescript (1980).

The Anderson Golf Course, six miles from Naval Headquarters in Colombo, became the site of Far East Combined Bureau; St Peter's College on the Galle Road became a Wrennery, and Pembroke College, on the corner of Flower Road and Cambridge Avenue, became an intelligence interception centre. The national museum in central Colombo, with its elegant architecture and lofty galleries, its quadrangles, box hedges and huge banyan trees, was hastily requisitioned as Army Headquarters in March 1942. A mortuary and signals office were constructed in its grounds, and the museum's collections so speedily dispersed for the duration that some were lost or damaged. The museum library, dominated by slow-moving punkas and dark-wood bookshelves, was emptied. The museum 'sustained its greatest loss due to the hasty evacuation and the lack of preservatives to the zoological collection'. The study collection was sent to Jaffna, what was salvaged of the spirits collection to Pelmadulla, and rare books and manuscripts to Nuwara Eliya and Ratnapura.[19] The military also occupied a special archaeological reservation at Anuradhapura, their presence preventing the normal visits of pilgrims to the site.[20] A naval stores facility was built at Kochchikade, a Royal Engineers yard at Bentota, a Royal Army Service Corps petrol depot at Kolonnawa, and a Royal Engineers military hospital at Kankesanturai.[21] Koggala lagoon on the south coast became a 'protected area' as the flying-boat base was expanded.[22]

Large areas of central and northern Ceylon were taken over by the military for the accommodation and training of thousands of imperial troops. In addition to land required for runways and buildings, the development of the airbase at Katukurunda, being readied from spring 1942 to accommodate six squadrons of fighter aircraft, demanded large areas be set aside for bombing and air to ground firing ranges.[23] In the Palk Strait separating Ceylon from India, a Governor's Ordinance under the Defence (Miscellaneous) Regulations in June 1944 declared the island of Kachchativu a bombardment range for the Royal Navy, though pilgrims to the island's Roman Catholic shrine were allowed to travel there on a permit issued by the Government Agent of the Northern Province.[24] The enormous harbour and surrounding inlets and coast line all around Trincomalee were entirely dedicated to the war effort. Unlike Colombo, it did not have a large urban population, and those who lived there were heavily involved in the work of the air and naval bases. The whole area surrounding the harbour became a 'Special Area'. As Fortress Commander appointed in the desperate days of spring 1942, Rear Admiral Arthur Palliser had been given authority by Layton to annexe anything he liked around Trincomalee in order to get the port onto a 'proper war-like footing', and as the war progressed, it was expanded and developed to be able to accommodate and support a very large fleet of warships as the Eastern Fleet, and its replacements, the East Indies Fleet and the British Pacific Fleet, gathered in its waters. In the air, too, restrictions applied, rigid corridors of approach demarcated for aircraft approaching or crossing the island, and prohibited areas were declared around key locations.

19 P. H. D. H. de Silva, *Colombo Museum One Hundred Years 1877-1977 Souvenir* (Colombo, 1977), p. 60.
20 TNA, CO 968/12/7, Commander-in-Chief Ceylon war diaries, April to June 1943, War Council minutes, 12/4/43.
21 SNLA, Administrative reports 1944, volume 1.
22 SNLA, CFD 306/38, Defence Regulations (Miscellaneous).
23 TNA, ADM 20/2410, Defence of Ceylon, 3 March to 2 September 1942, Admiralty to Flag Officer Ceylon and Commander-in-Chief Eastern Fleet, 31/7/42.
24 W. T. Jayasinghe, *Kachchativu and the Maritime Boundary of Sri Lanka* (Pannipitiya, Sri Lanka: Stamford Lake, 2003).

Only defence patrol aircraft and aircraft launched from British warships were allowed within a five mile radius of Colombo and Trincomalee without special permission.[25]

Trincomalee had long been known as the 'finest harbour in the world' thanks to a pronouncement by Admiral Lord Horatio Nelson in an earlier age of global confrontation, and it rarely failed to impress visitors.[26] Edward Young, captain of the submarine *Storm*, wrote that it was 'a magnificent and extensive natural anchorage.[27] The harbour itself, 'truly, spectacularly huge with quite a small entrance', as Leslie Atkinson of the destroyer *Volage* described it, was home to warships of all classes.[28] At the outbreak of war, the naval base itself was ramshackle and only half-complete, something being added to it each year as money became available. An airfield and dry dock were in process of being built, and a large number of oil-fuel storage tanks were already finished.

The establishment at Tricomalee was administered from the shore base HMS *Highflyer*, commissioned in April 1942.[29] Admiralty House, with its large verandah and sprawling banyan tree, became 'the permanent Wardroom Mess of HMS HIGHFLYER and the grounds were filled with "Kadjan" huts containing living quarters and administrative offices. The basement of the house itself was occupied by, among other things, a chapel and a cookery school'.[30] After the loss of Singapore, Trincomalee became the navy's most easterly major base, and fleet support services were built up as rapidly as possible. The drawing room was adapted as the ante-room, with a full-sized bar, and the bedrooms were divided into cubicles. The old stables were commandeered by the Dockyard Fire Brigade. Given the port's new-found status following the loss of Singapore, urgent plans for expansion and the augmentation of defences were put in train. As the Admiralty decreed in June 1942, it was 'to be developed with highest priority as a main Fleet base capable of berthing up to 10 capital ships and carriers, 10 cruisers, 24 destroyers, 3 depot ships, 10 submarines, and 16 Fleet minesweepers'.[31]

In March 1943 Admiral Somerville wrote that he had:

25 TNA, AIR 23/4887, Defence arrangements Ceylon, Prohibited areas, corridors of approach, and flying restrictions, 18/8/43.

26 Gerald Graham, *Great Britain in the Indian Ocean: A Study in Maritime Enterprise, 1810-1857* (Oxford: Clarendon Press, 1967), p. 308. For the history of Trincomalee as a naval base, see H. A. Colgate, 'Trincomalee and the East Indies Squadron 1746-1844', M. A. Thesis (University of London, 1959); Colgate, 'The Royal Navy and Trincomalee', *The Ceylon Journal of Historical and Social Studies*, 7, 1 (1964); and 'The Rise and Fall of Trincomalee', in Graham, *Great Britain and the Indian Ocean.*

27 Young, *One of Our Submarines*, p. 198. Young offers a description of the appearance of the fleet in the harbour, after mooring alongside the depot ship *Wu Chang*.

28 BBC World War Two People's War oral history archive, Leslie Atkinson, 'Serving on HMS *Volage* in the East Indies Fleet, 1944-45', A3021779.

29 Brown writes that naval personnel at Trincomalee before this had been appointed to HMS *Lanka*, the 'Accounting and Nominal Base Depot Ship' at Colombo. *Highflyer* had been an armoured cruiser that served as East Indies Station flagship between 1900 and 1921. Brown, 'Admiralty House'.

30 Ibid.

31 Simpson (ed.), *The Somerville Papers*, Admiralty, 2/6/42, p. 422. Colombo, the document stated, was to be an operational base for Force A. 'The defence and berthing facilities already approved to be completed as soon as possible. It is anticipated that Force A will consist of 4 capital ships, 3 carriers, 2 cruisers, and 2 destroyer flotillas'.

> spent a day at Trincomalee and was impressed by the progress made in all directions. In particular the Royal Marines engineering companies have done some very good work and shown their value in accommodating themselves to situations were initiative and resource are the primary requirements. I think that by the end of September everything should be ready to accommodate any Fleet likely to be available in these parts at that time.[32]

There were now 48 heavy anti-aircraft and 44 light anti-aircraft guns at Trincomalee (and 40 and 38 at Colombo). In addition, the majority of the 40 Army anti-aircraft searchlights in Ceylon were installed there.[33] On 8 January 1944 Somerville held a flag officers and commanding officers conference in Trincomalee aboard the cruiser *Newcastle*, and visited three other cruisers and a hospital ship. Giving a sense of the range of facilities and installations that comprised the base, he also visited 'the Naval Picket House, the old Canteen, new Canteen, Services Clubs, Dilkush Bungalow, Wrens' Sick Quarters, new jetty Cod Bay, Ceylon North Transmitting Station and A/A [anti-aircraft] Range'.[34]

By 1944, Trincomalee was a well developed fleet base, housing the largest concentrations of British warships beyond Britain.[35] Brown writes that 'when the Fleet returned to "Scapa Flow in Technicolor" [referring to the return of Eastern Fleet headquarters from Mombasa], over 2,000 officers and rating were housed in the grounds' of Admiralty House alone.[36] Captain Charles 'Granny' Grantham, captain of the carrier *Illustrious*, wrote in July 1944:

> Trincomalee [is] an astonishing sight. It is packed and crammed with a large fleet and its appurtenances ... ships are very smart and boats are spotless ... A great fuss over colours, no black out, sailing races, RPC here and WMP there all add to the general spring cruise atmosphere. To a newcomer this is all very striking.[37]

From summer 1944 until the end of the war big raids on Japanese-occupied territory were conducted from Trincomalee, along with routine shipping sweeps and patrols involving all classes of surface and subsurface vessels.

> Throughout January 1945 the vast harbour at Trincomalee steadily filled up with new ships arriving from Britain. Battleships, heavy and light cruisers, destroyers, submarines and every variety of escort ship and supply vessel occupied every spare jetty, wharf and mooring. Moored at the heart of Trincomalee harbour was the 1st Aircraft Carrier Squadron – *Indefatigable*, *Indomitable*, *Illustrious* and *Victorious* – which carried a total of 238 aircraft

32 Simpson (ed.), *The Somerville Papers*, to Pound, 11/3/43, pp. 450-51.
33 Ibid., p. 466.
34 Ibid., desk diary 8/1/44, p. 502.
35 See IWM, MGH 3584, 'On Board the Escort Carrier HMS *Hunter*', an amateur film shot by a navy sub-lieutenant in 1945. It shows scenes from a voyage around the anchorage in the Bay of Trincomalee in a motor launch. Various warships are shown, including the light anti-aircraft cruiser *Royalist*, flagship of the 21st Aircraft Carrier Squadron, the heavy cruiser *London*, and the escort aircraft carrier *Ameer*, also the escort carrier *Hunter*. Text from Colonial Film Database.
36 Brown, 'Admiralty House'.
37 CAC, Edwards Papers, REDW 2/17.

> and was escorted by the battleship *King George V*, four cruisers and ten destroyers. It was the largest airborne force the Fleet Air Arm had ever assembled.[38]

Away from the ports of Colombo and Trincomalee, the place most affected by the physical transformations brought by war was the inland town of Kandy, capital of Ceylon's last independent monarch before its conquest by the British in 1815. Mountbatten described the set up in Kandy, South East Asia Command's home town from spring 1944: 'The new SEAC Headquarters consists of the Supreme Allied Command HQ in Peradeniya Botanical Gardens, the Army Group HQ and the Air Command HQ, all three of which are on different roads leading from Kandy, and each about four miles from the centre of town'.[39] The daily 'SEAC Special' train service shuttled people between the web of military headquarters in Colombo and those in Kandy. The beautiful Royal Botanical Gardens at Peradeniya just outside the town had been used for military purposes since their requisition in March 1942. On the banks of the Mahaweli River, where monkeys played among giant bamboo trees and elephants bathed, Mountbatten's headquarters fanned out from colonial buildings with pillared verandahs and red-tiled roofs. Temporary buildings sprouted amidst the giant Java figs and coconut avenues, all overlooked by the mountain range known as the Knuckles.

Kandy underwent a massive transformation as it became one of the Allies' most important headquarters establishments. Hotels such as the Hotel Suisse and the Queen's Hotel were taken over for senior officers and female officers. Kandy's Maduma Bandara Park was converted into a NAAFI recreation hall, where regular dances were held. A Wrennery for American and British female other ranks was constructed on the eighth and ninth holes of the golf course, the Automobile Association of Ceylon's Members' Garage was taken over as an army store, St Anthony's College became a military hospital, and RAF bases were established at Polgolla and Uyanwatte.[40]

On the roads the volume of traffic increased tremendously as hundreds of military vehicles were imported, such as the 120 lorries landed from India for the army in early April 1942 and the 1,674 vehicles (excluding motorbikes) sent for the use of East African troops destined for Burma in May 1943.[41] The issue of road accidents caused by reckless driving immediately became an issue as soon as large forces began arriving at the start of 1942.[42] There was a huge increase in road traffic leading to many hair-raising experiences for drivers and passengers on unfamiliar roads, often involving felled trees or wandering elephants and bullocks. In the towns, pedestrians and vehicles added to the general chaos. Cecil Callis remembers the hustle and bustle in Colombo caused by 'buses on roads charging around like berserk monsters, mad lumbering lorries, carefree taxis, wavering overloaded bicycles, plodding bullock carts, wandering cows,

38 Iredale, *The Kamikaze Hunters*, p. 180.
39 Ziegler (ed.), *Personal Diary*, p. 99.
40 Nihal Karunaratna, *Kandy Past and Present, 1474–1998* (Colombo: Government Printing, Central Cultural Fund, 1999).
41 For the 120 Indian lorries, see TNA, ADM 199/663, Commanders' Meeting minutes, 3/4/42. For the East African division's vehicles, see TNA, WO 106/4487, Ceylon reinforcement, 20/3/43 to 20/8/43, War Office to General Officer Commanding East Africa, 6/5/43.
42 Ibid., War Council minutes, 30/3/42.

dogs, goats, hens, and occasionally elephants'.[43] John Banks recalls an army dispatch driver who collided with an elephant on the jungle roads leading to Trincomalee. The motorcycle's exhaust scorched the tusker, and the rider spent an uncomfortable night in a tree, until the elephant was collected by its mahout in the morning.[44]

The night sky was pierced by the headlights of lorries, staff cars, and jeeps, their beams covered because of black out regulations. Not only was the island's road system transformed, but the skies above came alive with aircraft, from the slow and ungainly Catalina and Sunderland flying-boats to the solid frames of Dakotas and Liberators and the full throttle dash of Barracudas, Hurricanes, and Spitfires. As a measure of the weight of air traffic, 44 Fleet Air Arm squadrons were stationed at or passed through China Bay aerodrome during the war. Even the island's elephant population was enlisted in support of the war effort: 'At aerodromes such as that at HMS *Ukussa* at Katukurunda, 28 miles south of Colombo, one could see the most modern aircraft being hauled around by elephants, each one working with a mahout sitting on top', recalled a British serviceman.[45] A sailor from the escort carrier *Rajah* watched as an elephant took 'exception to a Fairey Swordfish torpedo-bomber, and set off at a steady trundle in a cloud of dust across the aerodrome and rammed it'.[46] At Puttalam 60 miles north of Colombo, Fifi, had her name painted on her sides, led a team of elephants employed to tow Corsairs around the airbase at HMS *Rajaliyah*.[47] At airbases conditions could be muddy and the porous metal sheets ('PSP' – 'pierced steel planking') that constituted the runways would become slippery when wet. Commander Sam Macdonald-Hall recalls:

> After a shower the runway (steel strips) turned to ice, you stamped on the brakes, locked the wheels, and the Corsair slid gracefully into the sand (which turned to mud after rain). Call for the duty elephant. Ropes were fixed to the jumbo's collar, and led to the undercarriage legs of the Corsair, just above the wheels. To get the outfit back on the runway, the elephant had to pull from the opposite side, as jumbo did not like padding around on the metal tracking. The jockey (mahout) sat on the elephant's neck, clad only in a loin cloth.[48]

Extended facilities at China Bay meant that in 1944 50 giant American B-29 Superfortresses were able to use Ceylon as a base for a strike on Palembang in Sumatra.

It was difficult for the public to avoid martial scenes, such as the movement of soldiers in open topped lorries, CLI mortar practice in Colombo or CPRC drilling on Galle Face Green, Royal Marines practicing beach assaults at Mount Lavinia, and the uniforms of a range of different services, and branches within those services, that thronged the streets and places of entertainment. There were many formal military occasions, such as the one on 11 June 1942 at which the

43 BBC World War Two People's War oral history archive, Callis, chapter 5, 'Kandy and Colombo', A4428038.
44 Banks, 'World War Two Memories – Ceylon'.
45 BBC World War Two People's War oral history archive, anonymous, 'Elephants in the Fleet Air Arm', A3433268.
46 Ibid.
47 Iredale, *The Kamikaze Hunters*, p. 178. A painting at the Fleet Air Arm Museum in Yeovilton by Robert Taylor is called 'Puttalam elephants'. See http://www.oliversart.co.uk/acatalog/Puttallam_Elephants_Robert_Taylor.htm
48 Roger Thiedman, 'Of Aeroplanes and Jumbos', at http://www.worldgenweb.org/lkawgw//aero.html

Governor and the Commander-in-Chief Ceylon took the salute on the steps of Queen's House during a formal parade, accompanied by an RAF fly past as the soldiers and sailors marched to the accompaniment of the CLI Band. Captain Lamar representing the US Navy, Vice Admiral Conrad Helfrich, Commander-in-Chief of the Royal Netherlands East Indies Navy based in Ceylon, the Dutch.[49] The following month, on the Esplanade at Trincomalee, the Duke of Gloucester 'performed his most pleasant duty, presenting Military Medals to Sergeant Thomas Brown and Gunner Allan Monaghan, heroes of the air raid on Trincomalee, when they fought a blazing fire threatening an ammunition dump'.[50]

A 1944 Air Ministry film shows a parade in the capital. It opens with high angle shots from the roof of the Secretariat building of a military procession moving though Colombo with civilians all around. Twelve Spitfires in four three-aircraft 'vics' fly over the camera. One aircraft breaks to the left and peels off. The film then shows the Spitfires firing at a target a short distance offshore, with plumes of water from impacts, and the Spitfires in arrow formation. The film shows shots of the crowd, with locals and British servicemen intermingled. Sixteen Corsairs of the Fleet Air Arm are seen in a triple-arrow formation, then firing at offshore target. A crowd shot shows a boy holding a Union flag with British servicemen alongside. There are scenes of a joint RAF and Fleet Arm Air aircraft exhibition at Galle Face Green, with Fairey Barracudas and Corsairs on display.[51]

RAF and FAA squadrons regularly flew, singly or in formation over the island. At the racecourse in January 1942 one of many large ARP practices was conducted, in which the RAF contributed fighters acting as 'enemy' aircraft. In June 1944 the band of the King's African Rifles performed on Galle Face Green.[52] As the Eastern Fleet war diaries reveal, when warships of the Eastern Fleet visited Ceylon's ports they would frequently conduct exercises with the island's army and RAF defenders. This involved the fleet's aircraft making mock attacks on military installations and the docks, and the RAF and Royal Artillery responding. There were also mock invasions and operations by landing parties designed to test the defences, sometimes leading to disturbing encounters between servicemen and local people. Trenowden writes of a Force 136 party that was landed south of China Bay with orders to see how far it could get towards Colombo before being apprehended. The soldiers soon met a group of Tamil fishermen. Masquerading as a German officer with Malayan Chinese men, the leader of the party said that they were a pre-invasion party. Undeterred, the fishermen helped them hide their stores, and the men were feasted in several villages and told how welcome the Japanese would be if they landed. The submarine that had landed the SOE party had been detected by radar, and the men were eventually rounded up by a Eurasian police inspector.[53] Ceylon and its environs also remained subject to 'real' military encounters between British and Japanese forces. For example, a Japanese flying-boat, probably originating from the Andamans, was picked up and tracked by coastal defence radar at Rocky Point Trincomalee. RAF Beaufighters were vectored to intercept, and shot it down into the sea.

49 SNLA, *Times of Ceylon*, 12/6/42.
50 SNLA, Dispatches 441.
51 IWM, ABY 46, 'Procession, air show and football match at Colombo', 11/11/44, description from Colonial Film Database.
52 SNLA, *Times of Ceylon*, 13/6/44.
53 Trenowden, *Operations Most Secret*, pp. 118-21.

The war also brought strict censorship to the island. Frederick Tippet was an Assistant Censor in Ceylon from May 1940, rising to become Chief Censor before the end of the war, after which he wrote a comprehensive report and history of the Ceylon censorship service.[54] Postal and telegraph censorship was first imposed on 1 September 1939 under government defence regulations. The postal censorship unit was accommodated in the General Post Office, telegraphic censorship at the Central Telegraph Office. As the service expanded, the former headquarters of the P. & O. Bank were taken over.

The main categories of censored mail were the Indo-Ceylon traffic, mail from and to enemy occupied territories, Red Cross mail passing through Colombo, Empire and Americas mail, and mail to and from the Middle East and neutral countries. Microfilm was extensively employed to copy material of interest to be forwarded to London. The Chief Censor dealt personally with matters relating to press censorship. There was an average traffic of 25,000 letters per day to and from India, and also a significant flow between the Dutch East Indies and Europe, the Far East and Europe, China and the Middle East (a missionary and his wife initially covering Chinese language mail), and letters to and from the Maldives (requiring the employment of 'Maldivish' translators). In terms of telegraphic and telephonic censorship, the main lines of traffic were Indo-Ceylon and the rest of the world, all managed by Cable and Wireless. The daily average of telegraph messages was 2,052 in 1939, rising to 3,479 in 1945.

It was also down to the Censorship Department to board all neutral ships visiting Colombo to inspect mail, leading to truculence and resistance from the captains of Italian and Japanese vessels before those powers became belligerents in the conflict. Unusual discoveries were sometimes made, such as German propaganda films and mail being sent by Japanese ships to German firms in Iran. The censorship of prisoner of war mail could also yield useful intelligence, such as the location of Italian military units, and even maps showing the approaches to Mogadishu harbour taken from a visiting Italian submarine. The need to censor the mail of imperial service personnel based in Ceylon and passing through its ports necessitated the creation of military base censorship teams to supplement the work of the civilian censors. A 100 per cent censorship was imposed on all mail to and from the Trincomalee area, reflecting its military importance.

The Civil Defence Department and the National Food Campaign

A senior Sinhalese politician of inestimable importance during the war was Oliver Goonetilleke, head of the Civil Defence Department, who was created a Companion of St Michael and St George in the New Year's Honours List 1942. The department was a powerful war ministry responsible for preparing the island to deal with an attack and assisting the imperial military authorities in any way possible. This the department did through manifold schemes and construction projects and a sophisticated propaganda and information campaign. One of the department's main tasks was the organization of Air Raid Precautions. Posters and leaflets abounded, in English, Sinhala, and Tamil. One read 'When the warning siren sounds: Put out all lights: LIGHTS BRING BOMBS'.[55] The Civil Defence Commissioner ordered the clearance of slums

54 Butler Papers, F. S. Tippet, 'Report and History of the Ceylon Censorship, September 1939-November 1945'.

55 SNLA, H. 29/1, War emergency department pamphlets, 1940-1946.

in Colombo so as to implement a fire-gap scheme.[56] Whole streets of houses and shops were knocked down so that fires caused by incendiary bombs would not spread beyond the immediate sector in which they had started. ARP and first aid posts were established throughout the city, each with 300 men working in shifts and trained by municipal doctors, and the department built underground air raid shelters, each accommodating about 50 people. Goonetilleke planned for 140 Air Raid Wardens' Posts in Colombo alone, requiring 2,400 Air Raid Wardens and a 50 per cent reserve. The Governor praised the wardens for their participation in a big air raid practice in Colombo on 21 February 1942, though was not so impressed by the behaviour of civilians, many of whom failed to take cover.[57] Sirens were installed around the country, and, as in Britain, church bells were to remain silent unless there was a general invasion warning (though they were rung to celebrate Montgomery's victory at Alamein). People were encouraged to join 'house fire parties' – of which there were 650 in Colombo by May 1942 – and to prepare sand bins with which to extinguish fires, and were also asked to contribute to blood banks.[58]

These preparations were in no way excessive; throughout 1942 the Japanese threat was real, and everyone was mindful of the complete failure in Malaya and Singapore to make adequate civil defence preparations. In December 1942 Air Vice Marshal D'Albiac, soon to be replaced by Air Vice Marshal Alan Lees as Air Officer Commanding Ceylon, wrote a newspaper article entitled 'When Zero hour came to Colombo: Island's probable role in future air operations', in which he contended that the Japanese 'intend to conquer and occupy Ceylon'.[59] Posters offered comprehensive advice on what to do and what not to do during a raid, and gave figures indicating the lifesaving potential of air raid shelters. The public were clearly worried about the prospect of invasion, particularly because stories of Japanese atrocities in captured cities from Shanghai to Singapore were common currency. In January 1942 the Governor noted that people were taking money out of savings banks and hoarding coinage, and that when air raid sirens sounded in Colombo, stampedes occurred. In the State Council there were 'clamorous demands for evacuation' of the coastal towns of Batticaloa, Colombo, Galle, and Trincomalee, and well-to-do families moved inland. The Civil Defence Department even prepared evacuation camps in case of the need for mass evacuations from coastal areas targeted by the enemy. In May 1943 the Officer Commanding Troops Ceylon placed posters around the country offering rewards of up to 5,000 rupees for information on enemy landings, parachutists, sabotage, and spies.[60]

After the Japanese raids of April 1942, the Commander-in-Chief Ceylon, the Governor, and the Civil Defence Department redoubled their efforts. The worst expectations had come true – Ceylon had seen neighbouring colonies fall to the enemy, including the Andaman and Nicobar Islands – and now was itself being attacked. A poster published by the department asked 'If the enemy comes again – will you be ready?' and advertised ARP literature including lecture notes on First Aid in three languages, the *Report on the Colombo ARP Scheme*, a *Wardens'*

56 In its 2 June 1942 issue the *Times of Ceylon* printed a picture of Siripina Lane after the creation of the fire gap.

57 RHL, Papers of the Fabian Colonial Bureau, Mss Brit. Emp. S365, box 151, Ceylon 1939-1965, A. R. Caton, 'Sketch of Ceylon' (Fabian Colonial Bureau: February 1942).

58 House fire parties figure from TNA, ADM 199/663, Commanders' Meeting minutes, 29/5/42.

59 SNLA, *Times of Ceylon*, 15/12/42.

60 This matter was discussed in the War Council and a publicity campaign launched to herald the new law.

Handbook, *ARP for Everyman*, and *Everyman's ARP for Animals*. Captions beneath illustrations asked: 'Have you a refuge room or trench?'; 'Have you removed or protected all glass?'; 'Have you water and sand for fire fighting?'; 'Have you joined a House Fire Party?'; and 'Do you know how to deal with incendiaries?'. As late as June 1944 the department was still placing adverts in the newspapers for its September 1942 publication *After a Raid: What Shall I Do?*, 'a book every householder in Colombo should possess'.[61] Even at this late date, Japan remained in control of Burma, the Royal Navy had only just begun striking at enemy-occupied territory in the region from its Ceylonese bases, and Japanese sea power remained considerable.[62]

Networks of regional and trans-regional food supply criss-crossed the British Empire. Ceylon depended heavily on imported food, as did other territories of the Empire, as indeed did Britain itself. The loss of key 'bread basket' colonies along with general wartime food shortages accentuated the importance of access to sea lanes for the movement of food. New land was taken under cultivation in Ceylon as food shortages developed because of the loss of import sources to the enemy – the fall of Burma being particularly felt as it severed Ceylon's major rice supply – and the worldwide shipping shortage. Through a range of initiatives, therefore, the State Council tried to build food reserves and hoped to make Ceylon permanently independent of imports.[63] Buildings in towns and villages were adorned with war posters, exhorting people to 'Grow more food', 'Dig harder for your larder!', or warning them that 'Looting is punishable with death'.[64] General food rationing was introduced in 1942, the Municipal Council of Colombo issuing 566,919 ration books, and the Civil Defence Department initiating a Milk Supply Scheme which produced and distributed milk through a network of depots.[65] In May 1944 the department was supplying thousands of pints of reconstituted milk per day in Colombo.[66] In September 1942 the State Council debated a motion of no confidence in the Minister for Labour, Industry, and Commerce. In that role G. C. S. Corea was responsible for food distribution and rationing, and the motion referred to 'very widespread discontent prevalent throughout the island regarding the most unsatisfactory the food rationing and Control Schemes are operating particularly regarding curry stuffs and sugar'.[67] After consulting with the Board of Ministers the Governor appointed Goonetilleke to take charge of food purchasing, pricing, and distribution, his civil defence work having inspired public confidence in him.[68]

Despite hopes and ambitious initiatives, Ceylon did not manage to become self-sufficient, an unrealistic short-term goal given the extent of its reliance on imports. In fact, rice shortages became severe, Burma having provided 70 to 80 per cent of Ceylon's rice. The island turned to India as a substitute, but was denied exports because of the subcontinent's own grave food situation as the Bengal famine loomed. Ceylon then turned for help to the Middle East Supply Centre, itself facing a general shortage of cereal supplies in the Red Sea area, augmented by the failure of rains in Yemen and the Aden Protectorate. The matter was discussed by the War

61 SNLA, *Times of Ceylon*, 13/6/44.
62 SNLA pamphlets.
63 See SNLA, Lot 29/1, 1/3, Food for propaganda adverts, and articles on the subject.
64 SNLA, poster and advert files.
65 SNLA, Sessional papers, 1944, *Administrative Report of the Commissioner of the Municipal Council of Colombo for the Year 1942* (Colombo: Government Printer, 1944).
66 SNLA, *Times of Ceylon*, 29/5/44.
67 De Silva (ed.), *Sri Lanka*, CO54/98/17, no. 2, 4 September 1942, p. 219.
68 Ibid.

Cabinet in London on several occasions. At its meeting of 16 November 1942, for instance, before discussing Sir William Beveridge's new report on social welfare, 'Ceylon food supplies' was the item on the agenda. The matter had previously been discussed on 14 September, and now it was reported that the island was unable to obtain adequate supplies from India and 'a grave situation was now developing' and 'food shortages were affecting morale'.[69] The island's minimum requirement was 30,000 tons per month, yet in October, only 1,250 tons arrived. The grain stock was now at 23,000 tons, less than two weeks supply. The Cabinet recommended that the Government of India be asked to 'take exceptional measures' to ensure Ceylon's supplies reached the 30,000 ton per month target. To supplement this, wheat and flour were to be imported from Australia at the rate of 15,000. But Sir Ramaswami Mudaliar, attending the November War Cabinet meeting along with His Highness Maheraja Jam Saheb of Nawanagar, Australia's S. M. Bruce, and South Africa's Jan Smuts, said that India was finding it difficult to supply Ceylon. The meeting concluded that 'in view of the strategic importance of Ceylon in connection with the defence of India, and the extent to which the Empire's war effort now depended on Ceylon's rubber production', it was felt that India should make strong efforts to provide the required rice'.[70]

'Egyptian rice stemmed a critical shortage in Ceylon', which became dependent on Middle East rice for the remainder of the war.[71] The United Kingdom Commercial Corporation undertook to buy as much of Egypt's surplus crop as possible, and of the first 75,000 tons acquired in 1943, 31,000 tons went to Ceylon, 24,000 tons to the army (mainly for Indian troops serving with the Eighth Army), the 20,000 ton balance being held in reserve. Given that there was expected to be a shortfall in the purchase of the next 75,000 tons, the Middle East Supply Centre put in a strong plea for Ceylon to be cut off, but London overruled this given the seriousness of the position there. On 13 February 1943 the War Cabinet considered a paper on cereals for the 'Indian Ocean Area' prepared by the Minister of War Transport. It said that the demand for supplies came from Ceylon, India, Iran, Kenya, Mauritius, Northern Rhodesia, Réunion, the Seychelles, South Africa, Southern Rhodesia, and Turkey. In the last few months, 130,000 tons of wheat had been exported from Australia because of India's inability to supply.

Fortunately for Ceylon, it was in a better position than most colonial territories to deal with its food problems: because of its 'large and well trained administrative staff control was possible over a wide range of commodities and to a high degree of efficiency'.[72] The island was divided into self-supporting and non self-supporting areas, rationing being introduced into the latter regions and later extended across the whole island. John Shuckburgh explains the system applied to distribute rationed foodstuffs. Once received in port they were 'taken to Government Granaries and thence distributed by rail and road to 125 Government Supply Stations; 1,000 wholesale dealers drew from these; 22,000 authorized distributors, cooperatives and estates

69 Ibid., CAB 65/28 WM 153 (42) 4, Ceylon: Food supplies, War Cabinet conclusions of the supply of rice to Ceylon, 16/11/42, p. 225.

70 Ibid.

71 Martin Wilmington, *The Middle East Supply Centre* (London: University of London Press, 1972), p. 127. Many files deal with Ceylon's food problems. See for example TNA, MT 59/919. Empire requirements: Ceylon general imports. They were also regularly discussed at War Council meetings.

72 TNA, 940.531 SHU, Shuckburgh, 'Colonial Civil History', volume 2, part 3, 'Rationing', 'Ceylon', p. 475.

drew from them for issue'.[73] Food under controlled distribution included chillies, sugar, pulses, and coriander, issued through cooperatives and authorized retailers. Flour was issued to bakers according to the number of consumers they served, and some milk products were issued only to invalids and children.[74] Ration coupons were required for rice, wheat, wheat flour, and kurakkan (or finger millet, made from a herbaceous plant an a staple in certain parts of the island).[75] Shuckburgh writes that great efforts were made to improve the food situation 'and safeguard the health of vulnerable groups'.[76] Nevertheless, only so much could be done, and some people suffered.

> The price of many essential commodities were certainly beyond the purchasing power of those sections of the poorer elements to which the war had brought no increase in income. Whether the lot of the poverty-stricken stricken villager was worse in 1944, tan before the war, it would be hard to say. The war, however, had brought increased rages to a large number of people, and in consequence an improved standard of food consumption; and the Government's policy since 1943, of subsidising essential foodstuffs and pegging prices had done much to improve the food situation generally.[77]

Food controls meant extra duties for members of the colonial civil service. In addition to his routine district duties and army liaison work, John O'Regan was assigned new food control tasks. As food shortages, rationing, and the black market became themes in the lives of ordinary people, O'Regan was made responsible for introducing rationing in the Kandy District and was appointed Deputy Food and Price Controller. He became Controller of the Internal Purchase Scheme responsible for organizing and enforcing the government's plan for the compulsory purchase of locally grown rice throughout the colony.[78] The Internal Purchase Scheme for rice, established in 1942, was a central feature of the island's food strategy. Commonly known as the 'Paddy Purchase Scheme', it was an 'extreme measure given the acute rice situation' in the light of the loss of Burmese supplies. The scheme offered guaranteed prices for rice set above the world market price. Investment in peasant colonization schemes in dry zones was increased, and the range of free services offered by government to agricultural colonists was expanded. Guaranteed prices were paid to cultivators, free artificial manure and seeds were offered and grants of Crown Land made available on easy terms, and state farms were opened as the acreage under food crops increased. There were also government farms producing food, tended by the recruits of the Agricultural Corps. The State Council formed this 'volunteer land army', which employed up to 15,000 labourers, in order to provide dedicated labour for the national food campaign.

With the new interest in increasing rice production, the Government of Ceylon's Director of Irrigation embarked on a tour of Australia in order to garner information that would enable

73 Ibid., p. 478.
74 Ibid., p. 489.
75 Ibid., p. 489.
76 Ibid., p. 478.
77 Ibid.,p. 479.
78 RHL, the Papers of John O'Regan, Mss. Brit. Emp. s. 385.

him to improve the irrigation of Ceylon's paddy fields.[79] In November 1942 Lieutenant-General Pownall, Officer Commanding Troops Ceylon, suspended rice rations to British troops so as to make more available for civilians.[80] Also in that month, questions were asked in the British House of Commons about the island's food situation, and it was announced that rations were at two-thirds of normal consumption. New sugar supplies also had to be found after the loss of Java and in 1944 several meatless days a week were introduced in Colombo and other main population centres.[81] Also in 1944, pork became the only meat served in city cafes, and vegetarian menus were introduced from 1 June.[82] At the beginning of 1944 the War Cabinet again considered the food situation in Ceylon and it was reported that rice supply was still 'causing considerable anxiety'. Allocations were being made in Egypt, though India remained unwilling to let any reserves go because of the situation there.[83] Rationing was introduced throughout the island, though this presented little problem for the privileged, remembers Monica Hulme, a colonial civil servant's daughter living in Trincomalee, 'where canned food, chocolates, and even clothing was available via the friendly soldiers and sailors, who were able to make purchases at the NAAFI'.[84]

The Civil Defence Department coordinated the National Food Campaign, a sophisticated enterprise that used propaganda – in the form of posters, calendars, newspaper adverts, booklets, certificates, and even adhesive stickers – to encourage the population towards greater food self-sufficiency, backed up by government funds and inducements such as land and agricultural implements. 'We must not relax until we are self-supporting', one poster trumpeted; 'make production equal consumption!'.[85] The food production drive featured an Emergency School Food Production Campaign involving 5,000 schools, and the department also opened at least 20 'CDC [Civil Defence Commission] Restaurants' across Colombo, modelled on the 'British Restaurants' in Britain and sporting plates baring the CDC monogram.[86] Extremely detailed and well produced information appeared, such as the pamphlets *Food for Everyone* and *Food in Wartime: What to Grow in Home Gardens*, the latter containing over 50 pages of information and diagrams. People were exhorted to experiment with new crops, particularly wheat and wheat flour, one poster showing a Sinhalese man showing off his muscles, gained through eating wheat, to his admiring family. Adverts suggested wheat recipes, encouraged the consumption of greens for irons and vitamins, gave tips on how to grow chillies and French dwarf beans, and

79 SNLA, sessional paper, 8 (1943), S. G. Taylor, *Notes on a Tour of Australia* (Colombo: Government Press, 1943).
80 SNLA, *Times of Ceylon*, 18/11/42.
81 SNLA, *Times of Ceylon*, 5/5/44. Shuckburgh writes that rationed fresh meat was available two days each week in Colombo. Shuckburgh, ,Colonial Civil HIstory of the War', volume 2, 'Rationing', p. 489.
82 SNLA, *Times of Ceylon*, 26/5/44.
83 TNA, CAB 66/47/40, War Cabinet report for January 1944.
84 Monica Hulme, letter to author, 21/5/99.
85 SNLA, poster and advert files.
86 SNLA, Lot 5/439, Dispatches 1942-1-12, R. H. Bassett, *Administrative Report of the Commissioner for Development and Agricultural Marketing from January 1940 to December 1945* (Colombo: Government Press, 1946).

explained crop rotation and 'How to prepare manure'.[87] On his April 1942 visit Alan Moorehead wrote that 'sensible decrees for conserving food, especially rice' had been promulgated.

> The coarse, split rice of the island is not normally eaten, but now it was needed and the Governor handsomely came forward as an experimenter. He fed himself a number of large meals based on the split rice and sent a long and fascinating letter about it to the local newspapers. It was rather like a piece from *Country Life*.[88]

The media played an important role in encouraging food production and experimentation with things such as poultry-rearing. 'All races of Ceylon are eating hoppers, string hoppers, rotti and pitta', said the *Times of Ceylon*, all made with wheat flour imported to make good the deficiency in rice flour.[89]

Family sentiment was used in inventive food drive posters, one showing a man tilling the soil with a hoe while his wife and two children looked on affectionately. 'For those you love – grow more food' read the caption in three languages. Nutrition Demonstration Vans toured rural areas demonstrating how to cook with unfamiliar ingredients. Over the winter of 1941-42 Colombo Town Hall was the venue for the All-Ceylon Food and Food-Craft Exhibition.[90] At a repeat exhibition the following year, the military provided entertainment for the public in the form of a military tattoo. There was a 'Physical Training display' by a Ceylon Light Infantry battalion, an aerial ropeway demonstration by the Royal Navy, a demonstration of 'Artillery in Action', RAF aerobatics displays, African tribal war dances, and music from massed military bands.[91]

One result of the food shortages that affected the island was the growth of the cooperative movement. 'Epoch-making' progress was made between 1942 and 1945, a period of 'phenomenal growth, accompanied by a strikingly new orientation of the organization', April 1942 bringing to an end a 30 year period of gradual advance. At that point – the month of the Japanese raids – the island's cooperative movement had 2,000 societies with 92,000 members and a capital of 7 million rupees. By the end of April 1945, this had risen to 6,400 societies with 1,100,000 members and a capital of 26 million rupees, a shift ascribed solely to 'war conditions'. The entry of Japan into the war and 'the new theatre of war in the East' that this inaugurated meant that 'the outlook for food in Ceylon assumed a new gravity', as the prospect of food imports became 'very gloomy indeed' when the European colonies of Asia and the East Indies were lost.[92] The cooperative movement was of considerable help to government in the distribution and price control of food and agricultural supplies, and the number of retail stores rose from 38 in 1942 to over 4,000 by 1946.[93] The staff of the cooperative societies, run as a government department, rose from 121 in April 1942 to 900 in April 1945.[94]

87 SNLA, poster and advert files. How to grow chillies advert, SNLA, *Times of Ceylon*, 23/5/44.
88 Moorehead, *A Year of Battle*, p. 153.
89 SNLA, *Times of Ceylon*, 18/6/42.
90 IWM, PST 15903 for the striking poster advertising the event.
91 SNLA, *Times of Ceylon*, 5/12/42.
92 SNLA, Ceylon administration reports 1944, volume 1, G. de Soyza, *Administrative Report on the Workings of Cooperative Societies from May 1942 to April 1945* (Colombo: Government Press, 1946).
93 Bodleian Library, Oxford, Command 7167, 'The Colonial Empire', p. 92.
94 SNLA, G. de Soyza, *Administrative Report*.

The Japanese raids on Ceylon and the attack on both coasts of India had led to 'a very serious dislocation of the vital trade traffic with India'.[95] The Food Control Scheme adopted to supervise the distribution of supplies through a network of approved merchants was considered satisfactory for basic foodstuffs such as rice and flour, but for other products the public reaction was to take distribution into their own hands. This is where the cooperative movement came into its own:

> The remarkable events of 1942-45 were the result of war conditions ... The economic background was one of severe scarcity and rigid economic controls. Despite these controls, profiteering in consumer goods had become so rampant by the beginning of 1942 throughout the country (the situation became very acute after the Japanese air raids of April 1942) that the people themselves were led to ask for cooperative distribution as the only effective remedy for their pressing ills.[96]

Food shortages could have dire ramifications for some people. As the Fabian Colonial Bureau in London noted, tuberculosis in Ceylon increased mainly due to malnutrition caused by increases in the cost of living and the reduction in available foodstuffs and overcrowding as the war stopped building projects and the military requisitioned real estate.[97]

Given the food situation the people of Ceylon were obliged to rely on their own resources for much of their requirements. Fortunately, the island enjoyed an abundance of natural flora. Pineapples, bananas, avocados, mangos, wood apples, jack fruits, papayas, breadfruit, and coconuts abounded. Certain areas of Ceylon were known for their agricultural specializations; there were banana plantations in Uva Province, the region between Matale and Dambulla contained many spice gardens, and in the hill country around Diyatawala and Nuwara Eliya vegetable terraces had flourished since the days of Sir Samuel Baker, the English explorer who introduced cabbages, carrots, and leaks to his adopted home.

'Give til it hurts!': War charities, propaganda, and advertising

Throughout the Empire, colonial governments and private organizations raised funds for the war effort, amounting all together to a massive transfer of resources, as gifts or loans, from the colonies to Britain. Official British government figures reveal that Ceylon made monetary gifts to Britain amounting to £1,096,101, second only, in the colonial empire, to the Federated Malay States, the Unfederated Malay States, and the Straits Settlements.[98] There were also gifts in kind, another common wartime practice, including 200,000 pounds weight of Ceylon

95 Ibid.
96 Ibid.
97 RHL, Fabian Colonial Bureau, Ceylon 1938-1965.
98 Bodleian Library, Oxford, Command 7167, 'The Colonial Empire', Appendix 2, list of monetary gifts only, not including monetary gift made direct to organizations in Britain or gifts in kind, p. 115. The Federated Malay States figure was £5,963,744; the Unfederated Malay States £1,151,411, the Straits Settlements £9,479,475. Behind Ceylon came Trinidad, with £929,095. The total for all colonies was £24,014,948. The figures are for the colonial empire, so don't include India and the dominions.

tea sent to the armed forces in the Middle East in December 1941.[99] In a War Loans broadcast on 14 February 1941 Governor Caldecott said that 'if we lose the war we shall lose everything that makes life worth living. Give til it hurts!'.[100] The government raised war loans for the British government and ran the Ceylon Government War Purposes scheme which contributed to numerous British and local war-related causes and had its own advertising campaign, including a poster bearing the words 'Britain's fighting power depends on her money power' above a picture of arms and ammunition.[101]

There were collections for the Spitfire Fund and the Gloucester and Local Sailors' Fund, along with many other war charities and fundraising drives. In August 1940 the Governor reported to London that the *Ceylon Daily News* and *Ceylon Observer* were 'affording great assistance, by propaganda and reports of progress, to the Ceylon War Purposes, St Dunstan's, and King George's (Sailors) funds'.[102] Two months later, he wrote that the Send a Plane fund, the Jaffna Plane Fund, the Ceylon Government War Purposes Fund, the Gloucester Fund (Red Cross and St John), the King George's Fund for Sailors, the Local Sailors' Fund[103], the St Dunstan's Fund, the Hospital Supply Association, and the Air Raid Distress Fund had all benefited from contributions, including 7,179,448 rupees from the Colombo Municipality.[104]

Most of these charities were linked to Empire-wide fundraising drives. In August 1940 the 'Send a Plane' fund invited subscriptions for the island's fifth fighter aircraft sponsored as a donation to the RAF, and each issue of the *Times of Ceylon* devoted a column to the 'Send a Plane' fund throughout the war, keeping a running score of the island's contribution. The column reported on latest figures, and offered ceaseless exhortations to donate. As it trilled on 16 November 1942, attempting to stir inter-regional fund-raising competition, 'Up-Country leads the way so BUCK UP Colombo'.[105] By that month the fund had already purchased 25 fighters for the RAF, at a cost of £7,500 apiece. A month later, Sir Stafford Cripps sent his thanks to the people of Ceylon for the 26th aircraft purchased with their latest donation.[106] By May 1944 the number had risen to 32 aircraft, eight of them Seafires (Spitfires adapted for use aboard aircraft carriers).[107] Another sponsorship connection between the island and Britain was 102 (Ceylon) Bomber Squadron, flying Whitleys and Halifaxs from bases in Britain. The squadron was adopted by Ceylon in February 1942, and contributions from the island paid for its aircraft.[108]

In order to aid fundraising and support for the war effort, warships in Colombo and Trincomalee put out the bunting and turned on the lights for propaganda and morale purposes, to the accompaniment of military bands. An outdoor fair called 'London Calling' was held at

99 SNLA, *Times of Ceylon*, 3/12/41.
100 RHL, MSS Ind Ocn s. 235, Caldecott's speeches.
101 SNLA, poster and advert files.
102 De Silva (ed.), *Sri Lanka*, CO 54/977/7, no. 10, Things Ceylonese, 20/8/40, p. 117.
103 The Local Sailors' Fund for the entertainment of warships in Colombo enabled the equipment 'of a fleet club as good as any in the world'. De Silva (ed.), *Sri Lanka*, p. 134.
104 Ibid., CO 54/977/7, no, 12, 'Things Ceylonese, 18/10/40, p. 133.
105 SNLA, *Times of Ceylon*, 16/11/42.
106 SNLA, *Times of Ceylon*, 19/12/42.
107 SNLA, *Times of Ceylon*, 13/5/44.
108 For a squadron history, see Chris Gross, *It's Suicide But It's Funny: History of 102 (Ceylon) Squadron RAF, 1917-1956* (Crecy, 1995).

the racecourse, and there was a floating extravaganza in Colombo harbour called 'Harbour Lights', with Royal Navy cruisers dressed overall entertaining visitors and a Royal Marines band providing musical accompaniment. On 4 November 1942 the front page of the *Times of Ceylon* was taken up by an advert for Haig's Fund (Poppy Day), and there were also figures for contributions to the Duke of Gloucester's Fund, the Air Raid Distress Fund, and Red Cross Aid to Russia. Private institutions also organized fund raising events and made contributions to diverse war charities. At an emergency meeting of the Dickoya branch of the Ceylon Planters' Society at the Darrawella Club on 15 August 1940, it was decided to allocate funds to the Gloucester Fund, the Send a Plane Fund, the St Dunstan's Fund, the King George's Fund for Sailors, and the Government of Ceylon War Purposes Fund. The Association also ran a One Day's Pay Fund, through which members could donate to a war fund or charity of their choice.[109] In December 1941 a large dummy tank running on tram wheels travelled around Colombo to advertise the Printers' Pie Tank Week Carnival.[110]

Another distinct area of contributions from Ceylon for the war effort was the funding of equipment and facilities for use in Britain itself to help with the war effort, and the *Times of Ceylon* sometimes printed photographs of war items in Britain that had been paid for by the colony's people. On 13 November 1942, for example, there was a picture of a 'Hot Meals Service' provided by the people of the Central Province. This was a Mobile Canteen that toured bomb-damaged residential areas dispensing hot food and drinks. Another Mobile Canteen was funded by the Girl Guides of Ceylon.[111] Photographs in the archives depict a series of scenes from RAF Chicksands Priory taken in December 1942 on the occasion of the handing over ceremony of the Station's Women's Auxiliary Air Force (WAAF) Recreation Room and other facilities furnished by the people of Ceylon. They show the Station Commander, Group Captian Wigglesworth, Mr Sidebotham of the Colonial Office, and Air Chief Commandant Trefusis Forbes CBE, Director of the Women's Auxiliary Air Force.[112]

Efforts were made to involve the population with the war effort. For example, in 1942 the War Efforts Picture Committee was formed on the advice of the Ministry of Information in London in order to 'encourage the depicting of any activity in connection with the Colony's war effort'. The Special Board constituted to run the programme received 240 pictures, of which 66 were accepted for an exhibition held at King George's Hall, University of Ceylon, in July 1943.[113] Getting the message across to the population was important because of the enemy threat and the need to maintain morale and offer explanations as to why the British were not initially doing well in the war. A dramatic poster showed a hapless native of Singapore 'in the grip of Japanese Co-Prosperity', a looming, demonic Japanese figure holding him aloft in his fist. The Japanese were presented stereotypically as smiling, slant eyed sneaks – be our friend, they would say in an ingratiating manner, and then take over. 'Beware Japanese broadcasts! They clear the way for Japanese bayonets', one poster warned.[114] It was also important to present

109 Author's collection, minutes, Ceylon Planters' Association Ltd, emergency meeting, Dickoya Branch, 15/8/40.
110 SNLA, *Times of Ceylon*, 26/12/41. For the poster advertising the event, see IWM, PST 15970.
111 SNLA, *Times of Ceylon*, 13/11/42.
112 SNLA, H. 29/4/12.
113 SNLA, Lot 4, 29/4, section 4, War and emergency departments.
114 SNLA, poster and advert files.

Britain's lack of success to date as a result of the sneakiness of the enemy, and to highlight the fact that it was only a matter of time before the growing strength of the Allies was brought to bear. As an advert in the press put it on 30 April 1942:

> The Power of the British Commonwealth of Nations and its Allies grows with every hour as armament factories, shipyards and aircraft factories all over the world overhaul the advantage hitherto held by the Axis through its long-planned campaign of aggression. Britain's power rests not only on guns and planes and ships but on the INDOMITABLE SPIRIT OF HER FREE PEOPLE. Give generously today to the Ceylon Government War Purposes Fund.[115]

Another poster (featured on the cover of this book) showed a Ceylonese man looking out to sea, where a fleet of warships was visible in the distance and a flight of aircraft was heading towards the island, forming a massive 'V' for 'victory' in the sky. The poster, designed by the Survey Department Ceylon, was issued by the Department of Information, Colombo, on 22 January 1943.

Posters adapted familiar British war messages: 'Careless talk costs lives' showed two Sinhalese men in sarongs conversing while the 'snake in the grass', the reptile complete with a Japanese face and Rising Sun flags on its slithery body, moved unobserved at their feet. A similar poster contained a ditty beneath the warning 'Careless talk kills' and a cartoon showing a man writing a letter at a desk, watched by cunningly disguised Japanese spies looking at a map of Ceylon:

> Edgar in his letter home
> Described our latest aerodrome
> Reuters report a loss of mail
> And Tojo smiles at Edgar's tale.

Another poster of this genre relied on a rather flaccid pun, depicting Ceylon as a drip falling from a piece of sealing wax: 'Keep a Ceyl-on your lips', the text declared; 'Careless talk costs lives'.[116]

As in Britain, the public were exhorted to collect scrap metal, artistic posters explaining that old pots, pans, and sardine tins could be turned into bombs and tanks. On 2 November 1942, for example, the front page of the *Times of Ceylon* carried a large poster explaining 'What happens to waste metal'.[117] 'Throw your scrap into the fight', was the message – or as a poster from the Information Department put it, 'Get in the scrap – knock out the Jap', depicting a stereotyped Japanese soldier looking surprised as he was hit by old saucepans, wheels, and a clothes iron. 'Here is our chance to literally "get in the SCRAP". Every sixteen ounces of Salvage are another pound behind the Allied punch – the punch that is going to knock the Nazi and the Japs right out of business'. It further announced that the Colombo Municipality would launch a 'Salvage

115 Ibid.
116 IWM, Art PST 15972.
117 SNLA, *Times of Ceylon*, 2/11/42.

Drive' and make every Monday thereafter 'Salvage Day', a scheme subsequently 'extended to all parts of the island'.[118]

Consumer products were advertised in a manner that sought to capitalize on patriotism and a sense of the 'blitz spirit'. Commercial and retail advertisements in newspapers made multiple references to the war and mimicked the bullish tone of government propaganda. Peak Frean advertised its products by drawing attention to their absence from the shelves; against a picture of battleships at sea, the company claimed that for the duration sources were being diverted to the navy.[119] U. N. Wijetunge, a retailer operating from premises at 153 Main Street, Colombo, advertised his wristwatches thus: 'Here is proof of British naval supremacy: This fresh stock of wristlets has "done a goodly round" before reaching us, yet they have arrived all right, and so licked the enemy'. Capstan cigarettes had the nautically-inspired slogan 'Capital Ships Capital Men Capstan are Capital'. Standard cars, made 'in the world famous tradition of fine British engineering', were pictured on a quayside with a mighty fleet out to sea.[120] Whiteaway, Laidlaw and Company of Kandy, Colombo, and Nuwara Eliya advertised Sam Browne belts (complete with sword frog) and officers peaked caps.[121] GEC was, patriotically, 'in war, as in peace – at the service of the Empire'.[122]

Labour and war production

Apart from the production of food, the war called for an ever-increasing work force in order to satisfy the demands of the military authorities as Ceylon became one of the Allies' main bases. Military labour was derived from several sources, the most significant of which was directly-employed civilian labour. The remainder was provided by a range of military units or specially constituted civilian war labour units, the former including, as an example, the arrival in August 1943 of 'Maharaja' personnel of the Cochin State Labour Unit No. 10, 843 labourers.[123] Another representative example of the Indian labour units sent to Ceylon were the two Madras labour units landed in May 1944, each numbering 1,400 men, destined to work at Hingurakgoda, the latter the Ceylon-recruited Essential Services Labour Corps.[124] A set of statistics compiled by the Director of Pioneers and Labour reveals the extent of labour employment on behalf of the military. In August 1944 92,449 civilians were directly employed by the military (39,566 navy, 37,476 army, 15,407 air force). A further 24,015 people drawn from military labour units were also employed. This was divided among the Essential Services Labour Corps (1,258), ISLU (12,410), MLU (2,294), the Ceylon Pioneers (3,014), Italian pioneers (1,461), the 3rd

118 SNLA, *Times of Ceylon* front page advertisement, 2/11/42.
119 SNLA, *Times of Ceylon*, 5/5/44.
120 Ibid.
121 SNLA, sessional papers, 1944.
122 SNLA, *Times of Ceylon*, 5/5/44.
123 TNA, WO 106/4487, Ceylon reinforcement, 20/3/43 to 20/8/43. They were accompanied by 30 tons of equipment, and arrived alongside 610 tons of ordnance, 8 tons of stationery, 20 tons of naval stores, six tons of medical stores, and seven hundredweight of Red Cross packages.
124 TNA, WO 203/2924, Labour situation Ceylon, Movement Control order no. 97, No. 2 Madras Labour Unit, arrival from India, 19/6/44, and Movement Control order no. 91.

Indian Pioneer Battalion (871), Indian pioneer companies (2,375), and the 5th Company (East African) Auxiliary African Pioneer Corps (332).[125]

The tasks performed by these labourers were legion. A government plywood factory produced 152,000 square feet of the material for the armed forces in the first three months of 1943, at the expense of tea chest manufacture.[126] In December 1941 the Department of Development and Agricultural Marketing contracted to supply 16,000 charpoys (beds) for the 34th Indian Division which was arriving the following month. The department then received an order for one million panjies from the army, a panjy being a defensive spike placed in the ground at an angle of 45 degrees facing towards the enemy, two feet six inches in length and an inch thick, clearly to be employed if Japanese troops landed. One hundred and forty men were employed in their manufacture in the Harbour area of Colombo, though the Japanese raid on 5 April caused the entire workforce to flee, and only half ever returned.[127] Nevertheless, 2,212,200 panjies made. The foreman was told that it was secret war work, and so when anyone enquired what they were making, they were told that they were toothpicks for the Australian soldiers. The department also made 5,000 'donkey camp beds' of folding jute Hessian for the army, 23,000 bamboo telegraph poles, 2,500 latrine screen posts, 2,620 bivouac posts, and 700 camouflage nets. Other tasks undertaken by the Department of Development and Agricultural Marketing included building stores for thousands of tons of paddy rice imported from India, including the construction of 18 sheds using 27,000 sheets of corrugated iron. Rice was also stored in requisitioned and evacuated buildings and even in a tunnel under York Street in Colombo, and by the end of March 1942 over 30 institutions in the capital had been filled with rice stockpiles. The department was also preparing 5-6,000 meals a day for labourers in Colombo harbour in 1942, a figure rising to 15-20,000 meals a day by January 1945.[128] Over 70,000 people were served from canteens elsewhere.[129]

Other important war work was performed by the Essential Services Labour Corps (ESLC) recruited to provide mobile, disciplined, emergency labour. The unit had it own uniform – blue drill shorts and shirt and a white turban with blue edging, and for officers white uniforms with a steel helmet or blue forage cap. The Corps' crest was a lion with the initials 'ESLC' set in a border of palm leaves.[130] Sir John Kotelawala was Commander-in-Chief of this several thousand-strong outfit based at camps in Maharagama and Trincomalee. Its first emergency tasks took place during the Japanese raid on Trincomalee, and included salvaging a Japanese aircraft that crashed near one of the ESLC camps. In Colombo, units of the ESLC stepped into the breach caused by the Japanese raid, filling public service posts that had been deserted. ESLC personnel replaced railway staff that had fled, selling tickets and manning trains. They coaled a ship in the harbour, loaded coal wagons, and even ran deserted shops so that people could buy goods after the shopkeepers had fled.

125 Ibid., Brigadier, Director of Pioneers and Labour, 'Labour in Ceylon, August 1944'.
126 TNA, CO 968/12/7, Commander-in-Chief Ceylon war diaries, April to June 1943, War Council minutes, 31/5/43.
127 SNLA, Lot 5/439, Dispatches 1942-1-12, Bassett, *Administrative Report*.
128 Ibid.
129 TNA, 940.531 SHU, Shuckburgh, 'Colonial Civil History', volume 2, chapter 2, 'Rationing', 'Ceylon', p. 478.
130 SNLA, sessional papers, 9 (1943), Weerasinghe, *Report of Assistant CDC in Charge of the Essential Services Labour Corps (Maharagama), March 1942-March 1943* (Colombo: Government Press, 1943).

The war record of Walker Sons and Company offers an indication of the extent of the war work that Ceylonese companies and labourers undertook. Walker's was a Colombo-based firm supplying machinery to the rubber and tea planting communities. During the war, the company's ability to take on new tasks helped make Ceylon a base suitable for large military formations. Its most important work was repairing and refitting naval and merchant vessels, including 10 battleships, 29 aircraft carriers, 50 cruisers, 46 destroyers, 32 submarines, 91 troop transport liners, ten hospital ships, 138 tankers, and 1,932 merchant vessels.[131] This involved mounting guns, de-gaussing (to defend against magnetic mines), the installation of anti-aircraft devices, and the fitting of ASDIC equipment, and included tasks as diverse as working on the giant liners *Queen Mary* and *Queen Elizabeth* whilst they were packed with Australian soldiers to repairing the gouges made all along the casing of the submarine *Tally Ho* by the propellers of a Japanese cruiser. During the war Walker Sons dry docked 798 ships, of which 65 per cent were Royal Navy. Walkers also built collapsible boats for the invasion of Malaya and coastal defence motor launches.

Away from Colombo, at its up-country stations Walker Sons took on work for the army and the RAF. Of particular note was its contribution to the island's defences through the manufacture of items designed to fool Japanese aerial reconnaissance and convince the enemy that Ceylon was better defended than it actually was. This included the construction of full scale, accurately modelled IIb Hurricanes. 'The framework was composed of local wood covered with linen and afterwards painted in Service camouflage and given RAF markings'. Silhouette dummies were also made, along with Bofors guns and 38 wooden radar and lookout towers, the largest, at 185 feet in height, requiring 32 tons of uncut timber to construct. Walker Sons also made 186 lorry bodies, 1,200 bicycle pedals, church and chapel furniture for the RAF, and even wooden clogs for military cooks. Extensive air conditioning work was carried out in military buildings, and in January 1942 the company won a contract to maintain the vehicles of the newly-arrived 34th Indian Division. Part of the company's Colombo works was requisitioned by the British 16th Brigade, and 'our main garage space was used for repairs to heavy vehicles and Bren gun carriers and the paint shop for twenty-five pounders'. With the arrival of Mountbatten's SEAC Headquarters, the demand for new buildings, and furniture and fixtures within those buildings, accelerated, and Walker Sons built 39,000 pieces of furniture for the forces including desks, chests, chairs, and glass-topped tables for use in map rooms. As the last two chapters have made abundantly clear, the war had a profound effect on Ceylon's home front.

131 D. Bennett, 'Walker Sons and Company War Record' (1945), unpublished manuscript sent to Ashley Jackson by Gill Bennet in 1999. For a detailed account drawn from the company's war narrative, see Jackson, 'Refitting the Fleet in Ceylon: The War Diary of Walker Sons and Company', *Journal of Indian Ocean Studies*, 10 (2002). The company exists to this day under the name of MTD Walkers PLC.

11

Victory in Ceylon

According to the Government of Ceylon – not an institution inclined to exaggerate on such matters – the war 'so profoundly affected the economic and social structure of the country [that it] made a return to anything like pre-war conditions most unlikely'.[1] The report might have mentioned the political structure too, for a mere two-and-a-half years after the war had ended, Ceylon was independent and the governor gone forever. The sheer scale of wartime activity in Ceylon, and the seismic political changes wrought by the conflict across Asia, could not help but leave a profound mark on the colony, even if it had managed to avoid the deep scars left in places such as Burma and Malaya.[2]

The year 1945 saw a significant build up of British forces in the Indian Ocean in anticipation of an escalating deployment of British warships, divisions, and bomber squadrons for the American-led assault on the Japanese home islands, as well as for the operations planned by SEAC to complete the reconquest of Burma and begin that of Malaya, Singapore, and the Dutch East Indies. In the war's final nine months, as a matter of routine air and maritime forces regularly raided Japanese positions in the Indian Ocean from bases in Ceylon and India, including heavy carrier strikes on targets in the Dutch East Indies. Compared to 1942, the boot was now firmly on the other foot.

Operation Dracula, the airborne and amphibious assault on Rangoon, had gone in at the end of April 1945, operations extending into the early days of May. The East Indies Fleet ships involved, as well as those participating in the decoy operation in the Andaman and Nicobar Islands, Operation Bishop, were returning home to Trincomalee when Victory in Europe day, 8 May, dawned.[3] The destroyer *Rotherham* was one of the ships returning from the Nicobar

1 NMSL, *Post-War Development Proposals* (Colombo: Government Press, 1946).

2 The work of Bayly and Harper captures the seismic activity that occurred across the arc from India to Singapore during and after the war. See Christopher Bayly and Tim Harper, *Forgotten Armies: The Fall of British Asia, 1941-1945* (London: Allen Lane, 2004) and *Forgotten Wars: The End of Britain's Asian Empire* (London: Allen Lane, 2007).

3 I have refrained in this book from repeating sections found in its partner volume, *Of Islands, Ports, and Sea Lanes*. Though inevitably some of the same ground is covered, it is not repetitive and, for example, in the chapter in this volume regarding the Japanese raids, the focus is on the attacks on the island, whereas in the other book, it is on the naval engagements. In this section, however, things are repeated, as it seemed silly not to cover the ground relating to VE and VJ celebrations that took place on the island.

Islands 'when there was received a signal from the King: "To all ships and establishments: Splice the mainbrace"'. All ships did the same.

VE Day found Cyril Battell at HMS *Bambara*, the Royal Naval Air Station at China Bay:

> The navy have spliced the main brace [sic] and most people seemed to be quite drunk. Celebrations go on until midnight when we are turned out of our hut and paraded at the navy Reg office and threatened with a mutiny charge. Celebrations continue next day with a combined church parade held in the bombed out hangars down on the airfield. Lunch is also special with turkey on the menu and the whole camp again spliced the main brace.[4]

'The men of the East Indies Fleet listened to Winston Churchill broadcasting to the nation and then later, during the Middle Watch by Ceylon time on the 9th, to HM the King'. As Midshipman John Robathan wrote, still tired from days at sea aboard *Venus*, 'all we could do was think of home and wish we were there to join in the celebrations and hear the church bells'.[5]

> At Trincomalee there were few facilities for celebrations but the men of the destroyer flotillas, spurred on by an extra tot to splice the mainbrace and an extra pint of Australian beer to mark VE Day, did their best. When the radio in the Fleet Canteen announced that celebratory bonfires were being lit at home, some men of the 26th Destroyer Flotilla shouted, 'There's a bonfire here!' and burned down part of the canteen and nearby *basha* huts.
>
> Meanwhile the 11th Flotilla had an unarmed combat with ratings from *Richelieu*. In *Cumberland* the celebrations included the throwing overboard of a mounted fragment of a French shell which had inflicted damage on the ship at Dakar in 1940. But for many of the fleet, it was a quiet evening on board, with a film on the fo'c'sle, reminiscences on the messdecks and in the wardroom. It was still a long war in the east, but just for this evening, there seemed to be time for a smoke and reflection.[6]

'VE Day celebrations passed off quietly in Kandy', wrote Mountbatten. Not that he was there to witness them, as he was in bed with dysentery, Lieutenant General 'Boy' Browning, his Chief of Staff, deputizing in his stead, the parade also marking the recapture of Rangoon. 'There were considerable festivities that night, during which Gordon Lennox played the piano and Boy performed his Cossack dance'.[7] Browning also deputized at a big inter-Allied parade in Colombo.[8]

4 BBC World War Two People's War oral history archive, Cyril Battell, 'VE Day Ceylon', A4034314. *Bambara* was commissioned on New Year's Day 1944 and was new collective appellation for Royal Naval Air Station China Bay, the navy's Aircraft Maintenance Yard at Clappenburg Bay, and the Naval Accommodation Camp Nachchikunda. From 'Naval Air Stations', Fleet Air Arm Officers Association, at https://www.fleetairarmoa.org/fleet-air-arm-naval-air-stations

5 Winton, *Sink the Haguro!*, p. 55.

6 Ibid., p. 55-6.

7 Mead, *General 'Boy'*, location 4164.

8 Ziegler (ed.), *Personal Diary*, p. 206. Browning had arrived in theatre at the end of 1944, just in time to witness the unique investiture in which Field Marshal Wavell, Viceroy of India, knighted generals Slim and his three corps commanders, Philip Christison, Geoffrey Scoones, and Monty Stopford on

Alan Brundrett, the young sailor working in the Naval Secretariat, recalled the 'great excitement' that accompanied the event. 'Flags and coloured lights were everywhere on buildings. Crowds of people were talking in the street. There was plenty of celebrating going on in the bar of our hotel'. Cinemas were open to men and women in the armed forces for free. The Governor's House was

> bathed in floodlighting of pale rose and turquoise. Over the arch at the entrance were the letters 'GR' [George Regina] and the crown, formed by light bulbs ... Many of the public buildings and the Galle Face Hotel displayed an illuminated 'V' sign. Crowds gathered here to watch a fireworks display. Bonfires were lit. Dancing, eating and drinking were going on everywhere. Even the snake-charmers were out in force. An altogether memorable sight; one we shall have etched in our minds for a long time.[9]

On 13 May Brundrett attended the Victory Parade on Galle Face Green. Service personnel marched past a saluting base where the governor, Sir Henry Monck-Mason Moore, and the Commander-in-Chief Ceylon, Admiral Layton, took the salute, while 'ships of the Royal Navy steamed by close in shore, and planes flew over in formation'.[10] But VE Day meant little, from a working point of view, for the personnel of the East Indies Fleet and the airmen, soldiers, and sailors engaged in the ongoing war against Japan. They still had a job to do, and continued to face the prospect of potentially fatal encounters with the enemy. Indeed, even at this significant moment, celebrations had been cut short when it was learned that the heavy cruiser *Haguro* was loose in the Indian Ocean, escorting a convoy. 'At 10pm that evening a general alarm was flashed around Trincomalee, ordering almost every ship there to raise steam and prepare to leave harbour at 6am the next morning'.[11] A task force of 16 ships left Ceylon on 8 May to intercept the convoy – indicative of the sledgehammer to crack a walnut situation now pertaining in the region, where the Allies were now remarkably strong, the Japanese correspondingly weak. The British force comprised the battleships *Queen Elizabeth* and *Richelieu*, the cruisers *Cumberland*, *Royalist* and *Tromp*, the escort carriers *Emperor*, *Hunter*, *Khedive* and *Shah*, and eight destroyers. In an action resembling a fox hunt, the riders going pell-mell after their quarry, soon the ships remaining in Trincomalee, including the cruiser *Nigeria* and three destroyers, joined the chase.

Ceylon also continued to operate as a base for special forces preparing the ground in occupied territories for the moment when Allied invasions would free them from years of Japanese rule. One of the more famous Force 136 operatives, Freddie Spencer Chapman, was extracted from Malaya to Ceylon in May 1945. Collected by submarine, he spent six days on board sleeping on a camp bed under the wardroom table, 'the crew tripping over his feet as they repeatedly rushed to crash dive when enemy aircraft were picked up on on radar'.[12] *Haguro* had just been sunk off Penang by a British destroyer flotilla, and these aircraft were out looking

the field of battle. See *General Boy: The Life of Lieutenant General Sir Frederick Browning* (Barnsley: Pen and Sword, 2010), Chapter 23 'Kandy (December 1944-May 1945')'.

9 Brundrett, *Two Years in Ceylon*, pp. 204-205.
10 Ibid., pp. 210-211.
11 Winton, *Sink the Haguro!*, p. 55-6.
12 Brian Moynihan, *Jungle Soldier: The True Story of Freddie Spencer Chapman* (London: Quercus, 2009), p. 315.

for them.[13] Upon entering Trincomalee harbour on 19 May, the submarine moored next to its depot ship, Innes Tremlett, head of the Malaya Section of Force 136, waiting on the dockside to greet Chapman. He was taken to a Force 136 camp, where he bathed, shaved, sent his ragged clothes to be burnt, and drank 'large quantities of pink gin', before being flown to Colombo.[14] Believed dead, he now had the unnerving experience of discovering that his belongings had been auctioned off in order to pay his debts. Furthermore, he learned that a manuscript he had written had been published 'posthumously' as a book, entitled *Memoirs of a Mountaineer*.[15] There were benefits, however, as Chapman discovered that he had three and a half years back pay owing, as well as royalties on the sale of the book.[16]

Victory Japan

SEAC's long-anticipated amphibious invasions of Malaya and Singapore were never fully executed, the enemy's formal capitulation on 15 August rendering the plans redundant. In the aftermath, tens of thousands of Allied troops were put ashore, accompanied by East Indies Fleet ships sailing from Rangoon and Trincomalee. On 14 August, wrote Alan Brundrett, 'news came through that Japan accepted unconditional surrender … Everyone here went wild. Although we had expected it any time, its impact nevertheless hits us'.[17] Corporal L. V. Wills celebrated Victory Japan at 145 Repair and Salvage Unit Ratmalana, drinking beer with his pet monkey Jenny.[18]

Ken Waterson, meanwhile, was on the middle watch aboard *Relentless* in Trincomalee harbour when the news was received:

> That night Trincomalee had its celebrations. There were rocket (distress flares) displays, jumping jacks and concerts. The weather was cooler, the oppressive heat had subsided. VJ evening started just before sunset. Ships were dressed, every colour of flag was flown. There were lots of nationalities. The alphabet went down the USA (America) and USSR (Russia), the latter flew the hammer and sickle. All the flags were hauled down at sunset but were then immediately re-hoisted. The dark night showed up illuminated Vs made up of coloured light bulbs. Some of these were in many colours.

13 Ibid.

14 Ibid.

15 Freddie Spencer Chapman, *Memoirs of a Mountaineer: Helvellyn to Himalaya and Lhasa, the Holy City* (London: Reprint Society, 1945).

16 Moynihan, *Jungle Soldier*, p. 316. Given the minor celebrity status the handsome covert warrior was likely to attract, fellow officers formed a 'Freddy Protection Society in Colombo for women seeking a trophy affair', judging that, following his ordeals, he was vulnerable. Chapman wrote a report on conditions in Malaya, went home to Britain for three weeks leave, and then returned to Colombo two weeks before the atomic bombs were dropped. He returned to Malaya from Ceylon, the first British officer into Raub, dropped by parachute into Kuala Lipis, capital of Pehan. On 30 September he took the Japanese surrender in Kuantan.

17 Brundrett, *Two Years in Ceylon*, p. 255.

18 *RAF News*, 26/9/08.

When the last shadows had gone, the ship next to us let loose with her siren. It was a horrible noise, worse than a air-raid siren. After an interval of about 15 minutes every ship in the harbour was blowing off a different note. The result was an awful din. In time various Vs could be distinguished on different sirens. Some put in a J after the V making VJ in Morse code; Rockets (distress flares) and Vary lights (bright light flares) were being fired freely by now all over the harbour. Green, red, yellow and white ones. These offset the regular starboard and port navigation lights, green and red. Green and red lights shooting up into the sky and then down into the sea. Rustic VJs on hooters and much cheering completed an unreal atmosphere. Blackout was abandoned.

By 09:00pm the fun increased in tempo. Many were drunk now, where they got spirits and beer from is a mystery. We had none. Early an attempt had been made to mount a concert but the hooters drowned out any attempt to sing. Shooting pretty lights into the air became tame after a while. Ships started firing rockets at each other. Then they all started firing at the aircraft lined up on the upper deck of the aircraft carrier. An urgent signal was sent round the harbour to stop firing rockets. Various petty officers went round their ships to put a stop to the practice. It says something for discipline that the rocket shooting stopped. How it started I know not as I thought all rockets were kept under lock and key.

Instead jumping jacks were fired from rocket launchers. These were fearsome projectiles. They came in various colours and shot from left to right, from front to rear. Shooting down between deck awnings they scattered all and sundry. They were powerful, much stronger than bonfire night jumping jacks. They possibly were Chinese ones but who got them and from where is not known. The awnings were burnt in various place and a fire arose on one of the gun covers.

This led to hoses being turned on to put out all the small fires that had started. Generously ships put out each other's fires by hose. After that the hoses were turned on the other ship's crews. Everybody was wet through. Chaps coming back on board from shore leave were caught in this deluge.

After that things died down; various concert parties were got up impromptu. We were tied up alongside the Woolwich, the destroyer parent ship. We got up a singing party and wheeled our piano out onto the quarter deck so that others could see and hear us. The quarter deck was beautifully decorated with bunting. Out came our players in their costumes and started to sing. The stokers on the Woolwich did not seem to appreciate our singing, they turned a hose pipe on us. The drums were soaked as was the piano, the bunting all bedraggled. They did have the foresight to close the bulkhead that gave us access to their ship. Had we made contact, World War III would have broken out between us. By now a lot of people were drunk, where they got their booze from is not known we had none.

After all this excitement things quietened down, just Vary lights now and then. A 'feel good factor' abounded. The only alcohol we had was from the splicing of the main brace (an extra tot of rum).[19]

19 BBC World War Two People's War oral history archive, Ken Waterson, 'HMS *Relentless*: The End of the Japanese War, 1945', A2237591.

On 16 August there was a Victory March, wrote Brundrett, from 'village hall to Camp restaurant in which we all have to take part'. On 25 August he was back in Colombo for the big Victory Parade on Galle Face Green, the stretch of open space on the sea front flanked by the Galle Face Hotel and important government buildings. Mountbatten took the salute, and there were 'formations of Flying Fortresses, Sunderlands, Hellcats, and Barracudas. Meanwhile ships of the East Indies Fleet steamed up and down the coast'.[20] Mountbatten wrote proudly in his diary that 'the great Victory Parade was held in Colombo, at which some 3,500 representatives of all the services marched past in 35 minutes. At this rate, the 1,380,000 men in SEAC would take nearly 9 days and 9 nights to march past!'.[21] Considering the size of his command, he continued:

> Incidentally, few people realize the immense scale of the enlarged South East Asia Command, which includes a million and a half square miles of territory, has a population of 128 millions, nearly half a million Japs and over 200,000 prisoners of war and internees to be repatriated. From the northwest corner of SEAC, which starts a few hundred miles west of Karachi, down to the easternmost limits, halfway through New Guinea, is a distance of 6,050 statute miles. This is 150 miles more than the distance from the northwest corner of SEAC to St Johns, Newfoundland![22]

First and foremost, after the formalities of taking the surrender of scattered Japanese garrisons and ensuring order, the liberation of prisoners of war became SEAC's number one priority. As soon as the surrender came in to effect, aircraft from Burma, Ceylon, the Cocos-Keeling Islands, and India commenced Operation Mastiff, dropping food, medicine and radios to all prisoner-of-war camps in Japanese-held South-east Asia and the Dutch East Indies. Later still, many of the inmates of the prisons were air evacuated to Ceylon and to freedom. Bernard Longstaff was an engineer working on Douglas Skymasters in Ceylon, his job now to to assist prisoners of war as they were unloaded from transport aircraft.[23]

Tens of thousands of Allied prisoners of war returned home to Europe via Ceylon after their liberation in South-east Asia, the Dutch East Indies, and the Far East.

> As the first ship carrying prisoners of war arrived in Colombo, every ship saluted with its horn. Barges, lighters, and RAF craft ferried them ashore. Most looked like men from Belsen, wearing brand new uniforms. Many attractive young ladies had been recruited as escorts. Marquees had been erected and Colombo did its very best to welcome and entertain them.[24]

20 Brundrett, *Two Years in Ceylon*, pp. 262-263.
21 Ziegler (ed.), *Personal Diary*, p. 238.
22 Ibid.
23 BBC World War Two People's War oral history archive, Bernard Longstaff, 'Wartime Engineer', A4684179. IWM, JFU 315, 'Released Prisoners of War Arrive in Colombo', shot on 17/9/45, shows men, many suffering from beri beri and malnutrition, disembarking from a ship in Colombo and being hosted ashore.
24 BBC World War Two People's War oral history archive, anonymous, 'Colombo Harbour', A5330260.

Squadron Leader Sachs was an RAF engineer based in Ceylon working on Skymasters, DC10 transport aircraft. When the war ended his squadron's job was to receive aircraft loaded with released prisoners of war. 209 Squadron's Sunderland flying-boats had been modified to take stretchers, and they were the first into Singapore to bring prisoners back from Changi gaol. Most of the former internees arrived in Colombo by ship.

Lady Edwina Mountbatten had made arrangements for the men to be cared for by the tea-planters in up-country Ceylon to recuperate before heading home for Britain. Peggy Wightman described assisting POWs returning from camps in Thailand in September 1945, issuing gifts such as packets of tea to the men:

> I am exhausted now from a very worthwhile day. I have been with the prisoners; we had to be at the Officer's Club to meet them when they came ashore. I can't begin to tell you how dreadful it is. When they first come in they are all so dazed and nervous … The Club, run by the NAAFI, had put up a wonderful show; it is closed except to the repatriated prisoners and their friends, everything is free, and they are showered with chocolates and cigarettes and provided with a lively lunch. Actually another officer and I brought two naval commanders up to our Mess for lunch, they were so grateful it was pathetic, they looked like very old men though they can't have been more than in their early forties … They were terribly hopeful and talked as though everything would be as they left it at home. They said their last letters were two years old, it worried us that they seemed to think that their wives and girlfriends would be just where they had been in October 1943.[25]

Lady Mountbatten arrived at the King's Pavilion in Kandy. Her husband wanted her to rest up after her punishing schedule of visits to camps and hospitals. She had a quick ride 'a glorious mountain road on delightful ponies'. But then it was back to work; 'I then did a quick change and started off on a Hospital round'.[26] She took a jeep tour of the country north of Kandy and had a brief break at Dimbula, a tea planter's bungalow in the hills, interspersed with hospital visits in Colombo, Jaffna, and Trincomalee. As well as hospitals, she visited hospital ships, convalescent depots, cafeterias and clubs, dental surgeries, YMCAs and the Hospital Supplies Association. She also addressed the Wrens, Welfare and Canteen workers, and VADs, inspected parades of St John and Red Cross representatives and tasted the beer at the Royal Stag in the Services Holiday Camp run by the NAAFI.[27]

On the other side of the fence, Ceylon also became a holding place for Japanese captives, some of whom were accommodated in a prisoner-of-war camp in Trincomalee. Many British servicemen who had been engaged in the war against Japan also returned home via Ceylon. John Mills, who had served aboard the East Indies Station destroyer *Volage* for 18 months, had to stay a while in Ceylon to recuperate following an operation. Finally he left Ceylon on board the carrier *Formidable*, converted to a troopship by putting rows of beds in the hangars. She carried 2,000 passengers home. Once at sea, Mills and 20 others were detailed to push a number

25 Quoted in Aldrich, *The Faraway War*, p. 815.
26 Janet Morgan, *Edwina Mountbatten: A Life of Her Own* (London: Fontana, 1992), p. 349.
27 Ibid., p. 350.

of brand new Hellcat and Corsair aircraft overboard, so that under the terms of Lend-Lease the Royal Navy would not have to pay for them.[28]

The military bases and installations scattered around Ceylon were downsized or closed down for good. A senior RAF officer broadcast a valedictory speech on the radio as 222 Group, the umbrella organization for all RAF units in Ceylon, was wound down:

> It's never an easy thing to say good-bye and in saying good-bye to their Colombo associations many of 222's staff know that they are leaving behind friends of many months standing. In saying good-bye to 222 Group the people of Ceylon, in their turn, will recall how the last four years saw the building up of an island aircraft-carrier from the jungles and forest lands of their country.
>
> 222 Group came to Ceylon soon after the fall of Singapore. Before that there was one permanent RAF station on the island – at China Bay. There was a civil airport at Ratmalana which soon became a station for fighters. The racecourse at Colombo itself was taken over as fighters installed there. Experts went out to survey the jungle and select sites for new airfields. They are there today – Sigiriya, Minneriya, Vavuniya. At Koggala, a lake and the swampy ground around had just been turned into a RAF base which soon became the largest flying-boat base in the east.[29]

Slowly, things returned to normal in Ceylon, though adjustment was not easy. Military spending, for example, had led to a boom in the economy, but an artificial one as spending had been on non-productive goods and services as the island was 'converted into an advance base for military operations'. Towards the end of the war military expenditure was running at well over 400 million rupees a year. As S. A. Wickremasinghe of the Ceylon National Congress Executive Committee told British Labour MPs, because of the emergency situation 'all unemployed were absorbed by emergency essential services and auxiliary services'. The logical fallout from this was that when the war ended, 'half a million people were likely to be unemployed by the end of the year'.[30]

Politically, Ceylon managed to avoid the turmoil that afflicted the post-war period in the surrounding region, largely because of the harmonious relations that had prevailed between local British authorities and indigenous political elites, and the advances towards dominion status and independence that had been the result. As De Silva writes:

> The political leadership of the mainstream nationalist movement who shared power with the British colonial administration actively supported the war effort, unlike their Indian and Burmese counterparts. This association in the war effort, indeed active participation in

28 BBC World War Two People's War oral history archive, John Mills, 'Homeward Bound Somewhere', A8888115.

29 TNA, AIR 23/4802, An Officer of the RAF, 'A Resume of the Activities of 222 Group', prepared for a radio broadcast, 19/10/45.

30 RHL, Fabian Colonial Bureau papers.

> it, did not lead to any notable political agitation and controversy and the war left few scars in the collective memory of the people of Ceylon.[31]

Nevertheless, though the British were prepared to accede to demands for political advancement towards independence, they were keen to retain Ceylon as a member of the British Commonwealth, more alive than ever to the island's strategic significance, especially in a world where they could no longer rely on India as a base. The Second World War cemented Ceylon's place in the British Empire's system of imperial defence, and symbolizing Britain's continued strategic needs and the amity that was to characterize the transition from colony to nation, it was to remain an important Royal Navy base for another decade. Even before the war ended, strategic planners were thinking about the next war, which contained some apparently new, but in reality, surprisingly old, concerns. The battle lines of the Cold War were already being drawn, and as in all previous world wars British thinking focused on the defence of India and the utility of seapower. A Foreign Office report of February 1945 stated that 'it is inevitable that a study on the defence of India should picture the Soviet Union as the enemy', and that in countering the threat, Ceylon was essential as a fleet base. A fleet based on Ceylon 'would be capable of controlling the approaches to the east coast of India', and air and naval forces in the Andaman Islands 'could control the sea routes leading north from Penang'. It would be 'essential to retain Ceylon as the main naval operational base in the area'.[32]

The Allies had cause to be grateful for the island of Ceylon, and its people. 'When Singapore and other British strongholds in the East fell to Japan, Ceylon was described as "the last bastion of Empire"'.[33] As this book has attempted to demonstrate, though the war in Ceylon and its environs was not, mercifully, to be dramatically coloured by the combat and occupation that afflicted other parts of the world, the island had played a very notable part in the war, and been deeply affected by it.

31 De Silva (ed.), *Sri Lanka*, pp. xlvi-xlvii. Serving in Ceylon right at the end of the war and the immediate post-war period, John Lindop noted an edginess among British forces and their awareness of the demands of the nationalists to get the British out of the island. See Lindop, *Reminiscences of a Radar Plotter*.

32 TNA, FO 371/50774, Security of India and the Indian Ocean, including Post-Hostility Planning, 44, 28, 0, Map A, Atlantic and Indian Ocean communications. Note on file, 22/2/45. On the Royal Navy's use of Ceylon in the post-war years, see Jackson, 'The Royal Navy and the Indian Ocean Region since 1945', *Royal United Services Institute Journal*, 151, 6 (2006).

33 Stanley de Zoysa, 'Ceylon Survey', *New Vision*, n. D. C. 1944.

Bibliography

Primary sources

Papers have been consulted in London at The National Archives, the Imperial War Museum, the National Army Museum, the Naval Historical Branch (since moved to Portsmouth), and the British Library. Don Kimble has done a great service by making available online the text of Admiralty war diaries and reports of proceedings. The Colonial Film Database (http://www.colonialfilm.org.uk/) is an excellent finding guide for wartime films, many of them belonging to the Imperial War Museum, and contains superlative descriptions of them. In Cambridge, I have used the Churchill Archives Centre at Churchill College, and in Oxford, Rhodes House Library and the Bodleian's official papers. I have also made extensive use of the National Archives of Sri Lanka, as well as the Library of the National Museum of Sri Lanka, and some papers at St Andrew's Hotel Nuwara Eliya. The Singapore National Archives were briefly consulted, but regrettably not used. In terms of private papers, Frederick Tippet's material relating to censorship in Ceylon belong to the Butler Papers, a private collection, and Gill and Ian Bennett allowed me to see the 'Walker Sons and Company War Record' written by David Bennett. K. M. De Silva's *Sri Lanka* volume of the British Documents on the End of Empire project reproduces many key documents from the British national archives.

In terms of oral material the BBC World War Two People's War oral history archive has been a boon, as have the letters and typed and handwritten memoirs sent to me in the late 1990s by the people named in the acknowledgements. These were supplemented by interviews with Joan Gottelier in Martock, Somerset in 1999, and William Dempsey in Woodstock, Oxfordshire, in 2007.

Printed and secondary sources

Oscar Abeyratna, *The History of the Ceylon Light Infantry* (Colombo: Ceylon Daily News, 1945).
Augustus Agar, *Footprints in the Sea* (London: Evans, 1961).
Richard Aldrich, *Intelligence and the War Against Japan: Britain, America, and the Politics of Secret Service* (Cambridge: Cambridge University Press, 2000).
——, *The Faraway War: Personal Diaries of the Second World War in Asia and the Pacific* (London: Corgi, 2010).
Robert Aldrich, *Colonialism and Homosexuality* (London: Routledge, 2002).

H. M. Queen Alexandria of Yugoslavia, *Prince Philip: A Family Portrait* (London: Hodder and Stoughton, 1960).

Charles Allen, *Plain Tales from the Raj: Images of British India in the Twentieth Century* (London: Futura, 1976).

'Allied Chinese Ships', https://en.wikipedia.org/wiki/Allied_Chinese_Ships.

D. T. Aponso-Sariffodeen, 'How DS [Don Senanayake] Saved Ceylon from a Food Crisis', *Sunday Times* (Sri Lanka), 24/3/02.

Max Arthur, *Forgotten Voices of the Second World War: An New History of World War Two in the Words of the Men and Women Who Were There* (London: Ebury Press, 2004).

S. R. Ashton, 'Ceylon', in Judith Brown and William Roger Louis (eds), *The Oxford History of the British Empire,* volume 4, *The Twentieth Century* (Oxford: Oxford University Press, 1999)

Arthur Banks, *Wings of the Dawning: The Battle for the Indian Ocean, 1939-1945* (Malvern Wells: Images Publishing, 1996).

Desmond Ball, *Signals Intelligence (SIGINT) in South Asia: India, Pakistan, Sri Lanka (Ceylon)* (Canberra: Strategic and Defence Studies Centre, 1996).

John Barrass, '30 Squadron and the Battle of Ceylon' (HQ Strike Command: Command Media Services, n. d.).

——, '30 Squadron and the Air Battle Over Colombo 5 April 1942', at 30 Squadron Association website, http://www.30squadronassociation.com/history/ceylon.html.

——, 'The Battle of Ceylon – 1942 – Part 2', '30 Squadron and the Air Battle Over Colombo – 5 April 1942', https://www.raf.mod.uk/history/ceylon2.html.

——, 'The Battle of Ceylon – 1942 – Part 3', 'Eyewitness Recollections of 5 April 1942 at Ratmalana by D. A. McDonald, then a Pilot Officer on 30 Squadron', at https://www.raf.mod/history/ceylon3.html

G. M. Bayliss, *Union Jack, a Scrapbook: British Forces Newspapers* (London: HMSO/Imperial War Museum, 1989).

Christopher Bayly and Tim Harper, *Forgotten Armies: The Fall of British Asia, 1941-1945* (London: Allen Lane, 2004).

——, *Forgotten Wars: The End of Britain's Asian Empire* (London: Allen Lane, 2007).

N. M. P. Billimoria, *Seventy-Five Years at Mount: A History of St Thomas' College Mount Lavinia, 1918-1993* (Colombo: The College, 1993).

Leonard Birchall, 'The Japanese Ceylon Attack and Afterwards', in *The Empire Club of Canada Speeches, 1945-1946* (Toronto: The Empire Club Foundation, 1946).

Brian Bond (ed.), *Chief of Staff: The Diaries of Lieutenant-General Sir Henry Pownall,* volume 2, *1940-1944* (London: Leo Cooper, 1974).

Andrew Boyd, *The Royal Navy in Eastern Waters: Linchpin of Victory, 1935-1942* (Barnsley: Seaforth, 2017).

Britain's Midway: The Royal Navy versus the Imperial Japanese Navy: The 'Easter Sunday' Raid', at http://www.armouredcarriers.com/battle-for-ceylon-hms-indomitable-formidable/.

Katrin Bromber, 'Do Not Destroy Our Honour: Wartime Propaganda Directed at East African Soldiers in Ceylon (1943-44)', in Ashwini Tambe and Harald Fischer-Tiné (eds), *The Limits of British Control in South Asia: Spaces of Disorder in the Indian Ocean Region* (London: Routledge, 2008).

J. H. Brown, 'Admiralty House and the Royal Navy at Trincomalee, 1810-1957', unpublished paper, Naval Historical Branch (1980).

Alan Brundrett, *Two Years in Ceylon: The diaries of a Naval Secretariat Member, 1944-1946* (Lewes, Sussex: Book Guild, 1996).
Hugh Campbell, *Notable Service to the Empire: Australian Corvettes and the British Pacific Fleet, 1944-1945* (Garden City, New South Wales: Naval Historical Society, 2000).
'Ceylon and its People' (1944).
Winston Churchill, *The Second World War, volume 2, Their Finest Hour* (London: Cassell, 1949).
——, *The Second World War, volume 4, The Hinge of Fate* (London: Cassell, 1951).
Tom Clancy, *'The Most Dangerous Moment of the War': Japan's Attack on the Indian Ocean, 1942* (Oxford: Casemate, 2015).
H. A. Colgate, 'Trincomalee and the East Indies Squadron 1746-1844', M. A. Thesis (University of London, 1959).
——, 'The Royal Navy and Trincomalee', *The Ceylon Journal of Historical and Social Studies, 7, 1* (1964).
Artemis Cooper, *Cairo in the War, 1939-1945* (London: Penguin, 1995).
Noël Coward, *Future Indefinite* (London: Methuen, 2004)
Brian Crabb, *Passage to Destiny: The Sinking of the Troopship* Khedive Ismail *in the Sea War Against Japan* (Stamford, Lincolnshire: Paul Watkins, 1997).
Noel Crusz, *The Cocos Islands Mutiny* (Freemantle: Freemantle Arts Centre Press, 2000).
Alex Danchev and Dan Todman (eds), *War Diaries, 1939-1945: Field Marshal Lord Alanbrooke* (London: Weidenfeld and Nicolson, 2001).
Russell Davies (ed.), *The Kenneth Williams Diaries* (London: HarperCollins, 1994).
——, (ed.), *The Kenneth Williams Letters* (London: HarperCollins, 1995).
Barry Day (ed.), *The Letters of Noël Coward* (London: Methuen, 2007).
K. M. De Silva (ed.), *Sri Lanka*, part 1, *The Second World War and the Soulbury Commission 1939-1945, British Documents on the End of Empire* (London: The Stationery Office, 1997).
P. H. D. H. de Silva, *Colombo Museum One Hundred Years 1877-1977 Souvenir* (Colombo: National Museum, 1977).
Sergei DeSilva-Ranasinghe, 'A Historical Account of the Ceylon Defence Force (1881-1949)', Sabretache, xlix, 2 (2008).
——, 'Forgotten Campaigns, Forgotten Veterans', *Sunday Times* (Sri Lanka), 5/11/06.
Somasiri Devendra, 'Ceylon Navy's Prize "Catch"', *The Sunday Times* (Sri Lanka), 29/5/16.
G. de Soyza, *Administrative Report on the Workings of Cooperative Societies from May 1942 to April 1945* (Colombo: Government Press, 1946).
David and Percy De Zilwa, *The Spirit of St Andrew's* (Nuwara Eliya: St Andrew's Hotel, 2006).
Ken Dimbleby, *Turns of Fate: The Drama of HMS Cornwall* (London: William Kimber, 1984).
Charles Eade (ed.), *Secret Session Speeches by the Right Honourable Winston S. Churchill* (London: Cassell, 1946).
Empire Division, Ministry of Information, 'Ceylon for Victory' (1943).
'Evacuation and Rescue Ships 1942', at https://www.cofepow.org.uk/armed-forces-stories-list/evacuation-rescue-ships-1942.
'Fan Tan', 'Soldiering in Ceylon', *Journal of the United Services Institute of India, LXXIII* (1943).
Rodney Ferdinands, *Proud and Prejudiced: The Story of the Burghers of Ceylon* (Melbourne: Rodney Ferdinands, 1995).
Ferguson's Ceylon Directory 1945 (Colombo: Ceylon Observer Press, 1945).
Walter Gibson, *The Boat* (London: W. H. Allen, 1952).

Gerald Graham, *Great Britain in the Indian Ocean: A Study in Maritime Enterprise, 1810-1857* (Oxford: Clarendon Press, 1967).

C. Green and A. D. Maclean (eds*), A Skilled Hand: A Collection of Stories and Writings by G. F. Green, with Memoirs and Criticism* (London: Macmillan, 1980).

Chris Gross, *It's Suicide But It's Funny: History of 102 (Ceylon) Squadron RAF, 1917-1956* (London: Crecy, 1995).

Sanji Gunasekara, 'Target Ceylon, 1942', *Travel Sri Lanka* (September 2008).

Uthpala Gunethilake, 'Old Soldiers Never Die', *Sunday Times* (Sri Lanka), 5/11/00.

Peter Haining, *The Banzai Hunters: The Forgotten Armada of Little Ships that Defeated the Japanese, 1944-1945* (London: Robson Books, 2006).

Duff Hart-Davis, *Man of War: Officer, Adventurer, Agent* (London: Arrow, 2003).

Tim Heald, *The Duke: A Portrait of Prince Philip* (London: Hodder and Stoughton, 1991).

F. H. Hinsley and Alan Stripp, *Codebreakers: The Inside Story of Bletchley Park* (Oxford: Oxford University Press, 2001).

James Holland, *Fortress Malta: An Island Under Siege, 1940-1943* (London: Orion, 2003).

Christopher Hudson, *Colombo Heat* (London: Macmillan, 1986).

Ronald Hyam, *Empire and Sexuality: The British Experience* (Manchester: Manchester University Press, 1990).

William Iredale, *The Kamikaze Hunters: Fighting for the Pacific, 1945* (London: Pan, 2015).

Ashley Jackson, *Botswana 1939-1945: An African Country at War* (Oxford: Clarendon Press, 1999).

——, *War and Empire in Mauritius and the Indian Ocean* (Basingstoke: Palgrave Macmillan, 2001).

——, 'Refitting the Fleet in Ceylon: The War Record of Walker Sons and Company', *Journal of Indian Ocean Studies*, 10 (2002).

——, *The British Empire and the Second World War* (London: Continuum, 2006).

——, 'The Colonial Empire and Imperial Defence', in Greg Kennedy (ed.), *Old World Order: Imperial Defence, 1856-1956* (London: Routledge, 2007).

——, '"Defend Lanka Your Home": War on the Home Front in Ceylon, 1939-1945', *War in History, 16, 2* (2009).

——, *Distant Drums: The Role of Colonies in British Colonial Warfare* (Brighton: Sussex Academic Press, 2010).

——, 'Ceylon's Home Front during the Second World War', in Mark Crowley and Sandra Trudgen Dawson (eds), *Home Fronts: Britain and the Empire at War, 1939-1945* (Martlesham, Suffolk: Boydell and Brewer, 2017).

——, 'Military Migrants: British Service Personnel in Ceylon during the Second World War', *Britain and the World, 6, 1* (2013).

——, *Of Islands, Ports, and Sea Lanes: Africa and the Indian Ocean in the Second World War* (Solihull: Helion, 2018).

——, *Persian Gulf Command: A History of the Second World War in Iran and Iraq* (London: Yale University Press, 2018).

David Jacobs, *Jacobs' Ladder* (London: Peter Davies, 1963).

H. G. P. Jayasekera, 'Japanese Raided Colombo This Day in 1942', *Daily News*, 5/4/02.

——, *How Japan Bombed Tiny Ceylon* (Pannipitiya, Sri Lanka: Stamford Lake, 2013).

W. T. Jayasinghe, *Kachchativu and the Maritime Boundary of Sri Lanka* (Pannipitiya, Sri Lanka: Stamford Lake, 2003).
Denis Judd, *Prince Philip: A Biography* (London: Sphere Books, 1991).
Nihal Karunaratna, *Kandy Past and Present, 1474-1998* (Colombo: Government Printing, Central Cultural Fund, 1999).
'Kelavan', *Two Leaves and a Bud: Tales of a Ceylon Tea Planter* (Colchester: Bloozoo Publishing, 2000).
Terrence Kelly, *Battle for Palembang* (London: Robert Hale, 1985).
——, *Hurricanes in Sumatra* (London: Arrow Books, 1991).
——, *Hurricanes Over the Jungle* (Barnsley: Pen and Sword, 2004).
William King, *Dive and Attack: A Submariner's Story* (London: William Kimber, 1983).
Rudyard Kipling, *Plain Tales from the Hills* (Calcutta: Thacker, Spink, and Company, 1888).
Arthur Lane, 'Evacuation and Rescue Ships 1942', at https://www.cofepow.org.uk/armed-forces-stories-list/evacuation-rescue-ships-1942.
Brian Lavery, Churchill's *Navy: The Ships, Men, and Organization, 1939-1945* (London: Conway, 2006).
Geoffrey Layton, 'Ceylon – A Vital Point in Communications', *Journal of the Royal Empire Society*, 34, 4 (1943).
John Lindop, *Reminiscences of a Radar Plotter: Life in the Royal Navy in Ceylon at the End of World War Two* (Wigton: Mercianotes, 2016), p. 103.
Eugene Liptak, *Office of Strategic Services, 1942-45: The World War II Origins of the CIA* (Oxford: Osprey, 2009).
E. F. C. Ludowyk, *The Modern History of Ceylon* (New York: Praeger, 1966).
Andrew Lycett, *Ian Fleming* (London: Weidenfeld and Nicolson, 1995).
J. E. Macdonnell, *Valiant Occasions* (London: Constable, 1952).
Donald Macintyre, *Fighting Admiral: The Life of Admiral of the Fleet Sir James Somerville, GCB, GBE, DSO* (London: Evans Brothers, 1961).
Arthur Marder, *Old Friends, New Enemies: The Royal Navy and the Imperial Japanese Navy*, volume 2 (Oxford: Oxford University Press, 1990).
Richard Mead, *General 'Boy': The Life of Lieutenant General Sir Frederick Browning GCVO, KBE, DSO, DL* (Barnsley: Pen and Sword, 2010).
Alan Moorehead, *A Year of Battle* (London: Hamish Hamilton, 1943).
Janet Morgan, *Edwina Mountbatten: A Life of Her Own* (London: Fontana, 1992).
Rex Morgan, *The Hermes Adventure* (Manly, Australia: The Runciman Press, 1985).
Brian Moynihan, *Jungle Soldier: The True Story of Freddie Spencer Chapman* (London: Quercus, 2009).
Carl Muller, *Spit and Polish* (New Delhi: Penguin, 2000).
Anton Muttukumaru, *The Military History of Ceylon* (New Delhi: Navrang, 1987).
Michael Ondaatje, *Running in the Family* (London: Picador, 1984),
John O'Regan, *From Empire to Commonwealth: Reflections on a Career in Britain's Overseas Service* (London: Radcliffe Press, 1994).
Christopher Owen, *The Rhodesian African Rifles* (London: Leo Cooper, 1970).
Timothy Parsons, *The African Rank and File: Social Implications of Colonial Military Service in the King's African Rifles, 1902-1964* (Oxford: James Currey, 1999).
Janaka Perera, 'The Day Death Rained Over Colombo', *Ceylon Daily News*, 6/4/07.

Ruhanie Perera, 'Deep into History', *Sunday Times* (Sri Lanka), 9/11/05.
Hugh Popham, *Sea Flight: The Wartime Memoirs of a Fleet Air Arm Pilot* (Barnsley: Seaforth, 2010).
Andrew Roberts, *Eminent Churchillians* (London: Phoenix, 1995).
Gerard Robinson, *Fading Edge of Empire* (Sydney: ???, 1998).
Frank Rose, 'Last Voyage of the Wuchang' at, http://www.thepeacockscall.co.uk/sites/thepeacockscall.co.uk/files/images/Voyage-Woo-Chang.pdf.
Stephen Roskill, *The War at Sea*, volume 2, *The Period of Balance* (London: HMSO, 1956).
——, *Churchill and the Admirals* (Barnsley: Pen and Sword, 2004).
Trevor Royle, *Death Before Dishnour: The True Story of 'Fighting Mac'* (London: St Martin's Press, 1982).
Nicholas Sarantakes, *Allies Against the Rising Sun: The United States, the British Nations, and the Defeat of Imperial Japan* (Lawrence, KS: University Press of Kansas, 2009).
John Shuckburgh, 'Colonial Civil History of the War', 4 volumes (1949).
Michael Simpson (ed.), *The Somerville Papers: Selections from the Private and Official Correspondence of Admiral of the Fleet Sir James Somerville, GCB, GBE, DSO* (Aldershot: Scholar Press for the Navy Records Society, 1995).
Ian Skidmore, *Escape from the Rising Sun: The Incredible Journey of the Sederhana Djohanis* (London: Futura, 1974).
Michael Smith, *The Emperor's Codes: Bletchley Park and the Breaking of Japan's Secret Ciphers* (London: Bantam, 2000).
Peter Smith, *Fist from the Sky: Japan's Dive-Bomber Ace of World War Two* (Mechanicsburg, PA: Stackpole Books, 2006).
Christopher Somerville, *Our War: How the British Commonwealth Fought the Second World War* (London: Weidenfeld and Nicolson, 1998).
Alan Stripp, *Codebreaker in the Far East* (Oxford: Oxford University Press, 1995).
Robert Stuart, 'Leonard Birchall and the Japanese Raid on Colombo', *Canadian Military Journal* (Winter 2006-2007).
——, '91 Bombs: The Japanese Attack on Trincomalee', at www.combinedfleet.com/Stuart-91%20bombs-at-Trincomalee.docx.
——, 'Air Raid Colombo, 5 April 1942: The Fully Expected Surprise Attack', *The Royal Canadian Air Force Journal, 3, 4* (2014).
Kazuo Tamayama and John Nunneley, *Tales by Japanese Soldiers of the Burma Campaign* (London: Cassell, 2000).
Ashwini Tambe and Harald Fischer-Tiné (eds), *The Limits of British Control in South Asia: Spaces of Disorder in the Indian Ocean Region* (London: ?? 2008).
S. G. Taylor, *Notes on a Tour of Australia* (Colombo: Government Press, 1943).
The Colonial Empire (1939-1947) (London: HMSO, 1947).
Roger Thiedeman, 'Of Aeroplanes and Jumbos', *Sunday Times* (Sri Lanka), 2/2/97.
——, 'How Tamils Sent Plane Named "Jaffna"', *Sunday Times* (Sri Lanka), 1/8/99.
——, 'Conquering the Skies', *Sunday Times* (Sri Lanka), 2/1/00.
——, 'Koggala, Catalinas, and the Double Sunrise', *Sunday Times* (Sri Lanka), 27/2/00.
Kris Thomas, 'A War Story: Ceylon During World War II' (2017), Roar Media, at https://roar.media/english/life/history/a-war-story-ceylon-during-world-war-ii/

Julian Thompson, *Forgotten Voices of Burma: The Second World War's Forgotten Conflict* (London: Ebury Press, 2009).

J. Alan Thompson, *Only the Sun Remembers* (London: Andrew Dakers, 1950).

Peter Thompson, *The Battle for Singapore: The True Story of the Greatest Catastrophe of World War Two* (London: Portrait, 2006).

Time magazine, 'World Battlefronts: New Pacific', 16/3/42.

Michael Tomlinson, *The Most Dangerous Moment: The Japanese Attack on Ceylon, 1942* (London: Mayflower, 1979).

Ian Trenowden, *The Hunting Submarine: The Fighting Life of HMS Tally-Ho* (London: William Kimber, 1974).

——, *Operations Most Secret: SOE, the Malayan Theatre* (N. P.: Crécy Books, 1978).

J. Tudor Jones, 'Ceylon on Guard', *The Spectator*, 20/3/42.

A. Weerasinghe, *Report of Assistant CDC in Charge of the Essential Services Labour Corps (Maharagama), March 1942-March 1943* (Colombo: Government Press, 1943).

Kenneth Williams, *Just Williams: An Autobiography* (London: HarperCollins, 1993),

H. P. Willmott, *Empires in the Balance: Japanese and Allied Pacific Strategies to April 1942* (Annapolis, MD: Naval Institute Press, 1982).

——, *Grave of a Dozen Schemes: British Naval Planning and the War Against Japan, 1943-1945* (Shrewsbury: Airlife, 1996).

Martin Wilmington, *The Middle East Supply Centre* (London: University of London Press, 1972).

Brian Wilson, *A Submariners' War in the Indian Ocean, 1939-45* (Stroud: Tempus, 2000).

F. W. Winterbotham, *The Ultra Secret: The Inside Story of Operation Ultra, Bletchley Park, and Enigma* (London: Weidenfeld and Nicolson, 1974).

John Winton, *Sink the Haguro! The Last Destroyer Action of the Second World War* (London: Seeley, Service, & Co., 1979).

Bruce Wright, *Frogmen of Burma: The Story of the Sea Reconnaissance Unit* (London: Kimber, 1970).

Edward Young, *One of Our Submarines* (Barnsley: Pen and Sword, 2004).

Philip Ziegler, *Mountbatten: The Official Biography* (London: HarperCollins, 1985).

——, (ed.), *Personal Diary of Admiral the Lord Louis Mountbatten, Supreme Allied Commander South-East Asia, 1943-1946* (London: Collins, 1988).

Index

Ceylon Daily News 17, 147, 173, 196, 199, 234, 249, 253